THE V-CHIP DEBATE:
CONTENT FILTERING FROM
TELEVISION TO THE INTERNET

LEA'S COMMUNICATION SERIES

Jennings Bryant/Dolf Zillmann, General Editors

Selected tiitles include:

For a complete list of other titles in LEA's Communication Series, please
contact Lawrence Erlbaum Associates, Publishers.

THE V-CHIP DEBATE: CONTENT FILTERING FROM TELEVISION TO THE INTERNET

Edited by
Monroe E. Price

LEA
1998

LAWRENCE ERLBAUM ASSOCIATES, PUBLISHERS
Mahwah, New Jersey   London

The final camera copy for this work was prepared by the author, and therefore the publisher takes no responsibility for consistency or correctness of typographical style. However, this arrangement helps to make publication of this kind of scholarship possible.

Ratings icons reproduced with the permission of the TV Parental Guidelines Council, Inc.

Lawrence Erlbaum Associates, Inc., Publishers
10 Industrial Avenue
Mahwah, NJ 07430

Cover design by Kathryn Houghtaling Lacey

Library of Congress Cataloging-in-Publication Data

Price, Monroe E.
The V-chip debate : content filtering from television to the Internet
/ edited by Monroe E. Price.
        p. cm.—(Communications)
Includes bibliographical references and index.
ISBN 0-8058-3061-8 (alk. paper).
ISBN 0-8058-3062-6 (pbk.: alk. paper)
1. Television programs—Rating. 2. Violence in television.
3. V-chips.
I. Price, Monroe Edwin, 1938 - . II. Series.
PN1992.8.R3V2 1998
302.23'45—dc21
                                                      98-26402

                                                          CIP

Books published by Lawrence Erlbaum Associates are printed on acid-free paper, and their bindings are chosen for strength and durability.

Printed in the United States of America
10 9 8 7 6 5 4 3 2 1

For Edith Bjornson

Acknowledgements

This book is a publication of the new Programme in Comparative Media Law and Policy, Oxford University, located at the Centre for Socio-Legal Studies, Wolfson College. The Canadian Radio-television and Telecommunications Commission, which has been so extraordinarily careful in shepherding the V-chip's path in Canada, was willing to support the assembling of this book of essays. That is fitting because of the important contribution of the Canadian experience especially its early field testing of the system and the way its innovation, experience, and experimentation with the V-chip has led to an international pattern of inquiry concerning the technology. The essays are also, in part, the product of a symposium held under the auspices of the Howard M. Squadron Program on Law, Media and Society at the Benjamin N. Cardozo School of Law in New York. That symposium received funding from the John and Mary R. Markle Foundation. Mark Szafran was one of the principal organizers of that symposium and helped locate many of the writers included in this volume. Michelle Graham not only edited some of those papers into an issue of the *Cardozo Arts and Entertainment Law Journal*, but played a very considerable role in preparing manuscripts for this book. In addition, I participated in a seminar on the V-chip at the Freedom Forum's Media Studies Center where I later became a Fellow (and completed work on this book). The very able Melissa Mathis, assisted by Tamara Bock and Benno Weisberg, saw the project to conclusion. I want to thank, as well, Danielle Cliche, then research manager of the International Institute of Communications in London, who had the splendid idea of uniting these papers with the interests and support of the CRTC and was responsible for the book's creation. The book is dedicated to Edith Bjornson, Senior Program Officer of the Markle Foundation, for her extraordinary and persistent efforts to nourish scholarly understanding and humane administration of the wholesale and society-transforming changes that bewilder all of us in a time of rapidly changing communications technologies.

Contents

The V-Chip and the Jurisprudence of Ratings

Monroe E. Price

There's something that was and remains politically mesmerizing about the idea of the V-chip, a magic wafer or combination of wires and plastic that would help salve consciences, allow public responsibility to be satisfied, resurrect parenthood, and urge provenders of programming to be more forthcoming as to the content and impact of the material they purvey. The V-chip, or the concept of the chip, seemed to hit the marketplace of competing ideologies at a moment when legislators and decision makers in Canada, the United States, and elsewhere have had a real political need for this device, some because of the actual addition it could make in the architecture of program choice and screening, and some because of the expedient opportunity the technology presented to permit the inference that government was acting in a way that dealt with important cultural questions in the society. Its genesis was in Canada, but it was the kind of idea that mushroomed and spread throughout the world. The introduction of the V-chip, in a fascinating but subtle way, has been a time for revisiting, in a new guise, the protracted, perpetual analysis of the proper role of government, if any, in establishing cultural norms and protecting them from corrosion.

The V-chip, in its basic form, is specific to television and is part of a very long series of discussions about whether television (or broadcasting generally) deserves some special attention in terms of its accessibility to children, its particular power to affect conduct, and its invasiveness. But as this notion of filtering and labeling has caught the imagination of the regulator, the legislator, and all those who wish to consider new ways to alter bargaining over imagery in society, the very *idea* of the chip or its equivalent is now moving across technologies. The Federal Communications Commission, having found the broadcasting industry rating system "acceptable," might require the installation of a V-chip or its equivalent in computers (jurisdictionally because of their capacity to receive television signals) with implications for Internet screening and labeling.[1] The 1996 Telecommunications Act in the U.S. requires that manufacturers of "any apparatus" designed to receive television signals include the V-chip, and FCC officials have argued that computers, because they can be used to receive such signals, are potentially covered. The very request sent chills through the computer industry: "This could be a veiled attempt to back-door measures like the [Communications Decency Act]. Most computers are accepting video, and the distinction between what is going to be video for broadcast and video for the Internet is getting increasingly slim," David Banisar, an attorney at the Electronic Privacy Information Center in Washington, argued.

Within broadcasting, the V-chip approach may spread from the filtering of violent and indecent programming to filtering of advertisements of alcohol (or tobacco in some countries), to filtering of other kinds of messages that are unwanted or filterable because of political content.[2] Labeling and rating schemes proliferate: they are not only the province of motion pictures and now broadcasting. The video game industry and the music industry have responded to legislative pressure within the United States to develop labeling and rating methods of their own. One of the most important current discussions involves the development of PICS or the Platform for Internet Content Selection, a vigorous and still controversial approach to assuring a multiplicity of voluntary ratings and an architecture said to be free of government involvement.[3] School boards and libraries adopt policies that incorporate voluntary rating schemes into official regulation of access. Senator John McCain has introduced legislation, likely to be enacted, that conditions the receipt of federal subsidies on the adoption, by libraries, of particular kinds of filtering systems. Litigation over the use of awkward and relatively crude filtering software by libraries is already a First Amendment growth area. Communities design criminal ordinances that use government sanctions to enforce these restless labels. The concept of the V-chip is moving geographically as well. Its roots in Canada and the United States are discussed extensively in this book, but the V-chip is the subject of analysis in Australia, in Europe, and throughout the world.

The V-chip is the occasion for continuation of the debate about violence and sexual practices in society and how representations on television relate to those practices. As the essays in this book indicate, interpretations of the results of research on these questions vary wildly: there are those who think the connection is adequately demonstrated and those who think it is not proved sufficiently to justify government intervention. The V-chip's introduction is an occasion, as well, for a discussion, sometimes forced and artificial, about the role of parents in controlling the flow of images. There seems to be hardly any research on the specific and relevant relationship between parent (or caretaker) and child, and child and television set, yet speeches proliferate about the extent to which this device will enhance the parental or caretaking role. The technology's enthusiasts believe or claim to believe that the V-chip "empowers" parents, to use the term of the 1996 U.S. Telecommunications Act. There is no question that the technology has its doubters, both as to its inherent contribution, its neutrality and relationship to censorship, and to the plausibility of its implementation. Among these are skeptics who believe that the V-chip has merely allowed legislators and policymakers to *appear* to be addressing a problem of imagery and society while, in fact, nothing was done with respect to that virtually intractable issue. This skepticism is oddly reinforced by industry reports, based on early experiences with on-screen television labeling, that viewers seem indifferent to the labels, by and large, and their arrival, though much debated and heralded, has been a virtual non-event.

While the initial concept of the V-chip was simple, its flow into the public realm has raised so many extraordinary questions that the introduction and production of the chip can serve as a case study in problems of law and public policy. Here are a few of the questions that have emerged: What relationship between government and the image-producing industries can be characterized (for constitutional and other reasons) as voluntary as opposed to coercive? What role should governments learning from the U.S. experience play in terms of encouraging adoption of similar labeling schemes? If images are to be evaluated, who should do the evaluation—the producers, the distributors, or "objective" third parties? What role can a monitoring board play and how should such a board be composed? In a society barraged by images, how feasibly can rating or labeling systems emerge and be satisfactory? In television, should a rating system be scene by scene, program by program, series by series, or channel by channel? Indeed, how much information about content can be effectively redacted and communicated? As news becomes a forum for the salacious, is there diminishing integrity—in terms of cultural impact—to a system that exempts news (and sports) from labeling requirements? There are semiotic questions about the nature of the logos, the on-screen signals used to alert viewers: What kind of label or logo informs, and what kind persuades? What kind of logo is neutral and what kind carries its own shame-bearing or moral judgment? What kind of logo has a boomerang effect and attracts, as opposed to informs and repels, audiences for which it is to serve as a warning? What relationship is enshrined in the architecture of labeling between the industry that produces the images and the government that regulates them (how centralized or how distributed should the process of evaluation be)? What guarantees of integrity are there to the evaluative or rating process? What mode of assessment is there to evaluate whether the experiment is "successful"? What difference does it make how quickly or slowly there is V-chip penetration of households? What research should policy-makers require to enable them to adopt or transform a framework for labeling and rating? Many of these questions, though hardly all, are addressed in the essays in this book.

How a government introduces or furthers a technology of filtering is also worthy of study. This book includes essays that contrast the very different approaches in Canada and the United States in terms of the role of regulatory agency, industry, and government. These differences reflect political traditions and may demonstrate substantial distinctions in constitutional standards. Such a study of comparative processes—how different political and industrial systems evaluate these labels and mechanisms—ought to be of significance to the European Union, the United Kingdom, and other entities studying rating arrangements.

The V-chip experience is also intriguing as an exercise in cross-national regulatory influence. It is interesting to think of the impact of policy making in the United States on policy making elsewhere, particularly in Canada, especially at a time when globalization, wrapped in trade considerations, leads to a leveling of regulatory approaches. A principal motivation for this book has been to feature the Canadian processes—largely because of the origins of the technology in Canada—and to place them in the context of the very substantial industrial and governmental discussions that have now occurred in the United States as a consequence. In various ways, it is the reverse or mutual influence that is worth examining as well. The Canadian attitude was a more or less rational exploration of alternatives and the testing of alternatives; the United States approach involved the search for a political consensus and its wholesale implementation. The question then became whether the U.S. solution would (partly because of the complexities of transborder flow of entertainment programming and the dominance of the American industry) come to reshape the Canadian debate or the other way around. American advocacy groups, seeking what they perceived as a better outcome from the legislation, sought the disclosure of more information in ratings systems, an outcome that approached the Canadian system.

No matter what the solution to the debate over the V-chip, at bottom, the public outcry, intensive as it seems, generally glides over the basic concerns about modern culture, modern mores, and the impact of the influx of images. The V-chip exists largely because of unease about aspects of modernity—fixations on sex and violence, the loss of traditional kinds of literacy and the leveling of cultures. In this sense, the V-chip is an American-type solution to issues increasingly debated globally. It is a technical solution to a preoccupation with violence and indecency, a substitute for insignificantly addressed concerns about fundamental trends in the way children are acculturated. The overarching, almost religious questions are reflected only indirectly in the many studies of violence and media, including those in this book. These studies cannot satisfactorily rehearse the question of whether images on television affect behavior, or which images on television, in motion pictures, or on the Internet affect behavior in what ways. Scholarship, like the chip itself, tweaks culture at the margin, providing a filter, not a dam to modernity.

*****

In Canada, in the mid-1990s, a youngish scientist named Tim Collings wrote a short paper on a technology that, quite simply, permitted information about a program to stream down a vertical blanking interval and trigger a mechanism in the television set—preset by its owner—to block unwanted programs. Originally, the "V" stood for Viewer: a chip to give the viewer a choice. The very first transformation in this debate was over the meaning of the V: it has moved from Viewer, in Canada, to Violence in the United States (and, somewhat mysteriously, into Sex or Indecency). The Canadian Radio-television and Telecommunications Commission (CRTC) sought, systematically, to determine the best possible and most efficient means of classifying program content and conveying that classification to viewers. Industry and citizens together made decisions about what questions would be asked about a program—the subject matter of the information to be gathered—and the way in which that information should be conveyed.

An account of the contrasting processes of policy development is the subject of the first section of this book. Al MacKay, who was instrumental in providing assistance to government and industry, summarizes the history of the Canadian debate and provides a context for the various Canadian developments. An essay by Stephen McDowell, a political scientist, seeks to explore the contrast between the Canadian and U.S. experiences. As the essays by MacKay and McDowell indicate, in Canada there was a relatively open process of determining how the chip would be implemented, with relatively intimate, simultaneous, and cooperative discussion between regulator and industry. Furthermore, there was a period of experimentation, conducted under the supervision of the regulators. In the United States, because of the design of the 1996 Telecommunications Act and the supposed implications of the First Amendment, it fell almost purely to the entertainment industry to fashion the implementation of the device, at least in the first instance. Only if the U.S. industry developed an unacceptable approach would there be a government-appointed commission that might develop alternatives. This method, the result of political compromise and special U.S. constitutional considerations, had a profound impact on the initial industry offering and the process of debate that ensued. In the end, the paths seem to have converged; but that, too, is illuminating.

A dramatic "second act" in the United States debate provides insight into interest group politics and the competition between industry-legislator alliances and legislator-community group alliances. In the U.S., in contradistinction to Canada, the initial industry-originated plan led to well-coordinated objections by public interest organizations.[4] Advocacy group protest against the industry system proposed in early 1997 (see Appendix) led to changes that—depending on the critic—may or not have significance in the long run.[5] Heated discussion resulted in a revised system (also included in the Appendix), that added disclosure of content to the basic industry version of the Motion Picture Association of America classification system (a system that is largely age-based). Under the scheme, a three-year trial of a system would supplement age-based classifications with a V, S, L, or D rating, denoting violence, sexual content, coarse language, or suggestive dialogue, respectively. Further, children's shows that contain aggressive combat-style violence would carry an FV for Fantasy Violence (see Appendix). As a central element of the negotiated settlement between the industry and the advocacy groups (an agreement that NBC did not then join), key members of Congress were to agree to a three-year moratorium on legislation relating to television content.[6] Jack Valenti, the president of the MPAA and the central person negotiating the agreement, applauded this arrangement. He was candid in a vintage-Valenti way: "The purpose of doing a ratings system in the first place was to shut off this tidal wave of criticism. The gain, the singular gain, is that for three years we will keep the jaguars and bobcats off our backs, and have a period of legislative peace and perhaps a diminishing of carping and criticism in the marketplace." But in a press conference condemning the agreement, Senators Joseph I. Lieberman and Samuel Brownback opposed the moratorium. "Television content is the issue, not whether or not parents are provided with warning labels on bad programs," said Brownback. Acquiescence in the "voluntary" ratings approach scotched the snake of government intervention but did not kill it.

It is hard to know how to read the aggregated results of industry proposal, group advocacy, and industry change in Canada and the United States. There were many, including many in the creative community in Hollywood, who criticized the industry solution as compromising free speech values. In November 1996, for example, the Caucus for Producers, Writers and Directors proposed a ratings system similar to the one finally proposed by networks other than NBC. A year later, in November 1997, the Caucus, after inner turmoil, publicly voiced its opposition to the new television content ratings system and reversed its earlier position: "We actively oppose any interference with creative rights, whether it is the U.S. government, studios, networks or special interest groups," the Caucus said in an advertisement that appeared in trade papers as it applauded NBC's refusal to adopt the content ratings system. "We are appalled by the politically motivated tactics of legislators urging the FCC to reject the license renewals of television stations not using the new ratings system."

Other critics claimed that the industry had too much control over the U.S. rating system. Under its first proposal, the implementation would be wholly within industry hands and would be designed to interfere least with the marketability of the industry's products. The summer 1997 revision adjusted membership on a "monitoring board" to assure representation from groups other than the networks and producers of programming. No matter how much debate there was over the content of the labels, the size of their display on-screen, the number of seconds they would appear, and other details of hand-to-hand combat, the suspicion lingered that the whole exercise was merely a gambit, the minimum concession by industry necessary to avoid a renewal of attempts at government content regulation and the appropriate level of official noise to demonstrate concern while avoiding intervention in the economic activity of major constituents. Insufferably mild an intervention for some, the American scheme, even in its indirect mode, constituted censorship and government mind control for others. The ratings system, and the legislation that brought it about, could, with some winks, be viewed as a good faith effort to meet a public need, or, on the other hand, as a brilliant preemption of legislation that might more effectively and dangerously intervene and impose binding moral standards.

*****

A strong motivation for this book is that the V-chip phenomenon, trivial as it may be on the surface, masks important developments in the very conceptualization of speech in society. The ratings debate highlights a theoretically changed relationship between listener and speaker, one in which the viewer or listener is seemingly empowered. The place of the V-chip in this debate is increasingly important; indeed, it may be argued that the V-chip's contribution to legal argumentation may be greater than its ultimate contribution to the relationship between children and imagery. Already, the United States Supreme Court has used the V-chip and related ratings approaches as one reason to hold unconstitutional the Communications Decency Act (on the ground that a less restrictive alternative might be available for achieving the desired speech-infringing result).[7] The president of the United States has pointed to the V-chip or other built-in rating technologies as a key to the design of a deregulated Internet.

Speech rights have had an interesting cycle of use in the United States. Articulated as the domain of crusading pamphleteers, they have become, especially in the decisions of the 1980s and 1990s, a shield for the major enterprises of entertainment: the rights of broadcasters, the rights of program suppliers, the rights of cable operators.[8] The V-chip debate involves a slight tectonic shift to a once-articulated right of the listener to obtain information. Whether there is actually such a shift in rights or in the transfer of information and how important it is, requires a better understanding of differences across media—television, film, music recordings, the Internet, and motion pictures. Much of the free speech law in the United States is medium specific, with special cases for film, newspapers, television, music, and other carriers of culture. In this book, there is some effort to identify, at least historically, patterns of rating, labeling, censoring, and channeling that have been tied to specific media.

Examining the V-chip in theory means differentiating among various approaches to providing information to the listener. One approach is *information labeling*: requiring that distributors or producers of information place, in a cognizable way, indicators of the information. Some restrict the term "ratings" to a specialized form of labeling in which legal consequences attend the judgments the labels signify. In the V-chip context, however, "ratings" refers to the specific case where a labeling system is embedded in a compelled technology with a device to block, as desired, the labeled programs. In this book, different authors use the terms in different ways, often interchangeably. *Channeling* involves government requirements that programs in specified categories (indecent or violent, for example) be distributed only on certain specified carriers or at designated times.[9] The 1992 Cable Television Act required channeling of certain indecent programming to a specific, segregated channel, a requirement found unconstitutional in the *Denver Area* case.[10] *Blocking or censoring*, in comparison, involves government prohibitions on programming content.

As can be seen, labeling and rating schemes, as well as channeling proposals, are often welcome alternatives to the more onerous interventions such as blocking or censoring which implicate free speech concerns. Indeed, it is this quality of the V-chip that makes it so immediately embraceable, the quality that appeals to legislators who wish to appear to be doing something, to courts, which seek alternatives that are not so onerous, and to networks which seek to fend off criticism by adopting the mildest possible interventions.

These basic distinctions give rise to others and, as a result, when there are labeling or rating efforts, much more needs to be explored. One might ask whether the context of the ratings is so coercive that it amounts to a ban; whether disclosures necessary for a viewer's access to restricted channels unduly invade privacy; whether the evaluation—the determination of a rating or label—should be undertaken by the producer or whether there should be, for the particular segment of the media, centralized labeling. As implemented in the United States, the V-chip's significance depends on the dominant role of the producer or network, as with the role of the MPAA in film. Richard Mosk's short essay, recounting the practice of the Motion Picture Association of America, is helpful in describing the process. This is, as mentioned above, differently constructed in the approach of the PICS consortium. The U.S. V-chip system makes it less likely that there will be effective competition in the market for classifications. The industry determines hegemonically what ratings are embedded in the program; licensees therefore are not common carriers obliged to carry all possible ratings or even a representative bouquet.

Further questions deal with implementation: there may be different modes for reviewing the initial label or rating and determining consistency. The V-chip assumes that over time almost all television sets will be fitted with the technology. But in the shorter term, this will hardly be the case. Ratings systems will exist, then, independent of the V-chip technology. In addition, there are delicate questions about what program offerings should be covered by a rating system, news being the most important candidate for exclusion (and news and sports are both excluded under the U.S. plan). There is no question that news can be violent—there are those who believe that the primary *modus operandi* of the "late news" on American stations at 10:00 or 11:00 P.M. is to instill and build on the fears of the viewing public. And, if news is excluded, there is the question of which programs, particularly those that are of the new "real life" genre or tabloid television can be characterized as "news." It would be ironic but predictable to see violence and sexual innuendo come, even more, to shape news programming as a result of its exemption from a ratings scheme.

The Canadian discussion was far more deliberative on how detailed ratings would be (how sensitive to distinctions, how sensitive to context, how sensitive to program section). These were ultimately the questions debated by U.S. advocacy groups who successfully obtained modifications that made the American system more like the Canadian one. But the final criteria for disclosure may not be the most relevant factors in shaping the behavior of those watching television and providing suitable information about content. Little is known about whether one system of labeling or ratings, rather than another, may have an impact on the competitive structure of the media (facilitating entry by allowing freer play for violent and indecent programming or making entry more difficult by removing threats of competition based on "programming for the bottom").

Globally, another area of future inquiry is the standard, under constitutions or doctrines that approach constitutional status, of the validity or desirability of rating, labeling, or channeling systems. There is now quite a lot of writing about the applicability of the First Amendment of the United States Constitution to these systems.[11] A rather difficult aspect of that debate is the complicated, jurisprudentially brutal relationship between legislation or threatened legislation and private industry action, the coercive aspect of what is called, in the United States, jawboning. It was precisely the threat of legislation that called forth the "voluntary" action of the industry to develop a rating scheme, and, as indicated above, the U.S. industry extracted a moratorium on legislation (or even the serious discussion of legislation) as part of the deal for accepting the V-chip.[12] The U.S. Telecommunications Act of 1996 (set forth, in relevant part in the Appendix) was carefully drafted to respect an imaginary line between unconstitutional coercion and acceptably coerced voluntariness. Thus are raised fundamental free speech questions about the way in which government interacts with industry. The manner of adoption of voluntary rating schemes suggests a massive, moderately undisciplined, virtually unreviewable relationship between government officials and a particular set of industrial speakers. How does society place some bounds, rules, sense of appropriateness to the range of this swing between "voluntariness" and coercion? The new telecommunications law is part of a jurisprudence of jawboning: an interrelationship between the force of government and the self-regulation of industry. A pattern is developing in which more explicit steps in the dance of force versus voluntariness takes place. The ratings law is a useful moment for discussing changed modes of discourse between government and industry.[13]

All rating schemes, and all public policy discussions about them, bear within them some assumptions about the relationship of label to viewer or listener. I have already referred to what might be called the semiotics of ratings. How are ratings perceived by the consumer? What differences are there among the various industries that have tried or are trying ratings in terms of the nature of communication? The reader of this book should pay attention to the physicality of the labels, their drama or lack of drama, whether they are designed to communicate to the parent or to the child. We know very little about the connection between the physical placing of the label on the package (the screen, the compact disk container, the videotape box) and the interconnection between label and blocking device. There are practical questions about the shape and impact of the logo used as part of the rating system, how long it is on the screen, and the relationship between on-screen warnings and the reputed built-in screening capacity of the V-chip. In the future, it will be useful to know what observed relationship there is between ratings—information—and behavioral consequences. We need to examine, more carefully, the assumptions about human behavior that underlie the ratings schemes and how valid they are. Some symbols, in some industries, such as portions of the video game industry, seem almost designed to attract as well as inform the consumer.

The development of a labeling or rating system means that there will be a kind of "common law" of ratings, or different common laws depending on the industry. If ratings or labels are not arbitrary, rules will emerge. They may not be articulated in a published document or reduced to a code, but these rules will exist and be known to producers (this is somewhat the case today with respect to films). Such a common law would indicate to producers exactly what conduct or display would receive what kind of label or rating. Over time, such common law will surely evolve, with finely drawn distractions concerning dress, vocabulary, presentation of body. It would be interesting to determine how one would go about constructing or reconstructing that common law, determining what standards emerge, are articulated, become practices within companies.[14] One possibility is that the emerged common law will depend on the structure of the industry. An industry dominated by two or three providers may internalize a ratings scheme in a specific and documented form more rationally than an industry where there are many independents and constant testing of the limits and meaning of the ratings scheme. It would be useful to know whether there are studies within any industry that try to codify accumulated practices, as Llewellyn and Hoebel did with Native American determinations in their book, *The Cheyenne Way.*

As I suggested earlier, the V-chip contributes to the way in which speech is defined and defended in modern society. One can say that labeling and rating systems mandate speech about speech. They do not seek to change speech, but, like content descriptors on packages of food, only provide a sense of what the consumer is to receive. "This is a simple matter of truth-in-labeling," Senator Dan Coats of Indiana is quoted as having said. "We don't want Hollywood telling parents what is age-appropriate. We just want Hollywood telling parents what is in their shows." On the one hand, that is naive: just as information on a package is designed to alter eating behavior (and the very things that are supposed to be listed are probably clues to public attitudes), so the information on a rating or label is designed to influence what people see or hear. On the other hand, one can think about the change in speech doctrine, alluded to earlier, in terms of a shift toward the listener, a peculiar rebirth of the Jerome Barron theories imbedded in the Supreme Court's decision in *Red Lion*.[15] The idea here is that the "listener's right" cannot be fully implemented unless the listener knows, in advance, what is about to come into his ken. If the listener selects, if the listener affirmatively chooses (as is the case in pay television), the information requirement is less pressing. But even there, the government's power to require information to assist the listener to be a better consumer may be what is at stake. And in a world where listeners are atomized while speakers tend to be corporate, the corrective role for government may be growing.[16]

Another way to think about the change will be treated in what might be called the "open" versus "closed" terrain of speech.[17] Under this theory, there is more government interest and more government activity in speech that is broadly open to public view and display. Speech that follows channels that are narrow, selective, chosen, often bilateral, are not considered so much in need of or so much warranting regulation. The impulse toward ratings would, under this mode of thinking, be more intense for broadcast television than for cable, more for basic tier or "free" cable channels than for pay channels. Ratings or labels are more important where the speech that is ordinarily called entertainment is not specifically the subject of contract or a careful degree of choice. Here the theory does not turn on whether or not children are listening and watching, but on the method by which information reaches a household.

A third way to think about the increased emphasis on ratings and labeling alternatives is that we are witnessing a kind of "tobaccoization" of certain kinds of speech. Speech is treated as a public health question, and statutory findings and government statements concerning indecent and violent speech and images trace the rhetoric or regulation with respect to smoking (and alcohol). Until recently, not much had been written about a "public health" exception to the First Amendment and other speech standards, but that is an area that deserves more attention than could be provided in this book.[18]

*****

This book is a collection of essays designed to touch on many of the questions discussed in this introduction. The book begins with essays on the regulatory history by Al MacKay and Stephen McDowell, tracing the U.S. and Canadian experiences. Andrea Millwood Hargrave, a British lawyer who has had experience in administering program standards in the United Kingdom, introduces examples from European and British perspectives. Marjorie Heins, director of the Art Censorship program of the American Civil Liberties Union, casts a skeptical eye on the entire enterprise of regulating content to protect young people from the harms of certain kinds of television content. Professor Balkin develops an important theory of information and its filters, information, as it were, about information. Donald Roberts attempts to draw distinctions between rating systems and labeling systems and builds on his own experience constructing a system for video games. Professor C. Dianne Martin very specifically alludes to that system and the choices made by the Recreational Software Advisory Council. Professor James Hamilton analyzes the relationship between government legislation and private incentives to portray or submerge depictions of violence. In separate chapters, Daniel Weitzner and Jonathan Weinberg discuss the opportunities, implications, and shortcomings of proposed "empowerment" technologies or filtering systems as means of addressing public concerns about content on the Internet.

The V-chip exists within a history of rating and labeling systems, ranging from comic strips to motion pictures and encompassing voluntary and mandatory solutions. The book cannot cover all of this history, but Richard Mosk, who heads the administration of the rating system of the Motion Picture Association of America provides a description of that process for purposes of comparison. An essay by Professor Jack Balkin deals with ways in which the existence of filtering technology has led to a reconceptualization of free speech issues. The book includes two additional reports: a five-country study by Joel Federman specially updated for this book, and *The UCLA Television Violence Report (1996),* by the UCLA Center for Communication Policy.

Many of the significant issues in the debate are not front and center in this book because they are the subject of so much discussion elsewhere. One such question is the constitutionality, under the U.S. Constitution, of the congressional action that led to the V-chip. What has been interesting is how popular it has been to contend that the statue was of questionable constitutionality at the same time that most of the industry conformed to it. All networks agreed to ratings, even though NBC earned the badge of outsider or champion of broadcaster freedom for not agreeing to the last jot and title of the final arrangements. This is a book more about law than it is about accepted ideas of psychology. Therefore, the thicket of actual harms—whether violence or sexually explicit programming actually causes harms to young people—is left for the thriving debate of others.

The V-chip, as it turns out, may not have a great impact on the quality of society in the ways that are intended. The broadcasters who are preparing for its implementation have indicated that they do not believe, based on early returns, that rating and labeling systems are effective in "empowering" parents or saving the souls of their children. Still, the V-chip is a phenomenon. It is cause for rethinking the regulation of speech, for revisiting issues of imagery and society and for reinventing a relationship between parent and child. Not bad for a simple chip and a mass of labels.

Notes

1. The general rulemaking of the Federal Communications Commission is to be found at "In the Matter of Technical Requirements to Enable Blocking of Video Programming based on Program Ratings; Implementation of Sections 551(c), (d) and (e) of the Telecommunications Act of 1996," 12 FCC Rcd 15573 (September 26, 1997). Paragraph 22 discusses the possibility of extension of ratings to "any receiver meeting the screen size requirements . . . [including] any computer that is sold with TV receiver capability and a monitor that has a viewable picture size of 13 inches or larger." On March 12, 1998, the FCC found acceptable the industry video programming rating system.
2. *See* Mark Steyn, *TV Cynics zap Clinton's Cure-all The V-Chip, the In-home Censor, Is Coming Soon to Small Screens in the* U.S., SUNDAY TELEGRAPH, Mar. 3, 1996, at 24. *Meeting the New Chip on the Block: And Imagine the Joy of Watching Television without the Dross,* THE GUARDIAN, Mar. 19, 1996, at 16; Reference to President Clinton and B-chip; Frank Rich, The V-Chip G-String, N.Y. TIMES, Feb. 28, 1996, at A17; Roger Simon, Skip Chips to Stop Violence; The Problem's Not In the Set, THE SUN (BALTIMORE), July 16, 1995, at 2A; Hearings on "Music Violence: How Does It Affect Our Youth? An Examination of the Impact of Violent Music Lyrics on Youth Behavior and Well-Being in the District of Columbia and Across the Nation" Before the Subcomm. on Oversight of Gov't Management, Restructuring, and the Dist. of Columbia, 105th Cong. (1997) (statement of Hilary Rosen, President and Chief Executive Officer, Recording Indus. Assoc. of Am.).
3. See C. Dianne Martin, "An Alternative to Government Regulation and Censorship: Content Advisory Systems for Interactive Media" (in this volume).
4. An example of the reaction to the initial rating system is the response of Mark Honig, of the Parents Television Council in Los Angeles. According to Honig, at the time,

if we're going to have a rating system, it has to be content based. As everyone has been pointing out, and as the debate has been shaped from time eternity, this industry rating system is too vague. It doesn't give parents enough information. It doesn't tell them exactly what to expect to find on a TV show.

We did a ratings study. We looked at the first two weeks of the rating system, and we found that more than three-fifths of prime time programming is thrown into this black hole that they call TV-PG. Well, that's included stuff from "Promise Land," one of the most family friendly shows on television that had no sexual dialogue, no violence of any extreme nature, and no vulgar language. That got a PG.

You tune in a hour and a half later to an ABC show called Spin City, where you heard the "A" word twice, you heard the "B" word once, and you had dialogue centering on men downloading naked pictures of Amish women on the Internet. That got the same rating. That's too confusing to parents. They don't know from one show to another what to expect. (CNN Talkback Live, February 27, 1997, Transcript # 97022700V14)

During her testimony before Congress on the initial network ratings system, in February 1997, Joan Dykstra, National PTA President, stated that the National PTA was requesting,

1. A v-chip band that is broad enough that would allow parents to receive more than one rating system. Although this issue is covered [sic] another set of regulatory proceedings, it is complementary to the amount of information that parents have access to in determining their watching venue.

2. A rating icon on the screen that is larger, more prominently placed on the screen, and appears more frequently during the course of the program.

3. A rating board that is independent of the industry and the FCC, and that the board include parents. Currently, the industry rates itself, which is a conflict of interest. The producers could hardly be an impartial audience, or capable of providing consistent and impartial information.

Lastly, in this current period when is FCC is requesting comments to aid its decision-making responsibilities, and the industry is seeking public opinions itself, the National PTA recommends that the industry work with parents and advocacy organizations to fund an independent research study comparing their age-based system with a content-based system, such as HBO's to determine which better meets the needs of parents. After the study is conducted, the various stakeholders in this issue should convene to review the study and make final recommendations to the FCC based on the study results.

5.   The opposition came from public interest groups linked both to liberal and conservative causes. Andrea Sheldon, Executive Director of the Traditional Values Coalition, testifying before the Senate Commerce, Science and Transportation Committee on the initial television ratings system in February 1997 complained that TV-PG shows had nearly as many obscenities as TV-14. "Receiving the TV-PG rating were 'Wings,' 'Friends,' 'Beverly Hills 90210,' and 'Savannah' all featuring pre-marital sex, sex with various partners and sex with no commitment. In addition, all of this took place during the family hour. I doubt that many parents would consider these situations acceptable for a 14 year old. . . . Obviously, we need a rating system which is content-specific. Television viewers have a right to know what is coming into their homes. And parents should know this in advance."

6.   According to Rosalyn Weinman, head of Standards and Practices at the network, NBC decided not to add content-based labels because "we do not believe that they add any level of information to parents when they want to make decisions for their children. We believe quite the contrary that the content labels add nothing other than misconceptions and confusion to a system that was working and working well."

7.   *Denver Area Educ. Telecomms. Consortium v. FCC,* 116 S. Ct. 2374, 1996 U.S. LEXIS 4261, at *53.

8.   *Turner Broad. Sys., Inc. v. FCC,* 117 S. Ct. 1174 (1997)

9.   Professor Kevin Saunders of the University of Oklahoma School of Law has called for channeling of violent programming. In testimony before the Senate Committee on Commerce, Science and Transportation on February 27, 1997, Professor Saunders said that "the V-chip only allows parents to counter the effects of violent images within their own children. Parents cannot protect their children from the children of other parents who are not so vigilant. . . . If someone else's child becomes violent, he or she does not do violence only to himself or herself. Your child may be the victim of that violence. Parents do have legitimate concerns over limiting the access of all children to violent images. Channeling of violent television into hours when children are not likely to be in the audience will address those concerns."

10. *Denver Area,* 116 S. Ct. 2374, 1996 U.S. LEXIS 4261, *at* *12–19.

11. *See, e.g.,*Marci A. Hamilton, *Reconceptualizing Ratings: From Censorship to Marketplace*, 15 CARD. ARTS & ENT. L.J. 403 (1997); Matthew L. Spitzer, *An Introduction to the Law and Economics of the V-Chip*, 15 CARD. ARTS & ENT. L.J. 429 (1997); Howard M. Wasserman, Comment, *Second-best Solution: The First Amendment, Broadcast Indecency, and the V-Chip*, 91 NW. U. L. REV. 1190 (1997); J. M. Balkin, *Media Filters, The V-Chip, and the Foundation of Broadcast Regulation*, 45 DUKE L.J. 1131 (1996); Steven D. Feldman, Note, The V-Chip: Protecting Children from Violence Or Doing Violence to the Constitution?, 39 How. L.J. 587 (1996); David V. Scott, *The V-Chip Debate: Blocking Television, Sex, Violence, and the First Amendment*, 16 LOY. L.A. ENT. L.J. 741 (1996).
12. In February 1997, when opposition to the networks initial ratings submission was accelerating, Senators Hollings and Dorgan introduced legislation that would impose a "safe-harbor" limit on TV violence limiting such programming to specific late night hours.
13. In a letter to NBC head Bob Wright, after NBC refused to be part of the industry compromise, Senator John McCain promised to use law and regulation to pressure NBC into adopting the new ratings system, perhaps by compelling the dissenting network to run only family friendly fare in primetime. McCain was also thought to be urging the Federal Communications Commission to consider the network's practice during renewal for NBC's 11 station licenses if they didn't fall in line. As Jeff Greenfield said, on ABC's Nightline, putting a question to Senator McCain, "I can't think of a more direct use of government power than the chairman of the Commerce Committee telling prospective FCC commissioners he wants NBC's licenses looked at very carefully because they won't adopt this ratings system. How in heaven's name is that voluntary?" Senator McCain answered as follows: "Because when the affiliates sign voluntarily a piece of paper that they will act in the public interest, that's what has motivated the FCC to force them to show children's educational programming and other kinds of programming and if they're not acting in the public interest, then it's the FCC's obligation, not right, but obligation to determine that. And I believe that by refusing to provide parents with the information that they need, then they may not be acting in the public interest." When Greenfield asked, "Can we not concede or agree that that is at least a very powerful use of a high government official's power?" McCain responded "I think it's a use of my obligation to see that the broadcasters live up to their obligation, which they freely entered into when they said they would act in the public interest in return for obtaining billions of dollars of taxpayer owned assets" (ABC *Nightline*, October 17, 1997, Transcript # 97101701-j07).
14. In an interview with ABC, producer Dick Wolf of *Law and Order* gave this example: "It can get really crazy. We had one show where the opening was a woman who was found naked in a 60 story office building elevator vent. The standards called and said it's not acceptable. I said but she's faced down in the elevator. Well, you see too much of her breast. And I said well how could I prevent something like this happening in the future? She said, choose smaller breasted actresses." In the same program, Roland McFarland, head of the Standards and Practices Department at Fox Network said, "I suppose the question would be okay, so I've got four damns and a hell, you know, is that the tilt factor as far as the language is concerned? A kiss wouldn't necessarily, we wouldn't consider that as, a take down on a couch, not necessarily so. If there's a bed scene and a slip dropped, maybe" (ABC *Nightline*, October 17, 1997, Transcript # 97101701-j07).
15. *Red Lion Broad. Co. v. FCC*, 395 U.S. 367 (1969).
16. Jack Balkin discusses other limitations on the government's power to mandate labels on speech in his essay "Media Filters and the V-Chip" (in this volume).
17. Monroe E. Price, *Free Expression and Digital Dreams: The Open and Closed Terrain of Speech*, 22 CRITICAL INQUIRY 64 (1995).
18. *See, e.g.*, Martin H. Redish, *Tobacco Advertising and the First Amendment*, 81 IOWA L. REV. 589 (1996); Halberg, Note & Comment, *Butt Out: An Analysis of the FDA's Proposed Restrictions On Cigarette Advertising Under the Commercial-Speech Doctrine*, 29 LOY. L.A. L. REV. 1219 (1996); Rachel N. Pine, *Abortion Counselling and the First Amendment: Open Questions After Webster*, 15 AM. J.L. & MED. 189 (1989); Kenneth L. Polin, *Argument for the Ban of Tobacco Advertising: A First Amendment Analysis*, 17 HOFSTRA L. REV. 99 (1988).

PART ONE

ADOPTING THE V-CHIP SYSTEM: CANADA AND THE U.S.

CHAPTER ONE

In Search of Reasonable Solutions:
The Canadian Experience with Television
Ratings and the V-Chip

Al MacKay

> . . . television may be the perfect scapegoat
> for a host of well-intentioned organizations
> wishing to criticize society.[1]

On June 18, 1997, with little fanfare, the Canadian Radio-television and Tele-communications Commission (CRTC), handed down its decision on a television program classification system developed and tested by the Canadian broadcast industry.

The federal broadcast regulatory agency quietly approved a six-level classification system (plus an exempt category) for violence in television programming aired by English-language programming services. The CRTC said it was satisfied that the system—with its levels of C, C8+, FAM, PA, 14+, 18+, which went beyond the commission's requirement for violence to include coarse language, nudity and depictions of sexuality—met the criteria set out in its Policy on TV Violence.

It also agreed that Canadian broadcasters could, as an interim measure, display the ratings on-screen in the fall of 1997 while they worked out the technical bugs holding up the actual encoding of the programs to work with V-chips. The CRTC ruling drew only modest media attention—and no political outcry.

The contrast on that day could not have been more remarkable, for at precisely the same time in Washington, American broadcast industry executives were engaged in a pitched battle with senators, members of Congress, and activist lobby organizations. They were trying to work out a deal that would salvage their TV Parental Guidelines System, and get rid of a raft of antibroadcasting legislation, which was hanging over their heads in Damoclean fashion.

It was a brawl that would go on for nearly another month, until a deal was struck July 10 with public advocacy groups and congressional leaders. The major U.S. networks, with the exception of NBC, agreed to add a series of initials to their existing system that would highlight the presence of fantasy violence, sexual situations, violence, coarse language, and suggestive dialogue in television programming.

The Canadian broadcasters would later opt not to take exactly the same course, stating that their violence-based rating system—working in tandem with already established comprehensive industry codes and the use of advisories—would be of more use to parents than the emerging U.S. contingent.

It was not surprising that these two parallel processes had resulted in similar, yet slightly different, television rating systems. What was fascinating, was the manner and environment in which each was created.

In Canada, the debate about violence on television, classification systems, and the role of the V-chip had been on the government and regulatory agenda far longer than in the U.S. Yet the Canadian broadcast and cable industry had delicately managed to weave together industry, public, and regulatory consensus in a low-key approach that attracted no political heat.

Trina McQueen, president of the Canadian Discovery channel and one of the country's most respected broadcasters, had led the industry team in developing the rating system. She described it as quintessentially Canadian: practical, sensible, and rooted "not in dramatic rhetoric but in reality."

However, in the United States, the entire process was engulfed in controversy almost from the moment it began, when the Clinton administration enthusiastically embraced the technical "magic bullet" offered by V-chip technology. Having initially vowed to take to court any attempt to have their programming rated, the American broadcasters were now bickering with the politicians over how many different types of warning labels should be put on *Ellen*'s closet door.

They were searching for rational solutions in an environment that saw a Republican congressman castigate NBC for its 1997 broadcast of *Schindler's List*, thereby exposing the children of America to "violence . . . vile language, full frontal nudity, and irresponsible sexual activity."

To understand how this all began in Canada, the genesis of rating systems and the evolution of the V-chip, one has to go back to the 1980s.

The Canadian circumstance was shaped by the confluence of three things: two singular events and the personality and character of one particular individual who happened at the time to occupy an influential and critical policy-making position within the federal government bureaucracy.

The first pivotal event took place on December 6, 1989, when Canada had its first experience with horrific mass murder. A gunman walked into the École polytechnique in Montreal, Quebec, and began shooting. When it was over, fourteen young women, all engineering students, were dead.

The country was deeply and massively traumatized. It had lost its innocence in a fusillade of bullets, much the same way Scotland would in the aftermath of the Dunblane horror yet to come. After years of pointing to similar events in the United States and disdainfully saying "that type of thing can't happen here," it did. Canadians did not understand how—or why.

One man profoundly affected by the massacre was Keith Spicer, the chairman of the Canadian Radio-television and Telecommunications Commission.

The CRTC is the Canadian government's federal regulatory authority for broadcasting and telecommunications. It issues radio and television licenses, sets telephone rates, and sees its primary mandate as the protection and promotion of Canadian culture, via Canadian content regulations on radio and television. Its statutory authority is similar to the FCC in the United States, the Independent Broadcast Authority in Britain, and other comparable regulatory agencies in Australia, New Zealand, and France.

Keith Spicer came to the role of chairman with an eclectic background. He was the country's first Commissioner of Official Languages, promoting and monitoring French/English bilingualism within federal government institutions. He often joked that the best place to learn another language was in bed with an attractive partner of the opposite culture. He had been an author, a motivational speaker, the editor of a major Canadian daily newspaper, and had conducted a major study on Canadian unity at the request of an unpopular prime minister. Spicer was a master of the grand vision and dismissive of practical details.

The CRTC chairman was deeply shocked by what had happened in Montreal. While there was no suggestion of a link between the massacre and violence on television, he nonetheless ordered that two substantial studies be undertaken on the subject. The first looked at how other countries were addressing the issue of violence on television; the second reviewed over two hundred existing scientific studies on the subject.

These reports were released in 1992, and the commission concluded that the evidence was strong enough to say that there was a link—although not necessarily one of direct cause and effect—between violence portrayed on television and violence in society.

The CRTC used these studies as a lever to "request" broadcasters to improve and strengthen their code on the depiction of violence in programming, first developed in 1986. This revised code, while "voluntary," would still have to be approved by the CRTC. The cable industry was at the same time also told to develop its own antiviolence strategy.

As all this was in progress, the second principal event occurred, again in Quebec. A young teenage girl was raped and murdered. While there was yet again no direct linkage between this tragedy and the portrayal of violence in the media, the victim's thirteen-year-old sister, Virginie Larivière, was convinced there was.

She initiated a petition, demanding action on television violence. By the time she was finished, she had one and a half million signatures, which she brought to the capital city of Ottawa for presentation to the federal government.

Sensing an unproblematic photo opportunity, the prime minister's office invited her to bring the petition to Brian Mulroney for him to sign. As he was penning his name with cameras rolling, he chatted with the thirteen-year-old and said that his government would urge the television networks to voluntarily address the issue of violence on television. Ms. Larivière shot back in French and said, not urge, legislate. The prime minister responded with words to the effect that, yes, of course, there would be legislation. All of sudden, a major commitment was made by the prime minister, captured on news tape, from which escape would be problematic.

The prime minister sent the petition to the House of Commons Standing Committee on Communications and Culture and asked for a full investigation of the issue. He said that if the broadcasting industry did not voluntarily take action, the government would be willing to adopt strict laws and regulations. Never mind that any such laws and regulations might not withstand a freedom of speech challenge under the Canadian Charter of Rights and Freedoms. The prime minister's office had put its weight behind the issue of violence on television and had given it additional momentum.

The Parliamentary Committee held public hearings. The CRTC organized a major conference in Toronto, Ontario, at the C. M. Hincks Institute of Child Psychology, involving all elements of the broadcasting industry, educators, social scientists, politicians, community activist groups, and parents.

And a young, inventive professor from Simon Fraser University in British Columbia wrote to Keith Spicer and told him about a computer chip device he was working on. Tim Collings called his gadget the viewer control chip, or V-chip, for short; he said it could screen out inappropriate programming for children if the programming was coded for violent content.

In general, the Canadian broadcast industry adopted a politically astute and socially responsible approach to this delicate issue, learning from what had happened in the United States. Every time a new academic study was issued supporting the causal link between violence on television and violence in society, the American broadcasters would commission another study that would come to the opposite conclusion.

The Canadian broadcast industry collectively said it was time to move past the "my study against your study" confrontational approach. The broadcasters admitted that if they aired advertisements hoping to influence people to buy this brand of soap or that brand of car, how could they definitively say there was no causal link between violence on television and violence in society? Chairman Spicer also had helped set the tone at the various conferences he instigated by making it clear he was not interested in more acrimonious finger-pointing, but rather in building consensus on developing creative solutions.

The broadcasters also declared that Canadian programming was not the problem, that the problem was with the portrayal of violence in U.S. programming. As well, they moved the discussion into other areas that had heretofore not been the subject of much focus: the home VCR and the corner movie video store, and violent blood-and-gore video games. Broadcasters, who found a surprising ally in some parents' groups, pointed out that just because the violent programming was seen on the television set did not mean it had necessarily come from a television station.

The unregulated video rental business, combined with the advent of inexpensive VCR technology, was bringing video material into the home that five to ten years before had only been available in movie theaters. Unsuspecting parents, unfamiliar with the content of these films, often received a rude shock when they found out what they had rented. During a session of the House of Commons committee investigating violence on television, one member of Parliament admitted that his family had gone through that exact experience.

Of equal or even greater concern was when the video went down into the basement "rec" room, and the kids watched on their own, with parents oblivious to what Freddie was doing on Elm street.

There was one illustrative story of a Canadian sixth-grade teacher who had asked her students if any of them had seen *Silence of the Lambs*. All hands but one went up. At that point in time, this film had not yet played on conventional television. It had been shown on pay TV, which then had a national penetration rate of about 15% of cabled homes. Given the film's rating, children of this age would not have been allowed into a theater to see it. Only one conclusion was possible: most of these eleven- to twelve-year-olds had seen it at home, via the corner video rental store.

With video games, it was much the same story. Did parents know about the content of the action video games, where young players had the choice of half a dozen different ways to decapitate the bad guy, complete with splattering blood? There was indeed much more to video violence than just television programming.

The Canadian broadcast industry responded to this increased concern about violence on television by government and the regulator by creating a pan-industry organization called the Action Group on Violence on Television (AGVOT), in February 1993, in the wake of the Hincks conference.

Membership included over-the-air broadcasters, both private and public, the cable industry, cable-delivered specialty channels, program producers, and advertisers. AGVOT was assigned to coordinate the industry's approach to the development of codes and classification systems, and to generate public education on issues related to media literacy. The industry—cajoled by Chairman Keith Spicer—had agreed to a collective approach, something that had not happened before.

As all of this was taking place in Canada, there were other international catalysts that kept the issue very much on the public and media agenda. There was the murder of two-year-old James Bulger in Britain. Two boys under the age of twelve had lured Bulger away and murdered him in a fashion similar to the plot scenario of a horror film, *Child's Play III*. In the U.S., a two-year-old girl died in a house fire, set by her five-year-old brother. He said he was re-creating what he saw on an episode of *Beavis and Butthead*, an animated program developed for the teen market. Two teenage boys were killed when they lay down on the center line of a highway and were run over by cars. They had been mimicking a scene from a film called *The Program* in which a similar stunt had been tried. The movie was recalled, and that section edited out.

In June of 1993, the Canadian House of Commons received a report from the Standing Committee on Communications and Culture entitled *Television Violence: Fraying Our Social Fabric*. The report called for strong voluntary industry codes, for a program classification system to be designed by the CRTC, and for parents to take more responsibility for what their children were watching.

American broadcasters were also under the spotlight of governmental scrutiny. Just a month before, in the May 1993 ratings sweeps, the U.S. networks had gone all out with murder and mayhem in an effort to garner viewership. Much to their chagrin, they scored high ratings where they did not want them: on Capital Hill. They were called to explain themselves in front of Senator Paul Simon's committee. U.S. Attorney General Janet Reno outraged First Amendment advocates when she suggested that limiting violent content would not be unconstitutional.

A number of members of Congress launched bills to tackle the violence issue, talking about rating systems, family-viewing hours, and other initiatives. The White House waded in as well. President Bill Clinton spoke directly to the Hollywood creative community and asked it to take a closer look at what messages it was creating for American youth with its movies and television programs.

Faced with this uproar, the American networks—in spite of loud protests from the production back lots—agreed they would use advisories to warn viewers about violent shows, beginning with the 1993 fall season.

In October 1993, after a number of revisions and considerable negotiations over the wording, the Canadian broadcasters' new Voluntary Code on Violence in Television Programming was accepted by the CRTC. The code banned outright the telecast of gratuitous or glamorized violence. It put in place tough new restrictions on violence in children's programming and set a 9:00 P.M. watershed hour, before which programming containing violence for adults could not be broadcast. Acceptance of the code by the CRTC was conditional on the development of a program rating system by the industry.

Having put their own house in order, the Canadian broadcasters then told the CRTC it was going to have to deal with the violent U.S. programs or else face the fact that the Canadian code would accomplish very little. The tenuous broadcast/cable coalition was badly fractured when the broadcasters suggested the commission consider ordering cable to black out or scramble any American programs that did not meet Canadian standards.

Talk of blackouts, scrambling, and other consumer-unfriendly proposals set alarm bells ringing in the Canadian cable industry. Its response was to fund the development and testing of the V-chip, the blocking device invented by Professor Tim Collings of Simon Fraser University in British Columbia. The cable position was that if anyone was to black out programs, it should be the individual consumer who made that decision, not the cable industry.

By mid-1994, again under prodding by U.S. Senator Paul Simon, American broadcasters agreed to the creation of an independent, third-party monitoring organization, which would examine and report annually on the violent content in their programming over a three-year period. At the same time, the V-chip was being put though its first field trial, in Edmonton, Alberta, with sixty families and one broadcaster participating.

In the fall of 1994, the Canadian broadcaster's Violence Code was given its first real test. The Canadian Broadcast Standards Council, an independent organization set up by private broadcasters to administer its various codes, acted on a viewer complaint. It ruled that the program *Mighty Morphin Power Rangers* violated the children's section of the code.[2] The decision prompted international media attention.

Several Canadian stations and networks took the show completely off the air. One network went back to the American producers and asked for modifications to the program, to have some violent sections deleted so that the program would comply with the code. Eventually, even that network dropped the program from its schedule.

In its decision, the Canadian Broadcast Standards Council pointed again to the dilemma with which the CRTC had not yet been able to come to grips. For even though

Canadian stations had either modified or dropped the program, *Power Rangers* was still available in Canadian homes from an American network. Publicly, the commission praised the council's decision as a validation of its self-regulatory approach. Privately, it knew it was going to have to do something about the lack of a level playing field between Canadian and U.S. signals. Canadian broadcasters were insisting on nothing less.

Through the early part of 1995, there was intense debate within the CRTC. There were suggestions that Chairman Spicer and some of the staff were seriously considering forcing the Canadian cable industry to black out American programs that did not meet Canadian standards. Other CRTC commissioners were just as vehemently opposed to taking any action that would see the commission (therefore the government) placed in the role of censor. Questions were also raised about whether a blackout order would stand up to a court challenge under the Charter of Rights, and whether it would be valid under the provisions of the Canada-U.S. Free Trade Agreement.

The commission had no stomach for another massive consumer revolt. The Canadian broadcast regulator was still showing the bruises from its last exchange with cable subscribers who had been furious over the introduction of a new group of Canadian specialty channels. They blamed the CRTC for forcing them to subscribe to these new services, whether they wanted them or not.

The cable industry, also badly tarred by the specialty service debacle, was lobbying hard against any blackout regulations. They said individual parental control, made possible by the V-chip, was the most practical and consumer-friendly option. If only broadcasters would create a program rating system, the problem could be solved.

Spicer was faced with an impasse within the CRTC. He did get agreement from the other commissioners to take the issue to a public hearing process. If there was enough public support via the hearings, a blackout or scrambling regulation would be more tolerable within the commission.

In April 1995, the CRTC announced it would hold hearings to obtain public input on what it described as its long-term and short-term approaches to dealing with television violence. The long-term strategy involved developing a Canadian rating system and giving parents new tools like the V-chip. On a short-term basis, the commission wanted to hear what should be done about what it described as the unequal application of restrictions on television violence across the broadcasting system, in particular, the programming broadcast by Canadian stations and the programming on American signals distributed by cable in Canada. The hearings would be held that September across Canada.

In June of 1995, bills were introduced in the U.S. Congress, calling for the creation of a television programming rating system and the addition of V-chip technology in all new TV sets.

Two months later, in August of 1995, the cable industry had begun its third and most extensive test of the V-chip in a number of markets across Canada.

The public hearing process did not give Spicer any strong endorsement of blackouts. The creative community and civil libertarians were strongly opposed to anything resembling censorship by government. Some intervenors also tried to tell the CRTC they were concerned as much about sex, language, and nudity as violence. But Spicer derailed that conversation quickly whenever it was raised. Part of his violence strategy was to deliberately keep these touchy issues off the agenda. He was fearful the focus on protecting children from unsuitable violence in programming would be hijacked by those who would muddy the waters with discussions about morality.

At the final public hearings in Ottawa, cable heavily promoted the V-chip and brought in consumers who had used it in the second trial. The commission listened closely. Less than two hundred households had actually experimented with this new technology, and now two parents were at the witness table, talking about their experiences with the cable-designed rating system, and how the V-chip worked.

Cable also faced the blackout issue head-on, warning the commission that any regulation to scramble or black out U.S. programming would be a technical nightmare, a financial disaster, and would not withstand a legal challenge in the courts. Cable operators suggested that American border stations would go along with a Canadian rating system because they would want to continue to be distributed in Canada. Cable said the V-chip was ready; all it needed was a Canadian rating system.

The Canadian broadcasters told the commission *they* could not proceed on a rating system for Canadian shows until the issue of foreign signals was addressed. They said it was unfair to them and unfair to Canadian families if there were different rules for Canadian and American signals. Would cable rate the U.S. shows? Would there really be an American rating system? While there was pending legislation in the U.S. dealing with a program classification system, American networks had said, at that point, that they would not accept government intrusion into their First Amendment rights. They muttered darkly about going to court if forced to classify the content of their programs.

The Canadian public hearings were generally inconclusive. No easy answers emerged at the end of September 1995.

By January 1996, there was still no agreement at the CRTC on what to do about the American signals. There was an impasse within the commission on any blackout regulations. In the United States, the debate over the multifaceted Telecommunications Act, which now contained the V-chip and program classification system provisions, was heating up. The measures appeared headed for passage.

Spicer and two of his commissioner colleagues trooped off to Washington to find out what was going on. They heard from half a dozen or so members of Congress that the V-chip and rating system legislation would be approved. They also heard that any attempt by Canadian cable operators to interfere with American signals would be fought by the U.S. government. Washington would, however, agree to have U.S. border stations participate in the development of a Canadian classification system that would work with the V-chip.

Within a week of Spicer's return, President Bill Clinton, in his State of the Union speech, said the V-chip legislation would pass. He challenged broadcasters to develop a program classification system to protect children from unsuitable television programming. Clinton also upped the ante, inviting the heads of the American networks to the White House for a television summit to discuss the issue. It was a neat political maneuver that effectively sandbagged the Republicans on a key family values issue running up to the November elections.

On February 8, 1996, the new Telecommunications Act containing the V-chip provision was passed. It required a V-chip to be built into all television sets with screens larger than thirteen inches. The V-chip would allow consumers to block "sexual, violent, and other material about which parents should be informed before it is displayed to children." The bill gave the American networks one year to develop a program rating system. If the industry did not or could not accomplish that, a television ratings committee would be established by the U.S. Federal Communications Commission, to provide an advisory rating system that might lead to an imposed structure.

On February 29, 1996, the U.S. network heads met with President Clinton and Vice President Al Gore at the White House. They emerged with the creation of an Implementation Committee, an industry group under the chairmanship of Jack Valenti, president of the Motion Picture Association of America. This committee would be responsible for development and implementation of a rating system, to be in place by January 1997.

It was an incredible sea change. The American broadcast industry, which less than six months before had promised to take to the Supreme Court any attempt to have them classify their programs, had now agreed to develop a classification system.

CRTC Chairman Keith Spicer was thus given room to move. The Americans were going to have a classification system and the V-chip. In a matter of months, the U.S. environment had moved from several years behind Canada to ahead of it. Talk of blackouts and scrambling was now not necessary. On March 14, 1996, the CRTC released its decision, which included the following:

- Canadian broadcasters, by September of 1996, must encode their signals with a V-chip-compatible rating, which would be applied at the very least to children's programming (programming intended for children under 12), drama programming, reality-based shows, feature films, as well as promotional spots for these programs and movie trailer advertisements;
- The broadcast industry, through the pan-industry Action Group organization (AGVOT), would be expected to develop a four-to-six-level informative and user-friendly program classification system, which will have to be approved by the CRTC;
- The cable industry would have to make available by September 1996 an affordable V-chip device to any customer who wants one;
- By January 1997, all distribution systems in Canada would have to ensure that the American signals they distribute are encoded with a V-chip-based rating;
- If, by that time, the U.S. broadcasters had not implemented a rating system the CRTC judges to be effective and parent-friendly for Canada, Canadian distributors would be required to develop an alternative way to encode these signals with the Canadian rating system.

The Canadian broadcast industry reactivated the AGVOT infrastructure in April 1996. A twenty-six-member committee, comprised of programmers from all the major conventional broadcast services and specialty channels, along with representatives from the production industry and the cable industry, was assigned to develop a classification system. With blackouts off the table and the focus being on the development of a classification system—a subject now of as much interest to cable as to broadcasters—the broad-caster/cable alliance was back on again.

The committee's mandate was to develop a simple, parent-friendly rating system for violence in programming, which would work with the V-chip technology. Under the direction of the AGVOT Executive chaired by Trina McQueen, president of the Canadian Discovery Channel, the committee would look at how many levels should be developed, keeping in mind a four-to-six-level system seemed to be viewed as being most useful, based upon the public hearing process and previous consumer research undertaken by AGVOT.

The committee was also asked to see how to make the Canadian system meet the needs of Canadian families yet be compatible with the one to be developed in the United States, given the extensive cross-border flow of programming. Research from previous V-chip trials had indicated that consumers strongly thought compatibility with the American system was very important.

It is important to appreciate that the rating system that was being developed by the AGVOT classification committee would be used only by English-language conventional (over-the-air) stations and networks and by English-language specialty services.

Quebec French-language services had made a strong case during the public hearing process that they should be able to use the provincial film classification board ratings, the *Régie du cinéma* rating system, for their programming. They argued their viewers were already familiar with the nomenclature of this system and that it reflected the uniqueness of the French-Canadian culture. The commission agreed.

No similar approach was possible on the English-Canadian side because all the provinces had different movie ratings, and attempts to create a uniform system for English-language feature films were bogged down in bureaucracy. However, as the Canadian pay and pay-per-view cable channels were telecasting uncut feature films, they made the case that they too should continue to use the provincial rating systems, again citing consumer familiarity.

The CRTC accepted that argument as well, and while its decision urged harmonization of the three classification systems, it tacitly acknowledged that Canada would probably end up with a multiplicity of rating systems, in both official languages.

That reality, plus new developments on the technical front, made it quite clear early on in the AGVOT process that another V-chip test would be required before the technology could be considered ready for broad consumer rollout.

One of the most important considerations was just where the encoding data that would trigger the V-chip would be placed in the broadcast signal. The first Canadian tests had placed it in the vertical blanking interval, the VBI. It had been inserted in field 1 of line 21, where the closed-captioning data was transmitted. It had been the least expensive way to do it in the early field trials, as all broadcasters already had encoding equipment for closed captioning. However, in those early trials, the program encoding information sometimes interfered with the captioning data and jumbled the caption text when it was displayed on the receiving television set.

As well, the American Electronic Industries Association (EIA), in establishing technical standards for VBI, had decided V-chip encoding data should be placed in field 2 of line 21. This decision, in essence, created a North American standard. Canada could not follow a separate technical path if it hoped eventually to have V-chip-equipped television sets in the Canadian market. Sets are built for the entire North American market, and technical compatibility with American standards was deemed essential.

AGVOT was thus faced with the need for a V-chip that would have to be able to read multiple rating systems, function in both English and French, and handle encoding data in field 2 of line 21 in the VBI. It also wanted to field-test its program classification system. The Action Group went back to the CRTC in early August 1996, and asked for more time. It said the September 1996 deadline would be impossible to achieve and requested a one-year extension, to September 1997.

The CRTC demanded a detailed report justifying the delay.[3] In early October 1996, it granted the extension and instructed AGVOT to submit its classification system for final approval by the omission no later than April 30, 1997.

During the summer and early fall of 1996, work continued on the development of the classification system. As protection of children had been the underpinning of the Canadian approach to the issue of violence on television, the first key question for the Classification Committee was how to deal with content in children's programming.

It is important to remember that in Canada, the classification system would not be a stand-alone entity. It would, in fact, be a key module of the industry's Voluntary Code on Violence in Television Programming. Therefore, it was important to build the ratings for children's programming on the foundation of the children's section of the CRTC-approved code, where there were strict rules clearly established for the portrayal of violence in children's programming. This was the same code that had been responsible for taking *Power Rangers* off Canadian stations.

While the CRTC itself defined children as all youngsters under the age of twelve, the committee felt that a single children's category would be too broad an age spectrum, and that it needed to be divided into two levels.

Committee members turned to research undertaken by Dr. Wendy Josephson of the University of Manitoba. In her study prepared for the Department of Canadian Heritage,[4] she noted that age eight had been identified as a watershed stage in connection with how children processed what they saw on television, particularly in terms of being able to distinguish reality from fantasy. The result was a rating level for programming suitable for all children, and one for those eight years and older.

With these two categories in place, establishing the levels of the rating system for nonchildren's programming emerged over subsequent committee sessions. After exploring a number of combinations, the programmers decided that four classification levels could accommodate the scope of programming, ranging from that designed for a broad general audience to programming with content intended only for adult audiences.

The guidelines for violence content were built word by word. The goal was to provide useful information for parents and ensure there were demonstrable gradations of content as the rating level increased. The descriptive information was structured to make the system easy to understand and use.

The challenge of building the classification system was substantial. It would have to be capable of dealing with the wide range of programming offered by English-language services through over-the-air local stations, national networks, and cable-delivered specialty services. It would be applied to programming aimed at preschoolers, to unedited material targeted at adult audiences, and everything in between.

A key difference between the Canadian and American environment was that the CRTC had mandated AGVOT to develop a classification system that would rate *only* violent content. In the U.S., there were broader priorities. The wording of the 1996 Telecommunications Act said the industry must "establish rules for rating video programming that contains sexual, violent, or other indecent material."

However, as the Canadian programmers constructed their system, they felt that a rating scheme that dealt only with violence would not adequately serve the needs of viewers, particularly parents. These programmers who regularly dealt with the public knew what the commission had not wanted to hear, that parents were just as concerned about content other than violence.

It was their view that a system that rated only violent content could cause negative feedback from viewers. There would be occasions when a program would contain no violence yet not be suitable for younger audiences due to language, nudity, sexuality, and/or mature themes. A violence-only rating system would not be functional in informing parents about this other content.

Furthermore, in research conducted for AGVOT in 1994,[5] 70% of respondents had strongly agreed that coarse language, nudity, depictions of sexuality, and mature themes should be included in a television classification system, even though violence would be the most important content element to be rated.

The committee then developed a rating structure that blended all of these content elements into a comprehensive classification system, providing even more information to parents than had been requested by the CRTC. The compatibility issue with the Americans was also important. The Americans would be rating for content other than violence. If the two systems were to be similar, Canadian programmers would have to include more than just violence in their rating system.

The Canadian rating system was pretty much finalized by late November 1996. The preliminary framework of what had been developed in Canada had been informally conveyed to the Americans. The Canadian system had to be completed to allow enough time for the manufacture of the integrated circuitry that would be installed in the new, stand-alone V-chip boxes developed by Tim Collings and a Toronto manufacturer, which the cable industry wanted to field-test in January.

While the system, assigned the working name of The Canadian Television Rating System (CTR), was designed to blend all the controversial program elements into a comprehensive system, the broadcast community was firm in its intent to follow the letter of the CRTC's public notice. It would submit only the *violence* portion of the system to the commission for its approval.

The hearings had dealt with violence but not the other content elements. Broadcasters would not agree to have the CRTC pass judgement on these other content issues. There was no quarrel from the commission on this, as senior officials admitted privately that the last thing they wanted was the CRTC to become a moral censor or an arbiter of good taste or decency. Therefore, the system was laid out for submission to the regulatory body in an "above the line, below the line format" with all the violence content information above the line, and all the other content descriptors below the line.

By December 1996, AGVOT was well into organizing an extensive V-chip trial, scheduled to begin early in the new year. On December 19, preceded by dozens of leaked reports, the U.S. Implementation Committee released its initial (later revised) TV Parental Guidelines System to mixed reviews. While some congressional leaders and lobby groups argued that it did not go far enough, President Bill Clinton said the industry should be given a chance to make it work, and change it later if that was what American parents wanted.

In January 1997, the American networks began rating their programs. Because there were no V-chips in the United States, and none expected until they were built into television sets sometime in 1998, the networks put small icons on the screen to advise viewers of the rating.

In Canada, the V-chip trial had been scheduled to commence at the beginning of January and continue for sixty days. However, there were delays in manufacturing and shipping the five hundred V-chip boxes necessary for the trial; therefore, the test did not officially begin until February 7, 1997.

Families were being recruited for the trial, and boxes were being installed in homes as they became available. Programming services were testing their new equipment, ensuring that the encoder in particular interfaced smoothly with their existing operational configuration. It was a critical issue, as the V-chip information would be feeding into their programming stream, and broadcasters did not want to jeopardize in any fashion the integrity of their signal.

The 1997 trial had almost three times as many broadcasters taking part compared to the previous trial nearly a year earlier. A total of 28 programming services participated: 14 conventional stations in 5 markets, 3 national networks, 7 specialty services, and 4 U.S. border stations, who volunteered to take part in this Canadian experiment.[6]

A national research firm was hired to recruit the five hundred families for the trial, which the cable industry had agreed to fully fund. To qualify, respondents had to be cable subscribers and parents or guardians with children aged three to twelve living in the household. Participants had to agree to have the V-chip installed in their homes for a three-to-four-week period, commit to use the system, and to participate in subsequent research interviews.

It was much more difficult to recruit families for the trial than had been expected. In one market alone, almost five thousand households were contacted before eighty-nine were found who were eligible and agreed to participate. It was validation of separate research conducted for the Canadian cable industry, which indicated that consumer interest in technology to block programming had dropped significantly from 66% in 1995 to 55% in 1997.

Consequently, rather than the recruitment goal of 500, only 374 households actually took part. The trial ended on March 16, and the research data collection began, with V-chip households interviewed through a combination of telephone interviews and focus group sessions.

Concurrent to the trial, AGVOT undertook a national public opinion survey on the proposed rating system. Some 1,548 English-speaking adult Canadians were interviewed between March 11 and 31, 1997. (This sample size provided a margin of error of plus or minus 2.5 percentage points, 19 times out of 20.)

These interviews were conducted in-home, giving participants the opportunity to thoroughly read a description of the Canadian rating system. The research findings were very positive.

- 91% approved of a system that rated programming mainly according to the level of violence it contained but also took into account the presence of coarse language, sexual content, or nudity;
- 86% approved of rating children's programs as either C, meaning they are suitable for all children, or C8+, meaning they are suitable only for children age eight and older;
- 88% approved of rating those programs not made for children with one of four levels: programs that are suitable for all ages; programs that contain content that may not be suitable for younger viewers; programs suitable for viewers 14 years and over; and programs suitable for viewers 18 years and over.

After reading a one-page description of the classification system that outlined the content elements in each level, a large majority of respondents gave the system high marks.

- 84% approved of the Canadian Television Rating System;
- 85% of parents with children under 18 approved of the rating system, while 84% of parents with children under 12 approved it;
- 86% of parents with children under 18 said the system will be helpful for making choices about what their children will be able to watch; the number was 87% for parents with children under 12 years of age;
- 85% of respondents thought the system was easy to understand.

There was also a strong desire for compatibility between the Canadian and American rating systems, with 71% believing it important that the Canadian and U.S. systems be the same or similar.

The approval level from the families who had actually used the system with the V-chip was equally high. They gave it high marks for clarity and ease of distinguishing between the rating levels. Some 80% indicated it was easy to understand the different rating levels. The theme of compatibility with the U.S. system also came through in this research, with 78% saying it was very important or somewhat important that the Canadian and U.S. rating systems be the same or similar.

There were also focus group sessions with parents from the V-chip test households. While some focus group participants found the ratings too broad, there was general consensus that the age and content combination was useful. They said they used the age level as the starting point, then looked at the content elements contained in that level. If their children were more mature than most children their age, they might stay at that level or go higher. Or if they wanted to be extra cautious with their children's viewing, they might use a V-chip setting that would block more content.

They also appreciated the effort to keep the descriptors simple to understand. However, there was a not-so-subtle warning from these parents: for broadcasters to gain the confidence of the population, they would have to classify their programming appropriately, as the system was introduced across the industry.

They also reaffirmed their support for compatible rating systems, suggesting it would be nonsensical that different ratings be applied to the same program by Canadian and American services, given the large number of identical programs.[7]

In addition to the public opinion surveys, the Action Group also consulted a diverse range of individuals and organizations with an interest in children and television and with expertise in classification issues. The reaction to the system overall was quite positive. The endorsement of a number of key groups was important for AGVOT to have in hand when it submitted the rating system to the federal regulatory agency for approval on April 30, 1997.

While AGVOT's regulatory mandate was limited to developing and submitting a classification system to the commission, the broadcasters and cable industry felt it important to give the CRTC a full report on the technical issues that came to the fore during the trial.

There were a number of critical ones. Broadcasters said the software program used to encode their programs needed more work. Because the equipment needed to send the rating data in field 2 of line 21 was so new, there was only one reliable encoding device that had passed the test with flying colors.

Another other key issue for broadcasters was the CRTC requirement that program promotional spots and paid theatrical advertisements also needed to be rated and encoded. With the lack of integration between the encoding hardware and software and a station's overall automation systems, the broadcasters found that they just could not fulfill this requirement at this time.

The other key finding from the trial was the only modest consumer interest in the V-chip box in the configuration that was tested. In the focus groups particularly, it became evident that the high awareness of the V-chip prior to participation in the trial affected the participants' expectations for the technology and their subsequent disappointment with it.

The test families generally spoke highly of the V-chip technology as an important and useful means of monitoring their children's television viewing. However, they did not see it as a replacement for parental involvement and control of what their children watched, merely an additional tool. Furthermore, they believed that what they had tested was not in its final form, expecting that changes and improvements to the technology would be made before it was widely available in the marketplace.

Therefore, there was a general unwillingness to acquire the technology, either by renting or purchasing, at that time. They did not like having an additional set-top box and an additional remote control (a small one at that). They also were frustrated by problems with their VCRs, where the V-chip installation interfered with their ability to tape one program and watch another at the same time.

When asked how they thought the V-chip would work best for them, over half (64%) wanted to have the V-chip integrated in television sets, 18% in a converter, and only 11% in a stand-alone box.

On April 30, 1997, the Action Group filed its inch-and-a-half-thick report and supporting research with the CRTC. In its Summary Conclusions section, AGVOT under-lined that the V-chip, while an important development, was only one piece of the solution.

> Canada has the best framework anywhere to deal with violence on television. We have stringent industry codes. We have the Canadian Broadcast Standards Council. Canadian pay and pay-per-view services were the first in the world to rate their unedited feature films. We produce the best non-violent children's programming in the world. We are the only country to have tested V-chip technology, not once, but four times. With the Commission's approval, we will soon have a classification system that works with the V-chip. We have done better than most countries and have avoided the acrimony and political posturing extant in other jurisdictions.

> In this report we are submitting a solid classification system for violence in television programming. It tests well with consumers and is supported by extensive and serious research. It answers the criteria set by the Commission.

> The comprehensive Canadian Television Rating System which the industry intends to adopt includes other content elements and moves the industry beyond the expectations of the Commission. Canadian programming services are voluntarily undertaking to provide even more information to parents.

> With the approval of the Canadian Television Rating System for violence, broadcasters can begin encoding their programming by the end of September. However, there are caveats to that commitment, complicating factors beyond our control. There are issues which need to be settled before full implementa-tion in Canada is possible.

> There are serious technological problems, as well as limitations on the soft-ware. The encoding software, for example, is less than reliable, a critical factor for programming services which will be adding this rating information into their main programming stream. Certain program elements which should be encoded—promotions and movie advertisements—will have to wait until the technology catches up.

> While consumers support the concept of V-chip technology and can see its value as a means of monitoring their children's television viewing, they want it built into their television sets.

> As the research indicates, there is a high degree of public support and interest in harmonization of the Canadian system with the American system. We have that now. However, the Americans are uncertain of their direction and timetable.

We are continuing to work on solving the technology issues and on harmonization of the three Canadian systems. Our technical experts acknowledge it will be problematic if Canada maintains three to four different rating systems, as it is highly unlikely that all these systems can be accommodated in V-chip-equipped television sets—the clear preference for consumers.

Canadian programming services and cable companies have demonstrated, by means of the considerable resources and effort they have expended on developing the rating system and the new generation of V-chip technology, that they accept their responsibilities towards Canada's children.

We respectfully request the Commission approve the Canadian Television Rating System for violence, which is clearly supported by solid public opinion research.

This is the beginning of a new dialogue with viewers. It is another principal element of the Canadian approach to violence on television—an approach that is unequalled in the world.

On May 5, 1997, AGVOT made its report to the commission public. Trina McQueen, president of the Canadian Discovery Channel and chair of AGVOT, described the proposed system with these words:

> ...a six-level rating system that uses consistent and clear guidelines to evaluate the content of television programs. The guidelines centre on violence, but include language and sexual content as well. The content evaluation is assigned a rating according to the generally accepted stages of child development. Parents are already familiar with this approach in classifying movies, books, games, toys and other children's products.

Explaining the system was based on extensive research and consultation with parents and with public interest groups, she added:

> The classification system will work with the broadcasters' Code on Violence and the independent compliance mechanism of the Canadian Broadcast Standards Council to give Canadian parents the most comprehensive and advanced parental control system in the world.

In releasing its report, AGVOT also indicated it was prepared to go further than required by the broadcasting regulator. Pointing out that there were issues still to be resolved that made a launch of the V-chip unlikely by the fall program season, AGVOT informed the commission that it had achieved agreement with all sectors of the industry to display the AGVOT program ratings on-screen as an interim measure.

McQueen added that French-language programmers and premium services had also agreed to use on-screen icons, but using their established rating systems, as had been agreed to by the CRTC.

Michael McCabe, president and CEO of the Canadian Association of Broadcasters was also at the May 5 news conference. He said this voluntary initiative by all program services would give parents the benefits of the new classification system by the fall of 1997, when the on-screen rating system would be in place. He reiterated that all sectors of the industry remained committed to achieving program coding that worked with V-chip technology and said the industry would continue to work through the unresolved issues.

During the news conference, Ms. McQueen was asked about the multilevel, multicategory rating system that had been used in earlier trials, and why it had not been adopted by the industry. She indicated that while the earlier system had been developed exclusively by the cable industry to test out the evolving V-chip technology, this one had been created by drawing on the expertise of programmers from over twenty different television services.

She also noted that while the earlier cable system had tested well, with a satisfaction rate of around 77%, the AGVOT system tested higher, with approval ratings of between 84% and 88% on various elements of the system. Furthermore, research on the AGVOT system involved a much larger sample size than in the cable industry tests.

McQueen also said that, given the high priority placed by all those surveyed on the harmonization of the Canadian classification system with the rating system used in the United States, developments in Washington would be closely monitored. She added:

> If the Americans really make dramatic changes in their Parental Guidelines system, the Canadian broadcasters would look at them, but would not change the principles of the Canadian system which is based on recognizable stages of child development.

She also said the AGVOT proposal was not being presented as a perfect system but rather as "a good system that will evolve and get better with the help of parents and everyone else who cares about children."

Canadian media coverage of the release of the report was low key and generally favorable. In the United States, the report was embraced by MPAA President Jack Valenti, who had chaired the American rating committee, and was dismissed by Ed Markey, the Massachusetts congressman who was the most outspoken critic of the U.S. rating system.

For the Canadian broadcast and the cable industry, all it could do now was wait and see if its million dollar investment in the development and testing of the classification system and the next generation of V-chip technology would bear fruit.

Within seven weeks, they had their answer. On June 18, 1997, the CRTC released its decision, describing the proposed rating system as a meaningful, parent-friendly program classification system. The commission also said it was confident that the system would be another mechanism to protect children against TV violence.

In its decision,[8] the CRTC pointed out that the foundation of its violence policy had always been based on protecting children from the harmful effects of television violence, while preserving freedom of expression for creators, and choice for adult viewers.

It noted that its criteria for a classification system was that it be informative and readily understandable to the viewer, and consist of four to six levels. The commission also said any rating system should be responsive to the public's concerns but also be practical for the industry to implement.

The commission said it considered the proposed AGVOT rating system to have met the criteria set out in its violence policy and that it was confident that the implementation of this system, together with the continuing application of the Canadian Association of Broadcasters' Voluntary Code on Violence in Television Programming, would effectively protect children from the harmful effects of television violence.

The CRTC also endorsed the broadcasters' interim proposal to use on-screen icons:

> The Commission considers on-screen icons to be a valuable service since they raise public awareness of the classification system and provide all viewers, not just those who choose to acquire V-chip technology, with program content information. Furthermore, the Commission is satisfied that the use of on-screen icons in a manner that will complement the viewer advisories provided for in Sections 5.1 and 5.2 of the Code will assist parents in making informed program choices for themselves and their families.

On-screen icons had never been part of the commission's or broadcasters' plan, but the industry submitted it as a temporary measure. The decision left it up to the broadcasters to establish the protocols for use of the icons, such as the design, size, and frequency of use.

As to the future of the V-chip, the CRTC made it clear that broadcasters were not off the hook. It stated it expected the implementation of encoding and deployment of V-chip devices to occur as soon as feasible. However, having seen other deadlines come and go— defeated by technical developments—the commission wisely avoided placing a date on the consumer rollout of the V-chip in Canada, other than to say it wanted it as soon as possible:

> The Commission reaffirms its support for the development of parental control technology, and reiterates that it will continue to monitor all developments and take whatever steps are needed to ensure that the protection of children is a permanent feature of the Canadian broadcasting system.

With the CRTC's approval of both its rating system and implementation strategy, the Canadian broadcast industry began working on the launch of on-screen rating icons for late 1997. However, it also kept a close watch to see how the American system would finally shake out. During the news conference in early May at which the Canadian broadcast industry unveiled its rating system, AGVOT Chair Trina McQueen was asked about the American situation as of that moment. She responded:

> I just can't predict what the Americans are going to do, because they have gone through so many evolutions of saying we will never do this, we will always do that. We will go to court, we won't go to court. This is the right system. That's absolutely the wrong system. I don't know anybody who can

forecast what they are actually going to end up with. So, as Scarlet O'Hara said, we'll think about that tomorrow.

When the U.S. broadcasters eventually finally made their deal in mid-July to add the S, V, L, D, and FV initials to their TV Parental Guidelines, AGVOT polled Canadian program services to assess whether there should be any modifications to the Canadian system. In the end, they decided not to add any initials. While the major reason for the implementation of a television program classification in Canada had been violence, the Americans were now much more focused on other agendas, given that three of their four content indicators had nothing at all to do with violence in programming.

The Canadians also strongly believed that their overall system—industry codes, the Broadcast Standards Council, and the most extensively tested rating system in the world—was better than what had evolved in the U.S.

The Americans, for example, had added an FV (Fantasy Violence) option to their rating for programming for older children, to alert parents when the violence was "more intense or more combative." However, the Canadian broadcast system already had strict provisions in place about violence in children's programming, spelled out in various industry codes. This FV label would be the rating applied to programs such as the *Power Rangers*, which had already been taken off the air in Canada because it did not meet violence code guidelines.

Canadian broadcasters therefore thought the FV designator redundant for their system and, furthermore, felt it could possibly be misunderstood by parents to be a "Family Viewing" label, which would add to viewer confusion.

At the other end of the scale, the Canadians considered that no initials to protect children were required for their 18+ rating, as it was clearly designated for adult viewers.

As for sensitive content in other ratings categories, Canadian programmers had a long tradition of using viewer advisories at the beginning of programs, and industry codes even mandated their use in specific circumstances. These advisories enabled broadcasters to supply even more detailed information about content than could be conveyed with initials added to the ratings designators.

On August 28, 1997, Canadian broadcasters unveiled the icons they would use to rate their programming. As AGVOT had indicated to the CRTC when it filed its report, the industry changed the names of two categories because of parental familiarity with the terminology: FAM (Family) became G (for General), and PA (Parental Advisory) became PG (Parental Guidance) (see Appendix).

As was the case with the introduction of the rating system itself, media coverage on the icons was subdued, and there was no reaction from politicians.

Why had things evolved so smoothly in Canada compared to the tumult that occurred in the United States? There were a number of plausible explanations.

The first involved an important change in leadership at the CRTC. Chairman Keith Spicer had adopted television violence as his personal crusade and had made it a priority at the commission. But by the end of the process he was gone, his term expired. His replacement did not have the same emotional attachment to the issue. Madame Françoise Bertrand had quietly and firmly insisted that the integrity of the CRTC's decision on a classification system and the V-chip be respected by broadcasters. But she was prepared to accept a more pragmatic implementation framework proposed by the industry. If Spicer had still been there, it might well have been a different story.

The second reason involved how the two rating systems had been built and tested. The American system had been fashioned not by programmers but by senior lobbyists. In its first version, it was extremely Spartan in its descriptive information and had not actually been used by consumers before it was introduced as "the final system." The process was so plagued by leaks that by the time the American rating system was finally made public, it had already run aground on the reefs of congressional opposition and had drawn the ire of advocacy groups.

The Canadian system, on the other hand, had been crafted by programmers, who were actually going to have to use it on a daily basis in their jobs. They knew the type of information the public wanted by the phone calls and letters they received from viewers, and they felt comfortable with the more extensive content information. The key individuals and organizations sought out in the public consultation process also generally endorsed the system's format and the amount of content information provided. This consultation process was viewed by AGVOT as critical in obtaining CRTC endorsement of the system.

AGVOT was also successful in keeping its system out of the media scrum until it was tested by consumers and submitted to the CRTC. The families who experimented with it and who reviewed it so positively in the national surveys, did so without having their perceptions influenced by inflammatory headlines and editorial punditry. The extensive field trial, which generated a high level of acceptance from the parents who had used the rating system, again provided the CRTC with a solid degree of comfort in approving it. The Americans had no such field testing with which to make their case.

A fourth—and possibly the most important factor—was that in Canada, the rating system would be part of a broad set of instruments already in place to deal with violence on television. The classification system and V-chip would be added to existing strong industry codes that contained prescribed rules for the depiction of violence and the scheduling of programming with violent content. These were rules the industry had drawn up itself and with which they were generally comfortable. There was no such infrastructure or comfort level in the U.S., where some Hollywood program producers talked blackly about how the rating system and the V-chip were the first steps on a dangerous path toward government controlling what went into people's homes.

There was also an established and valid self-regulatory regime functioning in Canada, the Broadcast Standards Council, which had actually been responsible for taking a program (*Power Rangers*) off the air because it did not meet violence code standards. In the American plan, there would be an as yet unproven Monitoring Board with responsibility to oversee how the ratings were applied.

In addition, there were creative media literacy initiatives under way in Canada such as the Internet-based Media Awareness Network.[9] This educational site advocated that having children understand how the media worked was the best protection against its influences, and it then provided parents and teachers with the tools to do just that. In the United States, there were none of these supporting devices. All the "eggs were in the one basket" of a rating system.

Another fundamental factor was that television programming produced in Canada is not, for the most part, very violent. Canadian children's programming in particular has an international reputation for its quality and nonviolent approach to storytelling. While there was concern expressed from the production community that a classification regime would result in constraints on creativity, the focus of the debate in Canada stayed on the protection of young children under the age of twelve. The producers were constantly reassured by the broadcast regulator that it had no interest in telling adults what they could or could not watch.

The final reason was that in the United States, for whatever reason, the issue became a political football. Members of Congress and senators became instant experts on program classification, and each asserted they knew best what the parents of America needed. For the conservative right and family values advocates in particular, television was an easy and convenient target for what ailed America. The Dan Quayle/*Murphy Brown* fight had not gone away.

In Canada, how television programs should be classified was a nonstarter as a political issue. With some trepidation, the broadcast industry had released the details of its ratings system submission to the CRTC right in the middle of a federal election campaign. It was a timetable not of their choosing, but the deadline for filing the AGVOT report had been set long before the election was called. However, the politicians ignored the whole classification issue. It was not raised once during the campaign and continues to remain only a hillock on the Canadian political landscape.

Notes

1.   Television and Violence—A Few Primary Considerations, Jacques DeGuise, Professor, Department of Information & Communications, Université Laval. Excerpted from *Summary and Analysis of Various Studies of Violence and Television*, published by the Canadian Radio-television and Telecommunications Commission, June 1991.
2.   More information on the Canadian Broadcast Standards Council can be found at its Web site: <http://www.cbsc.ca>.
3.   "Progress on Implementation of a Television Programming Classification System and the V-chip in Canada." AGVOT Report to the CRTC, September 6, 1996.
4.   Television Violence: A Review of the Effects on Children of Different Ages. Report for the Department of Canadian Heritage.
5.   "Canadian Public Attitudes Toward a Classification System for Television." Environics Research Group, June 1994.
6.   A list of participating program services in the five test markets is in Appendix 4 of the AGVOT Report to the CRTC, April 30, 1997.
7.   The full research reports are appended to the AGVOT April 30 report to the Canadian Radio-television and Telecommunications Commission.
8.   CRTC Public Notice 1997-80.
9.   Media Awareness Network Web site: <http://www.schoolnet.ca/medianet>.

Developing Television Ratings in Canada and the United States: The Perils and Promises of Self-Regulation

Stephen D. McDowell
With Carleen Maitland

I. INTRODUCTION

In Canada and the United States, the design and development of program rating systems, planned to be used in conjunction with so-called V-chip technologies, was not undertaken by public authorities or by boards or task forces representative of a variety of groups in society, but was undertaken by select parts of the broadcasting industry. In the United States, only if the system proposed by the industry was seen to be unacceptable to the regulator, would the public authority appoint a representative advisory committee to designate a system or informally pressure the industry group to try again. In Canada, no other strategy than that of seeking a voluntary ratings system from industry groups was proposed in public documents.

These cases raise a number of important questions: Why was self-regulation chosen as a strategy to achieve what was supposedly a very important public policy objective? Why did the Canadian and U.S. cases of self-regulation take such very different trajectories in 1997 after very similar industry standards were proposed? Why did Canada end up with a less detailed system than the United States, after several years of work by the regulator on this issue? In more general terms, what benefits or costs does self-regulation have as a way to achieve public goals? What elements need to come together for self-regulation to be seen as a legitimate complement to communications policy or guidance?

It is the argument of this paper that for self-regulation to "work"—that is, to be seen as historically acceptable in the face of the overwhelming conceptual contradictions of being a judge in one's own case and excluding other nonindustry knowledge and expertise—it must address, manage, and placate at least three sets of political relations and social conflicts. Building and managing self-regulation as a social institution in a specific instance involves negotiating and balancing: (1) government-industry relations, (2) relations among different industry groups (including among the core chosen to direct self-regulation and other industry groups not included), and (3) the relations between industry and other societal and advocacy groups that might form around an issue.

The largest peril, however, remains. Self-regulation in specific instances may be a "success" and "work" as a strategy of political management. This success may occur while at the same time self-regulation may restrict speech rights and freedoms, entrench the power of capital in certain sectors, or effectively restrict and silence fuller democratic participation in decisions that concern society as a whole.

II. SELF-REGULATION

Public regulation by government-appointed boards or commissions, whether at the national, state/provincial, or local level, is one set of methods of governing the activities of private professional and industry groups to promote the public interest. Another major mechanism that has been used in market economies and especially in North America is the self-governing bodies of professional and industry groups (Rueschemeyer, 1986; Torstendahl, 1990). Self-regulation goes beyond the self-governance by individual actors or the magical self-regulating interactions of egoistic actors in market relations. It involves conscious collective effort of professional or industry groups to informally guide, regulate, or at least set norms for behavior through the development of codes, ethics, and guidelines. Professional self-governance in market economies is justified by the claim that it is inefficient and unsafe for consumers of certain services to constantly have to prejudge the ability of a provider to successfully undertake a service. After the doctor, architect, or lawyer has provided a service, it is often too late to evaluate the service. In some cases the state grants a sort of franchise or licensing authority to professional groups. In exchange for allowing professional bodies to limit entry into a profession, the public asks those bodies to ensure a minimum level of training and to police or regulate members of the profession who do not live up to certain standards (Randall Collins, 1990).

There are several promises or potential benefits, from a functional or administrative perspective, in pursuing a strategy of self-regulation to complement more direct regulation or legislation. Self-regulation may reduce the load on public officials or regulators, allowing the industry or professional groups to handle many of the administrative and operational details that a more active and attentive regulatory strategy would entail. State agencies may still have final approval or veto power over self-regulatory schemes proposed by industry groups.

Self-regulation offers a number of promises. Many industries seeking to avoid a legislative response to public complaints or preempt calls for state regulation introduce guidelines or self-regulation. In the traditional justification, self-regulation is seen as being preferable to formal regulation both by industry groups and by some groups in government. Additionally, public officials often offer the promise that self-regulation would be abandoned if in fact it did not work, and legislation or regulation would be introduced to serve society's objectives.

One example is found in a discussion of advertising self-regulation. It is claimed that "self-regulation is usually faster and less expensive, as well as more flexible and up-to-date, than government regulation because industry knows better what the problems and their realistic solutions are" (Boddewyn, 1992, p. 3). Self-regulation does not require that injury or complaints be proved with the same rigorous standards of evidence as legal procedures; it complements and assists legal processes; it promotes greater moral adhesion to codes by industry members who designed the codes; it minimizes the friction between businesses and consumers that might arise in formal legal or regulatory settings; and it may be supported by self-regulation in other industries, such as with the interaction of advertising and broadcasting codes (Boddewyn, 1992, pp. 5–6).

A general conceptual difficulty is encountered in the term itself, which runs against a basic precept of natural justice that one should not be a judge in one's own case. Thinking clearly—and setting aside for the moment the historical rationales proposed by defenders of professional and industry power—on the face of it, the idea that industries will regulate their own activities seems absurd. As well, self-regulation portrays most problems or complaints as arising on the margins, as a result of the actions of the few individuals or firms who are not following appropriate practices, rather than a whole social and political arrangement that may be fundamentally skewed in industry's favor. People who might be offended by the assumptions of self-regulation are not only the members of the general public but also the experts and advocates who deal with similar subject matter as industry groups, yet whose knowledge and experience is not consulted, acknowledged, or respected in the industry self-regulatory solution.

Self-regulation by professions and industry involves a number of problems or perils. Boddewyn, for instance, lists some criticisms of advertising self-regulation, arguing "some of which are more hypothetical than real" (p. 6). Self-regulation impairs business competition and innovation due to restraints by trade associations; it may be hampered by antitrust laws that preclude compulsory membership; it lacks effective judicial tools, rules of procedure and evidence, and penalties; it may be accompanied by little publicity and financing to make consumers aware; and industry-dominated participation in complaints processes may overwhelm the few outsiders. Boddewyn also states (hypothetically): "Self-regulation [may be seen as] a transparent device used by members of the industry (including the media) to subvert the adoption of more rigorous government standards by pretending that business will do the job when, in fact, voluntary standards might be set at minimal levels in order to avoid low membership or schism within the industry. Besides voluntary enforcement may be lax" (p. 7).

III. SELF-REGULATION AS A TELEVISION RATINGS IMPLEMENTATION STRATEGY

The V-chip initiatives in Canada and the United States provide contrasting studies in self-regulation. At bottom, while they were similar in many respects, their technological components and configuration differed in several key characteristics (see Maitland and McDowell, 1997). The U.S. system required the introduction of hardware in television sets to detect rating signals, while the Canadian system required cable companies to offer the blocking technologies and capabilities as part of a service package. The technologies closely parallel existing technologies to provide closed captioning for the hearing impaired (Andrews, 1996). The U.S. initiative was driven by legislators, while the Canadian changes were driven by the regulator, with no new legislative mandate or direction. The U.S. system was the first policy move in that country to reflect social concerns and the widespread and long-standing concerns arising from the findings of social science and health research regarding television violence, while the Canadian proposals were offered in addition to industry self-regulation of program content that had been in place since 1987 and that had been recognized by the regulator.

Canadian Broadcast Policy and Regulation

Differences in modes of self-regulation are imbedded in contexts. The Canadian ratings system had to be sensitive to the wide availability of programming originating in the U.S. Concern over program content in Canada is primarily about the origins of programming (Communications Canada, 1992; Ellis, 1992; Information Highway Advisory Council, 1995). The vast majority of programming available on Canadian television screens originates in the United States. Canadian cultural and broadcasting policies have attempted to use various measures to promote "Canadian content," whether through the public broadcasting network (the Canadian Broadcasting Corporation), through content requirements, or through program development funds and tax credits. The private Canadian broadcasting and cable industry exists as it does because of the national protections given to it by communications policies. These protections—such as national ownership require-ments, tax laws to direct advertising revenue streams to Canadian media, and programmers' continued access to audiences through carriage by cable television distribution networks—are also supplemented by broadcasters' and cable companies' profits from reselling programs and channels originating in the United States (see Jeffrey, with McAninch, 1996). Following from this support of the broadcasting system to achieve national cultural objectives, one might surmise that the CRTC has the possibility of exercising considerable influence and authority in its relationship with Canadian broad-casters. However, the regulator and government have been very circumspect in actually enforcing many performance requirements or imposing what are seen by the industry as onerous requirements (see Babe, 1979; Richard Collins, 1990).

Throughout the last two decades, the CRTC and the Canadian government have attempted to choose and to support specific Canadian cultural "producers" as vehicles to achieve the goals of Canadian cultural policies. This term "producers" has increasingly been translated to mean a small number of nationally owned communications oligopolies, dependent on the government for protection while at the same time restricting public policy options to the tasks of promoting the "bottom line" of cultural industries (Babe, 1979; Raboy, 1990). This is seen as a way of making certain cultural goods and services available to the Canadian public. Cultural producers include Canadian book publishers, magazine publishers, the sound recording and music industries, television program producers, and film production companies. At the same time, state support for public cultural agencies, such as the Canadian Broadcasting Corporation, the National Film Board, and the Social Sciences and Humanities Research Council, has diminished significantly in the last decade (see Dorland, 1996).

Along with a focus on production, in the last decade there has been considerable attention given to the distribution of communications and cultural services. Canadian films, it is argued, cannot reach Canadian audiences because film screens are controlled by contracts made for North American distribution. On the other hand, the Canadian cable television system offered a uniquely Canadian distribution channel for audiovisual programming, and also allowed for the introduction of a number of successful specialty cable services in the 1980s and 1990s. This has resulted in the existing distribution industry being seen as a very important partner in the Canadian cultural policy project. This has also meant that Canadian broadcasters required a ratings system that did not put them at a disadvantage compared to U.S. competitors.

The Canadian Television Industry's Ratings Proposal

Prior to the introduction of the V-chip policy, the Canadian Association of Broadcasters (CAB) had already introduced a Violence Code in 1987 (CBSC, 1997). The 1987 Violence Code, according to the Canadian Broadcasting Standards Council (CBSC), was "appropriate to its time, [but it] came to be viewed as insufficient for the public's needs in the 1990s." As a result of a number of public outcries over several cases of violence, convictions by the government and others that media was implicated in this violence, and a request from the CRTC in May of 1992, the Canadian broadcasting industry decided to rework the 1987 code. In February 1993 it created an Action Group for Violence on Television (AGVOT). A new Voluntary Code on Television Violence was proposed to the CRTC in September 1993, which approved it in October 1993 (CRTC, 1993a). This new code went into effect in 1994 without any new legislation being passed. The pay television programmers also adopted a standard in 1994 (CRTC, 1994a).

Critics, such as the Coalition for Responsible Television (1995), have noted that the CAB code defines "gratuitous violence" in its own unique way, quite differently from a dictionary definition: gratuitous violence is that which is not germane to the plot or story line. This allows television programs to tell stories that include violence if the story is about violence. The code for industry self-regulation allowed viewers to take complaints first to the Canadian Broadcast Standards Council (CBSC), and then to the CRTC if industry responses were not perceived to be sufficient.

The subsequent formation of television violence policy in Canada was guided more directly by the regulator. While no new legislation was introduced as a mandate for these significant changes in the broadcasting industry and in communications policy, they did take place in the context of a number of other political developments. In 1992, the CRTC's stated goal was to make "violence on television socially unacceptable." The approach, the CRTC stated, was to work by building "cooperation and consensus" and was to be guided by several principles, including:

1.   abandon an ideological, legalistic, and therefore combative approach in favor

      of a cooperative strategy recognizing TV violence as a major mental-health
      problem for children;

2.   adopt the goal of protecting children, not censoring adults, in order to strike a
      balance between the right to freedom of expression and the right to a healthy
      childhood;

3.   stick to a focused agenda on gratuitous or glamorized violence, not diffusing
      efforts by adding on sex, foul language, family values, specific feminist
      concerns, or other distinct, more controversial issues;

4.   bring all players to the table—broadcasters, advertisers, producers, parents,
      teachers, psychiatrists, and the regulator;

5.   have both a short-term and a long-term perspective. (CRTC, 1996c)

The CRTC commissioned background studies summarizing the research on the effects of television violence (Atkinson et al, 1991; Martinez, undated). Concerns about violence in society and violence in the media were also expressed in a number of other governmental forums in the early 1990s. A committee of Parliament looked into violence on television and issued a number of nonbinding recommendations encouraging greater control (Canada, Standing Committee, 1993). As well, Heritage Canada prepared a summary report (Josephson, 1995). These reports all concluded that violence in Canadian society, and violence on television, were serious problems that needed immediate and concerted action.

One high profile case testing the adequacy of industry self-regulation involved the *Mighty Morphin Power Rangers*. The Canadian Broadcast Standards Council (1994a; 1994b) required the removal of the program from the listing of a Toronto station following two separate complaints by parents. This CBSC decision also claimed that Canadian choices of this sort would be futile because a Buffalo station continued to broadcast the program, and that this broadcast was distributed on Canadian cable television distribution systems (CRTC, 1994b). Hence, despite the Canadian regulator's and industry's seeming willingness and ability to require content codes, the supposed openness of the Canadian distribution system to foreign programming was seen as limiting the effectiveness of these policies. This led to efforts to consider a ratings system that would be compatible with that being developed in the United States.

In April 1995 the CRTC (1995) called for written submissions on the problem of television violence, and announced that regional hearings and public hearings in Ottawa/Hull would be held that September. Only 232 written comments were received, and the hearings allowed, according to the CRTC, 141 individuals and organizations to "make oral submissions and discuss their views with CRTC Commissioners" (CRTC, 1996c). At the hearings, the Canadian Association of Broadcasters pointed to the problem of foreign programming, arguing that cable carriage of foreign signals and specialty channels would have to be addressed, and that any proposed solution should maintain an "equality of responsibility":

      Without assurance that other elements of the broadcasting system will classify
      the programming they carry—particularly programming on foreign signals

carried by cable companies and other distributors—it is not appropriate to require Canadian programming services to adopt a formal classification system.

Canadian programming services already adhere to approved violence standards that include scheduling and advisory provisions far in excess of anything that US services now [have] or are likely to have in the future. To leave foreign services unrated would deny Canadians information where they need it the most. (Nordicity, 1995, p. 25)

Public interest advocates argued that the consultation process had a very short time frame between the call for comments and the actual hearings. As well, to participate in the hearings, groups had to submit comments and agree to be available at some unspecified future date and place, at their own cost. The hearings themselves demonstrated the very significant imbalance in resources between industry groups (with large staffs of lawyers and representatives), and other groups and persons concerned about television violence. (In Canada, while telecommunications hearings allow for cost awards for public interest representation before the CRTC, these are not provided for in hearings concerning broadcasting matters [Canada, 1979].) These hearings also showed a very close relationship between the CRTC agenda and that of the largest cable television operator, Rogers.

The CRTC issued an order in March of 1996 (CRTC, 1996a) that mandated the development of a V-chip technology and a ratings system. In charging the industry group with both tasks, it noted, "the development of a classification system should involve input from the public, programmers, and distributors" (CRTC, 1997, p. 4). Following the March 1996 order, AGVOT began to work to develop a specific ratings systems and to test out the V-chip technology in Canadian homes for introduction in September 1996. AGVOT requested an extension of time from the CRTC in summer of 1996, in part because the U.S. ratings proposals were scheduled to be released in February of 1997 (CRTC, 1996b). It finally produced a report at the end of April 1997. The report proposed a ratings system that would designate the levels of violence that would be found in specific programs. This system, containing age-based categories, would not contain information about language or sexual behavior, although such features had been included in earlier tests and in public discussion of V-chip capabilities.

The AGVOT (1997) report also outlined the results from tests of proposed systems and the difficulty that AGVOT had in signing up households to participate in the tests. The Canadian Cable Television Association (1996) had noted in a January 19 report to the CRTC that the costs of introducing ratings after the program origination or production point (that is, introduction by the operators of cable systems) would be costly and involve many technical and administrative problems. It was also noted that various provincial film boards existed and that Quebec television used its own system (see Howell, 1997). Combined with the development of a ratings system in the United States that was anticipated to be a simple age-based system, the difficulties that Canadian households were having with new technology, and the pervasiveness of U.S. programming on Canadian cable distribution systems, the industry recommended an age-based program ratings system in its report of April 30, 1997.

The CRTC accepted the report on June 18, 1997 without any further public comment (CRTC, 1997), indicating that the industry group had, in its view, provided a ratings system that met the requirements the regulator had laid out in March of 1996. The report was presented as representing a consensus among the different elements of the Canadian industry. The CRTC noted that AGVOT had developed its ratings system "with the participation of representatives from both public and private broadcasters, specialty channels, the cable industry, and the independent production community" (CRTC, 1997, p. 5). The CRTC was also encouraged that the industry group, the CAB, had been expanded to include other industry sectors, such as specialty providers and cable distributors. One puzzling aspect of the report was the extent to which other types of information about program content had disappeared. An article in *Maclean's,* a national weekly newsmagazine, noted this shift and speculated that it was negotiations among the Canadian and U.S. industry groups while they were both developing standards proposals that were responsible for this drastic change in direction (McDonald, 1997).

The AGVOT report also made reference to the consultation process with nonindustry groups that it undertook in the development of the proposed ratings system. The CRTC acceptance of AGVOT's recommendations noted:

> The proposed system has been also evaluated by the public through a national public opinion survey, and through the cooperation of some 340 families who participated in the field trials. . . . Furthermore, community groups and professional associations concerned about violence on television were also consulted regarding the structure of the ratings system and the language of the descriptive and guideline information. (CRTC, 1997, p. 5)

However, some representatives of advocacy organizations depicted these "consultations" as appointments that AGVOT would call to inform other groups of what they were doing and give the results of selected surveys and studies it had prepared. Limited opportunity was given to others to participate in the design of studies, to conduct independent studies, or to check the methodology of the AGVOT studies. It is also notable that there was no further consultation with public interest groups by the CRTC between April 30, 1997 when the AGVOT proposals were offered and their formal acceptance on June 18. In fact, the last public input on this question was in the summer and fall of 1995, almost two years before any specific ratings system was proposed.

In general terms, the proposed use of a ratings system in Canada moved away from depending solely on broadcast standards to limit the depiction of violence at certain times of day and toward introducing the use of V-chip technology to allow parents to block out certain categories of programming. The ratings/V-chip option adopted by the CRTC and the industry was seen by many as, at best, a complement to existing, or even stronger, television violence codes. This approach was also seen by those supporting better quality children's television and an overall reduction of levels of violence in media and society, as quite possibly the beginnings of a diversion from more directive and positive anti-violence guidelines meant to keep certain types of programming off the air at certain times. Ratings systems, it was also argued, were like "media literacy" programs, in that they placed the responsibility for dealing with television violence with individuals and parents, rather than addressing more directly the responsibilities of the production and distribution industries. Despite these criticisms, it should be noted that the CRTC did reiterate the broadcasters' commitment to the Voluntary Code of 1993 in its acceptance of the AGVOT program ratings system.

Industry Proposals in The United States

The inclusion of the V-chip provisions in the Telecommunications Act of 1996 renewed debates about the appropriate role and meaning of self-regulation in the U.S. Self-regulation in broadcasting was long pursued "to limit or prevent regulation by the government," or "to prevent more stringent regulation by Congress or the FCC." In the 1920s, Commerce Secretary Herbert Hoover tried to let the radio industry solve the problem of radio-magnetic spectrum interference on its own, but Congress regulated radio when this was unsuccessful. The National Association of Broadcasters introduced a Radio Code in 1929 and a Television Code in 1952 (both were discontinued in 1982 following an antitrust suit initiated by the Department of Justice that was designed to address advertising rate setting). While companies neither had to belong to the NAB nor follow the codes, these were recognized as "standards of good practice" by the FCC, which also did not establish public rules in areas covered by the codes (Smith, Meeske, and Wright, 1995, pp. 107–8).

Television networks also had their own "standards and practices" divisions to monitor and remove potentially offensive or indecent dialogue or parts of programs. These offices were reduced in size because of network budget cutbacks in the 1980s and a changing regulatory climate. Cable television programmers made efforts in 1993 to discuss plans to curb violence and to provide advisories of violent content in programs (Smith, Meeske, and Wright, 1995, pp. 108–9). The Children's Television Act of 1990 was a more direct legislative and regulatory effort to improve the provision of quality programming for children (ibid., p. 281).

In the United States, from 1993 to 1997 the main focus of efforts to introduce television program violence ratings was the provisions in what became the Telecommunications Act of 1996 (Markey, 1996). Section 551 of this act introduced requirements that V-chip technology be included in new television sets with screens thirteen inches or greater in size sold after 1998. A program ratings system would not be required by law, but if programmers decided to rate their programs they should make use of the system as developed under the provisions of the act. The language of the section mandated the FCC to prescribe a ratings system for video programming, based on the recommendations of an advisory committee. The FCC, however, would only strike this committee if the industry had not voluntarily provided a ratings system within one year after the law went into effect, or if the FCC did not find that "such rules are acceptable to the Commission." Self-regulation was an important aspect of congressional debates. The fact that the industry would design the ratings system on a voluntary basis was repeatedly mentioned, as was the fact that the government would not take the lead in developing a ratings system. Even at this stage, many argued that "self-regulation" was a not very subtle cover for state intervention.

The proposed composition of the two types of committees designated by the legislation is notable. An industry proposal was to arise from "distributors of video programming," while the advisory committee to be struck by the FCC was to be "composed of parents, television broadcasters, television programming producers, cable operators, appropriate public interest groups, and other individuals from the private sector and is fairly balanced in terms of political affiliation, the points of view represented, and the functions to be performed by the committee." The narrowly constituted industry group, operating "voluntarily" only under the coercion of the provisions of the act, was seen as less of a threat to open communication than a broadly representative advisory committee constituted by the FCC.

In the debates in 1995 over the telecommunications bill, the broadcasting industry initially opposed any sort of ratings system or V-chip requirement, arguing that it would be an unacceptable infringement on their freedom to broadcast as a form of speech. After the passage of the bill in the Senate and the House of Representatives in the summer of 1995, and negotiations in conference committee in the fall of 1995, it became Public Law 104-104 on February 8, 1996. After meeting with administration and other officials in a White House summit on television in February 1996, the industry agreed to pursue the voluntary development of a ratings system (Andrews, 1996). The industry proposal for a ratings system was developed through 1996, made public in a press conference and White House briefing on December 19, 1996, and was formally submitted to the FCC on January 17, 1997 and amended in July 1997.

The Implementation Group and the Proposed Industry System

In the first phase, the development of the ratings system entailed much negotiation of different approaches and views among industry groups. The implementation committee was headed by Jack Valenti of the Motion Picture Association of America (MPAA), along with Decker Anstrom of the National Cable Television Association (NCTA), and Eddie Fritts of the National Association of Broadcasters (NAB). The implementation group also "represented all segments of the television industry: the national broadcast networks; affiliated, independent, and public television stations nationwide; cable programmers; producers and distributors of cable programming; entertainment companies; movie studios; and members of creative guilds representing writers, directors, producers and actors" (FCC, 1997).

The implementation group proposed an age-based system that contained only six categories. It did not provide specific information about "sexual, violent, or other indecent material," but referred to the age of the audience for which programming was designed and the types of content that the program "may contain." The small number of categories, rather than a series of scales for intensity of sexual, violent, or language content, was justified in that it "gave parents a simple, easy-to-use guide for deciding what programs are appropriate for children to watch" and that a simple system could be printed in television guides. The proposal also established an Oversight Monitoring Board, composed of six members from the broadcast television industry, six from the cable industry, a chairperson, and six members from the program production industry but with no nonindustry representation. Nonindustry views regarding the usefulness of the system to parents were to be solicited through focus groups and periodically commissioned quantitative studies.

In December of 1996, after the proposed system was announced, Mr. Valenti was being hailed as a lobbying genius, a masterful political magician who had pulled the solution out of the crosscutting industry interests and approaches, the pressures from legislators, and had bowled over the concerns of advocacy groups. On the day that the proposals were informally released, several senators and representatives wrote to the FCC in favor of the ratings system. President Clinton said that the system needed to be given time to work (Shogren, 1996; Mundy, 1997).

By law, effectively a check on self-regulation, the industry proposals had to meet the requirement of being "acceptable" to the FCC. The FCC would also, by law, make this determination "in consultation with appropriate public interest groups and interested individuals from the private sector." The key question was whether the industry had "established voluntary rules for rating video programming that contains sexual, violent, or other indecent material about which parents should be informed before it is displayed to children," and had "agreed voluntarily to broadcast signals that contain ratings of such programming." Hence, a key element of the industry-regulator relationship at this point was industry attempts to convince the regulator that the industry proposal was acceptable.

The industry proposal included a section arguing for a narrow definition of the term "acceptable," and also arguing that legislation had been primarily intended to let the industry develop a ratings system itself. The legislative history, the industry group claimed, and "Congress' use of the term 'acceptable' also confirmed that Congress did not intend for the Commission to demand that an industry-developed system conform to the Commission's own or anyone else's vision of an ideal program." The industry argued that "satisfactory" or "barely satisfactory or adequate" were among the dictionary meanings of "acceptable" that should be considered in the absence of specific legislative language about what acceptable meant (FCC, 1997). References to an age-based system similar to that used by the MPAA were included in Congressional debates about the legislation, while no one had specifically said that such a system would be unacceptable.

The development of the industry proposal had also involved consultation with "scores of parental, medical, religious, child advocacy and educational groups to get their views on how the parental guidelines should be structured," according to the background paper presented by the industry. The proposal also attempted, based on the legislative history of Public Law 104-104, to restrict any criticisms that it had not engaged in adequate consultation by noting that in the act the proposed composition of the industry group and the composition of the advisory committee were not similar: "No such requirement was proposed upon the industry in its development of guidelines, which shows that Congress did not intend the two processes be interchangeable." However, as became apparent rather quickly in the public comment process, many nonindustry groups thought that the age-based system in the industry proposal did not provide sufficient information and that there should have been more consultation in the development of this system.

The responses that arose in the months following the formal submission of the proposal undermined the quiet certainty of December 1996 that the proposed ratings system was a done deal. A sampling of the comments submitted to the FCC in the matter demonstrate concerns about the ratings systems itself and the process whereby it was developed. For instance, the submission of the Public Broadcasting Service indicated that more information about program content should be provided and that the rating system, "as currently implemented is too vague and unevenly applied to accomplish its professed objectives. The rating categories lack clarity; viewers are not provided with sufficient content-specific information; programs of particular value to children are not identified; and the 'TV-PG' rating appears to have become a catch-all category" (Public Broadcasting Service, 1997, p. 3). The submission continued:

> PBS chose not to implement the Proposed Industry System when it was launched by the commercial networks and some cable services for several reasons: (i) the industry system appeared to serve mostly the interests of networks themselves, and did not reflect the concerns of parents' groups and other public interest advocates who had attempted to participate in devising the system; and (ii) PBS was not convinced that the Proposed Industry System represented the best that could be achieved, and believed that PBS viewers and member stations would be better served by further efforts to improve the system. (Ibid., p. 4)

The comments of the Presbyterian Church (U.S.A.) also echoed these same themes. The industry proposal:

> fails to provide adequate and timely information about the nature of upcoming video programming, and thereby fails to assist parents in determining whether such programming would be harmful to their children. The industry guide-lines are overly broad as they include violence, language and sexual content in each category, but do not explain why a program falls within a particular category. The industry guidelines have excluded any description of the program's content, an omission which seriously limits a parent's ability to determine whether a program is suitable for children. The industry guidelines do not address the underlying social and public policy issue which has led to the need for a ratings system: i.e., the public awareness of the detrimental effects of exposure to programs containing violence, foul language and the exploitation of sexuality as well as an awareness of a lack of programs which contribute to the wholesome, fulfilling development of children. Finally, the structural mechanism proposed by industry to monitor the implementation and consistency of the ratings lacks sufficient input from non-industry orga-nizations, and cannot be trusted to amend the industry guidelines in a timely or adequate manner. (Presbyterian Church, 1997)

Other comments addressed the issue of industry consultation with other social groups. The submission of the American Medical Association stated:

The AMA is exceedingly concerned that the Industry Rating System was developed without adequate input from America's parents and other parties interested in and knowledgeable about limiting children's exposure to harmful programming. We would recommend that whatever rating system is ultimately approved be required to consult parents and other interested parties for their opinions and recommendations.

A system developed entirely by the television industry is not likely to address all of the critical issues that television violence involves. Without the valuable input of parents and other children's advocates, a television rating system cannot accomplish the task intended by Congress—to serve the compelling governmental interest of empowering parents to limit the negative influences of video programming that is harmful to children. (AMA, 1997)

The Benton Foundation argued that the industry monopoly over the design and administration of a ratings system could and should be broken. Rather than accepting the industry-proposed ratings system or that of an FCC-appointed advisory committee, there was room in the vertical blanking interval for a number of ratings systems:

Benton proposes that any alternative rating codes gain guaranteed rights of carriage on television broadcasts. Many parents may not feel comfortable with *any* ratings system devised by broadcasters and others with a commercial interest in the outcome. A ratings system devised by a Commission-appointed committee may not pass a constitutional test. The Commission should encourage noncommercial interests such as the National Parent Teacher Association, the American Academy of Child & Adolescent Psychiatry, and others to devise their own ratings systems. The Commission should then insist that broadcasters, cable operators, and other programmers include these ratings in the vertical blanking interval. Such rules for these codes will allow parents to choose the rating system they are most comfortable with. These codes would remain invisible in households that choose not to see them just as closed captioning does not appear in households that do not choose to use it. (Benton Foundation, 1997)

The advocates of a ratings system that included more information were assisted by the scheduling of Senate hearings in February 1997 by Senator John McCain (R-N.Mex.). These hearings provided a public forum for advocacy and industry groups at a time when the specific ratings proposals were made public and when comments were being prepared for the FCC. The hearings, which were held only in the Senate and not in the House of Representatives, allowed the legislators to shape additional input into the actual implementation of the 1996 Telecommunications Act by the FCC.

Following the initial round of comments, reply comments were also solicited so that groups could respond to the arguments made by other groups in the initial round. As the possibility that the system proposed by the industry might not be seen as acceptable became greater, a number of groups reiterated their opposition in principle to the FCC appointing an advisory group. The ACLU (1997) stated that it "believes that government-prescribed 'ratings' systems that single out sex, violence, or other controversial subjects for adverse treatment conflict with the fundamental principles of free expression enshrined in the First Amendment. The ACLU accordingly urges the Commission to resist the pleas of those dissatisfied with the television industry's new labelling system," though it took no position on the wisdom or efficacy of the industry's system.

The American Library Association stated that it "strongly opposes a government rating scheme. In our view, any such rating system is squarely at odds with longstanding First Amendment principles that 'foreclose public authority from assuming a guardianship of the public mind'" (American Library Association, 1997).

The reply comments of the industry group sought to clarify what was really at stake in the FCC decision, and also noted that the system that had been proposed in Canada in April 1997 subsequent to the announcement of the proposed ratings system in the United States was actually very similar:

> For the first time in the history of U.S. television, an industry-wide system has been implemented with the goal of providing parents easy-to-use, widely available information concerning the level and kinds of content in a program. The TV Parental Guidelines permit parents to quickly decide which categories of programming they wish their children to watch unsupervised, and they can also use the guidelines to help them decide which programs they should watch with their children. The TV Parental Guidelines are designed to be readily usable with the "V-chip" to give parents another tool to help control their children's television viewing. . . .
>
> Additional support for the Guidelines developed by the American television industry is contained in the May 5, 1997 announcement by the Canadian Action Group on Violence on Television of a rating system quite similar to the TV Parental Guidelines. The Canadian system is supported by extensive research and actual field testing. (NAB et al., 1997)

The FCC had initially scheduled a hearing for June 20. In the meantime, direct negotiations began between the main industry representatives, a number of key advocacy organizations, and central political actors. The industry groups included the NAB, the NCTA, and the MPAA, the joint proponents of the age-based ratings system. The advocacy organizations included the National Education Association, the National Parent Teacher Association, the American Medical Association, and the Center for Media Education. The legislative group included Representative Edward Markey (D-Mass.) and Senator John McCain.

The public advocates gained support as the first half of the year progressed (Fritz and Hall, 1997; Mifflin, 1997a). Negotiations broke down with much public attention on June 19 (just before the FCC hearing and after a press announcement supportive of the advocacy groups from Vice President Al Gore), and again on June 24 (just as an agreement was to be announced). Only on July 9 was an agreement on a ratings system concluded, and this was presented in a press conference on July 10.

This agreement would see the age-based system augmented by specific labels for sexual content, violence, language, suggestive dialogue, and fantasy violence. The industry, in return, sought and received pledges from individual legislators not to seek changes to the system for three years. Senator McCain prepared a letter to this effect which was signed by nine senators, Rep. Markey prepared a similar letter signed by four House members, and Rep. Billy Tauzin (R-La.), Chair of the Telecommunications Subcommittee in the House, sent a separate letter.

The process of developing a ratings system entailed direct negotiations and bargaining between the industry and advocacy groups, without the formal intervention of the FCC. Although the FCC mandate allowed for public comment, the intervention of legislators in the bargaining was not specified in the formal process outlined in the law or by the FCC. The FCC put off its hearing in order to allow the negotiation of a proposal that would be more acceptable and to avoid having to make a decision regarding acceptability of the industry proposal in the absence of an agreement.

The modified ratings system was not, however, acceptable to all involved. Industry groups that were not proprietors—specifically the guilds of writers, actors, and directors in Hollywood—"denounced the new system as a threat to their creativity and First Amendment rights" (Mifflin, 1997c). The NBC television network also broke with the industry and said it would not use the revised ratings system, as did Black Entertainment Television (Mifflin, 1997d).

Other legislators who wanted more than program labeling, that is, even tighter restrictions on program content, criticized both the modified ratings system and the agreement by others in Congress to allow three years for the system to be tried before introducing any new legislation or supporting any other legislation on television ratings or content.

This case of self-regulation under the public eye is instructive in the extent to which private, behind-closed-doors bargaining took the place of public hearings and procedures. One report noted that hearings and bills introduced in Congress in 1997 served as "leverage." However, "advocacy organizations have essentially served as Congress' proxy," and "Congress . . . deputized the PTA and others to work out a deal with broadcasters" (Farhi, 1997).

While self-regulation was a mechanism for moving the legislative mandate forward, in the process industry groups attempted to redefine the whole purpose of the ratings. The industry used two justifications to limit the amount of content in the ratings and attempted to shift the focus of the policy debate. First, the industry claimed that their system gave parents a simple guide for deciding which programs are appropriate for children to watch. However, the ratings system's primary purpose in the legislation was to work in conjunction with the V-chip to identify and potentially block programming with certain characteristics rather than deciding on specific programs. Second, the printing of program ratings is not mentioned in the act, which deals with a ratings system to be used with the V-chip technology. However, the space required to print ratings in television guides was presented by the industry as a limiting factor on the complexity of the ratings system. Both of these reasons were made less credible because cable television services had a detailed program advisory system in place which had been operating for many years, something with which the public was familiar.

IV. CONCLUSIONS

The use of self-regulation as a governance strategy involves a very careful process of building and managing consensus at a number of levels. Self-regulation is being promoted in the U.S. as a way to control minors' access to indecent Internet content, following the Supreme Court decision overturning the Communications Decency Act provisions of the 1996 Telecommunications Act. As well, a proposed Television Improvement Act of 1997 (S. 539) would provide the television networks with an antitrust exemption so they could engage in consultation and efforts to improve the quality of programming.

Government-Industry Relations

Does self-regulation actually serve the public interest and adequately respond to public concerns, or is it just a way of protecting an industry sector or for governments to avoid choices and actions that would be difficult politically? The relations between government and industry can easily be emphasized in accounts of the formation of self-regulation, in part because agents in both groups have reasons to portray this relationship as the central conflict. Regulators, legislators, and public officials act to be seen as responding to public concerns about industry actions and behavior, and do not try to emphasize conflicts between governments and nonindustry social groups. Industry officials, similarly, try to portray regulatory initiatives as those of power hungry and arrogant bureaucrats out of touch with common people and trying to build empires and make names for themselves, rather than as responsible actions of governance. However, focusing only on this part of the story would miss elements of what transpired in the development of ratings systems for television in Canada and the United States.

Rather than being a conflictual relationship, the interaction between the CRTC and the Canadian broadcasters and cable television companies was perhaps typified by too much "cooperation and consensus." As noted in the introduction, advocates of stronger policies limiting television violence to protect children, or at least a more detailed ratings system, were very disappointed at the CRTC's quick acceptance of industry proposals. The CRTC's ties to teachers, labor unions, parents' groups, and antiviolence groups were shown to be much weaker than its linkages with the cable television industry and Canadian broadcasters. The initial round of hearings in 1995 took place before specific proposals had been given a full public review. There was no open comment period after the industry proposed a ratings system in which these groups could formally register their views of the adequacy of the system.

Many Canadians might grudgingly admit that the CRTC and the Canadian government have difficult tasks in promoting the production and distribution of Canadian programming while sitting beside the world's largest film, television, and sound recording industries. Similarly, many in government and in the public have come to accept the claims that policy liberalization and economic globalization reduce the scope of communications policies (Comor, 1990). At the same time, the CRTC could always claim to have the objective of building and supporting a communications system that reflected a range of Canadian cultural values, these often being defined in opposition to some cultural expression and products originating in the United States. What therefore seems especially disappointing both about the process and the outcome in this case, is that when a clear difference between the views of members of the Canadian public and the communication industry representatives became apparent, the CRTC pursued the industry line and agenda. Given the perspective allowed by viewing a longer sweep of time, it appears that the CRTC worked to manage the potential social crisis created by shootings in Montreal and other emotion-stirring events. It deflected the attention away from Canadian television violence and toward media literacy and American programming, rather than take the concerns of Canadians seriously. This might be seen as deft crisis management, typified by: an early expression of support by the CRTC with the concerns and objectives of the public, the government, and Parliament in order to get out ahead and gain control of this policy initiative; referring repeatedly to cooperation and consensus rather than exercising the legally mandated powers and responsibilities of the regulator; the setting of ambitious goals, which are only later abandoned because they are no longer seen to be feasible; and making claims to open consultation while at the same time limiting public and nonindustry professional groups' consultation in decision making.

Although the industry group has met its objectives without any significant costs, the cost to the CRTC has been a further reduction of a directive role in shaping Canadian broadcasting in the public interest. The CRTC's legitimacy among public interest groups in forming telecommunications policies had already been undermined by its acceptance of telephone industry proposals to increase prices for local telephone services. Self-regulation has served as a vehicle for further reducing the public role in decision making about Canadian broadcasting content. The development both of stronger public interest groups and more open and effective formal processes of public regulation seem to be called for in the face of this successful case of self-regulation.

The relationship between the regulator and the broadcasters in the United States was characterized by a greater level of conflict over basic goals of the broadcasting system. FCC Chair Reed Hundt has long been an advocate of better quality television for children, and the reduction of violence levels in television programming. In a number of issues, the broadcasting industry has seen Mr. Hundt as a Commissioner less sympathetic to their concerns than others. The legislation that required the V-chip also specified the role that the FCC would play in determining the acceptability of the industry ratings system, and FCC procedures of public comment allowed the venue and adequate time for groups who opposed the proposed ratings to build alliances and prepare submissions. These elements of the government-industry relationship allowed for more effective and continuous public shaping of the self-regulatory solution.

Relations Among Industry Groups

The management of differences among industry groups in approaching specific problems must also be conducted effectively for self-regulation to be a viable option. Not all industry "players" may agree that a problem is serious enough to warrant a voluntary industry response or that a particular approach or solution is appropriate. Similarly, the core group that is selected as the "industry" for self-regulation may exclude other groups who believe that they have knowledge claims and membership in a profession or industry that is just as valid. Do property ownership and management control become the criteria for the selection of the core industry group, or do professional credentials also count?

The relations among different companies in the television broadcasting industry were also important in building self-governance. In Canada, AGVOT included almost all network and specialty service broadcasters. The group also made contact, and had extensive consultations, with other elements of the television broadcasting industry. The Canadian Association of Broadcasters also indicated that it would broaden its base and allow membership by other industry parties that were not members in order to allow for implementation of the television program ratings.

In the United States, trade associations were chosen to make up the implementation group, and they selected the MPAA chief Jack Valenti as their head. Valenti's credibility with the industry was reportedly essential in putting together the industry agreement on ratings proposals. However, the networks had less contact with other parts of the television industry. They also had serious disagreements among themselves regarding the appropriate strategy to pursue in dealing with the V-chip legislation, as shown by NBC's opting out of the final agreement.

Two chief problems with self-regulation emerge when considering intraindustry relations. Firstly, the debate and the reasoning used in deliberation were private and in forums that were not open even for observation by the broader public. We do not know what factors or arguments were considered to be important in making certain recommendations. Why, for instance, did printing ratings in television guides become such an important issue in the United States? Like private dispute resolution, this lack of knowledge and lack of a record of reasoning and precedents severely restricts the democratic palatability of self-regulation as a form of governance. Secondly, we do not know about the nature and extent of transnational negotiations between industry groups in Canada and the United States, between Canadian broadcasters and a group led by Jack Valenti, their long-time nemesis in Canada-U.S. trade disputes over film and television.

Industry Relations with Public Interest Groups

Self-regulation narrows the scope of consultation from all interested parties in a nation-state to a smaller group based on professional credentials or ownership and control of certain enterprises. Self-regulation may have been chosen as a way of managing conflicts between industry groups and societal groups, with less formal governmental or regulatory intervention. What is the nature of political, social, and economic conflicts that have led to this particular form of compromise? How adequately have industry groups consulted with and considered the views of other social groups? Does self-regulation as a form of social management reflect a practical historical bargain, a defense of market dynamics in face of possible incursions by the state, or a corporatist limitation on democratic participation? Is self-regulation indicative of aspects of unresolved social conflicts and social crises held in stasis?

The relations among industry and societal groups were most important in comparing the experience with self-regulation in Canada and the United States. In Canada, the industry body engaged in extensive consultations with most of the parties that had been involved in public consultations in earlier phases of the television violence proceedings. The Action Group on Violence on Television cited the comments and responses of these same groups and individuals in its report to the CRTC that presented the proposed Canadian Television Ratings Standard. It asked the Canadian Broadcast Standards Council, a group with a track record of regulating the broadcast industry's codes regarding violence in programming and in handling complaints for the Canadian public, to take responsibility in monitoring and handling complaints about the application of the ratings system to particular programs. This process was significant in that the recommendations of many analysts, health and education professionals, social science researchers, and advocates—who would in most instances be seen as holding expert knowledge on the issue of television violence—were largely ignored in the industry design of its ratings system. Public interest groups who did not speak the language of Canadian broadcast regulation were unwelcome and uncomfortable participants.

The Canadian case also showed the limitations of relying on self-regulation when neither the regulator nor the industry groups seem willing to consider public interest groups' input. Self-regulation in such a case becomes a cover for what has been seen as "regulatory capture" in more explicit and direct regulatory processes (Mahon, 1979). The CRTC structuring and definition of the problem of television violence narrowly channeled and limited the ability of public interest groups to become involved. The industry was successful in marginalizing nonindustry groups. The resource imbalance and weakness of the public interest groups suggest that the CRTC could make more provisions to include and support their participation.

In the United States, the report and proposal of the industry group tried to obscure and gloss over the weak support of public interest and advocacy groups for the age-based ratings system by referring to groups that had been consulted in designing the ratings system, without mentioning them very specifically. It also noted that the law did not require full consultation in developing the industry proposal. This was, however, a legalistic interpretation that did not carry much water practically. As mentioned above, by June 1997, the weaknesses of this strategy of nonconsultation became apparent as various groups that had been working for several months to modify the industry's proposed ratings scheme were able to shift media coverage of the story and persuade Vice President Al Gore to speak out in their favor, despite the administration's earlier support for the industry proposal. Whereas the industry groups had been able to manage a weak consensus-building process, the various interventions listed above show a strong agreement among diverse parents' and children's advocacy groups about the types of information that they wanted from a ratings scheme and the inadequacies of the proposed scheme. The FCC put off its public hearings in hopes that the industry and children's television advocates would arrive at some sort of agreement.

Implications for Other Countries

As more and more governments privatize broadcasting operations and seek policy mechanisms that are less interventionist than traditional broadcast licensing as practiced in North America, self-regulation may seem to be a strategy that can be applied in the new broadcasting environment with lower costs than formal legislation or regulation. The first question that must be asked is whether self-regulation is an appropriate institutional and policy response in the historical, political, and social conditions of a country. Will it actually achieve stated public policy goals, or will it prove to be an inadequate response to deal with certain types of questions? Would legal and regulatory measures be more useful and effective in serving important public goals, rather than the cooperation and consensus sought through self-regulation? Or, does self-regulation actually allow legislators and regulators to escape difficult decisions to protect certain constitutional principles and basic values in the face of short-term political gain?

This case has shown that for self-regulation to be seen as legitimate and effective, there are a number of difficult consensus building processes that remain. Policymakers and the public will have to assess the extent to which a responsible industry group can be formed that can mediate among various national and international firms and professions, such as those mentioned in this account. Since self-regulation is—more so than legislation or regulation—essentially a historical bargain, there are no guarantees that it will be a useful guide to policy in every nation-state.

Even if self-regulation of some form is used, the state still has a number of important roles. Public bodies should support the process of self-regulation, promoting and allowing consultation with other interested parties outside the industry, and ensuring that the intellectual resources and knowledge and political and social concerns of all groups in society are called upon and considered. The state does not whither away but serves as an important referee and forum for appropriate self-regulatory practices, and in maintaining the proper parameters and directions for the framework of self-regulation.

References

American Library Association (1997), "In the Matter of Industry Proposal for Rating Video Programming CS Docket No. 97-55, Reply Comments of the American Library Association," (May 8).

American Civil Liberties Union (1997), "In the Matter of Industry Proposal for Rating Video Programming CS Docket No. 97-55, Reply Comments of the American Civil Liberties Union," (May 8).

Action Group on Violence on Television (1997), "Report on a Classification System for Violence in Television Programming to be used in Conjunction with V-chip Technology," Report to the CRTC (April 30).

American Medical Association (1997), "RE: CS Docket No. 97-55 Industry Proposal for Rating Video Programming," Submission to the FCC (April 8).

Andrews, Edmund L. (1996), "TV Executives Reach Broad Agreement on a System to Rate Violent Shows," New York Times (February 29), p. A11.

Atkinson, Dave, and Marc Gourdeau, under the direction of Florian Sauvageau (1991), Summary and Analysis of Various Studies on Violence and Television (Ottawa: CRTC, June).

Attallah, Paul (1996), "Canadian Television Exports: Into the Mainstream," pp. 162–191 in John Sinclair, Elizabeth Jacka and Stuart Cunningham (eds.), New Patterns in Global Television: Peripheral Vision (Oxford: Oxford University Press).

Babe, Robert E. (1979), Canadian Television Broadcasting Structure: Performance and Regulation (Ottawa: Economic Council of Canada).

Benton Foundation (1997), "In the Matter of Industry Proposal For CS Docket No. 97-55 Rating Video Programming, Comments of Benton Foundation," (April 8).

Boddewyn, Jean J. (1992), Global Perspectives on Advertising Self-Regulation: Principles and Practices in Thirty-Eight Countries (Westport, Connecticut: Quorum Books).

Canada (1979), "CRTC Telecommunications Rules of Procedure," Canada Gazette, Part II, Volume 113, Number 15 (August 8).

Canada, Standing Committee on Communications and Culture (1993), Television Violence: Fraying our Social Fabric (Ottawa: House of Commons, June).

Canadian Broadcast Standards Council (1997), "Canada Deals with Media Violence," (http://www.cbsc.ca/).

Canadian Broadcast Standards Council, Ontario Regional Council (1994a), "Decision Concerning 'Mighty Morphin Power Rangers' on CII-TV (Global Television) (Toronto), April and May 1994," Files 9394-270 and 9394-277.

Canadian Broadcast Standards Council (1994b), "'Power Rangers' Too Violent, Says Ontario Council," News Release, Ottawa (November 1).

Canadian Cable Television Association (1996), "Final Report. The Classification of U.S. Television Signals for the Canadian Cable Industry," (January 19).

Coalition for Responsible Television (1995), "Taking the Razor Blade out of the Apple," Presentation to the CRTC Hearings on Television Violence 1995-5 (June 26).

Collins, Randall (1990), "Market closure and the conflict theory of the professions," pp. 24–43 in Michael Burrage and Rolf Torstendahl (eds.), Professions in Theory and History (London: Sage).

Collins, Richard (1990), Culture, Communication and National Identity: The Case of Canadian Television (Toronto: University of Toronto Press).

Communications Canada (1992), The Information Society: New Media, New Choices (Ottawa: Supply and Services).

Comor, Edward (1991), "The DOC under Free Trade," Canadian Journal of Communication Volume 16 Number 2, pp. 239–262.

CRTC (1997), (Canadian Radio-television and Telecommunications Commission) "Classification System for Violence in Television Programming," Public Notice CRTC 1997-80 (Ottawa, 18 June).

CRTC (1996a), "Policy on Violence in Television Programming," Public Notice CRTC 1996-36 (Ottawa, 14 March).

CRTC (1996b), "Revised Timetable for the Implementation of the Television Program

Classification System and V-Chip Technology," Public Notice CRTC 1996-134 (Ottawa, 4 October).

CRTC (1996c), "Canada and Television Violence: Cooperation and Consensus" (Ottawa: CRTC).

CRTC (1995), "A Review of the Commission's Approach to Violence in Television Programing," Notice of Public Hearing CRTC 1995-5 (Ottawa, 3 April).

CRTC (1994a), "The Pay Television and Pay-Per-View Programming Code Regarding Violence," Public Notice CRTC 1994-155 (Ottawa, 21 December).

CRTC (1994b), "CRTC Welcomes Broadcast Council Ruling on 'Power Rangers'," News Release (Ottawa, 2 November).

CRTC (1993a), "Voluntary Code Regarding Violence in Television Programming," Public Notice CRTC 1993-149 (Ottawa, 28 October).

Dorland, Michael (1996) (ed.), The Cultural Industries in Canada: Problems, Policies and Prospects (Toronto: Lorimer).

Ellis, David (1992) Split Screen: Home Entertainment and the New Technologies (Toronto: Friends of Canadian Broadcasting).

Fagen, Drew (1996), "Cross-border culture row looms," Globe and Mail (18 January), p. B1, B8.

Farhi, Paul (1997), "TV Ratings Talks Stall Over Threat of Hill Action," Washington Post (June 26), p. E1.

Federal Communications Commission (1997), "Commission Seeks Comment on Industry Proposal for Rating Video Programming (CS Docket No. 97-55)" (Washington, FCC, February 7).

Fritz, Sara and Jane Hall (1997), "Industry Watchdogs Claim Victory in TV Ratings Fight," Los Angeles Times (Thursday June 12).

Gardner, Gerald (1987), The Censorship Papers: Movie Censorship Letters from the Hays Office, 1934 to 1968 (New York: Dodd, Mead and Company).

Horwitz, Robert Britt (1989), The Irony of Regulatory Reform: The Deregulation of American Telecommunications (New York: Oxford University Press).

Howell, Peter (1997), "Don't call us censors," The Toronto Star (Friday, July 4), B1, B3.

Information Highway Advisory Council (1995), Canadian Content and Culture Working Group, Ensuring a Strong Canadian Presence in the Information Highway (Ottawa: Industry Canada, 1995).

Jeffrey, Liss, assisted by Fraser McAninch (1996), "Private Television and Cable," pp. 203–256 in Michael Dorlan (ed.), The Cultural Industries in Canada: Problems, Policies, and Prospects (Toronto: Lorimer).

Josephson, Wendy (1995), Television Violence: A Review of the Effects on Children of Different Ages (Ottawa: Canadian Heritage, February).

Mahon, Rianne (1979), "Regulatory Agencies: Captive Agents or Hegemonic Apparatuses," Studies in Political Economy 1, pp. 162–200.

Maitland, Carleen, and Stephen D. McDowell (1997), "Technology Choice in Canada and the United States: Themes and Variations in 'V-Chip' Design and Deployment," Paper for International Communication Association May 1997 Annual Meetings, Montreal, Canada.

Markey, Edward J. (1996), "It Takes a V-chip," unpublished mimeograph.

Martinez, Andrea (undated), Scientific Knowledge about Television Violence (Ottawa: CRTC, Television Programming Directorate).

McChesney, Robert W. (1994), Telecommunications, Mass Media, and Democracy (New York: Oxford University Press, 1994).

McDonald, Marci (1997), "A V-Chip Tug-of-War: Is Canada's new ratings system a concession to U.S. pressure?" Maclean's (May 5).

Mifflin, Lawrie (1997a), "Revisions in TV Ratings Called Imminent," The New York Times (Monday, June 16), pp. B1, B6.

Mifflin, Lawrie (1997b), "Industry Halts Talks on TV Ratings After Statement by Gore," The New York Times (Friday, June 20), p A12.

Mifflin, Lawrie (1997c), "TV Ratings Accord Comes Under Fire From Both Flanks," New York Times (Friday, July 11), pp. A1, A19.

Mifflin, Lawrie (1997d), "How NBC Could Gain From Stand on Ratings," New York Times (Monday, July 14), pp. B1, B4.

Mundy, Alicia (1997), "Valenti's presidential powers: by getting Bill Clinton to support his TV ratings system, Jack Valenti has foiled the naysayers—for now," MEDIAWEEK, Vol. 7 No. 1 (January 6) p. 15.

Mundy, Alicia (1996), "The clean-up man: Representative Ed Markey saves the V-chip from politics," MEDIAWEEK, Vol.6 No. 11 (March 11), p. 17(3)

National Association of Broadcasters, The National Cable Television Association, and the Motion Picture Association of America (1997), "In the Matter of Joint Voluntary Proposal for Video CS Docket No. 97-55 Programming Rating System of National Association of Broadcasters (NAB), National Cable Television Association (NCTA) and Motion Picture Association of America (MPAA), Joint Reply Comments," (May 8).

Nordicity Group Limited (1995), Approaches to Violence in Television Programming: Review of Responses to CRTC Notice of Public Hearing 1995-5 (Ottawa: Nordicity Group Limited, July).

Peers, Frank W. (1969), The Politics of Canadian Broadcasting 1920–1951 (Toronto: University of Toronto Press).

Presbyterian Church, U.S.A. (1997), "In the Matter of Industry Proposal For CS Docket No. 97-55 Rating Video Programming, Comments of the Presbyterian Church U.S.A.," (April 8).

Public Broadcasting Service (1997), "In the Matter of Industry Proposal For CS Docket No. 97-55 Rating Video Programming, Comments of the Public Broadcasting Service," (April 8).

Raboy, Marc (1990), Missed Opportunities: The Story of Canada's Broadcasting Policy (Montreal: McGill-Queen's).

Rueschemeyer, Deitrich (1986), Power and the Division of Labor (Stanford: Stanford University Press).

Shogren, Elizabeth (1996), "Clinton Supports Industry on TV Ratings Proposal," Los Angeles Times (December 14), p. A1.

Smith, F. Leslie, Milan Meeske, and John Wright (1995), Electronic Media and

Government: The Regulation of Wireless and Wired Mass Communication in the United States (White Plains: Longman).

Torstendahl, Rolf (1990), "Essential properties, strategic aims and historical development: three approaches to theories of professionalism," pp. 41-61 in Michael Burrage and Rolf Torstendahl (eds.), Professions in Theory and History (London: Sage).

United States (1996), Telecommunications Act of 1996.

Winsor, Hugh (1997), "CRTC adopts TV-show codes," The Globe and Mail (Thursday, June 19).

Winsor, Hugh (1996), "TV to be Rated for Violence," The Globe and Mail (Friday, March 15), pp. 1, 7.

CHAPTER THREE

Three Questions About Television Ratings

Marjorie Heins

In the 1996 Communications Decency Act, Congress mandated that all television sets manufactured or distributed in the United States after February 1998 contain "a feature designed to enable viewers to block display of all programs with a common rating"—that is, to have a so-called V-chip.[1] A chip enabling viewers "to block display of all programs with a common rating" is, of course, meaningless without someone to sit down and actually rate programming. Who will rate, how, and with what effect, have thus become critical issues for television producers and artists, for parents, children and teenagers, and for others who may rely upon the ratings. This article poses three questions worth pondering as the United States for the first time embarks upon a massive program of evaluating, labeling, and blocking hundreds of thousands of broadcast and cable television productions.

First, what exactly is the TV rating system that the industry created in response to the CDA[2] meant to accomplish? The answer is not so obvious, and looking beyond the conventional answer ("parental empowerment"), it becomes clear that the congressional purpose was to disfavor, and hopefully chill, broad categories of speech of which Congress disapproved.

Second, who will rate programming, and how will they decide? Unless one believes that the mandated V-chip combined with the industry's rating system will have no effect whatsoever on what is produced or viewed, these procedural questions are critical.

Finally, what are the likely political and artistic effects of the U.S. ratings scheme? The evidence is just beginning to come in, but it tends to confirm that the ratings will indeed be used to censor, chill, and pressure the industry into dropping controversial shows.

I. WHAT EXACTLY IS THE RATING SYSTEM
MEANT TO ACCOMPLISH?

The V-chip law, which forced the TV industry's creation of the rating system, is often touted as a form of parental empowerment; that is, its proponents characterize it as an innocent means of giving information to parents that will enable them to decide for themselves what programs their children should and should not watch. But the law is not quite so benign and noncensorial as its defenders sometimes would have it appear. For the CDA singles out certain categories of television content that Congress disliked (primarily violence and sexuality), and imposes, or at least very strongly encourages, the creation of a rating system to identify, and facilitate the blocking of, programs with just this content. The V-chip law is thus not simply an attempt to inform parents generally about the content of television programming.

Indeed, the "findings" portion of the law is quite explicit on this point. It reads, in pertinent part:

The Congress makes the following findings:

(1) Television influences children's perception of the values and behavior that are common and acceptable in society. . . .

(4) Studies have shown that children exposed to violent video programming at a young age have a higher tendency for violent and aggressive behavior later in life than children not so exposed, and that children exposed to violent video programming are prone to assume that acts of violence are acceptable behavior. . . .

(6) Studies indicate that children are affected by the pervasiveness and casual treatment of sexual material on television, eroding the ability of parents to develop responsible attitudes and behavior in their children. . . .[3]

These findings make clear that the purpose of the V-chip legislation was to target certain subjects and ideas with plainly stated censorial purposes. Those subjects and ideas, as spelled out in the law, are "sexual, violent, or other indecent material about which parents should be informed before it is displayed to children."[4]

But what is the basis for Congress's conclusions that "children exposed to violent video programming at a young age have a higher tendency for violent and aggressive behavior later in life," or that "casual treatment of sexual material on television [erodes] the ability of parents to develop responsible attitudes and behavior in their children"? Putting aside the constitutional questions raised by a law that imposes congressional value judgments about "responsible attitudes and behavior,"[5] what precisely are the subjects or ideas that Congress thought to be harmful, and what is the nature of the social science evidence that is said to prove the point? The two questions are related, for without defining what we are talking about (*all* violence? only "excessive" or "gratuitous" violence? explicit sex? implied sex? irresponsible attitudes *about* sex?), it is impossible to say whether "violence" or "sex" cause harm, or whether labeling and blocking TV programs is likely to reduce such harm.

One of the weaknesses in the social science literature on minors, television, and violence is precisely the inconsistency among researchers in defining these terms. Some studies attempt to identify the effects of films or TV shows with realistic physical violence; others look at make-believe play or cartoon violence; still others include verbal aggression. Some researchers attempt to distinguish "good" from "bad" violence—that is, they would excuse war movies, educational documentaries, or situations in which the hero uses force in self-defense. As a recent report by the Committee on Communications and Media Law of the Association of the Bar of the City of New York points out,

> The subject of violence and aggression in psychology is vast. These topics are fundamental to the models and theories created in the fields of psychology, biology, ethnology and evolution. One author estimated that there were 20,000 to 30,000 references on the subject of human aggression. What is most striking, even after sampling only a small part of this literature and thought, is how little agreement there is among experts in human behavior about the nature of aggression and violence, and what causes humans to act aggressively or violently. There is even difficulty defining the words "aggression" and "violence."[6]

The report goes on to note that aggression and violence themselves

> are necessarily defined relative to culture, intent, and context. While all societies condemn murder, the same act may be seen as treason or heroism. Physical discipline of a child may be viewed as appropriate or abusive, depending on viewpoint and culture. Physical assault may be viewed as reprehensible conduct or as an appropriate part of a sport or entertainment, like hockey or boxing.[7]

Thus, despite numerous pronouncements over the past decade that a causative link between television violence and social or psychological harm has been definitively proven, the ambiguities in scientists' own use of definitional terms is in itself enough to raise questions about the "findings" that Congress made.

The social science literature is too vast and technical to review in detail here; in any event, excellent critiques have been published elsewhere.[8] The report of the Association of the Bar of the City of New York, however, does provide a useful summary of the types of studies that have been done and of what, if any, political, scientific, and legal conclusions can reasonably be drawn from them. The report notes first that there are many schools of psychology, only one of which considers "social learning" to be the primary cause of aggressive or violent behavior:

> [P]sychologists do not even agree on the basic mechanisms that cause aggression—and therefore on the possible role of stimuli such as media

depictions of violence in contributing to it. Some see aggression as innate in human beings, a drive which demands discharge in some form. Evolutionary psychologists see human aggressiveness and destructive violence as a naturally evolved response to particular environments. Violence is simply the route to status in certain social environments. Another psychologist sees human destructiveness and cruelty not as an instinct but as a part of character, as "passions rooted in the total existence of man." For psychologists who emphasize the social needs of humans, violence is a reflection of psychological trauma in establishing relations to others. The failure to develop a mediating conscience because of a deficient family structure may lead to an inability to control aggressive impulses which arise.

Finally, there are psychologists who believe aggressive behavior is learned from the environment. It is primarily these theorists who have looked particularly at television and violence. But, although it is sometimes sweepingly said that television violence causes violence in society, the research of these psychologists by no means supports so broad a statement. For over thirty years researchers have been attempting to discern the relationship, if any, between aggressive behavior and viewing television violence. The results remain controversial and skeptics abound.[9]

The report then describes the four basic methodological approaches that have been used by this last category of social scientists, who believe that "aggressive behavior is learned from the environment." These four are laboratory experiments, field experiments, quasi or natural experiments, and longitudinal studies. After examining the strengths and weaknesses of each method, the report concludes that the results of empirical research

> offer only modest support, and to a greater extent contradict, the legislative findings drawing connections between media violence and violent conduct or predispositions that underlie most of the efforts to regulate violent media content.

This is because, first,

> most psychological studies of the effects of television are studies of aggression or aggressive attitudes, not violence. The distinction is significant: many behaviors which few would deem "violent" may be counted and measured by psychologists as aggressive. Yet the purported focus of most legislative efforts is violent behavior caused by media content. It would therefore be erroneous to rely on psychological studies of aggression to justify such regulations.

Second, as the report noted,

> research studies are generally influenced by more fundamental, underlying conceptions of the causes of human social behavior—issues on which there is

little agreement. For example, theorists who believe that behavior is learned by children from what they observe are more inclined to construct studies focusing on television or media than theorists who place more weight on the child's family structure or position in a social pecking order.

Finally,

determining psychological causation is problematic, difficult and the subject of a considerable amount of disagreement. The empirical findings normally speak in terms of correlation of events and not causation; the researchers' findings are usually carefully limited and, in general, do not make broad or definitive assertions about the causes of particular behavior. For many reasons, generalizing from research results to everyday experience can be perilous. It is difficult, for example, for psychologists to duplicate the mix and range of violent and non-violent programming that an individual may choose. There is also great variation in the population viewing violent programming: some persons may be unusually susceptible to imitation of violent media portrayals, and research populations may be skewed by over-representation of such individuals. It is also difficult to isolate everyday viewing of violent media portrayals from other experiences that psychologists believe may contribute to violent behavior. There is no consensus among even the researchers who have found some correlations that there is any clear causal link between media violence and violent behavior. Many psychologists point to other factors—such as watching television in general, or watching fast-paced programming—as the most likely causes of any aggressiveness associated with television viewing. And no researcher, to our knowledge, purports to demonstrate that eliminating media violence is necessary to reducing violent behavior.[10]

In short, Congress's "findings" about exposure to TV violence and subsequent behavior do not hold up to even the most cursory examination. The effects of art and entertainment on the complex and idiosyncratic human mind are still largely a mystery. The unavoidable conclusion is that Congress seized upon social science literature to cloak what was essentially a political and moral judgment that large, vague categories of television programming are offensive or at least inappropriate for youth.[11]

II. WHO WILL RATE PROGRAMMING,
AND HOW WILL THEY DECIDE?

The V-chip puts significant power in the hands of the people who will actually rate TV programming. Those parents who choose to activate the chip will not be evaluating programs themselves to determine if they are consonant with their own values or appropriate for the age and maturity levels of their children. Instead, parents will be blocking programs based on simple, conclusory V, S, L (for language), or D (for dialogue) labels, combined with the industry's originally proposed TV-G, TV-PG, TV-14, and TV-MA age-based recommendations.[12] The system will give no further information about the multitude of shows subject to the rating system—their context, purpose, viewpoint, quality, or educational value.

Those parents who block will thus do so based on *Congress's* determination that it is sex, "indecency," and violence that must be restrained, and the industry's apparent interpretation of "indecent," to the extent it differs from "sexual," to mean primarily "coarse" language (L) or "suggestive dialogue" (D).[13] Other types of content that have occasionally been blamed for juvenile delinquency or other ills—for example, racist speech, discussions of drug use, or paeans to "Satanism" or other disapproved religious beliefs—are not included.

Critics of ratings systems have pointed out the dangers of using broad, conclusory labels as measures of the value of speech, or of the harm it may cause. An often cited, and still powerful, example is Steven Spielberg's film *Schindler's List*, which will presumably receive V, S, L, and D labels because of its violent content (it is, after all, about the Holocaust) and occasional nudity (Schindler has affairs—sexual nudity—and the Jews who are being rounded up for slaughter are frequently deprived of their clothing—nonsexual nudity). Yet *Schindler's List* is probably among the most important and educational of commercial films in recent years. Whatever arguments might be made about the psychological effects on children of *gratuitous* violence, the violence shown in *Schindler's List* can hardly be deemed gratuitous, and indeed the film has been criticized in some quarters for not giving a vivid *enough* depiction of the horrors of the Nazi regime. What then, is the point exactly of shielding minors, particularly teenagers, from the knowledge of human pain and brutality imparted by this and other historical films? How are they to learn about human history without studying the evil that characterized one of its most gruesome episodes? Does it really help educate young people to airbrush the atrocities of history—or, for that matter, to pretend that the powerful force of human sexuality does not exist? Certainly, there is little basis to believe that viewing *Schindler's List* will cause young people to develop greater tolerance for violence, to behave more aggressively, or to acquire irresponsible attitudes about sex.[14]

Eyes on the Prize, to cite an example of a program specifically designed for TV, is a powerful documentary of the American civil rights movement, and contains violence galore—most of it visited by Southern white citizens or law enforcement officers against black protesters. The film would be historically false if it did not. Yet its educational value and dramatic power cannot be doubted. What is the justification for labeling with a V— and therefore suggesting to parents that they block it as unsuitable—this masterwork of documentary filmmaking?

On a more mundane level, the process of deciding whether a program merits a V, D, S, or L—or a TV-14 or TV-MA—will inevitably be subjective, value-laden and time consuming, as a Fox Broadcasting executive noted in September 1997.[15] Ellen DeGeneres, the recently "out" lesbian of the popular eponymous ABC sitcom, discovered in October 1997 that her completely nonviolent and nonsexually explicit show was slated to receive a TV-14, presumably because it deals approvingly with homosexuality. "How can I go forward?" DeGeneres was quoted as asking. "This is blatant discrimination. . . . This advisory is telling kids something's wrong with being gay."[16]

A December 1993 report from North Dakota Senator Byron Dorgan is pertinent here. The report summarized the results of a one-week survey of violence on prime time television conducted by college students earlier that year. Among the shows found to contain the highest number of violent acts per hours were *The Miracle Worker*, *Civil War Journal*, *Star Trek 9*, *The Untouchables*, *Murder She Wrote*, *Back to the Future*, *Our Century: Combat at Sea*, *Teenage Mutant Ninja Turtles*, and Alfred Hitchcock's classic *North by Northwest.*[17] Even if a TV ratings system purported to give pejorative V labels to only the programs on this list deemed to contain "bad" violence, which the industry's current plan does not, it would be difficult for a team of raters to make those judgments, expected as they will be to decide upon labels for dozens of programs daily. Indeed, the subjectivity of judgments about "value" or about the meaning or propriety of the messages contained in creative works, as well as long-standing First Amendment rules against "viewpoint discrimination,[18] are one reason that the ratings, like the Communications Decency Act itself, do not distinguish between "good" and "bad" violence or sex.

But if making value judgments of this type is both difficult and offensive to our anti-censorship instincts, a system that fails to do so, and thus encompasses *all* programming bearing on large subjects like sexuality or violence, is hopelessly overbroad. As Professor Burt Neuborne recently pointed out:

> The impossibly broad reach of a literal ban on all speech depicting violence inevitably requires a narrowing set of criteria designed to distinguish *Hamlet* from forbidden speech depicting violence. But any effort by the FCC, or anyone else, to decide when speech depicting violence crosses the line from an acceptable exercise in artistic creation, as in *Hamlet*, or *Oedipus Rex*, or *Antigone*, or *The Crucible*, to a forbidden depiction of "gratuitous" or "excessive" violence must involve purely subjective notions of taste and aesthetic judgment. Indeed, once it is recognized that the ban on violence cannot be applied literally, any effort to apply a narrower ban is utterly without objective guidance. In effect, efforts to ban violent programming would turn the FCC into a drama critic, forced to pass judgment on the artistic merits of any effort to depict a violent act.[19]

The problems Professor Neuborne identifies with respect to a ban are equally present in a ratings system. The American Psychological Association has acknowledged that "[t]elevision violence per se is not the problem; rather, it is the manner in which most violence on television is shown that should concern us."[20] But as Professor Neuborne points out, trying to distinguish between "excessive" or "gratuitous" violence on the one hand, and violent material presented in an instructive or morally approved way, as the APA suggests, would enmesh whoever is responsible for the ratings in a vast process of policing thought and censoring ideas.

Nor are these problems resolved if television companies decide not to assign the task of rating to in-house staff but instead force producers or directors to evaluate and label their own programs. Many of those on the creative side of the industry will object to being compelled to attached pejorative ratings to their works, or will bridle at the constraints of a system that substitutes overgeneralized and fundamentally uninformative labels for real contextual information about programs.[21] If, despite their objections, they are forced to label, the results are likely to be arbitrary and idiosyncratic. For example, the distinction between "strong, coarse language," requiring a TV-14 rating, and "crude indecent language," requiring a TV-MA,[22] is likely to elude many raters and lead to inconsistent results.

On the other end of the television continuum, there are countless programs with no violence, sex, "coarse language," or "suggestive dialogue," and also with little educational or artistic value. Mindless entertainment—the "idiot box" of popular discourse—may be a greater threat to healthy child development, to the nurturing of thoughtful young people who are knowledgeable about and capable of dealing with the complexities and tragedies of human life, than violent or sexual content per se. Justice Brandeis's much-quoted rhetoric about "more speech"[23] is pertinent here: teaching young people about responsible sexuality or other aspects of human behavior requires education and discussion, not censorship.

III. WHAT ARE THE LIKELY POLITICAL AND ARTISTIC EFFECTS OF THE U.S. RATINGS SCHEME?

Regardless of its unambiguously stated censorial purposes,[24] the 1996 V-chip law, it is sometimes said, will not have any speech-suppressive effect, or at least none attributable to the government. Parents will make their own decisions based on accurate information about programming—an outcome no more repressive of free speech than the existing operation of market forces as consumers choose some programs and reject others.

Let's examination this seductively simple proposition. First, even in the constitutional sense (as the First Amendment generally applies only to government), the television ratings are not likely to operate wholly in the unregulated sphere of private choice. Some public schools will rely upon the ratings in choosing—or, more accurately, disqualifying—what may be worthy and valuable TV programs for homework assignments or in-class viewing. Indeed, there are school districts that already rely upon the familiar Motion Picture Association of America/Classification and Rating Administration movie ratings in just this fashion,[25] despite the fact that MPAA/CARA raters have no background or expertise in education or child development.[26] Just as numerous students have been deprived of *Schindler's List* as part of their high school history courses because of its R rating from CARA, so *The Accused, The Miracle Worker, The Civil War*, and countless other educationally profitable TV movies or other shows with violent content will receive V ratings and be subject to at least a presumption against curricular use in many public schools.

Second, ratings necessarily imply that certain programs contain themes that are morally disapproved or psychologically harmful to minors. They thus provide an easy set of symbols for "family values" activists in local communities to seize upon. The average public school administration will not be particularly eager to countenance curricular use of S-, V-, L-, or D-rated material in the face of likely protest from such groups. Ratings thus advance censorship by giving private pressure groups easy red flags to wave in the faces of nervous government officials.

Moving from the local to the national government level, it is difficult to imagine that the Federal Communications Commission, which is so enmeshed in the regulation of "indecency" in broadcasting,[27] will not be drawn into disputes over ratings as well. It will no doubt receive complaints from politicians, members of the public, and perhaps rival broadcasters, that some companies are not accurately rating their programming, or are refusing to rate at all. Indeed, one member of Congress has already made such a threat explicitly. In September 1997, Senator John McCain wrote to NBC, which had so far resisted the addition of content-based letter labels to the original age-based industry ratings plan, that if NBC continued to "refuse to join with the rest of the television industry,"

> I will pursue a series of alternative ways of safeguarding, by law and regulation, the interests that NBC refuses to safeguard voluntarily. These will include, but not be limited to, the legislation offered by Senator Hollings to channel violent programming to later hours, as well as urging the Federal Communications Commission to examine in a full evidentiary hearing the renewal application of any television station not implementing the revised TV ratings system.[28]

Is the FCC to ignore the complaints of Senator McCain and others? It may, to be sure, be wary of initiating formal reviews of allegedly inaccurate or deceptive ratings, for fear of establishing the very "state action," and consequent vulnerability to a First Amendment court challenge, that the authors of the V-chip legislation attempted to avoid. Nevertheless, the agency is charged by law with evaluating a broadcast licensee's record of contribution to the "public interest" when reviewing requests for license renewals, transfers, or acquisitions.[29] Just as the commission has long considered broadcasters' records on community programming and their capacity to disseminate diverse points of view,[30] and just as it has threatened adverse licensing action based on complaints of "indecency,"[31] it is likely to consider allegations that broadcasters have rated programs improperly when it makes licensing decisions. At the very least, the possibility that it may do so, and the power of economic life and death that the FCC holds over broadcasters, will make the television industry cautious about displeasing the agency.

What about private censorship? Putting aside the legal question whether private marketplace choices made as a result of the V-chip law create First Amendment concerns,[32] it cannot be doubted that such private choices do have an effect on artistic freedom. Again, the analogy to movie ratings is instructive. Just as many theaters are reluctant to book NC-17 movies, some advertisers will be reluctant to support V-, S-, L-, or D-rated TV shows. Less advertising means less revenue, which in turn means less likelihood that the show will survive—unless, of course, its content is toned down. In many situations, advertisers' threats of withdrawal will not even be necessary, since for large entertainment companies the mere prospect of pejorative ratings may be daunting enough in terms of public relations to cause them to instruct producers to self-censor their material.

In recent years, the MPAA/CARA film ratings system has had just this effect.

Leading directors like the late Louis Malle have been forced to eliminate artistically important scenes from their work because of the studios' insistence on obtaining at least nothing more pejorative and audience-thinning than an R rating.[33] Self-censorship will thus be a predictable and intended effect of the V-chip law.

I have discussed in the previous two sections whether such pressures to self-censor are justifiable, given the ambiguity of the social science literature, the difficulty of defining what it is that is supposed to be harmful, and the dangers of reposing discretionary ratings powers in either program producers themselves or large numbers of industry-employed functionaries. The point here is that, regardless of the strength of the justifications or the fairness of the procedures, the inevitable pressures of the ratings system will in many instances lead to blander, less provocative programming—less coverage of controversial but important issues like sexuality, and less artistic freedom.[34]

V-chips and ratings will do nothing to solve the tough, persistent social problems we associate with youth: poor education, violence, alienation, high teen pregnancy rates. American political leaders, however, seem increasingly devoted to the art of making symbolic gestures while ignoring serious solutions to social problems. V-chips and ratings are such gestures, but they are not entirely empty ones. For although they will do nothing to reduce irresponsible sexual activity or violence, they will restrain artistic freedom. Moreover, they create the illusion that "something is being done," and reinforce the pernicious notion that information about such complex human phenomena as sexuality and aggression is better suppressed than examined.

Notes

1. 47 U.S.C. §303(x), Public Law 104-104, Title V, §551(c). The law only applies to TV sets with screens 13 inches or larger, and allows the FCC to alter the requirement consistent with advances in technology. *Id.*, §551(c)(4).

2. The law provided that if the television industry did not within a year develop a ratings system satisfactory to the Federal Communications Commission, the FCC must "prescribe" one that would identify "sexual, violent, or other indecent material," and then, "in consultation" with the industry, must establish rules requiring programmers to transmit the ratings in a manner allowing parents to block rated shows. 47 U.S.C. §303(w). Despite initial protests, the industry responded promptly by setting up a committee to design a ratings system. See n. 12, *infra*.

3. Section 551(a), Public Law 104-104 (1996), published in the Historical and Statutory Notes to 47 U.S.C. §303(w). Congressional "findings" may or may not be based on accurate empirical evidence, and in any event are not binding on courts, particularly not in First Amendment cases, where the judicial branch must make its own judgment about the facts on which the government relies to justify restrictions on free speech. See, e.g., *Sable Communications, Inc. V. FCC*, 492 U.S. 115, 129 (1989); *Landmark Communications v. Virginia*, 435 U.S. 829, 843 (1978).

4. 47 U.S.C. §303(w). The section goes on to assure that "nothing in this paragraph shall be construed to authorize any rating of video programming on the basis of its political or religious content." *Id.*

5. A fundamental First Amendment principle is that government cannot suppress ideas because it thinks them dangerous. See Marjorie Heins, "Viewpoint Discrimination," 24 *Hastings Con.L.Q.* 99 (1996); *American Booksellers Association v. Hudnut*, 771 F.2d 323 (7th Cir.), aff'd mem., 475 U.S. 1001 (1985);.

6. "Violence in the Media: A Position Paper," *The Record of The Association of the Bar of the City of New York*, vol. 52, no. 3 (April 1997), at 283–84 (citations omitted). Reprinted with permission from *The Record* of The Association of the Bar of the City of New York, copyright 1997, 52 *The Record* 273, 283–84.

7. *Id.* at 284.

8. See, e.g., Jonathan Freedman, "Television Violence and Aggression: A Rejoinder," *Psychological Bulletin*, Vol. 100(3), 372–78 (1986); Robert Kaplan, "Television Violence and Viewer Aggression: A Reexamination of the Evidence," *Journal of Social Issues*, vol. 32, no. 4, 35–70 (1976); Robert Kaplan, "TV Violence and Aggression Revisited Again," *American Psychologist*, vol. 37, no. 5, 589 (May 1982); O. Wiegman, M. Kuttschreuter & B. Baarda, "A Longitudinal Study of the Effects of Television Viewing on Aggressive and Prosocial Behaviours," *British Journal of Social Psychology*, vol. 31, 147–64 (1992).
9. "Violence in the Media," *Record of The Association of the Bar of the City of New York, supra* n. 6, at 286 (citations omitted).
10. *Id.* at 296–97 (citations omitted).
11. Social science studies with respect to sexual situations on television are quite limited compared to the extensive, if inconclusive, literature on violence. The few studies that do exist are at best suggestive of a correlation, not necessarily a causal relation, between viewing habits and sexual behavior. See, e.g., Charles Corder-Bolz, "Television and Adolescents' Sexual Behavior," *Sex Education News*, vol. 3 (Jan. 1981), p. 3 (survey showed that of seventy-five adolescent girls, half of them pregnant, the pregnant ones watched more TV soap operas and were less likely to think that their favorite characters used contraceptives). As the American Academy of Pediatrics, a proponent of more sexually responsible TV programming, acknowledges, "there is no clear documentation that the relationship between television viewing and sexual activity [among teenagers] is causal." American Academy of Pediatrics, "Children, Adolescents, and Television," *Pediatrics*, vol. 96, no. 4 (Oct. 1995), p. 786.
12. The industry's original plan, submitted by the National Association of Broadcasters (NAB), the Motion Picture Association of America (MPAA), and the National Cable Television Association (NCTA) to the FCC for its approval on January 17, 1997, was wholly age-based and gave no information about the content of specific programs. It encountered widespread criticism from politicians and advocacy groups. After a six-month period of negotiations with these groups, the three industry associations agreed to add V, S, L, and D labels to the scheme. See Letter Submission of Jack Valenti, President and CEO of the MPAA, Decker Anstrom, President and CEO of the NCTA, and Eddie Fritts, President and CEO of the NAB, to William Caton, FCC Secretary, Aug. 1, 1997 (hereinafter, "Valenti letter").
13. *Id.*, p. 2. As a legal term, "indecency" derives from the Federal Communications Commission's policing of radio and television broadcasting, as approved by the Supreme Court in *FCC v. Pacifica Foundation*, 438 U.S. 726 (1978). The monologue by comedian George Carlin found to be indecent in *Pacifica* consisted of the repetitive use of the so-called seven dirty words, not of any explicit description of sexual activity.
    Under the industry's plan, news and sports are to be exempt from labeling requirements. See Valenti letter, p. 3. Disputes may easily be anticipated about what programming qualifies as "news."
14. Many other examples of fine films with violent content could, of course, be cited: *The Accused, Bonnie and Clyde, The Burning Bed, Psycho*, and almost any war story or Biblical epic.
15. Lawrie Mifflin, "Helping or Confusing, TV Labels are Widening," *New York Times*, Sept. 30, 1997, p. E1 (quoting Roland McFarland, Vice President for Broadcast Standards and Practices at Fox, as stating that "the process had become much more time-consuming now that D, L, S, and V had to be considered." "Is it a punch? A gunshot? A gunshot plus killing? These are all subjective interpretations. The classic discussion here is around shows where there's heavy jeopardy involved, but not real on-screen violence. You might see a body, the aftermath of violence. . . . Where's the tilt factor, as far as giving it a V?" *Id.*, p. E8.
16. Bill Carter, "Star of 'Ellen' Threatens to Quit Over Advisory," *New York Times*, Oct. 9, 1997, p. E3.
17. Press Release from U.S. Senator Byron L. Dorgan (North Dakota), "Report on Television Violence Shows Fox Network Has the Most Violence Programming," Dec. 16, 1993, and attached report, "Television Violence Demonstration Project Conducted at Concordia College, Moorhead, Minnesota, Sept.–Dec. 1993."
18. See n. 5, *supra*.
19. Television Rating System: Hearings on S.409 Before the Senate Comm. on Commerce, Science and Transp., 105th Cong. (1997) (testimony of Burt Neuborne, Professor of Law, New York University).
20. Comments of the American Psychological Association to the Federal Communications Commission 3 (April 8, 1997) (in the matter of Industry Proposal for Rating Video Programming, No. 97-55).
21. In the analogous context of Internet ratings, producers of online information have loudly objected to proposals that they "self-rate" their sites: as one editor explained, "The rating of content, particularly in the area of violence—to tell people whether they should or shouldn't read about war in Bosnia—takes news and turns it into a form of entertainment." Amy Harmon, "Technology," *New York Times*, Sept. 1, 1997, p. D3.
22. As set out in the Valenti Letter, *supra* n. 12, p. 2.

23.   "Those who won our independence . . . believed that freedom to think as you will and to speak as you
       think are means indispensable to the discovery and spread of political truth; that without free speech and
       assembly, discussion would be futile; that with them, discussion affords ordinarily adequate protection
       against the dissemination of noxious doctrine. . . . [T]hey knew that . . . the path of safety lies in the oppor-
       tunity to discuss freely supposed grievances and proposed remedies; and that the fitting remedy for evil
       counsels is good ones." *Whitney v. California*, 274 U.S. 357, 375 (1927) (Brandeis, J., concurring).
24.   See *supra*, text accompanying notes 2–3.
25.   See *Borger v. Bisciglia*, 888 F.Supp. 97 (W.D.Wis. 1995) (rejecting First Amendment challenge to school
       district's ban on showing any R-rated film as part of curriculum, which resulted in inability of students
       to see *Schindler's List* as part of their study of the Holocaust); *Desilets v. Clearview Regional Board of
       Education*, 137 N.J. 584 (1994) (striking down school authorities' refusal to allow student newspaper to
       review R-rated films, *Rain Man* and *Mississippi Burning*); "'Schlinder' Blacklisted," *New York Times*,
       March 18, 1994, p. A28 (Letters to the Editor) (describing Plymouth, Massachusetts's school board's
       decision not to allow high school students to see *Schindler's List* because of R rating); "Twin Falls,
       Ohio," American Library Association *Newsletter on Intellectual Freedom* (Sept. 1997), p. 127
       (describing parent's challenge to use of films *Schindler's List* and *Macbeth* because of their R ratings).
26.   See Richard M. Mosk, "Motion Picture Ratings in the United States," in this volume. I do not mean to
       suggest that a ratings board composed of literary or psychological experts, as is found, for example, in
       Britain, would necessarily be an improvement.
27.   See *FCC v. Pacifica Foundation*, 438 U.S. 726 (1978); *Action for Children's Television v. FCC* ("ACT
       III"), 58 F.3d 654 (D.C. Cir. 1995), cert. denied, 116 S.Ct. 701 (1996).
28.   Letter from Senator John McCain, chairman, Senate Committee on Commerce, Science, and
       Transportation, to Robert Wright, President and CEO, National Broadcasting Company, Sept. 29, 1997.
       At around the same time, Senator McCain asked each of four new FCC commissioner candidates "to
       agree to consider a station's use or nonuse of the revised ratings-code as a factor in deciding whether to
       renew a station's license." Lawrie Mifflin, "Media," *New York Times*, Oct. 6, 1997, p. D11. Although
       refusing to use the letter labels, NBC was already giving "full-sentence advisories" about violent content
       at the start of some shows. *Id.*
29.   See 47 U.S.C. §§ 303-309.
30.   *See Metro Broadcasting, Inc. v. FCC*, 497 U.S. 547 (1990) (approving FCC's consideration of diversity
       of viewpoint in awarding licenses), overruled on other grounds in *Adarand Constructors, Inc. v. Peña*,
       515 U.S. 200 (1995).
31.   See *Action for Children's Television v. FCC* ("ACT IV"), 59 F.3d 1249, 1266 (D.C. Cir 1995), cert.
       denied, 116 S.Ct. 773 (1996) (Tatel, J., dissenting) (noting FCC use of administrative "indecency"
       determinations to threaten loss of broadcast licenses).
32.   In *Denver Area Educational Telecommunications Consortium v. FCC*, 116 S.Ct. 2374 (1966), Justice
       Stephen Breyer, writing for a plurality of four members of the Supreme Court, asserted that although a
       law authorizing private cable companies to censor "indecent" leased access cable programming was
       clearly "state action," it did not violate the First Amendment because, among other things, the law
       addressed "an extremely important problem"—"protecting children from exposure to patently offensive
       depictions of sex"—and it reflected a balancing of cable companies' and leased access programmers'
       free speech rights. *Id.* at 2385, 2382–88. As to public, educational, and governmental access cable
       programming, the Court reached the opposite conclusion. *Id.* at 2394–97.
33.   *See* Marjorie Heins, *Sex, Sin and Blasphemy: A Guide to America's Censorship Wars* 58–59 (1993)
       (describing Malle's cutting, over protest, of his controversial film, *Damage*); Stephen Farber, *The Movie
       Rating Game* 71 (1972) (recounting how line about pubic hair was cut from *The Reivers* to obtain GP
       rating and how pot-smoking scene and two short love-making scenes were eliminated from *Alice's
       Restaurant* for the same reason); see also *Miramax Films Corp. v. Motion Picture Association of
       America*, 560 N.Y.S. 730, 734 (Supreme Ct., NY County 1990) ("[t]he record also reveals that films are
       produced and *negotiated* to fit the ratings. After an initial 'X' rating of a film whole scenes or parts thereof
       are cut in order to fit within the 'R' category. Contrary to our jurisprudence which protects all forms of
       expression, the rating system censors serious films by the force of economic pressure"). Since the
       decision in *Miramax*, CARA's dreaded X has been replaced with the almost equally undesirable NC-17.
34.   Some critics of ratings claim that the censorial purpose may backfire—that is, the quest for adventuresome
       (especially teenage) audiences may in some cases cause producers gratuitously to *add* sexual or violent
       content to their work, for what self-respecting adolescent wants to attend a G-rated movie? Whatever the
       accuracy of this speculation, it seems evident that television ratings, like movie ratings, will distort
       artistic judgments and introduce extraneous pressures into the creative process.

CHAPTER FOUR

Media Filters and the V-Chip

J. M. Balkin

I. INTRODUCTION—TO V OR NOT TO V

One of the most controversial features of the Telecommunications Act of 1996[1] is its intervention in long-standing disputes about violence and indecency in the media. Due in part to the urging of President Clinton and his Democratic allies, the new act requires that all television sets over thirteen inches include a "V-chip," a device that would allow parents to block violent and indecent television programming.[2]

Despite its name, the V-chip is not a single chip at all, but a combination of different technologies. All television programs currently have the capacity to carry extra information—like closed captioning—as well as sound and pictures. An electronic circuit in a television or cable box can be designed to block programs by reading a numerical code broadcast along the same band used for closed captioning. Viewers then use a remote control device to select from a menu of choices as to how much violence, bad language, sex, and nudity they wish to tolerate. An experimental rating system developed in Canada, for example, features a five-number scale, with three separate categories for sex, profanity, and violence. Higher numbers signify higher levels of each category. When the V-chip circuitry reads a rating equal to or higher than the consumer's preselected standards, the picture is replaced by a large black box. A V-chip system can also be designed to recall previous settings and block all unrated programs. However, in order to prevent bad language from being transmitted, it must be able to block sound as well as pictures.[3]

In response to the passage of the Telecommunications Act, members of the American entertainment industry met with President Clinton on February 29, 1996, and promised the delivery of an industry-sponsored ratings system for the V-chip within a year. On December 19, 1996, an industry committee, led by Jack Valenti, president of the Motion Picture Association of America (MPAA), unveiled a ratings system quite different from the Canadian model described above. In its original formulation, this system did not offer separate categories for violence, sexual content, or bad language; instead it considered all three together and rated programming based on appropriateness to age, much like the MPAA ratings system. The current age-based ratings categories are TV-G (General Audience—suitable for children of all ages), TV-PG (Parental Guidance Suggested—material that some parents would find unsuitable for younger children), TV-14 (Parents Strongly Cautioned—material that many parents would find unsuitable for children under 14), and TV-M (Mature Audiences Only—specifically designed for adults and unsuitable for children under 17). There are also two special categories for programs designed specially for children: TV-Y (All Children—designed to be appropriate for all children), and TV-Y7 (Directed to Older Children—designed for children age 7 and above).[4] In response, Canadian broadcasters announced their own age-based system on May 5, 1997; it primarily rates violence as opposed to sexual content or bad language.[5] On July 10, 1997, the major American networks (excluding NBC) agreed to supplement their age-based ratings with codes for violence (V), sexual situations (S), coarse language (L), or suggestive dialogue (D). Children's programming rated TV-Y7 may carry additional codes for "fantasy violence" (FV).[6] Although the V-chip system has yet to be fully implemented in mass-market televisions as of the date of this writing, broadcast and cable programmers have already begun displaying age-based ratings at the beginning of many different television shows; they intend to begin display of supplemental content-based ratings sometime in the fall of 1997.

Critics charge that the V-chip raises serious First Amendment problems. This essay explores a few of them. But my more important goal is to use the debate over the V-chip to rethink the foundations of broadcast regulation. The federal courts, including the Supreme Court, have justified content-based restrictions on broadcast indecency partly on the grounds of the special nature of the mass media. Yet their justifications for special treatment have been, on the whole, unconvincing. I will argue that the real issues have little to do with traditional justifications of scarcity, public interest, and pervasiveness. They have to do with how different media permit the filtering of information. Different communication technologies are better adapted to different kinds of informational filters. For example, broadcast media permit different and more limited filters than print media. The V-chip promises to change all that by creating a new system for filtering broadcast information. But this new technology raises many new and unexpected problems. In particular, it raises the possibility that in the Information Age, control of filters may be one of the most important forms of power over human thought and human expression. In the Information Age, the informational filter, not information itself, is king.

II. THE DIFFERENCE BROADCASTING MAKES

The constitutional status of the V-chip is inextricably linked to the special constitutional treatment of broadcasting in American constitutional law. For many years, broadcast media have been subject to much greater content-based regulation than print media. For example, in *FCC v. Pacifica Foundation,* the Supreme Court upheld the constitutionality of FCC restrictions on indecency as applied to a radio broadcast of George Carlin's "Filthy Words" monologue.[7] More recently, the D.C. Circuit upheld "safe harbor" provisions that permit indecent speech on broadcast television only from 10:00 P.M. to 6:00 A.M.[8]

First Amendment scholars are divided as to whether this special treatment is constitutional. They have good reason to be concerned. "Indecency," like violence, is an unclear and wavering category. By definition, it includes sexually explicit speech that could not be regulated as obscene. This is a much larger category than many people imagine. It includes, for example, not only expression expressly designed for sexual stimulation, but also expression that is offensive to some but not obscene because it has genuine literary, artistic, political, or scientific value. Thus, indecent expression can include not only the more salacious contents of the Playboy Channel, but also political speeches laced with four-letter words and serious discussions of AIDS and homosexuality.

Similar problems hound the regulation of violence.[9] It is not always clear what kinds of violence do the most harm to children. Is the violence in cartoons worse than the violence in live action programs? Does unrealistic violence do more harm than depictions that bring home the horrors of war and death? Does the violence reported on the local and national news contribute to the problem, and, if so, should it also be restricted in the interests of our children?

In assessing the constitutionality of restrictions on violence and indecency, it is important to remember that the programming at issue here would be constitutionally protected if it appeared in print media, in a movie theater, or on a videocassette. There must be some special justification for abandoning general First Amendment principles in broadcast regulation.

Traditionally, content-based regulations of the broadcast media have been justified on two basic grounds: the scarcity of the airwaves and the pervasiveness of the medium. Other explanations—the fact that broadcasters hold licenses from the government and the importance of empowering democracy—tend to be parasitic on the scarcity rationale. Unfortunately, each of these justifications becomes problematic when applied to questions of violence and indecency.

The most common argument for special content-based regulations of the media is based on the scarcity of the airwaves. The word "scarcity" is poorly chosen. All valuable resources are scarce. The scarcity problem in broadcasting stems from the fact that no two broadcasters can use the same frequency at the same time in the same geographical area, or they will block each other out.[10] But this problem can be dealt with by creating a system of property rights dividing up the airwaves according to frequency, time, place, and broadcasting power; it does not require a system of government licenses.[11] Moreover, the existing system has actually created an artificial scarcity in broadcast television. Many VHF and UHF channels go unused in many localities.[12]

The spread of cable television has increasingly made the scarcity argument implausible. More than half of all American homes now receive cable,[13] and cable television wiring passes by most of the rest.[14] If the government is really interested in reducing scarcity and increasing choices, it should simply subsidize cheap cable television for the remaining households instead of artificially limiting access through the award of broadcasting licenses.

In any case, scarcity is a particularly badly suited justification for content-based regulation of violence and indecency. At best, scarcity provides a reason to put things on the air, not to keep things off. Because airtime is limited, governments may require that stations broadcast certain kinds of public interest programming, like local news or children's programming; it may also require that candidates for public office have the opportunity to purchase airtime and respond to personal attacks. But limited resources do not justify keeping particular programming off the air if there is otherwise sufficient room for it. To be sure, requiring that some things be on the air will necessarily require broadcasters to leave other things off. But the scarcity rationale does not by itself give the government any right to choose what that forgone programming will be, unless it thinks that scarcity entitles it to dictate the whole of the broadcaster's day. The justification for keeping indecency off the air cannot be to make room for the presidential debates; it must lie elsewhere.[15]

The other major justification usually offered for special treatment of the broadcast media is that these media are uniquely "pervasive." Like the term "scarcity," the term "pervasiveness" is also badly chosen. In fact, courts seem to use the term "pervasive" to stand for a conglomeration of five different sorts of justifications about broadcasting, often not fully distinguished. The broadcast media are pervasive first, because they are the most powerful medium of communication, and second, because they are ubiquitous. Yet the fact that a mode of communication is particularly powerful or ubiquitous is not necessarily a reason for regulating it. That would suggest that the only speech that escapes regulation is that which doesn't do its job very well.

A third interpretation is that television is "pervasive" because it is constitutive of our culture. We now live in a television culture, in which an increasing number of our cultural allusions are drawn from television. If we are what we eat, then perhaps we are also what we watch. Hence, many people secretly, and not so secretly, worry that whoever controls television controls culture, and they want to make sure that our culture is not thereby debased. But when the matter is put so starkly, the desire to use government to control culture by controlling what people watch on television cannot be a constitutional justification for the regulation of free expression.

A fourth meaning of "pervasiveness" is a restatement of the captive audience doctrine: government may protect audiences when their privacy is invaded in an intolerable manner by offensive speech they cannot escape. Television is "pervasive" in the sense that there are significant cultural pressures to have a television set and keep it in one's home. Once television is in the home, it is difficult to protect unwilling listeners from encountering programs they don't want to watch other than by keeping the television turned off at all times. The captive audience doctrine, it is said, has special force in the home because expectations of privacy are higher there.[16] Although television can be watched outside of the home—in a sports bar, for example—the fact that the overwhelming majority of Americans watch it at home is said to justify content-based regulation that would be impermissible if applied to the print media. However, when applied to adults, the captive audience rationale tends to prove too much. One can also accidentally come across printed material in the home. A newspaper or magazine might have offensive language buried on page fifteen; a videocassette might have offensive language or pictures in a "coming attractions" segment. But the fact that such a "sneak attack" might occur in the home does not justify content-based regulation of print media or videocassettes.

The fifth and final interpretation of "pervasive" is, to my mind, the most important, and the only one that really justifies special content-based regulation for the broadcast media. It is a concern about parental control of children's viewing habits.[17] Television is pervasive because it is difficult to keep it away from children and children away from it. Once television is in the home, parents must continually supervise what children watch, which is difficult and time-consuming. Many households now own multiple television sets, so that children can watch in the privacy of their own room, away from parental supervision. It is always possible for parents to remove television completely from the home. However, because of television's cultural importance, many parents do not feel able or willing to deny their children the right to watch television at home, especially when the children can watch it at their friends' houses.

Although concerns about children make the most sense doctrinally, it's important to remember that they have little to do with scarcity. Even if there were 500 channels, the problem of parental supervision would still exist, and might even be enhanced. Nor does this justification for regulation turn on the fact that broadcast television is an especially powerful medium of communication, or that it is conveyed in the easily assimilable form of pictures. Parents can watch rented movies on a VCR that are every bit as unacceptable for children as anything one might watch on television. But these movies cannot be regulated in the same way that television broadcasting can.[18]

This final rationale for broadcast regulation is often described as the protection of children, but the real issue is parental control. The two are not necessarily the same. We generally assume that parents love their children and discipline them in ways that are, on the whole, best for them. But parents do not always do so, and we do not second-guess their decisions except in extreme cases. Parents are currently free to bring home R-rated videos full of violence and nudity and let their children watch them. They can subscribe to premium cable channels showing these movies and leave their cable lock boxes unused. If violence and indecency really are bad for children, and we think protection of children is paramount, we should take steps to criminalize such behavior, whether or not parents misguidedly believe such exposure is harmless. Yet I suspect that such proposals would be severely criticized, and not merely by civil libertarians. Most parents do not want the government deciding what is best for their children when the decisions are contrary to their wishes; they want the government to assist them in controlling their children in ways they think appropriate.[19]

In short, behind the slogans of "scarcity" and "pervasiveness" lurks the real issue of parental control. This explains, I think, how current calls for media regulation are tied to the underlying anxieties of the moment. Calls for censorship (which exist at all times) arise most heatedly in moments of great cultural change and uncertainty. After all, where cultural mores are relatively stable, censorship can be achieved informally and without the constraints of law. But we now live in a time of cultural upheaval, caused by significant economic and technological changes as well as changes in mores. Not surprisingly, many people are especially anxious about these changes; they see the world they once knew slipping away. Like the drunk who searches for his keys near the lamppost because the light is better there, people tend to fix upon the mass media as the likely cause of cultural ills and regulation of the mass media as a likely solution.

The First Amendment prohibits relatively direct control over what adults can be exposed to. Hence the focus naturally turns to control of children, who are under their parents' authority and whom parents see as the natural inheritors and perpetuators of their cultural values. The desire to preserve culture in the face of widespread cultural change (and, in particular, economic and technological change) leads to anxieties over children and the desire to reassert parental control over them.

The problem we face today, however, is that new forms of technology increasingly upset established patterns of parental control. Children can operate VCRs and computers better than their parents. They spend more time in front of the television than at the family dinner table. Technology threatens to render parents' means of cultural reproduction ineffectual. It is no wonder, then, that new forms of communication technology, whether they be movies, records, radio, television, or the Internet, produce new cultural anxieties and new calls for censorship and control.

III. THINKING ABOUT MEDIA IN TERMS OF FILTERS

It might be best to start over again and think about where the real differences between broadcast and other media lie. I believe that the answer to this question must begin with features that all communications media share in common. All media, I shall argue, whether voice, print, or broadcast, share two features in differing degrees. The first is the ability of the recipient to exclude information; the second is the presence or absence of filtering mechanisms. Filtering and excludability are related to each other, because filtering information usually depends on the present or potential ability to exclude it.[20]

Print media lend themselves easily to filtering precisely because print media are easy to exclude. If I want to avoid the information contained in a newspaper, I can simply avoid buying it. If I go into a bookstore, I can buy the book I want without buying other books. I can take the books I want home and then lock them up so that my children cannot see them. Print media are also easy to select and organize. Because my books are discrete units, I can organize them alphabetically. I can read them when I want and in the order I want.

Filtering mechanisms fall into three basic types or functions—they can organize information (for example, by classifying it), they can select information, or they can block information. Within the last category, one can block information for oneself or for others (for example, one's children). All of these functions have important relationships to excludability. Blocking information clearly involves exclusion, but so do selection and organization. To select information, I must be able to take it and not other information. To organize information, I must be able to create categories into which that information (and not other information) falls, and through which that information could (in theory) be selected.[21]

Although I have divided up filters into blocking filters, selecting filters, and organizing filters, these functions substantially overlap. The V-chip is a good example. The V-chip is a blocking filter for children, but it also is a selecting filter for their parents. It lets adults choose whether or not to view violent or indecent material. Equally importantly, the V-chip is an organizing filter, because it creates two types of programming—programming that is blocked by the V-chip and programming that is not. Or, if the V-chip has multiple settings, it creates multiple categories of programming.

Installing an informational filter simultaneously raises and lowers preexisting costs of searching for, blocking, and receiving information. A V-chip raises costs of receiving information substantially to children and moderately to adults. But it also lowers costs as well, because it subdivides the body of programming and makes certain types of choices easier.

Throughout this essay I shall speak in terms of "informational" filters. Nevertheless, because of its computer-age connotations, the term "information" is likely to be understood much too narrowly. Many people associate information with statements of fact, or with strings of ones and zeros that can be read by a computer. Yet much of what people want to and do filter out is not information in that limited sense. They want to filter out dirty language, violence, and nudity. They also want to filter out dangerous ideas and views they do not agree with or expressions that offend and anger them. "Information," in the broader sense I am concerned with, is cultural information. It does not consist merely of statements of fact, but includes anything that can be understood by someone in a culture, and have a corresponding effect on their reason, emotions, or behavior. Cultural information is the counterpart of cultural understanding. Hence it is involved in not only the production of knowledge or ignorance, but also persuasion or offense, refinement or coarsening, ennoblement or corruption.

Because there is too much information in the world, all communications media produce attempts at filtering by their audiences.[22] The desire to filter is not, however, always matched by available methods of filtering. Each medium offers different means of exclusion and different costs of exclusion. Filtering is an effective strategy precisely to the extent that excludability is possible and cost-effective. Each medium's ability to permit exclusion determines and limits the kinds of filtering that are available to it. Even when filtering is used to organize information or facilitate selection, it is still limited by the possibilities of exclusion characteristic of the medium. An example from the print media may illustrate this point. Suppose that *Time* magazine started publishing lots of four-letter words and sexually suggestive pictures. Eventually *Time* magazine would get a reputation as the sort of magazine that does that sort of thing. Parents would, after a time, discover this. Some of them would cancel their subscriptions to *Time* magazine; others would not keep it lying around the house. Advertisers would also notice the change. They would discover that the demographics of the readership had changed and would shift their money accordingly. A magazine's reputation can act as a kind of filtering device, although it is social rather than technological. It signals the likely content of the magazine. Many filters work by offering signals to the audience. Examples are titles of books and headers in the delivery of e-mail. Nevertheless, *Time*'s new reputation would have little practical effect as a filtering device unless parents could exclude it by refusing to buy it or by not bringing it into their homes. If they could not act on *Time* magazine's new reputation by excluding it, the use of reputation as an informational filter would do little good, other than perhaps to warn parents to discount what they read in the magazine (which is itself a filter of a different sort).[23]

IV. FILTERING AND CHOICE

At first glance, filtering seems to overlap with a much more familiar concept—choice. But the two ideas are distinct in important ways. Not all informational filtering involves conscious or deliberate choice by an audience. Indeed, the importance of filters consists precisely in the ways that they obviate or skew choice even as they enable it. "Choice" is a word with largely positive connotations of personal responsibility, respect for individual intelligence, and protection of personal autonomy. Filtering, on the other hand, is morally ambiguous; it may make little demands on individual intelligence, may involve consider-able surrender of personal responsibility, and may actually undermine personal autonomy. Filtering, especially in the Information Age, increasingly involves delegation of choice to another party. Thus, it is very important not to collapse filtering into choice, thereby absorbing the latter's positive moral connotations.

Let me give an example drawn from my own experience as a legal academic. Currently there is more literature being published in law and related academic fields than any person can possibly keep up with. Hence I and many other legal academics make use of filters. One is a periodicals list. Another is searching on databases like LEXIS and Westlaw. The periodicals list gives me the titles of articles in different law reviews. This filter is widely distributed in identical form to many academics; I do not receive a version tailored to my specific needs. By contrast, an informational filter like a LEXIS or Westlaw database is partially modifiable by the use of search terms.

Both the periodicals list and the computer databases already filter out publications even before they offer me possibilities for choice. For example, I do not have a choice about what law-related journals to include or exclude. In LEXIS and Westlaw databases, I am limited to the journals that are currently online and the databases' selected periods of coverage. They will show me nothing published before 1982, for example. Recently a fellow law professor wrote me asking for a cite to an article I wrote in 1990. She could not find the article on LEXIS because the article was published in *Cardozo Law Review* and LEXIS's coverage of that review begins in 1994. Any articles written before that time do not appear on the database. My colleague depended heavily on LEXIS because it was easy to use; looking outside of it took considerable effort.

The LEXIS database has an interesting effect on the cost of obtaining and filtering information. It lowers the costs of searching for materials if one uses the database, while the costs of more traditional hard-copy searches remain constant, at least in the short run.[24] Furthermore, if one shifts to LEXIS as a primary research tool, certain types of filtering choices (i.e., searches) become easier and less expensive to make than others, even if the latter choices would be easier or less expensive using a different filtering system.[25]

This example demonstrates one of the important side effects of informational filters. If everyone uses LEXIS to do basic legal research, articles that do not meet LEXIS's selection criteria will increasingly disappear from view because the filter changes the differential costs of searching for and receiving certain kinds of information. And this example suggests a larger point. The structure and content of public communication can be, and often is, shaped by the informational filters people most commonly use and depend on.

I use filters like the periodicals list and LEXIS and Westlaw because they have definite advantages. I do exercise choice in using them. Yet my choice is at the same time limited. In using a particular filter, I have delegated choice to some other entity—in this case, the people who put together the periodicals list and the people who run LEXIS and

Westlaw. I hope that they know what they are doing, and that, over time, they will include most of the journals I might want to read. But they might not, and, as a result, my choices may be limited or skewed without my even knowing it.

Literary critics have always known about filters. They call them canons and anthologies. Canons and anthologies are special kinds of filters that involve special forms of delegation. People who construct canons and anthologies decide what is important to read, and, by implication, what is less important to read. Canons and anthologies can be very helpful filters. They introduce people to the works most worth reading or most often discussed in the academic literature. In this way they can enable not only choice but also the search for truth. But as repeated debates over canonicity have shown, canons and anthologies can also skew or inhibit these values.

More generally, the marketplace produces any number of informational filters. Book publishers screen manuscripts to determine which ones are most likely to be worth reading. Bookstores stock, classify, and sell books by category and likely readership interest. Magazines specialize in particular kinds of stories and particular political approaches, and the public can use their reputations as informational filters.

All of these examples involve different filters that work in different ways, but each filter involves some form of delegation. When many people need to filter the same body of information, there are considerable efficiencies in delegating that task to someone else. The need for filtering gives rise to people who provide that service, either through market demand, through social custom, or through governmental regulation. Filtering and delegation thus go hand in hand. And because increasing amounts of information inevitably lead to the need for filtering, they inevitably lead to the need for delegation. This gives people to whom we delegate the construction of informational filters an important degree of power. It is a necessary power caused by the limited space in our minds and limited time available for absorption, as well as the positive need to block harmful, useless, or offensive information. The power of delegation is, if anything, enhanced in an age of exploding information. We must—and do—trust and rely on delegations to filterers to give a relatively appropriate picture of the world. For it is the picture of the world we get through informational filters that will largely determine whether we think that the people we have delegated this power to are, in fact, doing their jobs properly. There is something ironic about this. In the Information Age, we were told, information would be power. It is turning out to be quite the opposite. In the Information Age, it seems, power does not rest with those who have access to information. It rests with those who filter it.

V. FILTERING AND MASS MEDIA

Let me summarize the argument so far. All communications media produce too much information. So in that sense, all media have a problem of scarcity. But the scarcity is not a scarcity of bandwidth. It is a scarcity of audience. There is only so much time for individuals to assimilate information. And not only is there too much information, some of it is positively undesirable. As a result, all media give rise to filtering by their audience, or, more importantly, by people to whom the audience delegates the task of filtering. For a filter to operate properly, any criteria of filtering must be linked to an effective ability to exclude. Many desirable ways of filtering information may not be possible or cost-effective given the nature of the media.

The problem of practical filtering exists in all media. It is inherent to any form of communication. However, the problem appears differently for different media. Media differ in terms of the kinds of blocking, selecting, and organizing filters practically available to them. It is easy to block books and videocassette tapes because books and videocassette tapes are individual and separate units of consumption. They can be put in stores on shelves or locked behind counters. It is easy to keep some out and let others in. It is also easy to put them in different shelves according to category. They can be read or viewed in any order you choose, at any time of day.

If broadcast media are special, they are special in this respect: broadcast media offer limited practical means of filtering. Parents may want to keep their children from certain kinds of television programs, but their ability to do so is limited.

Broadcast communication is a linear stream of information in a predetermined and unchangeable order sent out at a predetermined and unchangeable time. This form of communication limits the ways one can filter information. There are basically only three: turning the receiver off completely, turning it on only at designated times, or changing the channel. Parental blocking is similarly limited. Parents can control children's viewing habits by turning the television off at specified times or forbidding children to watch certain channels. If children insist on watching television when their parents are not at home or cannot supervise them, parents have no choice other than to remove the television entirely. Because the number of filtering solutions is limited, there is a poor fit between desirable filtering mechanisms and practical excludability. Only very coarse filters can be made to work. This coarseness is the distinctive characteristic of broadcast media.

Consider the problem from the perspective of a single broadcast station attempting to organize information for the benefit of its viewers. Other than simply not broadcasting a program, the only means of organizing information is to segment it by time. And that is precisely what broadcasters do. They put different types of programming on sequentially, so that viewers can choose what programs to watch by time period. Broadcasters then try to turn these limitations to their advantage, through strategic scheduling of programs as regular series at preordained times, through the use of special blocks of programming, or through repeated showings.

Not surprisingly, temporal filtering is also a major method of FCC regulation. Examples are the Prime Time Access Rule and the safe harbor provisions.[26] These regulations organize programming in sequences of time and require that some programs not appear at certain times. They act like blocking or organizing filters.

It is theoretically possible, using a VCR, to convert broadcast communication into something like books or videocassette tapes. Imagine taping each half hour of the day on each channel on a separate videocassette tape. One could then shuffle the order of the tapes, watching them in the desired sequence. One could also keep television programming locked up in a dresser drawer away from children. In this way one could convert the television day into the equivalent of a video library. It could then be filtered and organized in much the same way as a library or video store. But this process is expensive and time-consuming; it would require constant attention and a separate recording machine for each channel. And it does little to block children from seeing what is actually being broadcast, unless parents can make sure that children only watch the tapes rather than the original.

I hope it is clear by now that the problems of filtering and regulating broadcast media—especially where children are concerned—have nothing to do with scarcity or ubiquity. They have to do with the kinds of filters effectively available for this particular medium of communication. Broadcast media differ from other media not because of limited bandwidth but because of limited methods of filtering. Nor are broadcast media special because they involve pictures and music on a screen rather than stationary text on a page. Videocassette tapes offer the same kind of expression and are also shown on television screens, but they lend themselves to much easier forms of filtering. Because broadcast information is broadcast—sent out in single sequential streams at predetermined times—it can be blocked, selected, and organized in only a limited number of ways. This is a kind of scarcity, but it is a scarcity of filtering mechanisms, not a scarcity of channels. Even if there were ten million channels, all broadcast simultaneously, these problems would still arise. The special nature of the broadcast media can now be revealed. It was never about scarcity. It was never about pervasiveness. It was always about filtering.

The V-chip and similar technologies promise to change the nature of broadcast media because they offer the possibility of new types of filtering mechanisms. They help the broadcast media become more like the library or the video store, although the former will never be the same as the latter two. The approximation would work best if broadcast and cable could offer literally hundreds of channels, so that there would always be something to watch as an alternative to blocked-out material, and so that the same or similar programs would be available at different times. Perhaps the best approximation would be a pay-per-view system, in which each home could order any available programming at any time of day. (This system could also be priced as a flat fee if that were economically feasible.) We are not yet at that point in video delivery. But we may well be in a few years' time.

The great promise of new filtering and broadcast technologies lies in these changes to the organization of the medium. When we think of the future of the broadcast media and cable, we immediately think of an increased number of channels and the end of scarcity. But this is a confusion. What matters is not the increased number of channels by itself but the increased number of channels coupled with new ways to block, select, and organize programming. If broadcast media can permit blocking and time shifting of programming easily, cheaply, and painlessly, they will have largely approximated the filtering status of the print media. At that point, it is hard to see why they should be denied the same First Amendment status.

Before discussing the special problems of the V-chip, it might be helpful to ask how this analysis of filtering mechanisms applies to two other current subjects of controversy— cable television and the Internet. In *Denver Area*, Justice Breyer argued that cable television posed problems of pervasiveness quite similar to those in broadcast television.[27] Senator Exon and others have argued that protection of children equally justifies regulation of indecency on computer networks.[28]

The traditional reason to differentiate cable television from broadcast television is that cable channels are not scarce. But, as I have argued above, the scarcity rationale does not justify the regulation of indecency in broadcast television; the problem broadcasting faces is not scarcity of bandwidth but coarseness of filtering mechanisms. Without something like the V-chip, cable television is in no better a position than broadcast television, and should be treated accordingly.[29] Thus, if the safe harbor provisions are justified for broadcast television, they are justified for cable as well. And if they are unconstitutional for cable television, they are equally unconstitutional for broadcast television.

Once a feasible V-chip technology is in place, differential treatment of cable and broadcast television will be even less justified. Mandatory segregation and blocking of indecent programming should be completely eliminated. The blocking technology available in the V-chip, coupled with temporary safe harbor provisions (as described more fully below), should be sufficient protection for both media; no greater restrictions on broadcast indecency should be constitutionally permissible.

The Internet presents an entirely different set of problems. In terms of available (and potentially available) filtering mechanisms, the Internet much more closely resembles a bookstore or a video store than a television set in the home. In particular, the Internet does not require temporal filtering. An Internet user can filter information on the World Wide Web by subject matter using search engines like Lycos or Infoseek. Indeed, filtering mechanisms on the Web are in many cases more advanced than those widely available for much of the print media. Usenet groups—the Internet equivalent of bulletin boards—are already differentiated by subject matter. Because of information overload, the messages in Usenet groups do tend to be removed after a certain time. But these messages can be selectively downloaded and viewed at the users' leisure. In any case, many Web sites and FTP sites are quasi-permanent, with an inventory that changes no more often than that at a local Barnes & Noble. From the standpoint of the possible modes of filtering, the appropriate model for the Internet is the bookstore, not the television broadcast.[30]

The real problem facing the Internet is not the lack of appropriate and powerful filters; it is possible to divide and subdivide the information coming from the Internet in any number of ways. The real problem is the abilities of parents. If filters cannot be made relatively costless for parents to use, they will be ineffective in practice even if available in theory. This very real concern brings me back to the V-chip.

VI. PARENTAL CONTROL AND THE V-CHIP

There are two standard objections to blocking filters like the V-chip. The first is that parents will be unable to use the blocking device. The second is that, even if they do, children will be able to break through and watch the programming anyway. One finds similar fears expressed about the Internet. Although parents may be able to use a program like SurfWatch to keep children off sensitive parts of the Internet, children are often more computer literate than their parents. The parents won't be able to use the software, and the children will easily be able to break through.

To address these concerns, we must distinguish between the costs of blocking access to information and the costs of breaking through the block. It does not follow that a blocking filter that creates high barriers must itself be difficult or inconvenient to operate. A double-bolted lock is a perfect example. It is easy for homeowners to use but difficult for burglars to break through. In like fashion, the goal should be to create filters that are relatively costless for parents to operate but very difficult for most children to bypass.

This is not a problem of constitutional law. It is a problem of technological design. Different kinds of blocking filters differ with respect to these two variables. Childproof caps are relatively ineffective because they are difficult for parents to operate as well as children, so the parents don't use them properly. But it's quite possible to design a V-chip that parents can easily use but children will find difficult to crack. A simple example would be a four-digit number, like that on an ATM card, that enabled access to the programming menu. No doubt even these minimal costs can be further reduced with sufficient ingenuity.

Similarly, in designing Internet blockers, the goal should be to create an interface that is easy to use and that offers powerful blocking results. This task is hardly beyond the capabilities of the private computer industry. Enormous sums of money are devoted each year by these companies to produce increasingly user-friendly and increasingly powerful interfaces. The whole point of designing security features in commercial software is to make them painless for the user but difficult for the hacker.

It is important, nevertheless, to recognize that some children will be able to "hack through" the blocking devices their parents use. In any population of children, some will be more clever and more computer literate than others. Some will be very clever, and a few may even be able to break into Defense Department computers. But a filter design need not be foolproof to be acceptable as a constitutionally preferable alternative to a total ban. It need only be able to block most children or make it very difficult for them to break through.

This principle is clear enough from the existing safe harbor provisions in broadcast television. In its ACT III opinion, the D.C. Circuit acknowledged that some children would be able to expose themselves to programming not intended for them simply by staying up late or sneaking a television into their room at night.[31] Indeed, statistics quoted by the court indicate that many, although not most, children watch television after 10:00 P.M.[32] This did not undermine the value of the ban on indecent programming between 10:00 P.M. and 6:00 A.M. Rather, the court reasoned, the safe harbor provisions are a reasonable balance between free expression concerns and the protection of children. If the temporal filters involved in the safe harbor rules need not be perfect in blocking all children, neither do the technological filters involved in the V-chip.[33]

VII. THE KEY ISSUE:
AVOIDING ADDITIONAL LAYERS OF REGULATION

I am concerned about the V-chip for different reasons. Unless FCC regulations are carefully designed, they will simply superimpose new content-based regulations over the restrictions we now have. Without care and forethought, the V-chip will not liberate broadcast programming from censorial power; rather it will increasingly subjugate it.

Ideally, the V-chip should be understood as proposing a sort of constitutional bargain. In return for offering parents a method of protecting children from violent and indecent programming, the government should henceforth be forbidden from engaging in other content-based regulation of violence and indecency in the broadcast media. If the V-chip technology is implemented properly, it will shift the focus of broadcast regulation from regulation of content to regulation of filtering of content. Most importantly, it will turn broadcast regulation toward more appropriate concerns: ensuring access to as many speakers as possible. It will move us away from an improper fixation with what should not be on television and toward a proper concern with what must be.

What I fear is that the V-chip will be used instead to impose an additional layer of content-based regulation on top of existing indecency prohibitions and safe harbor provisions. It will be used to ensure not just that children are not exposed to certain programming but that adults are not exposed either. Proponents of censorship are inevitably tempted to protect adults in the name of protecting children. The V-chip must not be allowed to facilitate this desire.

Courts must be especially vigilant to ensure that a "multilayered" approach to broadcast regulation does not result. I propose a general principle for assessing the constitutional use of technological filters like the V-chip. Because lack of effective filtering mechanisms is the real justification for content-based regulation, creation of new and more effective filtering devices should always create heavy presumptions against any remaining content-based restrictions. The more easily and broadly a V-chip or other technological filters can be implemented, the more suspect must be any restrictions on violent and indecent broadcast programming.

The safe harbor provisions offer a good example of how to apply this principle in practice. Even after the V-chip has been perfected, there still may be a limited and temporary need for the safe harbor provisions. By its terms, the Telecommunications Act of 1996 applies only to television sets over thirteen inches, and its requirements do not take effect until at least two years after the date of the act.[34] Not every television is likely to be replaced as soon as the V-chip is introduced; even though the V-chip can be encoded in a cable box, not all families will immediately rush out and get one. Televisions (and replacement cable boxes) cost money. Most likely there will be a significant period in which many families lack the V-chip. For this reason, it may be necessary to retain the safe harbor provisions for a "sunset" period of, say, seven years.[35] After that point, anyone who uses a non-V-chip compatible television would be on notice that it would not be able to block out programs. If they wanted that capability, they would have to purchase a V-chip equipped television or a V-chip equipped cable box. If they refused to upgrade their equipment after seven years, they would have only themselves to blame if they were shocked and surprised by what they saw while flipping channels.

The regulatory scheme should not, however, use the lack of V-chip capability as an excuse to pile on additional regulations that put broadcast programming in a worse position than it was in before the act. The regulatory scheme should not require that the safe harbor rules remain in force indefinitely merely because some televisions do not yet have V-chip equipment.

VIII. THE RATINGS SYSTEM

The development of a ratings system poses a second constitutional problem. The Telecommunications Act of 1996 was cleverly drafted to create an almost irresistible set of pressures on private industry to create and implement a voluntary ratings system. It did so because, as the drafters well realized, a government-created ratings system imposed against the will of broadcasters would pose serious constitutional issues. The result of these statutory provisions was an industry commission that produced a set of age-based ratings modeled on the Motion Picture Association of America (MPAA) ratings system; these ratings have been appearing on selected broadcast and cable programming since the beginning of 1997. Later pressure from children's advocacy groups, with the full blessing of the White House and other government officials, has led to a promise of supplementary content based ratings to begin in the fall of 1997.

How did the government persuade the industry to take action so quickly? The act prescribed that "distributors of video programming" had a year to come up with a workable ratings system acceptable to the FCC, "in consultation with appropriate public interest groups and interested individuals from the private sector."[36] If private industry did not come up with rules satisfactory to the FCC, the job would have fallen to an advisory committee appointed by the FCC. This advisory committee would be comprised of "parents, television broadcasters, television programming producers, cable operators, appropriate public interest groups, and other interested individuals from the private sector."[37] Not surprisingly, this committee sounds like many of the same groups the FCC would probably consult with to determine the acceptability of any industry ratings system.

This "fail-safe" provision deliberately stops short of requiring that broadcasters accept the ratings system devised by the advisory committee. It requires only that, if video programming already is rated by the broadcaster, the rating must also be encoded so that it can be read by a V-chip system.[38] Left unclear is whether the commission would be empowered to require that broadcasters accept the advisory committee's rating system. Also left unclear is whether the FCC would have the power to insist that all programming be rated before it can be broadcast.

The fail-safe provision was left deliberately toothless to avoid constitutional problems of prior restraint and compelled speech. Instead, the true goal of the legislation was to present broadcasters with a set of unpalatable alternatives. If they did nothing, they risked the appointment of an advisory committee telling them how to rate their programs. Even if the FCC could not constitutionally require that the industry accept a government-sponsored ratings system as a condition of broadcasting, there would have been enormous public pressure to accept a system already worked out with attendant public fanfare. Faced with this possibility, broadcasters and distributors chose to create their own ratings system.[39]

In fact, pressing the industry to create its own ratings system actually gives the FCC considerable power and influence without ever invoking the fail-safe provisions. The FCC can decide whether to approve the ratings system or not, using basically the same players that would have formed an advisory committee. If the industry does not conform sufficiently to the FCC's wishes, the FCC can declare the industry not to be in compliance and once again hold up the threat of an advisory commission.[40]

In the long run, the result of this calculated gamesmanship will be a set of guidelines largely acceptable to the FCC and implemented without government expense or the creation of a new governmental bureaucracy. Moreover, because the guidelines are "voluntary," the FCC does not have to require that broadcasters accept them, or issue regulations that all shows be prescreened. It need merely insist on these conditions as the price of its approval of the "voluntary" ratings system. In this way the FCC (and other government officials) can achieve through threats much of what it could not have achieved through direct regulation. The actual history of industry ratings has followed this general outline: pressures from various government officials, and from children's advocacy groups acting with the blessing of the White House, have led first to age-based ratings and later to supplementary content-based ratings.[41]

Although the clever drafting of the V-chip legislation was designed to avoid constitutional problems, the very idea of an advisory committee, whether as an actual ratings body or as a threat the FCC hopes never to employ, is constitutionally troubling. From one perspective, there is no problem with the government designing a content-based information organization system and leaving it up to private parties to decide whether to accept or reject it. For example, there is nothing unconstitutional about the development of the Library of Congress cataloguing system or its near universal acceptance in public and private libraries as a means of organizing information. The problem comes when the government insists that information must be organized according to content in a certain way or it cannot be published at all. And when the government uses threats, whether overt or concealed, to achieve this result, constitutional values are surely implicated.

Defenders of a government mandated ratings system might point to the Supreme Court's decision in *Meese v. Keene*.[42] In *Meese*, the Supreme Court held that the government could label three Canadian films critical of the government's policies on acid rain as "political propaganda" under the Foreign Agents Registration Act consistent with the First Amendment.[43] The plaintiff in the case was not a foreign agent and therefore was not bound by the reporting and disclosure provisions of the act. He merely argued that he should be able to show the films without being branded as an exhibitor of governmentally designated propaganda. The Court rejected that argument, because the government is usually free to engage in its own speech, even when that speech seems value-laden or even condemnatory. But *Meese* did not decide whether the government could require U.S. citizens who were not agents of foreign governments to put labels on expressive materials that the government determined to be "political propaganda." The mere existence of a government labeling system is not the same as a governmental directive forcing people to use it as a mandatory preface to their own speech.

The first problem that any ratings system will face is what to do about unrated programming. Must all television programming be given a V-chip rating or only some of it?[44] Must all programming be submitted for ratings, or can a broadcaster refuse to accept or provide a rating? Most importantly, if less than all television programming is rated, can the unrated shows still be broadcast?

The 1996 act does not specifically require that all programming be rated before it can be broadcast, yet this is clearly the eventual goal of the V-chip system (with the usual exceptions for certain news and sports programming).[45] Once a ratings system is in place, the FCC can then issue regulations to discourage or segregate unrated programming. Chairman Hundt has specifically contemplated such a strategy. He has argued that any programs that remain unrated can constitutionally be relegated to the safe harbor period.[46]

Yet this solution is too facile. It threatens to put enormous numbers of programs in a worse position than they were in before the implementation of the V-chip. It violates the key constitutional principle I have enunciated: that the development of new technological filters should decrease government restrictions on adult viewing, not increase them.

A governmental requirement that all programs be submitted to a private industry council before they can be screened has many of the features of a prior restraint. The problems would be even greater if the ratings (or the guidelines for them) were entrusted to a government-appointed television commission. But it should also be constitutionally troublesome for government to insist that speakers gain the imprimatur of a delegated private organization before they can be allowed access to the airwaves.

The goal of the 1996 act is that broadcasters will voluntarily rate their own programming, making the prior restraint problems vanish. But not all broadcasters will be able or willing to do this for all of their programming. Many people who speak over cable and over the airwaves are not networks or network affiliates. They will necessarily have to rely on third parties to prescreen their material. Thus, the problem of prescreening by some organization other than the speaker cannot be avoided. This is especially so if the government is seriously interested in ensuring conformity of ratings among different program distributors. For example, without a credible third-party enforcement mechanism, some distributors may be tempted to "underrate" programs because they fear that a more stringent rating would reduce advertising revenues.[47]

One might object that a requirement of prescreening and prerating is not really a prior restraint, because all unrated programming can still be broadcast during the safe harbor period. But this argument is deficient on two grounds. First, as argued above, the safe harbor regulations must gradually be phased out after the new system is adopted. Second, and more important, the unconstitutionality of a prior restraint is not avoided even if there is another means of expressing oneself. Imagine a city ordinance that required all leaflets in the downtown area to be prescreened for appropriate content by the city manager.[48] The constitutionality of this ordinance would not be saved by the fact that one could distribute the leaflets in the suburbs or simply write letters to the editor.

My view is that the government cannot constitutionally require that all unrated programming must be shown during the safe harbor period, although it can require that, during a seven-year "sunset" interval, all unrated indecent programming be shown during the safe harbor period. It can do so because—assuming that the current safe harbor period regime is constitutional—unrated indecent programming would be no less protected before the act than after it. Assuming that safe harbor rules for regulation of particularly violent programming would be constitutional under the current regime, a similar argument should apply here as well.

Nevertheless, the government must allow all other programming to be shown outside of the safe harbor period whether it is rated or not, and whether or not it has been submitted to a third party. When broadcasters cannot or will not rate programs by themselves, the government must place the burden on third-party ratings systems to provide ratings in time for broadcast. It cannot put the burden on broadcasters to obtain or accept a rating before broadcasting.

To see why the burden must rest on ratings boards or other third parties and not on broadcasters, consider the problems involved with blocking access to three different groups of unrated programs: The first are pre-Act programs, the second are news programs, and the third are broadcasts of live events, including sporting events.

There is currently an enormous backlog of programs produced before the development and implementation of the V-chip. They include literally everything heretofore recorded on movie film or videotape. If the concern is sexual content and violence, many parents might well want to restrict access to much of this pre-Act material. But if this material would not have fallen afoul of the indecency standard of Section 1464, it is doubtful whether the government could constitutionally require it to be shown only during the safe harbor period. The contrary result would be ludicrous: imagine the federal government holding that a rerun of *M*A*S*H* or *The Mary Tyler Moore Show* originally broadcast during prime time in 1975 must now be shown after 10:00 P.M. because it has not yet been rated.

The constitutional problems are even more obvious when we come to programs like news reports that often cannot be prepared well in advance. Should we say that the *NBC Nightly News* cannot be broadcast except in the safe harbor period because Tom Brokaw did not prescreen it with an industry council? And should the same reasoning apply to CNN broadcasts from the former Yugoslavia or the latest results from the New Hampshire primary?

Live performances present similar difficulties. Industry officials can surely prescreen scripts if they are available. But the government must not be able to shunt all live performance into the safe harbor period simply because a bureaucracy cannot prescreen it. It is important to stress that when we talk about live programming, we are not speaking primarily about raunchy talk shows at two o'clock in the afternoon. We are talking about the World Series and the Super Bowl, as well as late-breaking news and public affairs programming. I doubt Chairman Hundt would insist that President Clinton give his State of the Union Address during the safe harbor period because the speech had not been prescreened.[49]

The constitutional problems posed by unrated programming can easily be solved. V-chip technology should be designed to allow viewers to block out all unrated material. This puts the onus where it belongs, on the parent to avoid watching unrated material, rather than on the networks to rate it. In addition, the FCC should permit broadcasters to insert a special category code for news and public affairs programming, a code that could be routinely assigned to local and national news programs without prescreening for sexual and violent content. (Another code could be offered for sports programming.) Parents then would have the option of watching or not watching such programming on the assumption that the vast majority of news and public affairs programming will not be harmful to children even though it will not have been prescreened.

The agreement between President Clinton and media executives assumed that sports and news programming will be unrated, and that agreement is reflected in the practices of broadcasters after January 1997.[50] Unlike its Canadian counterpart, the present U.S. age-based system contains no special code for news and sports programming.[51] However, because much adult-oriented and experimental programming will also be unrated, the industry's solution is likely to cause problems in the future. By giving all news (and sports) programming a special ratings code, we would prevent these programs from being lumped together with all other "unrated" programming. This would allow parents to avoid all unrated programming and still watch news and sports without constantly having to change the settings on their V-chip. This approach is better in keeping with the general goal advocated earlier—of creating a filtering system that requires as little effort by (and as little technological sophistication of) parents as possible.

If news and sports programming remain unrated, the danger is not that people will refuse to watch news and sports programming. The danger is that there will be enormous political and financial pressures to ensure that all unrated programming is acceptable for all children, so that unrated programming becomes equivalent to a G movie rating. The latter result is the exact opposite of what a V-chip system should accomplish.

I have argued that the constitutional problems of prior restraint can be avoided only if programs can be shown without prescreening or prerating; the burden must be on an external rating organization to provide ratings in time for broadcast. One might object that my solution allows broadcasters to do an end run around the V-chip; they can simply refuse to provide or obtain ratings and put on violent and sexually charged programming without effectively being blocked out. But this result is unlikely to occur as long as parents are empowered to block out all unrated programs. Broadcasters, after all, are not insensitive to advertisers, and advertisers will be unlikely to spend their dollars on unrated programming if they believe that a substantial number of parents will block such programming. Thus, even without the use of a prior restraint, broadcasters will have considerable financial incentives to submit all programming to a private industry ratings board (or rate it themselves) when they can. In the case of live broadcasts, they will take whatever steps are necessary to guarantee a rating beforehand. Thus, for the vast majority of programming that most families want to watch, it will be possible to obtain a rating before broadcast. This is especially so if broadcasters are permitted to give news and sports programming a special rating without prescreening.[52]

This solution is not without costs. Local cable access programming and other programs that do not or cannot submit to ratings can still be shown under my proposed solution. However, they will not be picked up in the homes of parents who have blocked out all unrated programs. Moreover, my solution will still tend to segregate programming that does not submit to prescreening along with programming that remains unrated for strategic reasons—for example, sexually explicit and violent programming. This will result in a smaller audience for such programming and less advertising revenues. But it nevertheless ensures that people who want to watch this programming can have access to it, and at any time of day. In this, sense it is more consistent with First Amendment values than the alternative.

IX. THE V-CHIP AND THE DELEGATION OF INFORMATIONAL FILTERING

So far, I have spoken only about the constitutional issues raised by the V-chip. Yet the deeper problems that the V-chip raises lie elsewhere, and it is likely that these problems are not constitutionally cognizable ones. They concern the power over individual thought and national culture that arises with increasingly powerful forms of delegation of informational access. This problem is by no means new. Delegation of informational access has always existed in one form or another. But my concern is that, in the Information Age, the shape of culture will increasingly be determined by those persons and organizations that organize, filter, and present information for others and to others. I fear that neither the proponents nor opponents of the V-chip fully grasp this fact. Although these features already exist in the world we now inhabit, they will surely be magnified in the world we now enter.

The regulatory apparatus surrounding the V-chip will work an enormous new delegation of informational filtering to bureaucratic institutions, whether operated by the federal government or by private industry.[53] This new bureaucracy will be entrusted with the task of devising and implementing filters for virtually all of the television programs available in the United States. It will have to determine both the salient characteristics of all programming and evaluate which programs fit within the boundaries defined by these characteristics. These characteristics and these evaluations will in turn be employed by viewers and, more importantly, by advertisers, cable providers, video rental stores, public libraries, television production companies, writers, composers, and directors. As these evaluations become commonly employed, further choices and social arrangements will then be organized around them. In this way, the divisions of the cultural and informational world created by the custodians of the V-chip, however innocent, will be amplified throughout our culture, shaping and skewing the social world in unforeseen ways. It is possible that we shall have nothing to fear from these effects. But it is equally likely that there is much to fear. It is probable that some version of these effects is inevitable. But it is certain that no particular version is inevitable.

Filtering mechanisms are not neutral means of organization, blocking, and selection. They have important effects on what kinds of materials are subsequently produced and how social arrangements are subsequently organized. People who produce and receive information respond to and organize their lives around the existing forms of filtering. I do not yet know the many ways that the filtering mechanisms devised for the V-chip will affect our culture. Indeed, I am quite sure that we will not be able to recognize them for many years after they have already taken hold. All I can do here is offer the most minor examples of mechanisms that may have major consequences.

I want to focus on three basic kinds of effects. The first has to do with what characteristics are salient in forming categories—for example, bad language or nudity. The second has to do with coarseness—how fine-grained the filtering categories are. The third concerns equivalency—what kinds of things are seen as parts of equivalent categories. These factors overlap, but they are also distinct. Two ratings systems can be equally coarse and yet view different characteristics as salient. Moreover, two ratings systems can be equally coarse and view different sorts of things as equivalent in each category. Consider two ratings systems that each have only two categories. The first system holds that any profane language or any mention of contraception places a program in the adult category, while the second includes only profanity. The two systems are equally coarse, but they have different senses of equivalency. In the first system, profanity and discussions of contraception are treated alike as inappropriate for children; in the second system they are treated differently.

The first problem of any ratings system is what characteristics count in making programming unsuitable for children. The industry television ratings system in effect since January 1997 focuses on the categories of sexual content, nudity, violence, and profane language; these factors basically track the considerations currently employed by the Motion Picture Association of America (MPAA) ratings system.[54] Racist, sexist, and homophobic depictions are not specifically included as salient categories. Yet if parents are concerned with what their children pick up from television, they might be particularly concerned whether their children are picking up habits of intolerance. The harm to our children from these influences, one might think, would be equally as great as the harm from exposure to sex, violence, and bad language. And both sets of criteria involve content-based distinctions.

It is even less likely that an FCC-appointed television advisory committee would code for racist, sexist, or homophobic expression. The Telecommunications Act of 1996 expressly states that ratings systems are to avoid political and ideological categorizations.[55] Such a commission would probably argue that coding or blocking programming as racist, sexist, or homophobic would give the unmistakable appearance of political favoritism.

Nevertheless, this objection reveals the problems that already exist with a system of ratings organized around depictions of sexual conduct, violence, and profanity. The choice to protect our children from these things rather than others cannot be said to be truly apolitical, even if it can be assured to be mainstream. While overt expressions of homophobia are likely to remain uncoded, overt homosexual expressions of affection will probably be among the first to be coded as inappropriate for children. The social equality of homosexuals is currently a political hot potato, and one is quite sure in which direction this particular potato will get dropped.

Coding for violence and for homophobia both involve content-based distinctions of subject matter. One might object that coding for violence, unlike homophobia, is viewpoint neutral, and therefore less controversial. But the example of homosexuality shows how tenuous the distinction between subject matter and viewpoint neutrality can be in practice. Simple, ordinary demonstrations of affection between gays—the kind that would pass unnoticed between heterosexuals—are important means of showing the normalcy of gay lives and the commonality of their basic concerns with those of straight audiences. Yet these displays are more likely to be judged unsuitable for children while negative portrayals of gays will pass unfiltered by the system.

In any case, the very assumption that exposure to racist messages is less harmful to our children and our community than exposure to violence already carries considerable political freight. Although coding for violence but not for racism seems to exclude political and ideological controversy, it does not avoid politics or ideology. Rather it installs them in the very process of coding. The actual practice of political and religious "neutrality" will be achieved by the selective avoidance of topics; it will produce the appearance but hardly the reality of apolitical judgment.

My point in raising these difficulties is not to call for the coding of racist expressions. It is rather to note the politics implicit in a coding system that focuses on violence and indecency to the exclusion of other factors. Coding for racist messages, whatever its constitutional problems, would prove very difficult in practice. Often racial stereotypes are used in ironic ways, in which it is difficult to tell their actual meaning, much less their long term effects. Black-oriented comedy shows like *In Living Color* and *Martin* routinely employ exaggerated racial stereotypes of minorities. It is difficult to know where one would begin in classifying this material.

What advocates of rating systems may not realize, however, is that similar problems apply to depictions of violence. Violence is often used to show a character in a bad light or to punish the wicked and the violent. Much violence is portrayed in a cartoonlike fashion. The many ways in which violence can be depicted, and the many social meanings it can convey, underscore that, like racist expression, there will be no easy way to code it.

Many people would probably be content with a ratings system that, even if not guaranteed to be nonideological, would at least be doggedly centrist. That is probably the best reason to have an industry-sponsored ratings system, which will cater to the tastes (or, more appropriately, the fears) of advertisers. Of course, it is hard to know whether this is cause for rejoicing. In any case, industry-developed ratings will not be unaffected by politics. Any industry-developed ratings system must still be approved by the FCC. Moreover, it is likely that future politicians will attempt to make political hay by bashing any industry ratings system and threatening a government takeover. To be sure, such a threat would be of dubious constitutionality, but constitutional proprieties about the First Amendment have rarely deterred the pontifications of American politicians. Just as Senator Dole attempted to boost his 1996 campaign for the presidency by denouncing the wicked-ness of Hollywood, pseudopopulists of the future will discover an irresistible temptation to denounce whatever ratings system emerges as toothless and sinful, endangering the lives of our children and the future of America. Thus, even though the industry has adopted its own system, the eventual result may still be heavily politicized. The use of industry-developed ratings is only the lesser of two considerable evils.

Coarseness of the ratings system is a second major concern. The new industry-sponsored ratings are based on the MPAA motion picture ratings system, yet that ratings system is perhaps the best example of how coarseness operates in practice. The MPAA currently offers a rating system featuring six categories—Unrated, G, PG, PG-13, R, and NC-17.[56] Ratings are determined by a panel of full-time employees using a combination of factors, including theme, violence, sexual content, and language.[57] Because these factors are taken together rather than differentiated, motion picture producers face a relatively coarse filtering mechanism. In fact, the PG-13 category was added later on because the previous system included too much in the PG category.[58]

Some effects of the system occur at the far end of the spectrum. Producers know that an NC-17 rating will significantly cut into movie sales. Many movie theaters will not show NC-17 movies,[59] many newspapers and television stations will not advertise them,[60] and they are not carried by major video chains like Blockbuster.[61] Hence producers take great pains to gain an R rating from the MPAA board, often offering to cut out offending materials.[62] Although the desire to obtain an R rating may produce self-censorship, movies with an NC-17 rating can still be shown to consenting adults.

A more curious and perverse effect happens on the other side of the ratings spectrum. Although a G rating signifies that a movie is suitable for all audiences, it also tends to drive away teenagers and young adults, who are among the most avid consumers of movies. As a result, the ratings system produces a perverse incentive to "dirty up" pictures to make them attractive to a wider audience.[63] Apparently many Americans demand genuine family entertainment; they just don't want to have to see it themselves.

Any system of ratings will produce self-censorship because moviemakers fear losing a desired audience. A movie producer has to balance the potential gains that might come from a change in content with the loss resulting from a corresponding change in movie rating. But the more important coarseness effects occur in the middle of the ratings spectrum. A ratings system that does not differentiate between sex, violence, and profanity will actually encourage the use of all three. For example, suppose that as a result of using several four-letter words a movie gains an R rating. At that point the movie director has every reason to put in additional sexual content and violence if she believes this will increase audience attention, as long as she doesn't cross the line into NC-17. She is guaranteed not to lose audience share because of a change in rating but she can hope to gain audience share by strategically increasing sexual or violent content. As a result, movies in the middle range of ratings may tend to get progressively more violent and more sexually explicit at the same time.

If the current V-chip system uses ratings as coarse as the MPAA, we can expect that the broadcast world will display similar effects. The MPAA ratings resemble the anthropologist's two basic categories of the sacred and the profane. There is a category of that which is suitable for children (taking the role of the sacred) and a category in which everything else—violence, bad language, nudity, homosexuality—gets thrown in indiscriminately (the profane).[64] What is profane is then subdivided not by kind of expression but by degree of profaneness, resulting in a world consisting of what is sacred, a bit profane, a lot profane, and seriously profane.

By contrast, if substantive categories are increasingly differentiated—for example into three separate categories of language, sexual content, and violence, with ratings from 1 to 5 in each category—the ratings system produces a different set of incentives. It may pay for the director to produce a film with increased violence but not sexual content, and vice versa, because a change at the margins is better reflected in the ratings system. Of course, the more categories are added, the more difficult it becomes for parents to operate the system. As noted earlier, one of the most important constraints on the V-chip system will be ensuring ease of use to technologically challenged adults. So the result is likely to be a compromise between coarseness and adequacy of ratings.

The July 10, 1997 compromise (entered into by all of the networks except NBC) looks, at first glance, like a move away from the MPAA model to something more like the separate category-based system described above. In fact, it is not substantially less coarse than the original MPAA-inspired ratings system. There are still only four categories for nonchildren's programming—TV-G, TV-PG, TV-14, and TV-M. The compromise plan merely offers the viewer the rationale for the choice of category. For example, "moderate" violence or "some" sexual situations are sufficient to garner a TV-PG rating, "intense" violence or "intense" sexual situations gain a TV-14 rating, and "graphic" violence or "explicit" sexual situations produce the dreaded TV-M rating.[65] But under the current plan, a parent cannot set the V-chip to let in programs with "graphic violence" but not more than "some" sexual situations. She must choose either to blank out all programs rated higher than TV-PG (for whatever reason) or only programs rated TV-M (for whatever reason). To move to a truly more fine-grained system, the industry would have to consent to make the levels of violence, sexual content, coarse language, or sexually suggestive dialogue fully independent ratings categories.

A third and final set of problems with any ratings system concerns equivalency. Even after the basic categories are determined, any ratings system will have to decide what gets coded within each category. More important for present purposes, it will have to decide what gets coded as possessing equal levels of inappropriateness. Like decisions about the categories themselves, these decisions cannot avoid political controversy; they are likely to have wide-ranging effects.

Take, for example, discussions of homosexuality or of safe sex as a means of preventing AIDS. How should these be coded in a ratings system? And what should they be coded as equivalent to? Some parents would see a big difference between such discussions and a sexually titillating love scene, while other parents would find both categories equally unsuitable for people under the age of eighteen. Now imagine a made-for-television movie that depicts a fictional cover-up by the church hierarchy of child abuse allegations made against Catholic priests, and a movie in which Freddy Krueger murders a hapless teenage couple having sex in the woods at midnight. It is not difficult to imagine different groups of parents disagreeing heatedly about the relative inappropriateness for children of these two examples.

Questions of equivalency severely test any facade of political neutrality. Does the ratings system regard two men kissing as equivalent to a woman being raped or another being slashed with a knife? Does the system regard a discussion of contraception as more or less inappropriate than a discussion of drug use? Whether or not we regard these events as really being different in kind is irrelevant. What is important is whether the ratings system makes them equivalent, by coding them as equally appropriate or inappropriate for children. Once materials are coded as equivalent, they become equivalent for all purposes for which the ratings system is used. And, make no mistake, the ratings system will be used for purposes other than its designers intended.

Advertisers deciding where to invest their dollars, video rental stores purchasing and organizing inventory, parental groups demanding tighter controls on undesirable programming, and consumers searching for suitable entertainment will not easily be able to differentiate within categories created by a ratings system. They will not have to. Rather, they will use the ratings system to avoid having to engage in such differentiations. They will rely on the categories already provided to choose what to purchase, what to watch, what to protest, and what to invest in. The ratings system will come ready-made as a division of the programming universe, and the efficiency and ubiquity of the system will make its distinctions real in practice.

Just as parental groups today do not watch NC-17 movies before protesting their inclusion in suburban movie complexes or local video stores,[66] people will use the television ratings system as a guide to the content of rated programming. The categories produced by a ratings board, whether public or private, will be the key informational filters that others will use to organize their decisions, whether monetary, political, or aesthetic.

Nevertheless, it is possible that events will play out quite differently. If cable bandwidth is expanded—for example, through digital delivery systems—there may be room for several different ratings systems. Groups like the Christian Coalition may offer their own ratings system using V-chip technology, employing their own conception of what is family-friendly and what is not. Consumers can then subscribe to the ratings system of their choice, much as they now subscribe to magazines like *TV Guide*. Moreover, an explosion of space on cable systems promises the possibility of filtering systems based on any number of programming criteria. The only limitation upon would-be filterers is their ability to catalogue and categorize the millions of hours of materials that will eventually exist for television, and their ability to gain sufficient market share to underwrite the costs of rating this material.

We do not yet know whether the economy will produce and support a wide variety of V-chip ratings systems. There may be economies of scale in producing a commercially viable ratings system. If so, then the number of ratings systems that can survive will be quite small, and the results will not be too dissimilar from what I have described above. But the more interesting possibility is that ratings systems and related forms of media filters can and will proliferate. Consumers will be able to insulate themselves in increasingly special-ized programming universes. By delegating their choices to specialized media filtering companies, they can filter out the great mass of programming to focus narrowly on their own special interests. Some, I suspect, will see this as the ultimate vindication of autonomy. Others will mourn the loss of a common televisual culture. In any case, this scenario produces effects completely opposite of the first. Instead of a single filtering system (or a handful of systems) uncannily structuring and skewing thought and culture, the alternative scenario imagines an increasingly fractured community of individuals fixated on their personal programming universe and increasingly oblivious to everything else.

Standing as we are, still in the infancy of the Information Age, it is impossible to tell how events will play out. But we can already appreciate the deep irony of our situation. The call for the V-chip, like the call for censorship of the Internet, stems from a sincerely felt anxiety that our culture is spinning out of control and an earnest desire to strike back at those new technologies thought to form part of the cause. The promotion of the V-chip as the solution to this cultural anxiety is at once appropriate and perverse. It is appropriate because it uses technology to fight the perceived effects of technology. It is perverse in that, like all other technologies before it, our submission to it is destined to have immea-surable and unexpected consequences.

The inevitable emergence of filtering organizations, whether public or private, underscores the importance of distinguishing between delegation and choice—the distance between the informational future that awaits us and the attractive homilies of autonomy and personal empowerment now used to describe it. We are on the verge of installing a series of new filtering mechanisms that will transform the most important systems of mass communication available to us. We do this to satisfy the concerns of parents and the ambitions of politicians. But as we do this, we might be well advised to stop for a moment and try to imagine what is as yet unimaginable—the profound though unintended effects of this potent combination of bureaucracy and technology on the health of our democracy and the evolution of our culture.

Notes

1. Pub. L. No. 104-104, 110 Stat. 56 (1996) (to be codified in scattered sections of 47 U.S.C.).
2. section 551, 110 Stat. at 139–42. As its name implies, the V-chip technology has been touted primarily as a means of controlling television violence. But its uses are not limited to that category. The Telecommunications Act of 1996 specifically lists its concerns as "sexual, violent, or other indecent material." section 551(b)(1), 110 Stat. at 140.
3. Joseph A. Kirby, Device Would Let Parents Program TV for Children, Times-Picayune (New Orleans), Jan. 7, 1996, at A26.
4. *See* TV Parental Guidelines, http://www.tvguidelines.org/#Children.
5. *See* Canadians Propose 7-Point TV Ratings System, Communications Daily, May 6, 1997; Etan Vlessing, Canada Aims at TV Violence: Nation will go light on language, sex in its ratings system, The Hollywood Reporter, May 6, 1997.
6. Paige Albiniak, Ratings get revamped: networks, except for NBC, agree to add content labels; includes related articles on the rating system and the V-chip, Broadcasting and Cable Vol. 127 (July 14, 1997), at 4.
7. 438 U.S. 726 (1978), reh'g denied, 439 U.S. 883 (1978).
8. Action for Children's Television v. FCC (ACT III), 58 F.3d 654 (D.C. Cir. 1995) (en banc), cert. denied, 116 S. Ct. 701 (1996). The relevant law actually permitted stations to broadcast indecent programming from midnight to 6:00 A.M., but it also permitted public television stations that go off the air before midnight to broadcast the same programming starting at 10:00 P.M. Public Telecommunications Act of 1992, Pub. L. No. 102-356, section 16(a), 106 Stat. 949, 954 (codified at 47 U.S.C. section 303 note (Supp. V 1993) (Broadcasting of Indecent Programming; FCC Regulations). Because the court found the exception for public broadcasting to undermine the purposes of the legislation, it remanded the case to the FCC with instructions to limit the ban on indecent programming to the period from 6:00 A.M. to 10:00 P.M. ACT III, 58 F.3d at 669–670.
9. For an accessible (and skeptical) view, see Thomas G. Krattenmaker & Lucas A. Powe, Jr., Regulating Broadcast Programming 120–34 (1994).
10. See Turner Broadcasting Sys. v. FCC, 114 S. Ct. 2445, 2456 (1994) (citing National Broadcasting Co. v. United States, 319 U.S. 190, 212 (1943)), reh'g denied, 115 S. Ct. 30 (1994).
11. Critiques of the scarcity rationale are by now legion. For a sampling, see Lucas A. Powe, Jr., American Broadcasting and the First Amendment 197–209 (1987); Matthew L. Spitzer, Seven Dirty Words and Six Other Stories 1013–20 (1986); Ronald H. Coase, The Federal Communications Commission, J.L. & Econ., Oct. 1959, at 1, 12–27.
12. See Krattenmaker & Powe, supra note 7, at 87–88, 217–18 (discussing the FCC's restrictive channel allocation policies).
13. See H.R. Conf. Rep. No. 862, 102d Cong., 2d Sess. 56 (1992) (stating that nearly fifty-six million households and more than 60% of all households with televisions are cable subscribers); Robert S. Tanner, Note, The Data Transfer Industry: Communications Regulation for the Next Century, 17 Hastings Comm. & Ent. L.J. 917, 922–23 (1995) (citing Chesapeake & Potomac Tel. Co. v. United States, 830 F. Supp. 909, 915 (E.D. Va. 1993)).
14. Leland L. Johnson, Toward Competition in Cable Television 179 (1992) ("Cable systems have become accessible to more than 95 percent of the nation's homes."); see also US West, Inc. v. United States, 855 F. Supp. 1184, 1192 (W.D. Wash. 1994) ("Cable service is now available . . . at 96% of all U.S. homes . . . ."), aff'd, 48 F.3d 1092 (9th Cir. 1994), cert. granted and judgment vacated, 116 S. Ct. 1037 (1996).
15. Many other justifications for regulation of violence or indecency often tend to be parasitic on the scarcity rationale. For example, in Red Lion Broadcasting Co. v. FCC, 395 U.S. 367 (1969), the Supreme Court suggested that content-based regulation was permissible because broadcasters do not own the airwaves outright. Id. at 394. They hold licenses from the government, and therefore the government can impose conditions on that license. By itself, this argument tends to prove too much. The government's conditions may be unconstitutional conditions. The government does not license the airwaves as an act of governmental largesse—the usual means of justifying conditions on licenses. See, e.g., Rust v. Sullivan, 500 U.S. 173, 199 n.5 (1991) (stating that restrictions on abortion counseling by recipients of Title X subsi-

dies do not violate the First Amendment because the subsidy may be declined). Rather, the licensing scheme exists because the government decided to take complete control of the airwaves and parcel out licenses instead of auctioning off rights to broadcast at certain times in certain locations and with certain degrees of broadcast strength. The government does not license the manufacture and distribution of paper or printing presses. Even if it did so, it could not constitutionally justify imposing content-based conditions on their use. Thus, the conditions-on-licensing justification ultimately rests on the prior justifications for licensing, which depend in turn upon the scarcity rationale.

FCC Chairman Reed Hundt has suggested that restrictions on violence and indecency on television may be justified by the fact that the First Amendment is designed to protect democracy. Reed E. Hundt, The Public's Airwaves: What Does the Public Interest Require of Television Broadcasters?, 45 Duke L.J. 1089, 1097 (1996). He argues that violent and indecent programs were not what James Madison had in mind when he wrote the First Amendment; they do nothing to promote discussion of public issues. See id., at 1126. This seems to conflate an argument that some speech is of lesser constitutional value with an argument that the broadcast media are special. Assuming that Chairman Hundt's claim about degrees of constitutional value is sound, it applies equally well to violent and indecent depictions in movies and the print media. It cannot by itself distinguish broadcast media from other media.

In any case, the argument tends to prove too much: a great deal of nonindecent and nonviolent programming on television has only the faintest relationship to promoting democracy. Yet it does not follow that this programming is subject to content-based regulation because it is also of low constitutional value.

In fact, the argument from democracy is best viewed as an adjunct to the scarcity argument. Because airtime is scarce, television must make room for programming that enhances democratic values. But again, this argument does not justify keeping indecency or violence off the air; rather, it justifies keeping public interest programming on.

16. FCC v. Pacifica Found., 438 U.S. 726, 748–49 (1978), reh'g denied, 439 U.S. 883 (1978).
17. Id., at 749; ACT III, 58 F.3d at 661.
18. With a few exceptions—zoning regulations for adult movie theaters and procedures for prescreening obscene films—the regulation of movies is largely along the lines of the print model. See, e.g., City of Renton v. Playtime Theatres, 475 U.S. 41 (1986) (upholding zoning requirements for adult movie theaters), reh'g denied, 475 U.S. 1132 (1986); Young v. American Mini Theatres, 427 U.S. 50 (1976) (same), reh'g denied, 429 U.S. 873 (1976); Freedman v. Maryland, 380 U.S. 51 (1965) (establishing procedures for reviewing obscene films).
19. The D.C. Circuit recognized that parental control and protection of children were separate interests, but it did not acknowledge the degree to which they might conflict in practice. ACT III, 58 F.3d at 660–61. In fact, safe harbor rules do not perfectly mesh with the goals of enhancing parental control. As Chief Judge Harry Edwards has pointed out, safe harbor rules actually preempt some parental choice, because children cannot watch certain programming (for example, a documentary on AIDS prevention) even if parents want them to. Alliance for Community Media v. FCC, 56 F.3d 105, 145–46 (D.C. Cir.) (en banc) (Edwards, C.J., dissenting), aff'd in part and reversed in part, sub nom. Denver Area Education Telecom. Consortium v. FCC, 116 S.Ct. 2374 (1996); ACT III, 58 F.3d at 670 (Edwards, C.J., dissenting).
20. When we think of excludability, we think of captive audiences, and when we think of captive audiences, we think of justified expectations of privacy. Although excludability and privacy are related concepts, they are related in complicated ways. Practical excludability does not by itself determine whether we have a justified expectation of privacy. On the one hand, expectations of privacy seem to be based in part on the practical possibility of exclusion. Because one can be assaulted by billboards or by voices in the street, one's justified expectations of privacy are lower there. On the other hand, expectations of privacy are sometimes thought justifiable whether or not excludability is practically possible. Even though we may not be able to prevent electronic eavesdropping, we have a justified expectation that others will not eavesdrop.
21. Thus, in alphabetizing a list, I make selection by first letters possible. Placing books in the Library of Congress cataloguing system enables readers to find books on some subjects without having to look at others.

Some forms of organization have a more attenuated relationship to excludability. Suppose I merely imagine a system for cataloguing library books. Although this system organizes information, the organization is not implemented. The imaginary system merely gives directions for implementation, which, if enacted, would require selection, and hence the possibility of exclusion. Finally, purely mental organization of information does not involve physical selection and exclusion, but it does involve mental selection and exclusion.

22.   The desire by producers of information to gain an audience and the contrary desire by recipients to block out unwanted information creates an arms race between filters and ways of getting around filters; hence, the use of flashier graphics, louder music, and increasingly hyperbolic claims to attract people and gain a slice of their increasingly valuable and limited attention spans. Audiences use remote controls to flip through channels during commercials; advertisers respond by varying the content, length, and timing of their advertisements, and broadcasters respond by varying the length of time between shows. Marcia Mogelonsky, Coping With Channel Surfers, Am. Demographics, Dec. 1995, at 13. Occasionally methods of filtering and methods of evading filters start to merge. For example, best-seller lists are both means for weeding out books that might be interesting to read and means by which publishers promote books as worth reading. Kudos on the backs of books also have this dual character.

23.   This example also suggests that filtering is a heuristic device for dealing with information, and, as a heuristic device, it is usually imprecise. For example, I may use *Time* magazine's new reputation as a reason not to bring it into my home. There may be lots of things in the new *Time* magazine that are just like the old *Time* magazine—useful news stories, for example. But the overall reputation, and not the precise content of the stories, will determine whether parents subscribe and what kinds of advertising revenues the magazine generates.

24.   In fact, the costs of more traditional searches might even increase in the long run if older skills and sources atrophy as a result of mass shifts to LEXIS and Westlaw.

25.   Law librarians have long understood that the shift to computer databases alters the way legal research is conducted. See, e.g., James A. Sprowl, A Manual For Computer-Assisted Legal Research 14-15 (1976).

26.   section 16(a), 47 U.S.C. section 303 note (Supp. V 1993) (Broadcasting of Indecent Programming; FCC Regulations) (safe harbor provisions); 47 C.F.R. section 73.658 (j), (k) (1981) (Prime Time Access Rule).

27.   Denver Area Educ. Telecom. Consortium v. FCC, 116 S.Ct. 2374, 2386 (1996).

28.   142 Cong. Rec. S706-07 (daily ed. Feb. 1, 1996) (statements of Sen. Helms and Sen. Coats); 141 Cong. Rec. S9770-01 (daily ed. July 12, 1995) (letter introduced by Sen. Exon).

29.   *See* Denver Area, 116 S.Ct. at 2386–87 (Opinion of Breyer, J.).

30.   In cyberspace, the closest thing to the broadcast medium is the electronic chat line, but even that is really closer to the model of telephone communication. Chat lines can be segmented according to subject matter or age requirements, and parents can then use filters to ensure that children cannot enter certain chat "rooms" which have subject matter or age requirements. The existence of plentiful and adequate filtering mechanisms means that the broadcast model should not apply. Cf. Sable Communications, Inc. v. FCC, 492 U.S. 115 (1989) (rejecting total ban on "dial-a-porn" services in light of available blocking mechanisms).

        E-mail presents special problems. E-mail messages can be filtered by subject matter and by thread. However, the subject matter of an e-mail message may not disclose its indecent or harassing nature. Nevertheless, in this respect e-mail is very much like regular mail, and to this extent the constitutional forms of regulation of indecency should be the same.

31.   See ACT III, 58 F.3d at 665. Moreover, it is at least theoretically possible that children could tape indecent programs during the safe harbor period and view them during the hours they are awake.

32.   See id.

33.   It is important to stress that no parental control system, like no filtering system generally, can be foolproof. Because the V-chip will be installed only in sets larger than thirteen inches, children will still, in theory, be able to get around its blocking capabilities. They need only purchase a nine-inch set and a magnifying glass.

34.   section 551(c), 110 Stat. at 141; section 551(e)(2), 110 Stat. at 142.

35.   This figure depends on how one sees the likely future of technological development. If the V-chip is placed in standard cable boxes or in inexpensive add-on devices, it is reasonable to assume that most households that want them will purchase them more quickly, and the sunset period could be reduced accordingly. If, on the other hand, the V-chip is mainly implemented through new television sets, then something like ten years may be necessary for most old sets to wear out and be replaced. We must also factor in the possibility that the FCC's recent move toward digital television technology may tend to hasten the replacement of older sets.

36.   section 551(e), 110 Stat. at 142.

37.   section 551(b)(2), 110 Stat. at 140. The advisory committee is to be "fairly balanced in terms of political affiliation, the points of view represented, and the functions to be performed by the committee." Id.

38.   section 551(b), 110 Stat. at 140.

39   Alexandra Marks, TV Industry Problem: Rating 400,000 Shows, Christian Science Monitor, Mar. 1, 1996, at 3 (noting that media companies originally resisted V-chip ratings but ultimately decided to

"declare victory" and capitulate). CNN founder Ted Turner—who supports the V-chip—put it best when he wryly noted that "we're voluntarily having to comply." Kathy Lewis, TV Ratings Promised by January, Dallas Morning News, Mar. 1, 1996, at 1A.

A similar logic suggests that, if one broadcaster decided to rate its programming, others would feel enormous pressure to follow suit. Thus, when Rupert Murdoch broke ranks and announced that his Fox network would rate shows regardless of what the other networks did, he made it virtually inevitable that NBC, CBS, and ABC would agree to a ratings system. See March Gunther, Fox Leads Pack in Vow to Adopt Ratings System, Times-Picayune (New Orleans), Feb. 16, 1996, at C1.

40. At the time this essay was written, the FCC had scheduled hearings on the industry ratings system for early summer 1997.

41. As Valenti put it after the July 10, announcement, "This is not something we celebrated as a great victory. . . . This is something we did because we had to do it." Albiniak, Ratings get revamped, supra note 6.

42. 481 U.S. 465 (1987).

43. *See* 22 U.S.C. § 611(j).

44. Current estimates suggest that there are over 600,000 hours of programming yearly on a seventy-channel cable system, as opposed to around 1,200 hours of movie programming rated annually by the Motion Picture Association of America. Ed Bark, TV Ratings Sure To Be a Daunting Task, Dallas Morning News, Mar. 1, 1996, at 24A.

45. The act is deliberately ambiguous on this point. To avoid the fail-safe provisions, "distributors of video programming" must "establish[] voluntary rules for rating video programming that contains sexual, violent, or other indecent material about which parents should be informed before it is displayed to children," and "agree[] voluntarily to broadcast signals that contain ratings of such programming." section 551(e)(1), 110 Stat. at 142. The act does not say that all such programming must be rated—only that rated programming be broadcast as rated. However, it is hard to believe that the FCC would be satisfied with a result in which an industry ratings system was developed but not implemented on a virtually universal basis, at least for prerecorded programming other than news and sporting events. Even if individual members of the commission could accept such a fig leaf, political pressures against it would be almost unbearable.

46. Hundt, supra note 13, at 1129.

47. There is also the related danger that the same program might receive different ratings from different distributors. The February 29, 1996 agreement between President Clinton and major media executives sought to allay these concerns by promising to establish an oversight group that would periodically review ratings of specific programs and comment on whether they met the industry's ratings guidelines. Lewis, supra note 37.

48. Cf. Lovell v. City of Griffin, 303 U.S. 444 (1938) (striking down prohibition of distribution of literature in city streets without permit from city manager).

49. Of course, given President Clinton's natural propensities, the speech might go on into the safe harbor period anyway.

50. John M. Broder & Jane Hall, President Hears TV Executives Commit to Ratings System, L.A. Times, Mar. 1, 1996, at A1.

51. The new Canadian system specifically contemplates such a ratings category—CTR-E—which includes news, sports, documentaries, talk shows and other informational programming. See Canadians propose 7-Point TV Ratings System, Communications Daily, May 6, 1997.

52. The use of a special code for live news and sports raises its own problems. Among the most obvious is whether faux-journalism shows like *Geraldo* and *Hard Copy* should be classified as "public affairs programming" along with the *NBC Nightly News* and the State of the Union Address, or should be treated under the general ratings system. There are reasons to think that the latter solution is preferable, especially if a program devotes a substantial amount of its airtime to sexually charged material. But this leads to dicey questions about what is "really" news and public affairs and what is not. See Jane Hall, TV Content-Rating Planners Weigh Category Refinements, Dallas Morning News, Apr. 7, 1996, at 2C.

The concern about *Geraldo* is, of course, symptomatic of a larger problem. If media executives really played fair in assigning V-chip ratings, it might well turn out that the vast majority of daytime television—lurid talk shows and steamy soap operas—is unsuitable for children due to its pervasively sexual content. Perhaps it's a good thing most kids are in school during those hours.

53. The Telecommunications Act of 1996, for example, provides that the advisory committee shall be assigned "such staff and resources as may be necessary to permit it to perform its functions efficiently and promptly." section 551(b)(2)(B), 110 Stat. at 141.

54. One major problem with the current MPAA system is that the ratings are awarded by a committee of laypersons who have no particular expertise in what kinds of violence are actually the most harmful for children to watch. So it is likely that some movies rated R for their violence may actually be less harmful than some rated PG-13. Of course, there is no guarantee that an industry-produced ratings system will match the results of psychological studies any better.

55. The act insists that "nothing in [the requirement of ratings provisions] shall be construed to authorize any rating of video programming on the basis of its political or religious content." section 551(b)(2), 110 Stat. at 140. Furthermore, the advisory committee that informs the television commission is to be "composed of parents, television broadcasters, television programming producers, cable operators, appropriate public interest groups, and other interested individuals from the private sector," and is to be "fairly balanced in terms of political affiliation, the points of view represented, and the functions to be performed by the committee." Id.

     One assumes that the same caveats will apply to any industry-created ratings system, since under section 551(e)(1)(A) of the act the FCC will not issue guidelines for ratings if private industry has established rules "acceptable to the commission." section 551(e)(1)(A), 110 Stat. at 142.

     By contrast, under the experimental three-category ratings system tested in Canada, "language offensive to minorities or ethnic groups" can be blocked out by a V-chip. It gains a rating of 3 out of a possible 5 on the language scale, with 5 being the most offensive. Verne Gay, Ratings Soon: TV Industry to Code Shows by Next Year, Newsday, Mar. 1, 1996, at A3. In effect, this system equates the "F-word" with the "N-word"; hence, it raises many of the problems of equivalent degrees of offensiveness discussed infra. Moreover, under this system, even though racial epithets are coded, they are judged less offensive than many other possible expressions. Id.

56. The X rating originally devised by the motion picture industry has been abandoned and is now used primarily by adult video producers as a way of emphasizing the salacious nature of their product. See Leonard Klady et al., Sticks Can't Nix Naughty Pix: *Showgirls* Wide Release Pushes NC-17 Envelope, Variety, July 24–30, 1995, at 1.

57. Jack Valenti, The Voluntary Movie Rating System, in The Movie Business Book 396, 401–02 (Jason E. Squire ed., 1992); Richard P. Salgado, Regulating a Video Revolution, 7 Yale L. & Pol'y Rev. 516, 519–20 (1989).

58. Richard Zoglin, Gremlins in the Rating System: Two Hit Films Raise New Concerns About Protecting Children, Time, June 25, 1984, at 78.

59. Rachel Eisendrath, Film Industry Rates NC-17, Montgomery Advertiser, Oct. 29, 1995, at 1H (reporting decision by Carmike Cinemas, a chain of 2,104 screens scattered through the South, not to show *Showgirls* because of its NC-17 rating).

60. See Richard Corliss, What Ever Became of NC-17?, Time, Jan. 27, 1992, at 64.

61. See John Greenwald, Wayne's World, the Sequel, Time, Oct. 11, 1993, at 64, 67.

62. Although the director does not directly negotiate with the film board, strategic behavior is apparently not uncommon. Martin Scorcese was reported to have deliberately added ultraviolent material to his film *Casino* so that later cuts would seem tame by comparison, thus enabling him to keep in material he thought essential. Steve Daly, In the Ratings Game, Ultraviolence is the Ace in the Hole, Ent. Wkly., Aug. 18, 1995, at 8.

     Another possible alternative is to refuse the MPAA rating and release the film as unrated. See Edward Guthmann, Director Finds Gender Does Matter, S.F. Chron., Nov. 25, 1995, at C1 (describing the decision to release *When Night is Falling,* a drama which included two lesbian love scenes, as unrated). But this does not avoid stigma, and indeed, may even invite it.

63. Film Censors; Child-Minders, The Economist, Aug. 13, 1994, at 78.

64. Richard Corliss, It's Great! Don't Show It! A Misguided Rating System Slaps an X on a Discreetly Erotic Film, Time, Sept. 17, 1990, at 70 (discussing NC-17 ratings given to director Philip Kaufman's film, *Henry and June,* and controversies over other films involving lesbian scenes).

65. Kim Asch, Rating system to help parents pick programs, Washington Times, August 19, 1997, at E1.

66. See, eg., Michael Granberry, *Temptation*: Some Resist, Others Yawn, L.A. Times, Aug. 20, 1988, section 2, at 2; Julia McCord, Film on Fallen Priests Sparks Pastor Protest, Omaha World-Herald, Apr. 7, 1995, at 13SF; Sean P. Means, Pickets Organize to Protest *Showgirls* in Utah: Kids' Movies and Skin Flicks a Bad Mix, Protesters Say, Salt Lake Trib., Sept. 28, 1995, at B1; Victor Volland, Video Stores Have *Priest*; Groups Protest, St. Louis Post-Dispatch, Jan. 27, 1996, at 5D.

PART TWO

OTHER PERSPECTIVES, OTHER MEDIA

CHAPTER FIVE

The V-Chip and Television Ratings: British and European Perspectives

Andrea Millwood Hargrave

BACKGROUND

The United Kingdom has one of the most regulated broadcasting environments in the world. The British Broadcasting Corporation (the BBC) self-regulates through its Board of Governors. The Independent Television Commission (the ITC) grants licenses to, and regulates, the commercial television sector, including satellite-delivered services. The Broadcasting Standards Commission[1] (the BSC) acts as an independent body, established by statute, to consider complaints from the public on the issue of standards in broadcasting (such as the portrayal of violence, of sex and of matters of taste and decency, including bad language, stereotyping, and areas such as the treatment of disasters), and to consider complaints and offer redress on the question of unfair or unjust treatment in programs and unwarranted infringements of privacy. In addition, the BSC must monitor program content and may undertake research into all the areas within its remit, which covers all television, radio, cable, and satellite services.

Each of the regulatory bodies—the BBC, the ITC, and the BSC—produces a Code of Practice or guidelines that cover the areas within its remit. Each is aimed at slightly different audiences. The BBC's reflects its role as regulator and broadcaster, with detailed producer guidelines in certain areas. The ITC's reflects its role as licensor of commercial broadcasting. The BSC's Code of Practice aims to provide general principles for program makers but seeks to avoid what has been described as "the chilling effect" (an inherent danger to creativity in proscriptive regulation). The code seeks to reflect the BSC's role as a consumer voice, providing guidance and a framework within which broadcasters may work. It is laid down in the statute that the codes produced by the BSC must be reflected within the guidelines produced by other bodies and broadcasters. The former Broadcasting Standards Council has published a code on standards issues (to be revised in 1997) and the new commission will be producing, for the first time, a code dealing with fairness and privacy issues.

In addition to the codes, a well-established procedure has been adopted by the broadcasters, that of "family viewing time" or the Watershed. On terrestrial television this is at 9:00 P.M. and states that to help parents decide, under normal circumstances, the broadcasters will not show programs before that time that they believe unsuitable. The earlier in the evening a program is placed, the more suitable it is likely to be for children to watch on their own. On subscription payment satellite-delivered film channels a "twin" Watershed is in operation with material broadcast at 8:00 P.M. that would not be permissible before the 9:00 P.M. Watershed on other broadcasting services. The further Watershed is at 10:00 P.M. after which time more "adult material" is acceptable.

Nonetheless, despite the regulatory structure of British broadcasting, there are concerns expressed about the material carried on channels. Much of this concern focuses around public uncertainty about the influences and effects of television viewing. In this sense the United Kingdom has differed historically from the United States, arguing that the audience has a dynamic, active relationship with the screen. In recent years, however, there has been a gradual coming together of the two disciplines, with both sides of the Atlantic more prepared to share and acknowledge experiences of the "influence" of broadcasting.

A number of recent studies have underlined concerns about influences on the young and those that are deemed vulnerable.[2] It is interesting to note that these concerns are raised not only by parents and other interested adults but also by young people themselves who are particularly aware of the effect advertising has on them, for example.[3] "Ads are a bad thing for parents, with children demanding things" (fifteen-year-old boy).

Further, the ITC is (at the time of writing) in the process of awarding the first license to companies wishing to operate multiplex services. There is some uncertainty about what the future may hold in the rapidly developing media environment in which live pictures could be distributed through a variety of sources.

Concerns such as these about the power of broadcasting and its continued growth have led to the recognition, within the United Kingdom, that the V-chip offers a possible technological answer to the demands, made by some, for greater consumer control over broadcasting content.

In February 1996 the European Parliament voted in favor of an amendment to the 1989 Television Without Frontiers Directive to pursue V-chip technology (see Appendix). The proposed amendment was not included in the directive. However, in April 1997, the Council of Europe and Parliament agreed that the European Commission should carry out a study looking at ratings systems, technical devices (including the V-chip), and other strategies such as the family-viewing policy. The commission has been instructed to report back within one year.

Public attention in the U.K. has been drawn to the issue of on-screen violence most forcibly by a number of recent tragic events. This started with the (unsubstantiated) claim that two young boys who murdered a toddler had access to a violent horror film. Although this hypothesis was never proved, legislation was passed making it a criminal offense for video rental outlets to supply videos certified for a particular age to anyone under that age. The debate calmed until the outrage in Scotland in March 1996 when a man murdered a number of primary school children in their school. Although it has never been suggested that on-screen violence played any part in the tragedy, the media were held up as a negative reflection of society. Other, subsequent tragedies added to that unease and with them came a more focused concern not only about violence in society but also the part television plays in reflecting it.

With this refocusing on screen violence came media debate about the V-chip. In the debate surrounding the 1996 Broadcasting Bill, reference was made to the V-chip but only in the form of a demand for research into the issue by the BSC. It was also proposed that broadcasters should be required to set up a classification system for programs. These amendments to the bill were defeated, but they attracted substantial cross-party support.

The then secretary of state called together the chairmen of the BBC, the ITC, and the BSC and asked that on-screen violence be brought to the top of their agendas. She also asked that the BSC host a seminar into the issue. This was held in March 1997. Members of the regulatory bodies, the political parties, the broadcasting industry, and the audience all attended. Audience research was presented, and presentations were made by program producers and editors. In these, they described the decision-making process they had to go through, illustrating these with specific examples.

One of the outcomes of the seminar has been the formation of a Joint Working Party on Violence with representatives from the BBC, the ITC, and the BSC. The V-chip is one of the issues that it is considering.

THE V-CHIP

The key questions that have been raised with regard to the V-chip have been issues about the technological and technical competencies of the system, and also concerns about the subsequent effect of its introduction on standards in broadcasting. It may be useful to take some time to develop these issues further.

The Technology

Early interpretations of the way in which the system is functioning in other countries where it is undergoing trials create some concern here. However, it is assumed that these "teething" problems will be overcome. But can they be overcome to such an extent that the introduction of the technology is commercially viable and attractive both to the hardware manufacturer and to the consumer? Initial costs appeared to be reasonable but the trials will identify the true cost.

In the United Kingdom, as in other countries, there is the issue of retrofitting. In the United Kingdom, television sets (which might contain the new technology) are replaced on an average five-to-seven-year cycle. The newest television set tends to be the one placed in the "family" room, the area where most joint viewing takes place. Secondary sets are often placed in children's bedrooms or in spaces outside the "family" environment. These sets would not, therefore, be fitted with the V-chip or any other such device. Yet, it may be argued that the V-chip is designed with audiences such as children in mind. Retrofitting would be possible but may be inconvenient and too expensive for most homes.

Another issue for the U.K. is that the part of the broadcast signal that has been adapted in the U.S. and Canada to carry the V-chip signal is set aside in the U.K. for the transmission of teletext signals. It may be possible to adapt the teletext signal to carry the classification codes, but the difficulties created by out-of-date television sets are equally true for video recorders, which have varying capabilities with regard to teletext.

Within the U.K. it is believed that the advent of digital broadcasting offers the most scope for development. The likely introduction of electronic program guides (EPGs) may allow broadcasters to classify programs and feed the data into their schedule information. While this system is more flexible and may offer a way forward in the burgeoning multichannel environment, it is still reliant on the growth in the market of set-top boxes, in itself dependent on the introduction of digital broadcasting.

Security. Issues of security still need to be addressed, with both the key system and a PIN number system raising potential problems. Until a suitable mechanism has been found any technical "blocking" device would be rendered useless.

It may be worth noting that many of the experiments in the United Kingdom developing on-demand services use a mixture of methods—often comprising personal PIN numbers plus additional payment-related controls.

Standards in Broadcasting

Labeling. One of the possibilities under consideration is the labeling or classification of programs. This could be on-screen, using symbols, or pretransmission with warnings or with symbols or cinema-style classifications, or off-screen, through better prepublicity or information in listings. A previous fear on the part of the broadcasting regulators and advisers was that labeling systems might act as an attraction to viewers. There is some popular mythology in the U.K. that an early experiment with on-screen symbols on Channel Four (a commercial broadcaster) was unsuccessful. It was argued that viewers tuned in to see films with "red triangles" (the on-screen symbol used to denote an "adult" theme). This is not, however, clear from the patchy data available.

More useful may be a consideration of the system in France (being tested at the time of writing), which uses a mixture of symbols and colors to warn viewers about the suitability of material. This began in November 1996, voluntarily agreed to by broadcasters as a way of staving off political pressure. Films, fiction and documentaries are classified into five categories:

1. No broadcasting restrictions.
2. Parental guidance recommended. Use of a symbol and program cannot be broadcast in children's programming time. No other time restrictions set.
3. Parental guidance required—violence of particular concern. Use of a symbol on-screen if the film is broadcast before 10:00 P.M. Program may be broadcast after 10:00 P.M. without the symbol on-screen.

4.　Adults only—violence and eroticism of particular concern. Use of a symbol and program cannot be broadcast before 10:30 P.M. No trailers or advance publicity can be transmitted before 8:30P.M.

5.　Broadcast is forbidden.

The Conseil Superieur de l'Audiovisuel in France—which regulates commercial television and oversees this scheme—reports that, since its inception, it has been highly successful. Eighty percent of respondents to a survey said they were aware of the system, and over two in three said that they found it useful. Some other preliminary studies showed that fewer children were watching programs classified as unsuitable for them than previously. For example, on the most popular television channel those in the audience aged 4 to 10 watching classified material had fallen from 6.5% to 4% over the period of time measured. Similarly, those aged 11 to 14 had fallen as a proportion of those watching classified programs from 9% to 6%.

Similar findings were made in Australia where programs are classified by their target audience age group and have timing restrictions placed upon them.

V-CHIP AND CLASSIFICATION

In both France and Australia it has not been possible to establish a common national classification system for television. Film does not create a significant problem as there are national guidelines and classification systems in place, and these are often followed by the broadcaster. However, other material is left to the broadcaster's discretion, with an overview provided by the relevant broadcasting regulatory authority. Further, the experience of Canada and the United States suggests that a common classification approach is fraught with difficulties.

In Europe there is an additional overlay that needs to be taken into account. These are the significant cultural differences between countries, which are, nonetheless, subject to common directives regarding transfrontier broadcasting. These differences make it difficult to see how a Europe-wide classification system could be achieved. If it were considered desirable that a unified approach be adopted, then guidance would need to be given establishing the criteria for classification for all broadcasters. The difficulty of a national classification system has already been alluded to—how much more difficult an international and crosscultural one!

Allied to this would be the difficulty of defining "violence." In the United Kingdom analyses of violent content on television have been undertaken, but there is much debate about the way in which violence has been defined. The definition was taken to be "any overt depiction of a credible threat of physical force or actual use of physical force, with or without a weapon, which is intended to harm or intimidate an animate being or a group of animate beings. The violence may be carried out or merely attempted, and may or may not cause injury. Violence also includes any depiction of physically harmful consequences against an animate being (or group of animate beings) that occur as a result of unseen violent means." This is not dissimilar to the definition being used by researchers in the United States who are currently looking at violent on-screen material.

Their definition is "any overt depiction of a credible threat of physical force or the actual use of such force intended to physically harm an animate being or group of beings. Violence also includes certain depictions of physically harmful consequences against an animate being or group that occur as a result of unseen violent means." Nonetheless many within the audience and many broadcasters challenge such a broad meaning. They argue that fictional violence as seen in a Tom and Jerry cartoon should not be placed alongside the fictional violence in a Shakespearean tragedy or the fictional violence in an Arnold Schwarzenegger film. Again the aforementioned Joint Working Party on Violence will consider this as one of its tasks.

It has been suggested that factual programming, such as news and sports, will be exempt from any system, and "live" programming will also raise issues that will need to be addressed. It is possible that the oversight of such a system could work in a broadcasting landscape of twenty or so channels. But the difficulties of regulating content (and its classification) over the promised broadcast palette of many tens of channels will be significant. It is also worth reminding the reader that no regulatory or advisory body in the United Kingdom has the power to preview material any longer. Action can only be taken *after* transmission. The reasons for removing these powers (once held by the regulators) were twofold: (1) it was thought undesirable that censorship should be practiced in a free democracy, and (2) it was considered important that broadcasters should be freed, in the creative process, of direct intervention in the making of programs by those who regulate them (as far as is feasible in the case of an organization such as the BBC).

As this is the case, regulation would need to be retrospective. An efficient monitoring process would be too expensive and difficult, which would mean the system would become more reliant on complaints. It is recognized that less than 34% of those who have felt like complaining about something they have seen on-screen actually do so.[4] Further, it has been noted in a number of studies[5] that changing the relationship between viewer and broadcaster by payment affects how the viewer reacts to on-screen material. For example, respondents appear to be far more accepting of sexually explicit or violent material on a pay channel than on a free-to-air service.

Related to this of course is the economic argument of compliance. Concerns have been expressed about the cost of classification and encoding the relevant electronic signal. Smaller broadcasters, possibly catering to a minority interest audience, may find the expense prohibitive. It is also likely that advertising revenues will be affected as advertisers will not be able to predict audience size as well as has been done in the past, and measurement systems showing usage of the V-chip will not be available quickly.

On the other hand, it is possible that the commercial imperative may impact on the quality of British programming, that program makers will shy away from controversial material, or that the range and breadth of British programming will be reduced as "safe" audiences are sought.

The Responsibility of Broadcasters

It is possible that, in a more formally regulated environment than is currently the case in the United Kingdom, broadcasters might argue for a more liberal regime, with the

V-chip as a shield. It is also possible that the 9:00 P.M. Watershed might be put under pressure for similar reasons.

Parental Responsibility

A central plank of the U.K.'s broadcasting regulatory environment is self-regulation. Part of that is the determination to give viewers sufficient information on which to base their viewing decisions. There is a clear move among broadcasters—and their advisers and regulators—to ensure that such information is available and comprehensive. Indeed, this is one of the areas that the Joint Working Party on Violence will consider.

Other research by the BSC showed how widely video and film classifications were ignored by adolescents, particularly if a film took on "cult" status, or peer pressure came into play.[6] The data showed that nearly two in three respondents (aged up to seventeen) had seen at least one of a list of films classified by the British Board of Film Classification as being suitable for those aged eighteen and over. Nearly a third had seen three or more. Nevertheless it was interesting to note that the youngest of the respondents (those aged between ten and twelve years) were significantly more likely to say that they were not interested in seeing the film, and were least likely to say that they had already seen them. It would seem that there is some element of self-regulation in play here as well.

However, there are already some data available on the potential use of a blocking device. Many homes with cable or satellite television have access to a parental lock device that can be used to "block" programs. Recent research shows that only 37% of these homes (with children aged under 15 in them) were aware of this device. More importantly, only 8% said that they used it regularly. A further 11% said they used it "occasionally."

This in itself raises concerns about the nature of the vulnerable groups that need "protection." While the data referred to above do not suggest the demographic profile of those households that exercise their parental lock devices, questions must be raised about the far greater proportion who do not. It may be hypothesized that those who leave their children to watch television unsupervised are less likely to use the V-chip or any other such device.

CONCLUSION

It will be clear that many of the arguments in the United Kingdom are against the V-chip. It should be emphasized that these arguments do not stem from an antipathy toward regulation—far from it. The approach to broadcasting has combined legislation (through the existence of regulatory and advisory bodies and their duties) with encouraging self-regulation and responsibility. The Watershed is the prime example of this. The notion of a "contract" between the broadcaster and viewer is well understood by those involved in the industry.

Substantial amounts of money are spent to understand televisual violence and its attraction, its effect, its influence. The audience's role in the debate is never lost and the broadcaster's voice is always heard as part of a larger picture.

However, it is recognized that the V-chip may be a useful tool for those who would want to use it. The work that needs to be done will not only have to check the technological feasibility of the system but also the viewer's willingness to implement it. It is possible that a more rigorous approach to labeling and providing information may be the most logical way forward, especially on a pan-European dimension.

Notes

1.   The Broadcasting Standards Commission came into effect on April 1, 1997, as the result of the merger between two bodies—the Broadcasting Standards Council and the Broadcasting Complaints Commission. The Standards Council previously dealt only with standards issues while the Complaints Commission dealt with complaints regarding fairness and unwarranted infringement of privacy in a broadcast program.
2.   See for example, "Regulating for Changing Values," Broadcasting Standards Commission, Working Paper No. 1 (1997).
3.   "Young People and the Media," Broadcasting Standards Council, Working Paper No. 13 (1996).
4.   Broadcasting Standards Council, "Trend Data" (1995).
5.   "Television: The Public's View," Independent Television Commission (1996) and "Regulating for Changing Values," Broadcasting Standards Commission, Working Paper No. 1 (1997).
6.   'Young People and the Media," Broadcasting Standards Council, Working Paper No. 13 (1996).

Media Ratings Systems:
A Comparative Review*

Joel Federman

During the last decade, media ratings have been increasingly utilized as a means of addressing concerns about "objectionable" or potentially harmful media content. Politicians, entertainment industry leaders, and media advocacy groups alike have turned to media ratings as a "middle ground" solution to such concerns, somewhere between direct government censorship and not addressing the issue at all. While movie rating systems have been in place for several decades, there is currently a trend toward adopting rating systems for other media—such as television, video games, sound recordings, home video, and the Internet—both in the United States and abroad. The advent of content blocking technologies, such as the V-chip, which require some form of attendant rating system to be useful, has further spurred this trend.

This chapter provides a survey of media rating systems in five countries: Australia, Germany, Great Britain, Sweden, and the United States. The survey reviews rating systems as they apply to various media, including film, videos, sound recordings, television, video games, film advertisements, and the Internet. The review briefly describes the historical origins of each rating system, its organizational structure, decision-making process, and the ratings themselves. The chapter closes with a discussion of the social impact of ratings, as well as the relative merit of various rating system designs.

AUSTRALIA

Films and Videotapes

The Australian Commonwealth Classification Board is a government agency that administers a national classification code for films, videos, publications, and computer games. The board is part of the Australian Office of Film and Literature Classification (OLFC), which also classifies printed matter on behalf of New South Wales, South Australia, Queensland, Victoria, and the Territories.

According to law, the board has a maximum of twelve members, including the director, the deputy director and two senior classifiers. Appointments for up to six-year terms are made by the Governor-General, though customarily appointments are for three-year terms.[1]

Australian customs legislation empowers the Commonwealth Classification Board to refuse to register a film or video imported for public exhibition if, in the board's opinion, it is "blasphemous, indecent or obscene," "likely to be injurious to morality," or "undesirable in the public interest."[2] In addition, Australian law provides for the classification of films and videos, in order to protect children and young people from material considered to be harmful to them. The classification process is intended "to reflect what a reasonable adult person would consider within the acceptable limits of community standards for that age group."[3]

The process of rating a film begins with accumulation of information about the film, including reviews by critics internationally, as well as the ratings given the film in other countries. This information is reviewed by the senior classifier, who determines the size of the screening panel based on the degree to which the film or video may be controversial. Most screening panels consist of three censors, but potentially controversial films may be viewed by the entire board.[4]

Outside advice is sometimes solicited from experts, such as clergy and psychologists. In addition, the public is consulted via direct input in the form of letters concerning particular films. The board also has chosen to convene focus groups, discussing both particular films and censorship issues in general, in order to more thoroughly reflect public opinion. The final rating decision is made by a majority vote of the screening panel. If a panel is sufficiently divided on a particular film or video, a larger panel is convened to review it.

The Office of Film and Literature Classification (OFLC) rating system for films and videotapes, revised on July 11, 1996, includes five categories.[5] The OFLC criteria for inclusion in each category are extensive and are reproduced verbatim here:

G General (Suitable for all ages). This is a category which is considered suitable for all viewers. The G classification symbol does not necessarily indicate that the film is one that children will enjoy. Some G films contain themes or story-lines that are of no interest to children. Parents should feel confident that children can watch material in this classification without supervision. Material classified G will not be harmful or disturbing to children. Whether or not the film is intended for children, the treatment of themes and other classifiable elements will be careful and discreet.

Violence. Violence may be very discreetly implied, but should: have a light tone, or have a very low sense of threat or menace, and be infrequent, and not be gratuitous.

Sex. Sexual activity should: only be suggested in very discreet visual or verbal references, and be infrequent, and not be gratuitous.

Coarse Language. Coarse language should: be very mild and infrequent, and not be gratuitous.

PG Parental Guidance (Parental guidance recommended for persons under 15 years). The PG classification signals to parents that material in this category contains depictions or references which could be confusing or upsetting, to children without adult guidance. Material classified PG will not be harmful or disturbing to children.

Parents may choose to preview that material for their children; some may choose to watch the material with their children. Others might find it sufficient to be accessible during or after the viewing to discuss the content.

Violence. Violence may be discreetly implied or stylized, and should also be: mild in impact and not shown in detail.

Sex. Sexual activity may be suggested, but should: be discreet, and be infrequent, and not be gratuitous. Verbal references to sexual activity should be discreet.

Coarse Language. Coarse language should be mild and infrequent.

Adult Themes. Supernatural or mild horror themes may be included. The treatment of adult themes should be discreet and mild on impact. More disturbing themes are not generally dealt with at PG level.

Drug Use. Discreet verbal references and mild, incidental visuals of drug use may be included, but these should not promote or encourage drug use.

Nudity. Nudity outside of sexual context should not be detailed or gratuitous.

15+ Mature (Recommended for mature audiences 15 years and over). The Mature category is advisory and not legally restricted. However, material in this category cannot be recommended for those under 15 years. Films classified M contain material that is considered to be potentially harmful or disturbing to those under 15 years. Depictions and references to classifiable elements may contain detail. However, the impact will not be so strong as to require restriction.

Violence. Generally, depictions of violence should: not contain a lot of detail and not be prolonged. In realistic treatments, depictions of violence that contain detail should: be infrequent and not have high impact and/or not be gratuitous. In stylized treatments, depictions of violence may contain more detail and be more frequent if this does not increase the impact. Verbal and indirect visual references to sexual violence may only be included if they are: discreet and infrequent, and strongly justified by the narrative or a documentary context.

Sex. Sexual activity may be discreetly implied. Nudity in sexual context should not contain a lot of detail, or be prolonged. Verbal references to sexual activity may be more detailed than depictions if this does not increase the impact.

Coarse Language. Coarse language may be used. Generally, coarse language that is stronger, detailed or very aggressive should: be infrequent and not be gratuitous.

Adult Themes. Most themes can be dealt with, but the treatment should be discreet, and the impact should not be high.

Drug Use. Drug use may be discreetly shown. Drug use should not be promoted or encouraged.

Nudity. Nudity outside of a sexual context may be shown but depictions that contain any detail should not be gratuitous.

15+ Mature Accompanied (Restrictions apply to persons under the age of 15). The MA category is legally restricted. Children under fifteen will not be allowed to see MA films in the cinema or hire them on video unless in the company of a parent or adult guardian. Material classified MA deals with issues or contains depictions which require a mature perspective. This is because the impact of individual elements or a combination of elements is considered likely to be harmful or disturbing to viewers under 15 years of age.

Violence. Generally, depictions of violence should not have a high impact. Depictions with a high impact should be infrequent, and should not be prolonged or gratuitous. Realistic treatments may contain detailed depictions, but these should not be prolonged. Depictions of violence in stylized treatments may be more detailed and more frequent than depictions of violence in close to real life situations or in realistic treatments if this does not increase the impact. Visual suggestions of sexual violence are permitted only if they are not frequent, prolonged, gratuitous, or exploitative.

Sex. Sexual activity may be implied. Depictions of nudity in a sexual context which contain detail should not be exploitative. Verbal references may be more detailed than depictions, if this does not increase the impact.

Coarse Language. Coarse language may be used. Coarse language that is very strong, aggressive or detailed should not be gratuitous.

Adult Themes. The treatment of themes with a high degree of intensity should be discreet.

Drug Use. Drug use may be shown, but should not be promoted or encouraged. More detailed depictions should not have a high degree of impact.

18+ Restricted (Restricted to adults 18 years and over). The R category is legally restricted to adults. Material which is given a restricted classification is unsuitable for those under 18 years of age. Material classified R deals with issues or contains depictions which require an adult perspective. The classification is not intended as a comment on the quality of the material. Some material may be offensive to some sections of the adult community. Material which promotes or incites or instructs in matters of crime and/or violence is not permitted.

Violence. Depictions of violence which are excessive will not be permitted. Strong depictions of realistic violence may be shown but depictions with a high degree of impact should not be gratuitous or exploitative. Sexual violence may only be implied and should not be detailed. Depictions must not be frequent, gratuitous or exploitative. Gratuitous, exploitative or offensive depictions of cruelty or real violence are not permitted.

Sex. Sexual activity may be realistically simulated; the general rule is "simulation, yes—the real thing, no." Nudity in a sexual context should not include obvious genital contact. Verbal references may be more detailed than depictions.

Coarse Language. There are virtually no restrictions on coarse language at R level.

Adult Themes. The treatment of any themes with a very high degree of intensity should not be exploitative.

Drug Use. Drug use may be shown but not gratuitously detailed. Drug use should not be promoted or encouraged. Detailed instruction in drug misuse is not permitted.

18+ Contains Sexually Explicit Material (Restricted to adults 18 years and over*). This classification is a special and legally restricted category which contains sexually explicit material. That is material which contains real depictions of actual sexual intercourse and other sexual activity between consenting adults, including mild fetishes.

No depiction of sexual violence, sexualized violence or coercion, offensive fetishes, or depictions which purposefully debase or abuse for the enjoyment of viewers is permitted in this classification.

RC Refused Classification. As pointed out in the introduction, films, and videos must be classified. A film or video which does not have the authorized classification symbols or the consumer advice is either an unclassified film or video, or it has been refused classification.

Films or videos which contain elements beyond those set out in the above classification categories are refused classification. Films or videos which fall within the criteria for refused classification cannot be legally brought into Australia.

The Classification Code sets out the criteria for refusing to classify a film or video. The criteria fall into three categories. These include films that:

1. depict, express or otherwise deal with matters of sex, drug misuse or addiction, crime, cruelty, violence or revolting or abhorrent phenomena in such a way that they offend against the standards of morality, decency and propriety generally accepted by reasonable adults to the extent that they should be classified RC;
2. depict in a way that is likely to cause offense to a reasonable adult a person who is or who looks like a child under 16 (whether or not engaged in sexual activity), or;
3. promote, incite or instruct in matters of crime or violence.

Films and videos are refused classification if they appear to purposefully debase or abuse for the enjoyment of viewer, and which lack moral, artistic or other values, to the extent that they offend against generally accepted standards of morality, decency and propriety.

Films and videos are refused classification if they contain: (a) depictions of child sexual abuse or any other exploitative or offensive depictions involving a person who is or who looks like a child under 16; (b) detailed instruction in: (1) matters of crime or violence, (2) the use of proscribed drugs; (c) depictions of practices such as bestiality.

Films and videos are refused classification if they contain gratuitous, exploitative or offensive depiction of: (d) violence with a very high degree of impact or which are excessively frequent, prolonged or detailed; (e) cruelty or real violence which are very detailed or which have a high impact; (f) sexual violence; (g) sexual activity accompanied by fetishes or practices which are offensive or abhorrent; (h) incest fantasies or other fantasies which are offensive or abhorrent.

In addition to refusing classification of films and videos, the board may sometimes agree to an importer's request to cut certain scenes for the purposes of receiving a particular rating. If a distributor or producer wishes, he or she may appeal a decision of the board to the Office of Film and Literature Classification.

Ratings issued by the board, whether for films or videos, include additional "consumer advice," which informs the public as to the rationale for a given rating. Consumer advice is usually in the form of a several word descriptive and evaluative statement, such as "low level violence" or "medium level coarse language."[6] This consumer information is required by law to appear in advertisements for videos or films, and on the covers of videotapes for sale or rental. The consumer advice is in addition to the "code reasons for classification," which are published in *Discovery,* a government-run computer bulletin board service. In most Australian jurisdictions, stores selling or renting videotapes must have on display a sign that explains the videotape classification symbols.

Computer Games

The Office of Film and Literature Classification also classifies computer games. Titles sold or rented for home use as well as those played in arcades are subject to classification. Specific states and territories retain the right to vary classifications in their jurisdiction and are responsible for enforcement of the system. In addition, only those titles classified as G, G8+ and M are permitted for use in amusement arcades.

The classification system for titles is based on the categories for film and video but with significant alterations that make the title classification system more restrictive. In addition to the ratings, classification labels also provide consumer advice information similar to that provided for film and videotapes. Following are the OFLC computer game classifications and guidelines:[7]

General. This category is suitable for all persons under 15 years.

General (8+). This category is also suitable for persons under 15 years but may not be appropriate to younger children under 8 years who may have difficulty distinguishing between fantasy and reality.

Mature. This category is suitable for persons 15 years and over.

MA. This category is restricted to persons 15 years and over.

Refused Classification. Material so classified may not be sold, hired, exhibited, displayed, demonstrated or advertised. Material which includes any of the following is refused classification:

Violence. Depictions of realistic violence, even if not detailed, relished or cruel (e.g., excessive and serious violence such as realistic depictions of dismemberment accompanied by loss of blood to real-life images); extreme "horror" scenarios or special effects; depictions of unduly detailed and/or relished acts of extreme violence or cruelty.

Sex. Nudity, including genitalia *unless* there is a "bona fide" educational, medical or community health purpose; simulated or explicit depictions of sexual acts between consenting adults; any depiction of sexual violence or sexual activity involving non-consent of any kind; depictions of child sexual abuse, bestiality, sexual acts accompanied by offensive fetishes, or exploitative incest fantasies.

Language. Use of sexually explicit language.

Other. Detailed instruction or encouragement in matters of crime or violence or the abuse of proscribed drugs; depictions which encourage the use of tobacco or alcohol, or which depict drug abuse; depictions which are likely to endorse or promote ethnic, racial or religious hatred.

Although the OFLC is responsible for title classification, the industry has agreed to facilitate the classification process by providing the agency with clips of any "contentious material" contained in titles.[8] This alleviates the OFLC from the time-consuming task of reviewing every title in its entirety for such material. Industry accountability is enforced by the ability of the OFLC to automatically declassify and withdraw from sale any title found to contain "contentious material" not submitted to the agency for review.

Printed Matter

The classification scheme for printed matter, also administered by the Office of Film and Literature Classification, is voluntary. Most publications submitted for classification are of a "sexual nature."[9] There are four OFLC categories of classification for printed matter:[10]

Refused Classification. Material which exploits children, promotes crime or violence, or would be considered so offensive to a reasonable adult person that it should not be permitted.

Unrestricted. (No restriction as to sale or display) Photographs on covers and advertising posters must be suitable for display in public. They may depict discreet nudity if it is not overtly sexually suggestive or if it does not imply sexual activity. Depictions of genitals, pubic hair, fetishes or implications of fetishes are not permitted. Language on covers must not be assaultative or sexually suggestive. Some lower level coarse language is acceptable, but sexually suggestive combinations of words or colloquialisms for sexual acts or genitals are not permitted. (Covers or posters which do not comply with these guidelines are considered unsuitable for public display and would result in a Category 2 restricted classification.)

Regarding the contents of unrestricted material, the following requirements apply: photographs of discreet male and female nudity are acceptable but not if sexual excitement is apparent; depictions of sexual activity between consenting adults are acceptable only where they are discreetly implied or stimulated; illustrations, paintings, statues etc. which are considered bona fide erotic artworks and depict explicit sexual activity or nudity may be acceptable in Unrestricted when set in an historical or cultural context; written descriptions of sexual activity between adults are acceptable in mainstream works of literature and in publications not overwhelmingly dedicated to sexual matters.

Category 1 Restricted. (Sale restricted to persons 18 years and over, to be displayed in a sealed wrapper—not to be sold in Queensland) The requirements for covers are the same as for unrestricted materials. Regarding the contents of Category 1 Restricted material, the following requirements apply: photographs may include explicit genital detail or obvious sexual excitement, and may also include implied, simulated or obscured sexual activity between adults and touching of genitals; depictions of mild fetishes such as rubberwear and stylised domination are acceptable; illustrations and paintings which are considered not to be bona fide erotic artworks, and depict explicit sexual activity or nudity will warrant a restricted category classification; photographs of realistic and explicit violence, or its aftermath, may be accommodated in a publication that exploits violence, except in a sexual context, or if extremely cruel or violent; exploitative novellas may contain explicit descriptions of sexual activity between consenting adults but excluding bestiality, or incest, or sexual activity involving children, or relished or detailed descriptions of gratuitous acts of cruelty, or detailed or unjustifiable descriptions of sexual violence against non-consenting persons; publications which contain exploitative, realistic and gratuitous descriptions of violence will warrant a Category 1 restricted classification. They will not include relished or detailed descriptions of gratuitous acts of cruelty, or detailed or unjustifiable descriptions of sexual violence against non-consenting persons.

Category 2 Restricted. (Sale restricted to persons 18 years and over, only to be displayed in premises restricted to persons 18 years and over—not to be sold in Queensland) As the publications are not displayed in a public place there is no restrictions on what may be displayed on their covers. Regarding the contents of Category 1 Restricted material, the following requirements apply: photographs of sexual activity between consenting adults which include explicit genital detail; depictions of stronger fetishes are permitted but not if non-consent or apparent physical harm are evident; exploitative novellas may contain explicit descriptions of sexual activity of most kinds but excluding sexual activity involving children, or relished or detailed descriptions of gratuitous acts of cruelty, or detailed or unjustifiable descriptions of sexual violence against non-consenting persons.

Refused Classification. (Publications refused classification may not be sold or displayed) Materials with the following content are refused classification: photographs of sexual activity involving children or of exploitative child nudity; publications which promote, incite or instruct in matters of crime or violence; photographs of sexual activity between humans and animals; photographs which depict extremely cruel or dangerous practices, especially those which show apparent harm to the participants; photographs which show sexual violence against the consent of a participant (this will also apply when the non-consent is established from text which relates to a photo sequence); books which promote, incite or encourage the use of prohibited drugs (included are books that instruct in the manufacture or cultivation of prohibited drugs; exploitative novellas which include gratuitous descriptions of sexual activity involving children (this guideline does not apply to works of genuine literary merit); exploitative novellas which contain relished or detailed descriptions of gratuitous acts of cruelty, or detailed or unjustifiable descriptions of sexual violence against non-consenting persons (this guideline does not apply to works of genuine literary merit).

Television

Commercial, community, and subscription television and radio broadcasters in Australia are regulated by the Australian Broadcasting Authority (ABA), a government agency authorized under the federal *Broadcasting Services Act 1992.*[11] The ABA replaces the former Australian Broadcasting Tribunal, which had broader powers over broadcasting content. Under the 1992 law, the ABA retains control over children's television programming, while primary responsibility for all other programming standards falls to the broadcasters themselves. The broadcast networks are required by law to develop their own codes of practice.[12]

Broadcast network codes are developed in consultation with the ABA. To be included in the ABA Register of Codes of Practice, the codes must meet the following requirements: (1) the code must provide appropriate community safeguards for the issues covered in it; (2) the code must be endorsed by a majority of the providers of broadcasting services in that section of the industry; and (3) members of the public must have been given an adequate opportunity to comment on the code.[13] Primary responsibility for compliance with the codes and for resolving complaints is held by the broadcasters. The ABA's role is to supervise the operation of the codes and perform the role of an independent adjudicator when complaints are not resolved between the complainant and the relevant broadcaster.

Broadcasting licensees are required to ensure that all programs transmitted have a rating assigned to them. In practice, the classifiers from the broadcast networks aim for continuity and meet occasionally to discuss classification issues. These meetings include representatives from the ABA and from the Office of Film and Literature Classification.

As the arbiter for children's television programming, ABA maintains two program classifications specifically for children's television. The two children's categories are C-Children and P-Preschool. These categories denote programming that is made specifically for children within the preschool or primary school ages and intended to "enhance a child's understanding and experiences."[14]

The commercial television industry code of practice came into effect in September 1993, in accordance with the 1992 law. The classifications, and their explanations, are as follows:

> **The General ("G") Classification.** Material Classified "G" must not contain any matter likely to be unsuitable for children to watch without the supervision of a parent.
>
> *Violence:* Depictions of physical and psychological violence and the use of threatening language, weapons or special effects must not be likely to cause alarm or distress to children, must be strictly limited to the context or story line of the program, and must not show violent behavior to be acceptable or desirable.
>
> *Sex and Nudity:* Depictions of and references to sexual behavior must be limited and discreet. Discreet portrayal of nudity only when absolutely necessary to the story line or program context.
>
> *Language:* Mild expletives or language which may be considered socially offensive or discriminatory may only be used in exceptional circumstances when absolutely justified by the story line or program context.
>
> *Drugs:* References to the consumption of illegal drugs must be limited and discreet and allowed only when absolutely justified by the story line or program context. Use of legal drugs must be depicted with care.

Suicide: Reporting of suicide must be straightforward, and not include graphic details or images. Discreet references to suicide are acceptable only if justified by the story line or context, and not presented as romantic, heroic, alluring or normal act.

Other: Dangerous playthings may only be depicted where absolutely justified by the story line or context, and must be depicted in such a way as to minimize the likelihood of imitation.

Where music, special effects and camera work are used to create an atmosphere of tension or fear, care must be taken not to cause unnecessary distress to children. Care must be exercised in the treatment of themes dealing with social or domestic conflict.

General ("G") classification zones.
Weekdays	6:00 A.M.–8:30 A.M.
	4:00 P.M.–7:30 P.M.
Weekends	6:00 A.M.–7:30 P.M.

The Parental Guidance Recommended ("PG") Classification. Material classified "PG" may contain adult themes or concepts but must remain suitable for children to watch under the guidance of a parent or guardian.

Violence: Any violence depicted must be inexplicit, discreet or stylized and appropriate to the story line or program context. No overly realistic, bloody or horrific depictions of violence are permitted.

Sex and Nudity: Depictions of and references to intimate sexual behavior must be discreet and appropriate to the story line or program context, and must not dominate the theme of a program. Discreet portrayal of nudity only where justified by story line or program context.

Language: Low-level offensive language may only be used when justified by the story line or program context, and then only infrequently.

Drugs: Techniques for the consumption of illegal drugs must not be demonstrated, and illegal drugs must not be depicted favorably. Use of legal drugs must be depicted with care.

Suicide: The depiction of suicide or attempted suicide must be inexplicit and discreet, and must not be presented as the means of achieving a desired result or as an appropriate response to stress, depression or other problems.

Parental Guidance Recommended ("PG") classification zones.
Weekdays (school days)	5:00 A.M.–6:00 A.M.
	8:30 A.M.–12:00 P.M.
	3:00 P.M.–4:00 P.M.
	7:30 P.M.–8:30 P.M.

Weekdays (school holidays)   5:00 A.M.–6:00 A.M.
                               8:30 A.M.–4:00 P.M.
                               7:30 P.M.–8:30 P.M.
Weekends   5:00 A.M.–6:00 A.M.
                               7:30 P.M.–8:30 P.M.

The Mature ("M") Classification. Material classified "M" is *recommended* for viewing only by persons aged 15 years or over because of the matter it contains, or of the way this matter is treated.

Violence: May be realistically depicted only if it is not too frequent or impactful, appropriate to the story line or program context, and not unduly bloody or horrific.

Sex and Nudity: Intimate sexual behavior may only be implied i.e. at most inexplicitly simulated. It must be relevant to the story line or program context. Portrayals of nudity must be relevant to the story line or program context.

Drugs: No detailed instruction in the use of illegal drugs. Illegal drugs must not be depicted favorably.

Suicide: Suicide must not be depicted favorably, and methods of suicide must not be depicted in realistic detail.

Mature ("M") classification zones.
  Weekdays (school days)   12:00 A.M.–5:00 A.M.
                                 12:00 P.M.–3:00 P.M.
                                 8:30 P.M.–12:00 A.M.
  Weekdays (school holidays)   12:00 A.M.–5:00 A.M.
  and Weekends   8:30 P.M.–12:00 A.M.

The Mature Adult ("MA") Classification. Material classified "MA" is suitable for viewing only by persons aged 15 years or over because of the intensity and/or frequency of violence, sexual depictions, or coarse language, or because violence is central to the theme.

Violence: No sustained, relished or excessively detailed acts of violence. Violence occurring in a sexual context is to be assessed more stringently. Depictions with a high degree of realism or impact must be brief and contextually justified. Violence may not be presented as desirable in its own right.

Sex and Nudity: No explicit depiction of sexual acts, or depiction of exploitative or non-consenting sexual relations as desirable. Intimate sexual behavior may only be implied or simulated.

Language: No excessive and grossly offensive language. The use of offensive language must be appropriate to the story line or program context and not overly frequent or impactful.

Drugs: No detailed instruction in the use of illegal drugs. Illegal drugs must not be depicted favorably.

Mature Adult ("MA") classification zones.
All days between 9:00 P.M. and 5:00 A.M.

Material Not Suitable for Television. Material which cannot appropriately be classified "MA" or any lower television classification, because of the matter it contains, or the way that matter is treated, is unsuitable for television, and must not be broadcast.

The following categories indicate what will invariably be suitable for television.

Violence: Sustained, relished or excessively detailed acts of violence.

Sex and Nudity: Explicit depiction of sexual acts, or depiction of exploitative or non-consensual sexual relations as desirable.

Language: Excessive and grossly offensive language. The infrequent use of offensive language must be appropriate to the story line or program content.

Drugs: Detailed instruction or encouragement in the use of illegal drugs.

Display of Classification Symbols. An appropriate classification symbol must be displayed as close as is practicable to the start of those programs to be classified, and within any promotion for the program.

Consumer Advice for "M" and "MA" Programs. "M" classified feature films and all "MA" classified programs must carry, in addition to the classification symbol, brief consumer advice giving the principal elements which have contributed to the classification and indicating their intensity and/or frequency. The advice will be in a style consistent with the guidelines on consumer advice published by the Office of Film and Literature Classification.

Spoken and written consumer advice must be broadcast at the start of the program. The consumer advice is to be in a readily legible typeface, and is to remain visible for at least five seconds. Briefer written consumer advice is to be broadcast as soon as is practicable after the resumption of the program at each break.

Clearly visible consumer advice is to accompany all press advertising of programs placed by the licensee.

Warnings Before Certain News, Current Affairs and Other Programs. Where news, current affairs, or other programs not classified "M" or "MA" include for public interest reasons material which is, in the licensee's reasonable opinion, likely to seriously distress or offend a substantial number of viewers, the licensee must provide adequate prior warning to viewers. The warning must precede the relevant segment in news and current affairs programs and precede the programs in other cases.

As of October 1997, the subscription television broadcasting services are developing their own code for television practices, to include program ratings.[15]

GERMANY

Film, Video, and Video Games

There are three separate kinds of bodies which play a role in the rating and classification of films in Germany: the Voluntary Self-Regulatory Board of the Film Industry, in cooperation with the Länder (German states or provinces) governments; the Federal Institution for the Examination of Youth-Endangering Media; and the public prosecutors of the Länder.[16]

The Voluntary Self-Regulatory Board of the Film Industry (FSK) was created in 1949 by the Spitzenorganisation der deutschen Filmindustrie (SPIO), the German film trade organization.[17] In 1951, the German legislature introduced legislation for "protection of the youth," which delegated to the Länder the authority to decide whether a film can be shown to minors, as well as to determine the classifications of films. The Länder governments work in conjunction with the FSK to determine the ratings of films.

The classification process for most films involves a working committee of seven examiners. The examiners are part of a pool of 180 individuals who are appointed for three-year terms. Of the 180 examiners on the board, 140 are from public bodies such as youth organizations and religious institutions, in addition to 40 representatives of the film industry, chosen by the SPIO.[18] The examiners rotate onto the examination committees for three-week terms each year, and are paid a fee of DM114 ($50–$60) per day, plus expenses.[19]

On the FSK examination committees, four of the seven examiners are representatives of the Länder, the churches, or other public bodies, and three are representatives of the film industry. Film ratings are determined by a majority vote of the committees.[20]

The FSK administers five categories of film classification, in accordance with the German "Law Relating to Protection of Youth in Public":

Released without an age limit
Restricted for children younger than 6 years
Restricted for children younger than 12 years
Restricted for children younger than 16 years
Restricted for children younger than 18 years [21]

The FSK has no formal written guidelines concerning which behaviors earn films a particular classification. According to Folker Hönge, Chairman of the FSK, the main issue for raters is "the representation of violence and its consequences for the psyche and behavior of young people."[22]

A second organization responsible for the classification of film in Germany is the Federal Institution for the Examination of Youth-Endangering Media (BPjS). The BPjS, an agency of the Federal Republic, deals with the classification of videos and music recordings. Like the FSK, the BPjS only enforces restrictions on the access of minors to media products. Federal law restricts the distribution of videos that depict the glorification of violence, the promotion of racial hatred, excessive violence, and pornography. Videos are placed on the BPjS Index based on whether they fall under any of those categories. Videos indexed by the BPjS can not be on public display in video stores or in catalogues. Videos not classified by the FSK run a greater risk of being banned than those which have been classified. Approximately 2,300 videos are currently indexed as restricted for use by children under the age of eighteen.[23]

The third set of agencies responsible for the categorization of films in Germany are the public prosecutors of the Länder. These agencies operate under the auspices of the Penalty Law of the Federal Republic, and have the authority to ban films from public distribution in general.

Video Games

Since October 1995, the FSK is also responsible for the rating of video games with long film sequences.[24] The same rating codes are applied to video games as for films.

GREAT BRITAIN

Film and Video

The British Board of Film Classification (BBFC) is an independent, nongovernmental body, which classifies films and videos throughout Great Britain. Though the board is not an official entity, its decisions are usually followed by the local licensing authorities, who have statutory censorship powers over the films shown in their licensed theaters. It was founded in 1912 by the film industry.[25]

The creation of the Board was a response to a situation in which local authorities had begun to impose their own, widely varying, censorship decisions on films after the courts ruled in 1911 that prior censorship of film was legal in Britain. The film industry hoped that the Board would be "a body which, with no greater power than that of persuasion, would make judgments which were acceptable nationally."[26] By the early 1920s, the Board had accomplished that objective.

In 1984, the British Parliament passed the Video Recordings Act (VRA), which created a requirement that all video recordings of works not exempted under the act must be classified by an authority to be determined by the Home Secretary.[27]

The following year, the BBFC was so designated and, for the first time in its history, found itself "exercising a statutory function on behalf of central government."[28] The VRA makes sale or rental of unclassified videos, or videos that are inappropriate to the age of the purchaser, illegal acts punishable by fines or imprisonment. The regulations accompanying the VRA require that BBFC classification labels appear on the packaging for all classified home videos rented or sold in Britain; failure to do so is also a criminal offense.

Films and videos, as well as trailers and advertisements for them, are reviewed by a committee of at least two examiners, and the classification decisions of the reviewers are usually released within seventy-two hours of viewing. If there is objectionable material in the film or video, the board will suggest specific edits, either to avoid banning or to elicit a particular rating. In addition to its suggested cuts, the board elicits cooperation between itself and the relevant filmmakers in the editing process, and is available to view the material with filmmakers to devise mutually acceptable solutions to problem material.[29]

Under the terms of the Video Recordings Act, decisions of the board may be appealed to an independent Video Appeals Committee. In the first ten years since the act took effect, only nine of the board's decisions have been appealed.[30]

The BBFC classification system, which has undergone several changes since its inception, includes the following categories:

U, for Universal. Suitable for all.
Uc, for Universal. Particularly suitable for young children.
PG, for Parental Guidance. Some scenes may be unsuitable for young children.
12. Suitable only for persons of twelve years or older.
15. Suitable only for persons of fifteen years and over.
18. Suitable only for persons of eighteen years and over.
R18. Restricted distribution only, through cinema clubs and licensed sex shops.

Since the end of World War II, the BBFC has not maintained a formal set of criteria for determining classification decisions. Instead, each film is judged independently, "on its merits," with precedent, context, and the "evolution of public taste" taken into account.[31]

Interactive Electronic Games

The passage of the Video Recordings Act in 1984 provided a legal framework for the classification of interactive leisure software, including video games. Under the act, computer and video games are exempt from classification by the British Board of Film Classification (BBFC) unless they have significant sexual and violent content.[32] In such instances, the titles are to be referred to the BBFC by the software publisher for classification according to the BBFC ratings system. Historically, the vast majority of computer and video game titles have fallen outside the criteria requiring BBFC classification. However, in response to growing public and government concern regarding the content of video games, the video game industry has come under pressure to implement some type of ratings mechanism for non-BBFC classified titles.[33] In early 1994, the European Leisure Software Publishers Association (ELSPA), the trade association for the United Kingdom leisure software industry, unveiled a system of self-regulation for the game industry.

According to ELSPA, "[t]he system is designed to ensure responsible behavior by members and to allow parents to make informed choices about the game playing of their children."[34] The system was developed by ELSPA in cooperation with the Video Standards Council and the BBFC. It is comprised of two components: an age suitability classification system and an industry code of practice developed by the Video Standards Council (VSC).

All members of ELSPA, both in the U.K. and in other European countries, are bound by ELSPA membership requirements to include the ratings on their packaging. However, according to ELSPA Director General Roger Bennett, the ratings requirements are being enforced only with regard to titles marketed in Britain.[35] He notes that the monitoring and enforcement of titles packaged for non-U.K. markets are not a priority at this time. The reason for this is twofold. First, the broad cultural differences which characterize the European market limit the application of a uniform ratings system across the continent. Second, eighty percent of titles produced for the European market are by British-owned companies or British software subsidiaries.

The ratings classification system is voluntary. However, there is strong economic and political pressure for software publishers to support the system. Publishers who fail to submit the title to the BBFC in accordance with the 1984 Video Act are subject to heavy fines. Also, one criteria for ELSPA membership is compliance with the ratings system. In addition, most computer and video game retailers will only carry titles that are rated. The support of retailers and distributors has proven key to industry adoption of the ratings system. According to Bennett, as of July 1997, nearly 100 percent of all titles published and marketed in Britain are now rated.

The ELSPA age suitability ratings system includes four age categories: ages 3–10; 11–14; 15–17 and 18+. Games can be considered suitable for all or particular age groups depending on the extent to which the title contains violent and sexual content.

The rating for a specific title is determined through the completion of a Product Rating Assessment form by software publishers. The form is designed to assess the level of sexual and violent content of the title and age suitability. The effectiveness and credibility of the system are thus fundamentally based on the truthfulness of software publishers in completing the assessment form. Two checks exist in the system to reduce potential misclassification by the publisher. First, the form is reviewed by the Video Standards Council to ensure that the age rating is appropriate based on the information provided by the publisher. If the council suspects the rating is incorrect it can review the video game and require a change in the rating. Second, as was mentioned above, it is in the economic self-interest of the software publisher to abide by a ratings system increasingly supported by retailers and the general public.

SWEDEN

Film

The National Swedish Board of Film Classification was created in September 1911, making it the oldest public institution of its kind in the world.[36] There are five "censors" on the board; two, including the director, work full-time, while three work half-time.[37] All censors are appointed by the government. Currently, board members come from the following professions: psychology, sociology, education, and film.

Decisions as to how many censors review a given film are made on a case-by-case basis. A film can be reviewed by only one censor, though any for which cuts are recommended must be viewed by at least two.[38] For the board to classify a film within a category lower than its "15" rating, at least two censors must have seen the film, and at least one of those must have appropriate education in behavioral science.

Board decisions can be appealed to the Administrative Court in Stockholm, which is expanded in such cases to include one specialist each in "film science" and behavioral science.[39] The board also employs fourteen inspectors who ensure compliance with the rating law by video stores and film theaters.

The board is financed entirely by the government. Film distributors are charged a fee based on the length of the film, with much lower rates given for documentaries.

The National Swedish Board of Film Classification's film classifications are the following:

Allowed for All.
7. Allowed for children from the age of seven.
11. Allowed for children from the age of eleven.
15. Allowed for adults, that is, persons from the age of fifteen.

In 1991, a parental guidance policy was established whereby children under the age of seven may attend a film allowed for seven-year-olds when accompanied by an adult (a person eighteen or older), and children seven years and older may attend films allowed for eleven-year-olds with adult supervision.[40]

Swedish age restrictions apply only to *public* showings of films. Private showings are not restricted in any way, and can include invitation-only events, members-only organizations, and videos shown in the privacy of the home.[41] A teacher, for example, can legally show a picture that is given a "15" to a class of thirteen-year-olds, if he or she considers it valuable as a topic for discussion.

The board also rates videos for sale or rental on a voluntary basis. Since not all videos are reviewed by the board, there is some confusion as to whether the recommended age limits on the cover of videos for sale or rental are those of the board or of the video distributors themselves.[42]

UNITED STATES

Film

In the United States, films are rated by the Classification and Ratings Administration (CARA), a division of the Motion Picture Association of America (MPAA), a film industry trade group. The current rating system is one of a series of self-regulatory actions taken by the MPAA over many years. From 1931 to 1968, the MPAA sponsored the Hays Production Code, which required that films meet standards concerning sexuality, vulgarity, religion, "repellent subjects" and "national feelings," or not be released at all.[43] Then, in 1968, when two U.S. Supreme Court decisions gave state governments the right to control minors' access to films, the MPAA responded by adopting the Voluntary Movie Rating System. Less restrictive than the Hays Code, this system advises audiences about the age appropriateness of films and limits minors' access to films with adult themes.

The Rating Board is currently composed of eleven members, employed by the MPAA.[44] Producers/distributors present their films for review and pay a fee for this service. The board, by majority vote, determines a rating and provides a brief written rationale for the decision. Producers/distributors unhappy with the rating can edit the film and resubmit it for another review.

If they are dissatisfied with a ruling of the Rating Board and unwilling to edit their film, they can submit it to a separate twenty-one member Rating Appeals Board, whose membership is comprised of equal numbers of theater owners and producers/distributors. Board members are appointed by the MPAA member companies[45] and the National Association of Theater Owners. One representative of the American Film Marketing Association, which represents independent film production/distribution companies, also sits on the Appeals Board. The president of the MPAA serves as its chair. The board must achieve a two-thirds vote to overturn a rating.[46]

There are no special professional qualifications for CARA board membership. All board members must, however, be parents, "be possessed of an intelligent maturity, and most of all, have the capacity to put themselves in the role of most American parents."[47] With the exception of the board chair, the identities of CARA board members are kept secret to the public, though some family and occupational background information about them is released. The current board members include four homemakers, three teachers, a cabinetmaker, postal worker/social worker, microbiologist, and hairdresser.[48] Current board membership is diverse in terms of age, gender, race and national origin.[49]

The CARA Voluntary Rating System, revised several times since its inception, currently provides for five ratings categories:

G for "General Audiences. All ages admitted."
PG for "Parental Guidance Suggested. Some material may not be suitable for children."
PG-13 for "Parents strongly cautioned. Some material may be inappropriate for children under 13."
R for "Restricted. Under 17 requires accompanying parent or adult guardian." (Age varies in some jurisdictions).
NC-17 for "No children 17 and under admitted."

Film Advertisements

The enormous influence of movie advertisements becomes readily apparent when one realizes that far more people see or listen to such ads than see the movies they promote. Indeed, often, ad campaigns linger in the public consciousness long after the movies have faded from view.

Movie ads are found in every medium designed for advertising—from print and electronic media to online in cyberspace—with most advertising concentrated in newspapers, magazines, billboards, radio, and television. Unlike other products, movies can also be marketed through previews (trailers) of several minutes duration which highlight a movie's more enticing scenes, and which run in theaters before the showing of feature films.

Unlike the films themselves, all movie advertising is approved or disapproved by the MPAA. In the case of ads, such ratings are given out by the MPAA's five-member Advertising Administration department. Though a like set of standards are applied to magazine, newspaper, billboard, radio and television ads, movie trailers are judged on a different, and stricter, basis. Trailers are approved for either G/PG for general audience release or R for restricted audience release. G/PG-rated trailers are for movies that have been rated either G, PG, PG-13 R, or NC-17 by the MPAA. Restricted trailers can only play in a theater that is playing an R- or NC-17-rated feature.[50]

The approval or disapproval of trailers is based on their suitability for viewing by children. G/PG-rated trailers are prevented from showing any nudity, drugs or drug paraphernalia, and can only show mild depictions of violence. R-rated trailers are less restrictive and can display some depictions of nudity, drugs and drug paraphernalia, and some violence (though the act of pointing guns to actors' and actresses' heads is prohibited). However, restricted trailers are prevented from showing only the scenes from a film that have caused the film to be rated R or NC-17.

In other words, restricted trailers cannot be a collection of a film's R-rated scenes of sex and violence, which when edited together in a shortened clip, would possess a greater intensity than if the individual scenes were to appear in the context of a 90-minute or two-hour movie.[51]

Advertising for movies is sometimes submitted for rating to the Advertising Administration in advance of the movie being submitted to the MPAA for rating by the Classification and Rating Administration. Filmmakers are prohibited from displaying the MPAA-designated rating in their advertising until their advertising has been approved by the Advertising Administration. Failure to abide by this can result in the revocation of their rating.[52]

In cases when an ad has been disapproved, filmmakers can contest the judgment of the Advertising Administration by appealing to the president of the MPAA to overturn the disapproval. Some of the more well-known ad campaigns that have been appealed include the print advertisements for the 1993 film *Dazed and Confused* (which contained the subsequently changed ad line, "Finally! A Movie for Everyone Who Did Inhale"),[53] and *Jason's Lyric* (1994), which displayed partial female nudity.[54] In both cases, the appeals were turned down. In another publicized case, a print ad for *Ready to Wear* (1995) showing a seminude model was also turned down. However, MPAA officials said the ad was rejected because it was used before it was submitted for rating. The ad was later approved by the MPAA.[55]

Finally, an ad that showed frontal male nudity in the form of Michelangelo's Sistine Chapel fresco, *The Creation of Ad*am, used as part of a trailer for the film *Six Degrees of Separation*, was labeled "unsuitable for all audiences" by the Advertising Administration. Though the offending image was trimmed from the ad, in an unusual statement, the MPAA's president labeled the decision a mistake and said it would have been rectified if the filmmakers had chosen to appeal the rating.[56]

Television

TV Parental Guidelines

The United States Telecommunications Act of 1996, signed into law by President Clinton in February of that year, required the inclusion of v-chip technology in all newly manufactured television sets with screens larger than thirteen inches within two years of the law's enactment. The law also empowered the Federal Communications Commission to create a committee to develop its own television content code, should the television industry fail to create its own rating system compatible with V-chip technology within one year.

In December 1996, a television industry coalition comprised of the National Association of Broadcasters, the National Cable Television Association, and the Motion Picture Association of America, announced the creation of the TV Parental Guidelines. The industry insisted that its new guidelines were created "voluntarily," despite the Telecommunications Act's threat of a rating code designed by a government-created committee.[57]

The new rating system is divided into two groups: rating categories for programs designed for children, and categories for programs designed for the entire audience. The original ratings were: TV-Y (All Children), TV-Y7 (Directed to Older Children—age 7 and above), TV-G (General Audience), TV-PG (Parental Guidance Suggested), TV-14 (Parents Strongly Cautioned—may be unsuitable for children under 14), and TV-M (Mature Audience Only—may be unsuitable for children under 17).

The industry's guidelines immediately came under strong attack from parents groups, media researchers, members of Congress, public health associations, and media advocacy organizations.[58] The critics cited public opinion surveys that showed the overwhelming majority of the public—and, particularly, parents—preferred a rating system that described the content of shows rather than one which designated their suitability according to age.[59] They also cited studies that showed that age-based ratings can attract some children to those very shows that the ratings are intended to deter them from watching.[60]

As a result of this criticism, the industry entered into several months of negotiations with some of its major organizational critics (the American Medical Association, the American Academy of Pediatrics, the American Psychological Association, the Center for Media Education, the Children's Defense Fund, Children Now, the National Association of Elementary School Principals, the National Education Association, and the National PTA). The negotiations resulted in an agreement outlining modifications to the system, including the addition of certain content information to the rating system. As part of the agreement, the advocacy groups joined the industry in recommending to the Federal Communications Commission that the MPAA rating system and the new TV rating system be the only systems mandated for inclusion on the V-chip.[61]

Under the system, ratings are assigned to programs by broadcast and cable networks and producers. In addition, local television stations have the right to substitute the rating they deem most suitable for their particular audience. The ratings icons and associated content symbols appear for fifteen seconds at the beginning of all rated programming.

The guidelines are applied to all television programming except news and sports.[62] Unedited movies that are often shown on premium cable channels carry their original MPAA ratings; movies produced before the creation of the MPAA rating system (1968) and movies that are edited for television are given TV Parental Guideline ratings.

The industry has also established an Oversight Monitoring Board to "ensure that the Guidelines are applied accurately and consistently to television programming."[63] Board membership, as revised in the industry/advocacy group agreement, includes 24 members, six each from the broadcast industry, cable industry, and program production community, five from the advocacy community, and a chairman. The first chairman of the board is Jack Valenti, president of the Motion Picture Association of America.

Following are the revised TV Parental Guidelines rating categories, as submitted by the television industry to the Federal Communications Commission:[64]

The following categories apply to programs designed solely for children:

TV-Y All Children This program is designed to be appropriate for all children. Whether animated or live-action, the themes and elements in this program are specifically designed for a very young audience, including children from ages 2–6. This program is not expected to frighten younger children.

TVY-7 Directed to Older Children This program is designed for children age 7 and above. It may be more appropriate for children who have acquired the developmental skills needed to distinguish between make-believe and reality. Themes and elements in this program may include mild fantasy violence or comedic violence, or may frighten children under the age of 7. Therefore, parents may wish to consider the suitability of this program for their very young children. Note: For those programs where fantasy violence may be more intense or more combative than other programs in this category, such programs will be designated TV-Y7-FV.

The following categories apply to programs designed for the entire audience.

TV-G General Audience Most parents would find this program suitable for all ages. Although this rating does not signify a program designed specifically for children, most parents may let younger children watch this program unattended. It contains little or no violence, no strong language and little or no sexual dialogue or situations.

TV-PG Parental Guidance Suggested This program contains material that parents may find unsuitable for younger children. Many parents may want to watch it with their younger children. The theme itself may call for parental guidance and/or the program contains one or more of the following: moderate violence (V), some sexual situations (S), infrequent coarse language (L), or some suggestive dialogue (D).

TV-14 Parents Strongly Cautioned This program contains some material that many parents would find unsuitable for children under 14 years of age. Parents are strongly urged to exercise greater care in monitoring this program and are cautioned against letting children under the age of 14 watch unattended. This program contains one or more of the following: intense violence (V), intense sexual situations (S), strong coarse language (L), or intensely suggestive dialogue (D).

TV-MA Mature Audience Only This program is specifically designed to be viewed by adults and therefore may be unsuitable for children under 17. This program contains one or more of the following: graphic violence (V), explicit sexual activity (S), or crude indecent language (L)"

As of this writing, two television networks, the National Broadcasting Company (NBC) and Black Entertainment Television (BET), have refused to sign on to the TV Parental Guidelines system.[65] NBC argues that the new system will have "a chilling effect" on program content.[66] NBC has instead pledged to increase its use of on-air program advisories.

Premium Cable Television

In addition to the TV Parental Guidelines, four premium cable networks—Cinemax, HBO, The Movie Channel and Showtime—continue to use a previously developed content advisory system that provides descriptive advisories. This voluntary system was established to provide viewers with information about programming containing violence, sex, and offensive language.[67] Executives in the networks' programming departments are responsible for evaluating programs.[68] Because each network labels its own programs, however, it is possible that a movie might receive different advisory labels on different stations.[69] Showtime's Executive Vice President McAdory Lipscomb comments, "'It is possible that we would rank something different than HBO, but we both recognize our dual responsibility to provide information to our subscribers about what is graphic or perhaps unsuitable for children, and we think the common language we've developed will provide an acceptable parameter.'"[70]

As many as five labels, which appear both on the air and in program guides, may be applied to a movie or program.[71] The premium television content advisory system includes the following descriptive codes:

MV, for Mild Violence
V, for Violence
GV, for Graphic Violence
RP, for Rape
AL, for Adult Language
GL, for Graphic Language
BN, for Brief Nudity
N, for Nudity
AC, for Adult Content
SC, for Strong Sexual Content

Sound Recordings

In 1985, after a series of congressional hearings initiated by Tipper Gore and the Parents Music Resource Center (PMRC), the Recording Industry Association of America (RIAA), a trade association representing the major record producers, reached an agreement with the PMRC and the National Parent Teacher Association on the labeling of explicit lyrics. Under that agreement, record companies would voluntarily identify and label newly released sound recordings with lyrics that reflect explicit violence, explicit sex, or explicit substance abuse. In 1990 the RIAA standardized the label, which is still being used today. Under this system, labels reading "PARENTAL ADVISORY: EXPLICIT LYRICS" are affixed to some music cassettes, records, and CDs of an explicit nature. Beyond this advisory, however, no further distinctions in terms of content are made, such as whether the lyrics are "explicitly" violent, sexual, or profane.

The recording industry labeling system itself is wholly voluntary on the part of record companies, with no oversight or enforcement capability by the RIAA. Currently, any record company that wishes to identify any of its products with the official RIAA advisory sticker may do so, so long as the company uses and affixes the sticker correctly. There are no penalties for not placing the advisory stickers on music products that may be explicit, and there are no industry guidelines to determine which music products should be labeled. According to the RIAA, "given the vast number of songs (over 10,000) released each year, compared with the 577 films rated during 1993, developing a ratings board to review and rate every sound recording would be a near impossible task."[72]

In 1995, a coalition of groups led by former Education Secretary William Bennett and C. Delores Tucker, Chairwoman of the National Political Congress of Black Women, initiated a campaign against music they deemed objectionable. This was followed by a speech on media violence by then Senate majority leader Bob Dole, in which he specifically criticized Time-Warner's music division as marketing "evil through commerce."[73] Consequently, Time-Warner severed its distribution ties with Interscope, a record label with popular rap artists that had been targeted for criticism.[74]

As a result of this controversy, in October 1995, the RIAA, along with the National Association of Recording Merchandisers, representing record retailers, undertook a campaign to raise public awareness of the advisory system through merchandising and advertising.[75] Specifically, they pledged to encourage record companies, retailers, and distributors to include the advisory logo in consumer advertising; provide signs in retail outlets to identify the logo and describe its meaning; and create an internal process to ensure the correct size and placement of the logos on music products. The RIAA also announced plans to adopt a Parental Advisory logo for music videos, as well as a standard advisory notice for recordings that are distributed electronically.

Interactive Electronic Games

In response to congressional pressure, two major classification systems for interactive electronic entertainment have been created in the United States. These include the system developed by the Interactive Digital Software Association (IDSA) and that of the

Recreational Software Advisory Council (RSAC). Both systems began operations in late 1994. Sega, one of the largest producers of interactive entertainment, had its own rating system in place until the inception of IDSA; it has agreed to replace it with the ESRB system.[76]

Entertainment Software Rating Board

The Interactive Digital Software Association (IDSA) was established in 1994 by members of the software industry in part to coordinate the development and oversight of a self-regulating rating system for the interactive entertainment software industry. As part of these efforts, IDSA established the Entertainment Software Rating Board (ESRB) as a ratings body for software titles. The ESRB is independent of the software association, and its rulings are not subject to review by the IDSA.

The ESRB classification system applies to software for all platforms. The system is comprised of five ratings categories:[77]

Early Childhood (EC). Titles* rated "Early Childhood (EC)" are suitable for children ages three and older and do not contain any material that parents would find inappropriate.

Everyone (E). Titles rated "E" (Everyone) are suitable for persons ages six and older. These titles will appeal to people of many ages and tastes. They *may* contain minimal violence, some comic mischief (for example, slapstick comedy), or some crude language.

Teen (T). Titles rated "Teen (T)" are suitable for persons ages 13 and older. Titles in this category may contain violent content, mild or strong language, and/or suggestive themes.

Mature (M). Titles rated "Mature (M)" are suitable for persons 17 and older. These products may include more intense violence or language than products in the Teen category. In addition, these titles may also include mature sexual themes.

Adults Only (AO). Titles rated "Adult Only (AO)" are suitable only for adults. These products may include graphic depictions of sex and/or violence. Adults Only product are not intended to be sold or rented to persons under the age of 18.

*Title is the term used by the electronic game industry to refer to a specific product, such as a game or CD-ROM.

Accompanying these classification labels on title packaging are content descriptors relevant to each category. These descriptors provide consumers with additional content information and in many instances indicate the level of violence or sexual content of the title. Several descriptors are possible for each ratings category. Among the descriptors used are the following: Edutainment, Informational, Mild Animated Violence, Mild

Realistic Violence, Comic Mischief, Animated Violence, Realistic Violence, Animated Blood And Gore, Realistic Blood And Gore, Animated Blood, Realistic Blood, Suggestive Themes, Mature Sexual Themes, Strong Sexual Content, Mild Language, Strong Language, Gaming, Use of Tobacco And Alcohol, Use of Drugs, and Some Adult Assistance May Be Needed.

Submission of material for ratings classification is on a voluntary basis. As part of the ratings process, publishers submit a range of content-related materials. Each product is reviewed separately by three raters who are randomly selected from a pool of more than 100 specially trained individuals. The identity of all raters is kept anonymous.[78] The raters represent a cross section of demographic groups including sex, age, ethnicity, education, and marital status.

Submitted material must include a questionnaire on the game's content, as well as a videotape, demodisks, storyboards, scripts, and/or other narratives so raters can view the content of the product. Publishers are required to submit content excerpts representing the most "extreme portions" of the title, along with a full spectrum of game play.[79] Raters are randomly assigned by computer to rate the software title. Each rater reviews the title-related material and labels his or her observations and ratings recommendations, including suggested descriptors from among the standardized descriptors.

All three reviews are then submitted to an ESRB staff member. Upon review by the staff member, a consensus rating, based on the three individual ratings, are returned to the publisher. Prior to shipping, a copy of the final product must be sent to the board to provide a check that the final product corresponds with the original submission. The publisher can either accept or appeal the designated classification. An appeals board made up of persons unaffiliated with the software industry, but all with backgrounds in entertainment media, is available to hear appeals.

The ESRB has several systems in place that promote publisher accountability and honesty in submitting accurate product information. Submitting companies are required to sign judicially enforceable affidavits attesting to the accuracy of the submitted material. The ESRB's trademarks are registered and the board has a range of sanctions to use against companies which fail to provide full disclosure, including requiring that products be stickered in the field and/or revoking the rating. As a condition of accepting an ESRB rating, publishers must adhere to the IDSA Advertising Code of Conduct, which requires them to display the rating and content descriptor(s) on product packaging, and to include the rating symbol in all electronic and print advertising, as well as in other consumer marketing material. The ESRB has also established a toll free number for consumers to call to obtain rating information. An outside consumer and academic advisory board, whose members include representatives from the Consumer Federation of America and KIDSNET, meets periodically to advise the executive director on the system.[80]

Recreational Software Advisory Council Rating System

A second ratings system to emerge from the software industry is the product of a coalition of personal computer software companies organized as the Computer Game Ratings Working Group. The Working Group was formed with the purpose of developing an independent rating system for recreational software titles. The group was comprised of over twenty-five associations, including the Software Publishers Association (SPA), the Association of Shareware Professionals (ASP), the Educational Software Cooperative (ESC), Shareware Trade Association and Resources (STAR), the Software Entrepreneurs Forum (SEF), and the Computer Game Developers Association (CGDA).

The Recreational Software Advisory Council (RSAC) was founded by the Working Group to implement a game rating system. The council is an independent, non-profit organization comprised of various nonindustry representatives, including parents, teachers, and experts from various disciplines. The organization includes a Board of Directors, an Advisory Committee, and an Audit Group. The Board of Directors is responsible for the policy, operation and finances of the ratings program. The Advisory Committee advises the Board of Directors in developing and implementing the Game Ratings Program. The committee is comprised of media researchers, psychologists, and other experts in various disciplines. The Audit Group is responsible for viewing and rating randomly selected software titles. If there is a discrepancy between the rating assigned by the Audit Group and the rating determined by the software publisher's questionnaire, the title is sent to an Appeals Committee for a hearing. Appeals Committees are made up of a number of the Board of Directors which then reviews the contested rating.[81]

The ratings system developed by RSAC is based on a five-part classification scale ranging from titles suitable for all audiences to those considered extreme in violent and sexual content and language. For example, the content of titles considered suitable for all audiences (ALL) may contain violence that is considered harmless, must include no nudity or revealing attire, and involve language which is inoffensive or contains no profanity. Titles considered as having extreme content (Level 4) may contain wanton or gratuitous violence, torture or rape, provocative frontal nudity or explicit sexual activity and "four-letter" words or explicit sexual references. Levels 1 to 3 include content that varies between these two end points in terms of violence, nudity/sex, and language. Classification icons on title packaging and advertisements will appear in the form of thermometers, with four "temperature" readings, representing the four levels of intensity for each behavioral category. In addition, specific descriptors of the kinds of behaviors involved in determining the level of rating can accompany the icons, e.g. "bare buttocks," "blood and gore," "obscene gestures."

Title classification is determined through the use of an interactive software ratings program. Publishers complete a comprehensive, computerized ratings application that will indicate, through responses to specific questions, the extent of "potentially objectionable" violent and sexual content in the software title.[82] Rating classifications are automatically determined by the computer program according to the answers given.

The RSAC system is based on self-disclosure. The accuracy of the ratings recommendation is fundamentally dependent on the honesty of the software publisher in completing the application. However, several checks are present at both the pre- and post-distribution stages of the title, which encourage publisher accountability. For example, the questionnaire is designed to be highly specific and objective to limit ambiguity. If points of ambiguity arise publishers can seek a clarity ruling from RSAC. Also, if a publisher considers the recommended rating unfairly harsh, the publisher may appeal to an Appeals

Committee. In addition to these application-related checks, external checks also are present. These include the operation of a consumer complaint hotline and the random selection of titles by RSAC for review.[83] If it is found that a publisher has intentionally falsified responses to the questionnaire, sanctions include monetary fines, as well as removal of the title from the market while relabeling occurs.

Titles are assigned labels by RSAC prior to distribution to retail outlets. Software publishers are required to display the rating on all packaging, retail displays, self-running demonstrations, and splash-screens for interactive computer games.[84]

Online

Unlike other media, a rating system for the Internet need not be universally applied. In fact, ratings need only be used by those service providers who specifically want to target children. In order to protect children from other potentially objectionable areas of the Internet, parents can use a blocking technology to block out all materials that are unrated. This process can ensure that children are protected without interfering with the rights of adults.

Several Internet access providers have already added such parental control technologies to their services. America Online, CompuServe, and Prodigy, for instance, all have systems whereby parents can restrict children's access to adult-oriented areas of the Internet. In addition, several companies have introduced technologies that allow parents to filter out offensive language, sexually explicit materials, and other unwanted content. Many of these technologies also make it possible for parents to monitor their children's online activities.[85]

In addition to the online blocking technologies already available, efforts are being made to devise ratings and advisory standards to label content on the Internet. One such effort is the Platform for Internet Content Selection (PICS), developed by the World Wide Web Consortium as a "'practical alternative to global censorship of the Internet.'"[86] A technical protocol rather than a rating system, PICS has developed standards to allow for the voluntary rating of online content. These standards, based on such criteria as the amount of sexual content, the level of violence, or other references that parents may find objectionable,[87] enable companies to develop their own rating systems, distribute labels for Net content, and create label-reading software and services. Among the companies that will incorporate PICS standards into their products are Microsoft, Net Nanny Ltd., Netscape Communications, the Recreational Software Advisory Council (RSAC), and SurfWatch.[88]

This protocol is unique in that it does not rely on the judgment of a single ratings entity. Parents will be able to choose the system that best reflects their personal criteria. Hence, parents will be able to follow the advice of independent groups such as the Boy Scouts, *Parents* magazine, or the Christian Coalition.[89] Parents will have their choice of several PICS-compatible rating systems, such as those already created by RSAC, SafeSurf, Cyber Patrol, and SurfWatch, to control children's access to Internet content.[90]

An example of such a system is RSACi (RSAC on the Internet), created by the Recreational Software Advisory Council, which also provides a rating scheme for video games. RSACi provides detailed information about the content of an Internet site, based on the levels of sex, nudity, violence, and offensive language located within that site, and enables parents and teachers to block children's access to World Wide Web sites on the basis of such criteria.[91] Developed by Dr. Donald F. Roberts at Stanford University, the ratings questionnaire used to evaluate each site asks specific yes-or-no-type questions about the site's content. A numerical rating label, from 0 to 4 (0 being the mildest), is then assigned to the site based on its levels of language, violence, nudity, and sexual themes.[92] Another proposed Internet rating system is the Entertainment Software Rating Board Interactive (ESRBI), an arm of the video game rating board (ESRB) cited above.[93] ESRBI plans to rate Internet games and entertainment sites. ESRBI ratings symbols and content descriptors arc similar to those listed in the section on ESRB above.

CONCLUSION: DESCRIPTIVE VS. EVALUATIVE RATINGS

Accepting as given the trend toward increasing use of media ratings in many countries, experience with existing rating systems such as those documented in this chapter indicates that there are better—and worse—ways to devise such systems, not only from the standpoint of freedom of expression, but in terms of general practicality and social usefulness.

Here I would like to focus on one general recommendation concerning the design of rating systems: Rating systems should be designed to provide maximum information about media content while minimizing judgments about that content. An example of the latter approach is provided by the food labeling system. The "Nutrition Facts" label found on virtually all foods in the grocery store provides information about the fat, cholesterol, carbohydrates, etc., contained in food products. It does not, however, comment on the healthfulness or unhealthfulness of those ingredients. Such value judgments are left to the consumer.

Likewise, descriptive media rating systems are preferable to evaluative or prescriptive ones. A broad distinction between the two is that descriptive ratings tend to focus on relaying information about media content, while evaluative ratings tend to make judgments about the appropriateness of media content for particular audiences. Some have referred to this distinction as one between "rating" and "labeling."

In the context of ratings, description and evaluative are relative, not absolute, terms. No rating system is purely descriptive. The act of choosing to rate implies evaluation. Yet, there are rating systems that are more or less descriptive or evaluative. Table 1 provides some examples of the two types of ratings.

TABLE 1

Examples of Descriptive and Evaluative Ratings

Descriptive Ratings	Evaluative Ratings
Contains some violence	Parental Discretion Advised
Nudity/Sex Level 3	Teen: Ages 13+
Violence: Blood and Gore	R: Restricted
Language: Mild Expletives	Adults Only
Contains extreme violence	Mature: Ages 17+
BN: Brief Nudity	PG: Parental Guidance

There are four reasons why descriptive ratings are preferable to evaluative ones. First, evaluative ratings run a greater risk of having the opposite effect than the one for which they are intended. Such ratings have been shown to have boomerang/backlash effects. Attaching evaluative ratings such as PG-13, R, and "Parental Discretion Advised" to television programs can have the effect of attracting some children to watch those shows. By contrast, descriptive ratings, such as "This film contains extreme violence" have not been shown to have that effect.[94]

Second, evaluative ratings are less likely to be consistently applied than descriptive ratings. An evaluative rating system combines divergent categories of behavior—sex/nudity, violence, profanity—into ratings such as G or R. This requires that each rating decision includes an evaluation of the relative importance to the rating of the sexual, violent, or language component in the media product. Such a process "individualizes" rating decisions, which then must ultimately be made on an "I know it when I judge it" basis. By contrast, descriptive ratings can be more consistently applied, since the level of judgment is lower and simpler to apply, i.e., whether or not certain depictions occur in the story or game.

Third, because of their relative lack of consistency, evaluative ratings are less reliable as a source of information for those making media consumption choices. A typical conservative consumer, for example, may have different viewing preferences concerning violence, language, and sex than an average liberal. Evaluative ratings make the decisions regarding the relative appropriateness of these factors for the consumers. In contrast, by providing specific content information, descriptive ratings allow these very different consumers to make media consumption choices appropriate to their values and preferences. This point is especially relevant to the implementation of V-chip-style blocking technologies. Using an evaluative rating system, content would be blocked according to the *rater's* decision about what is appropriate or inappropriate for particular audiences, rather than according to the specific values and tastes of individual consumers concerning sex, violence, and language.

Finally, descriptive ratings are less likely than evaluative ones to be misused as representing a value system for society. All media ratings run the risk of assuming a moralistic tone, and ideas—or "unacceptable" portrayals of behavior or attitudes—can be suppressed in ways more subtle than direct government intervention. The simple act of "rating" a behavior can imply that it may be socially undesirable in some way. There is less scientific consensus on the social harm of depictions of sexuality or profanity than there is with violence, yet these are usually rated also. This is of particular concern for television ratings, since television in currently the most pervasive and influential medium. The more universalized a rating system, the more it runs the risk of appearing to represent quasi-official values for the society as a whole. Therefore, there is greater burden on its creators, from the standpoint of freedom of expression, to minimize value judgments in the rating process. A descriptive rating system accomplishes this to the greatest degree.

The recent American controversy regarding the TV-PG14 rating for an episode of the TV series *Ellen*, which contained a scene in which two lesbians kiss, can be used to highlight the distinction between descriptive and evaluative or prescriptive ratings. Using the TV Parental Guidelines, the ABC television network "appropriately" applied the *prescriptive* TV-PG14 standard that the show contained "material that many parents would find unsuitable for children under 14 years of age." By contrast, if the mostly *descriptive* Recreational Software Advisory Council rating system (reviewed above) had been applied to the *Ellen* episode in question, the kiss in question presumably would have received a "1" level nudity/sex rating,[95] just as any heterosexual kiss would have (a kiss is still a kiss). It is ironic that during the debate over the creation of the TV rating system, many within the television industry argued inexplicably that descriptive ratings would have a greater potential chilling effect on the range of program content than age-based prescriptive ones, though the arguments and *Ellen* example above indicate that the reverse is true.

While media rating systems are increasingly being used in many countries as a vehicle for addressing concerns about violent and other potentially problematic media content, this choice is not without its costs. A society that values freedom of expression should be extremely cautious about assigning warning labels to ideas, regardless of whether those ideas come in the form of political rhetoric or fictional stories. While ratings are preferable to direct government legislation of media content, they are by no means an ideal social policy. The cost to freedom of expression involved in rating media content can be limited through the use of rating systems that maximize description and minimize judgment. Ratings that simply provide descriptive information can enable individual parents and other consumers to make media consumption choices based on their own values and tastes, an approach far superior to those rating systems that attempt to make judgments about which kinds of entertainment or information are "appropriate" for other people's consumption.

Notes

*   This chapter is a revised and updated excerpt from the author's book, *Media Ratings: Design, Use and Consequences* (Mediascope, 1996). The revision effort benefitted greatly from the cooperation of all the relevant film rating organizations, as well as from outstanding research assistance by Melissa York. The original book was commissioned and published by Mediascope, Inc., a Los Angeles-based nonprofit media policy organization. It was funded by the Carnegie Corporation of New York and the California Wellness Foundation, and written while the author was Mediascope's Director of Research. For a copy of the full book, contact Mediascope at (818) 508-2080.

1.   *Report on Activities, 1991–92.* Sydney: Office of Film and Literature Classification and Film and Literature Board of Review, 1993, p. 8.

2.   Ibid.

3.   *Guidelines for the Classification of Films and Videotapes: Information Bulletin No. 7.* Sydney: Australian Office of Film and Literature Classification, 1993.

4.   Frank Marzic, Executive Officer, Australian Office of Film and Literature Classification. Telephone Communication, June 24, 1993.

5.   Office of Film and Literature Classification, *Guidelines for the Classification of Films and Videotapes,* July 1996, pp. 7–15.

6.   *Censorship Markings for Cinema and Video Advertising.* Sydney: Australian Office of Film and Literature Classification, 1993.

7.   Office of Film and Literature Classification, *Guidelines for the Classification of Computer Games,* Sydney: Office of Film and Literature Classification, October 1997.

8.   Attorney-General Australian National Government. *Computer Games and Censorship Reforms Agreed.* (Press Release) February 18, 1994.

9.   Office of Film and Literature Classification, *Printed Matter Classification Guidelines.* Sydney: Office of Film and Literature Classification, 1992.

10. Government of Australia Office of Film and Literature Classification, *Classification Board and Classification Review Board Annual Report, 1996–1997*. Sydney: Office of Film and Literature Classification, 1997, pp. 112–114.
11. *An Introduction to the ABA*. Sydney: Australian Broadcasting Authority, 1993
12. *Report of the Proceedings of the International Colloquium on Television Violence*. Montreal: Government of Canada Department of Communications, 1993, p. 27.
13. Letter from Rosie O'Neale, Australian Broadcasting Authority, to Joel Federman, University of California, Santa Barbara, October 10, 1997.
14. *Australian Broadcasting Tribunal Manual, Second Edition*. Sydney: Australian Broadcasting Tribunal, 1992, p. 1.
15. Ibid, p. 2
16. Since the unification of Germany, these originally West German bodies now apply to what was formerly East Germany.
17. "International Film Certifications." *The Business of Film*, October 1991, p. 38.
18. Ibid.
19. Bettina Buchler, Freiwilligen Selbstkontrolle der Filmwirtschaft (FSK). Telephone Communication, June 22, 1993.
20. Ibid.
21. Folker Hönge, op. cit.
22. Ibid.
23. Buchler, op. cit.
24. Letters from Folker Hönge, Freiwilligen Selbstkontrolle der Filmwirtschaft, to Joel Federman, University of California, Santa Barbara, October 2 and October 21, 1997.
25. *A Student's Guide to Film Classification and Censorship in Britain*. London: British Board of Film Classification, undated, p.1. The BBFC was originally named the British Board of Film Censors.
26. *Memorandum on the Work of the British Board of Film Classification*. London: British Board of Film Classification, 1993, p. 1.
27. Ibid.
28. Ibid.
29. *Video Recordings Act 1984: A Guide to Its Implementation and Practical Consequences*. London: British Board of Film Classification, 1985, p. 7.
30. *British Board of Film Classification (Fact Sheet)*. London: British Board of Film Classification, undated, p. 1.
31. *Video Recordings Act 1984: A Guide to Its Implementation and Practical Consequences*. London: British Board of Film Classification, 1985, p. 5.
32. Ibid., p. 1.
33. Roger Bennett, General Secretary ELSPA. Telephone Communication, September 1, 1994.
34. European Leisure Software Publishers Association, *Computer & Video Games Industry Announces System of Self-Regulation*, (Press Release) February 9, 1994.
35. Letter from Roger Bennett, Director General, ELSPA, to Joel Federman, September 29, 1997.
36. *Swedish Film Censorship: What It Is; How It Works*. Stockholm: National Swedish Board of Film Censors, 1992.
37. Erik Wallander, Censor, Swedish Board of Film Classification, Written Correspondence, October 20, 1997, p. 2.
38. Berg, op cit.
39. *Rules and Procedures in the Work of the Board as Censors*. Stockholm: National Swedish Board of Film Censors, 1991, p. 1.
40. Ibid.
41. *Swedish Film Censorship: What It Is; How It Works*. Stockholm: National Swedish Board of Film Censors, 1992.
42. Ibid.
43. Leonard J. Leff and Jerold L. Simmons, *The Dame in the Kimono: Hollywood, Censorship, and the Production Code from the 1920s to the 1960s*. Grove Weidenfeld, 1990.
44. Jack Valenti, *The Voluntary Movie Rating System*. Motion Picture Association of America, 1991, p. 5.
45. Buena Vista (Disney), Metro-Goldwyn-Mayer, Paramount, Sony Pictures, Twentieth Century-Fox, Universal, and Warner Bros.
46 Grimes, op. cit.
47. Valenti, op. cit., p. 6.

48. *CARA Board Members (Full and Part-Time)*. Los Angeles: Motion Picture Association of America, 1996.
49. Richard Mosk, Chairman, Motion Picture Association of America Classification and Ratings Administration. Telephone Communication, May 3, 1996.
50. Bethlyn Hand, Senior Vice-President, Classification and Ratings Administration, MPAA. Telephone Communication, November 2, 1995.
51. Ibid.
52. Ibid.
53. "MPAA Just Says No To Film Ad," *Los Angeles Times*, September 22, 1993.
54. Benjamin Svetkey, "Sex, Violence and Movie Ratings: Why the System Doesn't Work," *Entertainment Weekly*, November 25, 1994, p. 31.
55. Hand, op. cit.
56. "MPAA Makes Well-Known Member Exit MGM Trailer," *Daily Variety*, November 18, 1993.
57. Letter from Jack Valenti, President and CEO, Motion Picture Association of America; Decker Anstrom, President and CEO, National Cable Television Association; and Eddie Fritts, President and CEO, National Association of Broadcasters; to William F. Caton, Secretary, Federal Communications Commission, January 17, 1997, p. 1.
58. Heather Fleming, "Ratings Fail to Score in Peoria," *Broadcasting and Cable*, May 26, 1997; Heather Fleming, "Senate Pressuring for Content Ratings," *Broadcasting and Cable*, May 5, 1997; Letter from Joanne Cantor, Professor, University of Wisconsin, Madison, to Federal Communications Commission, April 7, 1997.
59. Silver, M., & Greier, T. Ready for prime time? *U.S. News & World Report*, September 9, 1996). pp. 54–61, Cantor, J., Stutman, S., & Duran, V., *What parents want in a television rating system: Results of a national survey*. Report released by the National PTA, the Institute for Mental Health Initiatives, and the University of Wisconsin-Madison, November 21, 1996; Media Studies Center/ Roper, *Poll finds public support for content over age-based TV rating system*. Arlington, VA: The Freedom Forum, December 12, 1996; Mifflin, L., New ratings codes for television get mixed reviews from parents,*New York Times*, February 22, 1997. p. 1, 6; Bash, A., Parents crave a clearer TV ratings code. (Yankelovich poll). *USA Today*, March 18, 1997, p. 3D.
60. Joel Federman (editor), *National Television Violence Study, Volume 2: Executive Summary*. Santa Barbara, CA: Center for Communication and Social Policy, 1997; Joanne Cantor, et. al., "Ratings and Advisories for Television Programming," in Center for Communication and Social Policy (editor), *National Television Violence Study, Volume 2* (pp. 267–322). Thousand Oaks: Sage Publications, 1997.
61. Motion Picture Association of America, et. al., *Agreement on Modifications to the TV Parental Guidelines*, July 10, 1997.
62. Jack Valenti, et. al., (January 17, 1997), op. cit., p. 4.
63. Letter from Jack Valenti, President and CEO, Motion Picture Association of America; Decker Anstrom, President and CEO, National Cable Television Association; and Eddie Fritts, President and CEO, National Association of Broadcasters; to William F. Caton, Secretary, Federal Communications Commission, January 17, 1997, p. 4.
64. Ibid., pp. 1 2
65. Rosalyn Weinman, "Rate the Ratings: 'C' for Complex," *New York Times*, July 15, 1997; Howard Rosenberg, "Holdout by NBC to Provide Real Test," *Los Angeles Times*, July 30, 1997.
66. Brooks Bolick, "NBC Steps Up TV Advisories," *The Hollywood Reporter*, July 25–27, 1997.
67. Steve Weinstein, "Premium Cable Channels Adopt Content Labels," *Los Angeles Times*, June 8, 1994; HBO/Showtime, *HBO/Showtime Content Advisories and Descriptions*, February 9, 1994, p. 1.
68. Pearlena Igbokwe, Director of Original Programming, Showtime Networks, Inc. Telephone Communication, April 17, 1996.
69. Steve Weinstein, "Premium Cable Channels Adopt Content Labels," *Los Angeles Times*, June 8, 1994; HBO/Showtime, *HBO/Showtime Content Advisories and Descriptions*, February 9, 1994, p. 1.
70. Ibid.
71. Ibid.
72. Paul Russinoff, Director of State Relations, Recording Industry Association of America, to Stephanie Carbone. Written Correspondence, December 1, 1995.
73. *Remarks by Senator Bob Dole, Los Angeles, California, May 31, 1995*.
74. "Time Warner to Abandon Gangsta Rap," *The Los Angeles Times*, Sept. 28, 1995.
75. RIAA/NARM press release, "Recording Industry Responds to Concerns About Music Lyrics—Announces Enhanced Parental Advisory Program," October 24, 1995.

76. Interactive Digital Software Association, *The Interactive Entertainment Rating System*, Fact Sheet, 1994.
77. Letter from Arthur Pober, Executive Director, Entertainment Software Rating Board, to Joel Federman, University of California, Santa Barbara, October 20, 1997.
78. Jack Heistand, Chairman, Interactive Digital Software Association, Testimony Before the Senate Subcommittee on Regulation and Government Information and the Senate Subcommittee on Juvenile Justice. July 29, 1994, p. 2.
79. Ibid., p. 7.
80. Arthur Pober, Executive Director, Entertainment Software Rating Board, to Joel Federman. Written Correspondence, May 2, 1996.
81. *Recreational Software Advisory Council—A Plan for an Independent Ratings Program.* Prepared by the Computer Game Ratings Working Group. Washington, DC. July 1994. pp. 3–5; Steven Balkam, Executive Director, Recreational Software Advisory Council. Telephone Communication, May 24, 1996.
82. Ibid., p. 6.
83. Mark Traphagen, Counsel, Software Publishers Association. Telephone Communication, September 14, 1994.
84. *Recreational Software Advisory Council: A Plan for an Independent Ratings Program.* p. 6.
85. For a review of these blocking technologies, see Joel Federman, *Media Ratings: Design, Use and Consequences.* Studio City, CA: Mediascope, 1996.
86. "PICS Picks Up Partners," *Multimedia Daily*, March 15, 1996, p. 1.
87. Clair Whitmer, "Browsers to Help Parents Monitor Net," *c/net news*, February 29, 1996.
88. "PICS Picks Up Partners," *Multimedia Daily*, March 15, 1996, p. 1.
89. Peter H. Lewis, "Microsoft Backs Rating System for the Internet," *New York Times,* March 1, 1996.
90. Leslie Miller, "System to Help Net Ratings Catches On," *USA Today*, March 14, 1996, p. 5D.
91. Peter H. Lewis, "Internet Ratings Backed Microsoft to Make Cyber-Filter System," *Los Angeles Daily News*, March 1, 1996, p. B1.
92. "Group Unveils Rating System for Online Content," *NetGuide's NetDaily News Roundup*, March 1, 1996.
93. Entertainment Software Rating Board Interactive, *ESRBI* (Draft Prospectus), October 20, 1997.
94. Joel Federman (editor), *National Television Violence Study, Volume 2: Executive Summary.* Santa Barbara, CA: Center for Communication and Social Policy, 1997; Joanne Cantor, et. al., "Ratings and Advisories for Television Programming," in Center for Communication and Social Policy (editor), *National Television Violence Study, Volume 2* (pp. 267–322*).* Thousand Oaks: Sage Publications, 1997.
95. The RSAC "Nudity/Sex" classifications give an "All rating" for romance and innocent kissing; a "1" for "passionate kissing;" a "2" for "clothed sexual touching," a "3" for "non-explicit sexual touching" or "non-explicit sexual acts;" and a "4" for "explicit sexual acts" and "sex crimes.

CHAPTER SEVEN

Who Will Rate the Ratings?

James T. Hamilton

I. INTRODUCTION

In January 1997, the presidents of the National Association of Broadcasters, National Cable Television Association, and the Motion Picture Association of America jointly presented the Federal Communications Commission with a description of the television industry's initial version of a rating system, the TV Parental Guidelines. After the industry submitted its initial plan, the Federal Communications Commission issued a notice seeking comment on the industry's proposal, specifying:

> In particular, we seek comment on whether the industry proposal is "acceptable." Parties should specifically identify the factors they believe the Commission should consider in making this determination. We also seek comment on whether the industry proposal satisfies Congress' concerns.[1]

In July 1997, the industry committee amended the TV Parental Guidelines to include indicators for violence (V), sexual situations (S), adult language (L), and suggestive dialogue (D).

In directing the FCC to determine whether the industry program rating system is "acceptable" without further defining this term, Congress potentially delegated significant decisions to the agency. Congress frequently transfers decision-making authority to agencies, in part to take advantage of their expertise and in part from a desire to pass symbolic legislation that earns credits with constituents.[2] Congress members may have had yet another reason for using a vague term such as "acceptable" in the Telecommunications

Act, since more specific language defining the parameters of a rating system could cause the courts to rule the rating system legislation violated the First Amendment. Spitzer (1998) argues that government pressure and legislation leading to the industry's adoption of the V-chip rating system mean that the courts may determine that the industry's "voluntary" system is in reality a product of state action, and hence subject to First Amendment scrutiny. If Congress had been more explicit in defining the form of the content ratings, then this might raise the probability that the system would be open to a successful constitutional challenge. As in many areas of media regulation, vague legislative language here may stem from concerns about possible First Amendment challenges.

In submitting the initial version of the TV Parental Guidelines system to the FCC in January 1997, the industry representatives who headed up the committee that designed the ratings made arguments consistent with the "congressional intent" and "plain meaning" doctrines (see Valenti, Anstrom, and Fritts, 1997). As the industry's filing noted:

> . . . if the industry develops a voluntary system of guidelines, as it has, Congress did not expect the Commission to develop its own rating system; the Commission is to act only if the industry fails to. To be sure, the Act authorizes the Commission to appoint the advisory committee if the industry-developed system is not "acceptable." But that proviso does not alter Congress' express understanding that it was principally looking for guidelines adopted by the industry. Nor does it permit the Commission to substitute its own judgment of what might be the "best" system for the industry's choice.[3]

The submission by Valenti, Anstrom, and Fritts presented quotations from the *Congressional Record* to bolster the industry's interpretation of congressional intent behind the V-chip legislation. The filing also offers a "plain meaning" approach to interpretation of the FCC's responsibilities under the legislation, noting:

> Further, Congress' use of the word "acceptable" also confirms that it did not intend for the Commission to demand that an industry-developed system of guidelines conform to the Commission's own or anyone else's vision of an ideal program. Given the absence of a specific definition of the term in the Act or its legislative history, the Commission should be guided by its general meaning. *Webster's Third International* defines "acceptable" as a thing that is "capable or worthy of being accepted;" as something that is "satisfactory: conforming to or equal to approved standards;" and as "barely satisfactory or adequate." Thus, if the industry-developed system is designed to accomplish Congress' stated goals, then it must be deemed "acceptable" by the Commission.[4]

When the initial age-based rating system was announced by the industry, children's advocacy groups were highly critical of the system because it failed to provide parents with specific content information about the levels of violence or sexual content in programs. In making its case, the coalition of interest groups that supported content-based ratings also relied on congressional intent and legislative history in arguing that the FCC should find that the initial TV Parental Guidelines were not "acceptable." As the reply comments filed by the Center for Media Education, et al. (1997) concluded:

> Finally, proponents of the industry system wishfully, yet mistakenly, claim that mere industry action in developing a ratings system satisfies the legal requirements of the V-chip provision. The provision expressly states that, in order to obviate the need for an advisory committee, the FCC must find that the industry has voluntarily established an "acceptable" ratings system. The legislative history clearly shows that an "acceptable" system must specifically identify violent content and provide parents with the information necessary for them to make programming choices for their children.[5]

Members of Congress filed comments with the FCC in a letter arguing their interpretation of congressional intent meant that the industry's age-based ratings should not be approved by the agency. They indicated that the industry rating system "has the effect of obscuring, not identifying the actual content of programming." They declared that:

> As Members of Congress who support the V-chip amendment to the Telecommunications Act of 1996, several of whom participated in the actual drafting of this amendment, we offer these comments concerning Congress's intent in approving this legislation and sending it to the President for his signature. It is our view that the age-based ratings system proposed by the industry undermines the usefulness of the V-chip to such an extent that the purposes of the statute cannot be fulfilled.[6]

In this essay, I explore factors that might be considered in evaluating a rating system. The Telecommunications Act of 1996 provides little in the way of guidance as to how this can or should be done. Under the legislation, the Federal Communications Commission was charged with determining—if video programming distributors submitted voluntary rules (as they did)—whether that rating system is "acceptable." The standard I will use in evaluating the rating system is efficiency, the utilitarian framework implicitly used in economic assessments of regulations across many federal agencies.[7] In this work I will examine the economic rationale for government intervention to facilitate a program rating system and describe the individual incentives faced by parents and programmers concerned about television ratings. Though I ultimately conclude that one cannot use cost-benefit analysis here to quantify the gains and losses associated with the implementation of the V-chip and rating system, viewing the development of the rating system as an economic problem does offer insights into what the agency should do to implement the Telecommunications Act of 1996. In particular, the analysis here suggests that the broadcast industry will generally be reluctant to provide parents with detailed content information about programs because of fear of advertiser backlash. The agency's freedom to develop rules on the design of the V-chip, however, provides it with an opportunity to encourage the spread of a technology capable of reading multiple rating systems. With the expansion of broadcasting to digital signals, ratings other than the industry classification may be broadcast to televisions equipped with viewing software. To the extent that the FCC can encourage the use of a V-chip architecture capable of reading multiple rating systems, the agency could accept the industry's revised rating system while fostering competition from other rating sources.

II. WHY INTERVENE IN THE MARKET FOR PROGRAM INFORMATION?

Television violence is a product of market forces. Men aged 18 to 34 are the top adult consumers of violent entertainment programming, while women aged 18 to 34 are the second highest consumers of such programming.[8] Companies trying to reach these demographic groups will support violent shows. Cable channels in search of younger viewers will also use violent content strategically to build audiences and establish a brand name. Though broadcast networks and cable channels use violence to attract young adult viewers, the exposure of children aged 2 to 11 or teens aged 12 to 17 arises as a by-product of programming strategies. Broadcast stations are not rewarded by advertisers for attracting children to violent prime-time shows, for children are not the target audience of the products advertised on these shows. Similarly, cable renewal decisions by heads of households are unlikely to be influenced by a desire to afford children the opportunity to view unedited theatrical films containing violence. The exposure of children to violent shows represents a market failure, since neither advertisers nor programmers will consider the costs to society of children's consumption of violent fare. Though substantial research indicates that violent programming may, among some children, increase aggressive behavior, fear, or desensitization toward violence, these concerns are external to the profit maximization decisions faced by those in industry. The negative effects generated by television violence are similar to those of pollution, since in both instances companies may impose damages on society without factoring these social costs into their production decisions.[9]

If violence on television harms children, then parents should want to shield them from exposure, thereby creating a demand for products to make television "safer" for children. Federman (1996) details the large number of consumer discretion technologies available that do allow parents to block particular channels or programs. These safeguards come at an extra cost to television purchasers, however, so that parents will weigh the cost of additional technology and additional time spent programming devices versus the benefits of shielding their children from violent content. Though some parents will buy additional technology and invest time in monitoring their children's viewing, from society's perspective they will do this in less than optimal amounts. Parents will consider the reduced likelihood that their children will become aggressive or experience fright in making their decisions about how much effort to devote to monitoring television viewing. Yet parents will not factor in the broader benefits to society from shielding their children from violent programming, such as the reduced likelihood that their children will impose negative costs on others as a result of aggressive or violent behavior. This means that parents will fail to devote enough effort from society's perspective to protecting their children from violent programming.

This argument is demonstrated more formally in the graph in figure 1, which describes how many hours of a child's viewing that a parent will monitor. The costs of

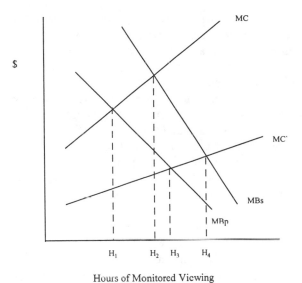

$
MC
MC'
MBs
MBp
H₁   H₂ H₃   H₄

Hours of Monitored Viewing

FIG. 1. Parental Monitoring

monitoring an hour of programming include information costs and other transaction costs (e.g., what type of violent or sexual content is in this program? how can I know what programs are on what channels?) and the opportunity cost of time spent checking to make sure that children are not watching a particular program. The costs of monitoring another hour of programming are reflected in the marginal cost curve MC in the diagram. Parents will consider the private benefits of shielding their children from objectionable program-ming, such as the reduced likelihood that the children will be stimulated to aggression. If parents block the most dangerous programs first, the marginal private benefits of moni-toring decline with each additional hour monitored, as reflected in the curve MBp. Parents trading off the benefits and costs of monitoring viewing would monitor up to the point where the additional costs of monitoring equal the additional benefits of shielding children from viewing, i.e., H₁ hours of viewing.

From society's perspective, the optimal amount of monitored viewing would be H₂ hours. If parents took into account the full benefits to society of shielding their children from television violence, then they would calculate the benefits by the values reflected in the curve MBs, and would therefore engage in H₂ hours of monitoring. The difference between the private and social benefits of monitoring creates an argument for policies designed to increase parental action to shield children from violent programming. If programs carried informative ratings about violent and sexual content and parents could easily access this information, this would lower information costs for parents. If televisions carried V-chips that allowed parents to block programs based on informative ratings, this would lower the opportunity costs of the time devoted to making sure that children were not watching programs the parents deemed inappropriate. In a world of informative ratings and V-chip technology, parents would thus face lower marginal costs to monitoring children's viewing, as reflected in the curve MC'. This curve is below the previous marginal cost curve and rises more slowly since the fixed costs of becoming informed and the opportunity costs of additional hours of monitoring are reduced by the V-chip (e.g., the parent only needs to check on viewing intermittently). Parents with the advantage of ratings and the V-chip would find shielding their children less costly and would end up monitoring more hours of viewing (H_3). Even in a world of enhanced technology, parents would not engage in the optimal amount of monitoring (H_4). Reductions in the costs of becoming informed about program content and acting on this information, however, would lead to more parental monitoring and the added benefits of shielding children from violent programming.

The graph in figure 1 leaves out many factors that a full cost-benefit analysis of a rating system and the V-chip would incorporate. It does not reflect the costs of developing and implementing a rating system, nor does it reflect the costs to parents of purchasing a V-chip. The analysis also leaves unanswered what "informative" ratings for parents would consist of and what incentives the industry would have to develop such ratings. The following sections explore in more detail evidence on the incentives of parents to demand and programmers to develop particular types of program rating information.

III. VIEWER INCENTIVES

A number of factors determine the success of systems designed to provide information about products, including the dimensions of product attributes described, the specific wording used, the availability of the information in the market, and the ease with which a consumer can process the information.[10] Each of these factors will influence how useful parents will find a given type of rating system for television programs. Three different types of evidence indicate how parents (and children) may evaluate and react to different program rating formats: public opinion surveys about the potential design of program content indicators; lab experiments that gauge the reaction of parents and children to various types of program labels; and field evidence from the implementation of viewer discretion warnings and the TV Parental Guidelines system.

Federman (1996) notes that program rating formats may be categorized as *descriptive* (e.g., providing information on the type of content in a television show) or *evaluative* (e.g., recommending parental discretion or indicating the appropriateness of the program for a given age group). In the debate over television program ratings in the United States, survey data have repeatedly indicated that parents prefer ratings that provide indications of content information rather than ratings that make recommendations about the appropriateness of programs for particular viewing audiences. For example, the survey by Cantor, Stutman, and Duran (1996) indicates the preference of parents for content-based rather than age-based ratings. This study, supported by the National PTA, found that parents expressed high degrees of concern about the effects of television programs containing violence, sex, and profanity.[11] The level of parents' concern about particular types of content varied with the age and gender of their children, which leads the researchers to note that content indicators would allow parents to evaluate programs more readily based on the importance they attached to specific types of content. When asked in the survey whether there should be "an overall summary rating of a program" or "separate ratings for different types of content, such as violence, sex, and language," 80% of the parents surveyed indicated a preference for separate indicators rather than a summary rating. When asked whether a program rating should indicate "what age of the child the program is appropriate or inappropriate for" or simply indicate "what the content of the program is (i.e., amount or type of sex, violence, and language)," 80% of the parents selected the content-based ratings rather than the age-based ratings. Although the initial TV Parental Guidelines system implemented in January 1997 used a summary indicator (e.g., TV-14) and categorized programs based in part on recommended ages of viewers (e.g., TV-Y7, TV-14), parents in survey data consistently reported that a content-based rating system would be superior to an age-based system.[12]

In addition to the Cantor, Stutman, and Duran survey, polls by the Yankelovich Partners and by the *New York Times* indicate that a substantial majority of respondents prefer a content-based system.[13] The Valenti, Anstrom, and Fritts January 1997 filing with the FCC included a summary of survey data entitled "National survey shows widespread support by parents for TV Parental Guidelines," which at first might seem to contradict the other polling information discussed here. Yet the survey of 1,207 parents conducted in December 1996 by Peter D. Hart Research Associates and Public Opinion Strategies frames the evaluation of the rating system in a different light. Rather than reporting the results of asking parents to choose among alternative rating systems, the Hart survey questions reported in the FCC filing have parents evaluate the TV Parental Guidelines alone. The Hart survey found that "90 percent of America's parents favored the TV Parental Guidelines system as it has been created, with 58 percent 'strongly' in favor and 32 percent 'somewhat' in favor." In their filing with the FCC, Valenti, Anstrom and Fritts indicate that the question before the Commission is whether the TV Parental Guidelines are "acceptable" rather than an "ideal program."[14] Their use of polling data to indicate approval or disapproval of the rating system chosen by the industry committee rather than reliance on polling data that gauged parental support for different types of rating systems is consistent with their interpretation of the standard (i.e., "acceptable" ratings) they are trying to meet.

Data from laboratory experiments offer another indication of how parents and children react to ratings. Cantor and Kremar found in a study of seventy parent-child dyads in a lab setting that these groups strongly avoided choosing programs carrying the advisory "Contains some violence. Parental discretion advised." Parents with younger children were especially likely to indicate in discussions with their children that programs with advisories had inappropriate content.[15] Most other lab studies of ratings have focused on how the wording of program labels may influence the viewing selection of child or teen viewers left to make their own viewing decisions based on program guide descriptions. In the 1996 National Television Violence Study, Cantor and Harrison found that varying the wording of viewer discretion warnings and varying the use of Motion Picture Association of America (MPAA) ratings in viewing guides affected children's willingness to select particular programs. They concluded:

The well known admonition, "parental discretion advised" had a strong and positive effect on boys' interest in viewing reality-action programs, and the effect was strongest for boys in the older group. This same advisory had no impact on girls' tendency to choose such programs. In contrast, another frequently used advisory, "viewer discretion advised," did not increase boys' interest in viewing police-detective shows, but it decreased girls' (and especially younger girls') choices of such programs.

The MPAA ratings "G," "PG," "PG-13," and "R" also strongly affected children's desire to see a movie. Older boys were especially interested in the target movie when it was rated "PG-13" or "R" and completely avoided it when it was rated "G."[16]

In the 1997 National Television Violence Study, Cantor, Harrison, and Nathanson tested different rating and advisory systems by examining how descriptions in viewing guides affected the program selections of 374 children between age five and fifteen participating in their experiments. They were particularly interested in examining whether some types of program information increase children's interest because of a "forbidden fruit" effect where restricted behavior appears more desirable or because of an "information effect" where some children may choose to view programs with advisories because they seek out more violent content. They concluded:

> Not only did the higher level MPAA ratings make movies more attractive to older children, they were the only one of six ratings systems tested to attract children to restricted content. Moreover, these restrictive ratings attracted younger children who like to watch television the most and who by their own admission get involved in fights with other children more frequently. Finally, the MPAA rating of "PG-13" was especially attractive to older children who like to watch violent television.

> Of all the rating systems tested, then, the "forbidden fruit" effect turned out to be strongest for the rating system most like the one that has been adopted by the television industry. The new rating system seems likely to produce the same effect, because it, too, provides guidance on the appropriate age for viewing while exhorting parental control over children's access to programs.[17]

"Field" evidence on how parents and children actually use program information offers a third source of data on viewer reactions. In 1993, the broadcast networks announced they would place viewer discretion warnings on violent programming. A study of the impact of viewer discretion warnings placed on prime-time broadcast network movies from 1987 through 1993 indicates that viewing does change if programmers provide information about content (see Hamilton, 1998). Broadcast network movies that carried viewer warnings had, other things being equal, Nielsen ratings among children aged 2 to 11 that were 14% lower than movies without the warnings.[18] This is consistent with parents acting on these warnings and intervening in the viewing decisions of their children, which may be more likely in prime time than in other periods when parents may not be home when children are viewing. The placement of a viewer warning dropped a movie's audience by approximately 222,000 children aged 2 to 11. Ratings among teens and adults were not affected by the viewer discretion advisories.

Six weeks into the implementation of the TV Parental Guidelines, the *New York Times* survey of parents indicated awareness of the program outpaced its use in viewing decisions. In the *Times* poll, "86 percent of the parents approve of the idea of such ratings, and 73 percent say they have noticed the ratings on their television screens, but only 37 percent say they have used the ratings to guide their viewing choices."[19] The level of ratings use by parents will depend, in part, on how widely available they are. Though *TV Guide* added two to three pages per issue in order to include the TV Parental Guidelines ratings, many newspapers appear reluctant to include the program rating information in their daily television grids.[20] The ultimate level of use of the TV Parental Guidelines should shift once the V-chip technology spreads. This will lower the transaction costs of parents of using program information, since parents can simply set the program indicator levels on the television and rely on this to screen out shows with higher ratings. Parents will still need to monitor children's viewing, but the costs of incorporating program information into viewing decisions will be radically lower once televisions carry V-chips capable of reading program ratings.[21]

IV. PROGRAMMER INCENTIVES

The debate over the format of a television program rating system is often framed as a disagreement between academics or interest groups concerned with children and industry participants concerned about parental demand for types of program information. This framing obscures the fact that parents are simply one of the many groups whose interests were considered by the committee that designed the TV Parental Guidelines. The concerns of program producers, who worried about impingement on creative freedom, and of advertisers, who were afraid of consumer backlash against supporting particular types of programs, also influenced the industry committee in its selection of rating formats. Controversy can be costly in the programming market. Some advertisers will fear association with a program's content if it raises the probability they will become the target of a consumer boycott or increases the chance their brand image will be otherwise damaged. When the American Family Association focused attention on *NYPD Blue* during the fall 1993 television season, advertising time on the program at first sold at a 45% discount because of sponsors' fear of consumer backlash.[22] By the fall of 1995 the program had won critical acclaim and controversy had dissipated, so that advertising no longer sold at a discount. Even if controversy is short-lived, programmers sensitive to advertiser concerns may fear initial impacts on advertising prices and long-term impact on demand for violent programs as they consider the effects of program content ratings on advertiser decisions.

Broadcaster experiences with the parental discretion warnings placed on network prime-time movies offer some evidence for the incentives created by program labeling. Hamilton (1998) demonstrates that the placement of a warning on a prime-time broadcast network movie between 1987 and 1993 reduced the viewership of the film among children aged 2 to 11 by 14%, or 222,000 children. The warnings had no impact on ratings of teens or adults. Since children are not the target of advertisers on prime-time broadcast network films, one might assume that the fact that adult audiences remain unchanged should mean that advertiser behavior does not change if a movie receives a warning label. The placement of a label on a film such as "Due to some violent content, parental discretion is advised," however, may make it more likely that a firm is associated with support for "violent content." In theory, advertisers will face different incentives to react to the prospect of consumer backlash caused by support of violent programming depending on the demographics of who consumes their products.

Assessments of advertiser reactions to movie warnings bear out that the amount of paid advertising and the identity of advertisers changes when viewer warnings are placed on network broadcast movies. Don Ohlmeyer of NBC has indicated that the placement of a warning on movies causes some advertisers to pull out of sponsorship, though these ad spots are sometimes sold to other firms willing to trade potential association with controversy for a lower ad price.[23] In studying a sample of over 19,000 commercials on 251 broadcast network movies shown during 1995 and 1996, I found that the violent theatrical films that carried warnings had fewer general product ads and more network promotions than violent theatrical films without warnings. This is consistent with advertiser pullouts causing prices to drop and leading networks to be more willing to run internal promotions. Companies with products whose customers are less likely to be offended by television violence, e.g., males or younger viewers, may be more willing to buy time on movies with warnings since they face less consumer backlash.[24] In analyzing ads on broadcast network movies, I found:

> Violent theatrical films with warnings were more likely to have products aimed at younger consumers, males, and households without children. Products aimed at these consumers, such as sports and leisure and alcoholic beverages, are more likely to advertise on theatrical movies with warnings. Products from industries where "family" brand images are important, such as food or kitchen products, are less likely to sponsor ads on theatrical films with warnings.[25]

If broadcasters fear that labeling programs will cause prices to drop and the mix of advertisers to change, then one would expect they would be less willing to label truly violent programming as "violent." The UCLA Center for Communication Policy studies, funded by the broadcast networks, and the National Television Violence Study, supported by the cable industry, all indicate that in the 1994–95 and 1995–96 television seasons violent programming often went unlabeled on the broadcast networks. For the 1994–95 television season, the UCLA Center (1995) found that of 118 theatrical films shown on the broadcast networks, 50 raised issues of concern with respect to violence but 22 of these films did not carry viewer warnings. The UCLA study (1996) found improvement in the 1995–96 season, with only 33 of 113 theatrical films raising issues of concern about use of violent content (and only 10 of the 33 films lacked warnings). In its analysis of a composite week of television on broadcast and cable channels during the 1995–96 season, the NTVS researchers found that overall only 5% of the programs that contained violence carried viewer advisories.[26]

Do the incentives of network programmers to avoid advertiser backlash affect their application of the TV Parental Guidelines? One way to measure this would be to examine the content of a sample of programs shown on television in 1997 and compare TV Parental Guideline ratings with the content of the programs. As another way to examine this question, I have compared how the TV Parental Guideline ratings relate to program ratings from the Parents Television Council (PTC). If broadcast networks fear advertiser backlash, they should be less willing to use "higher" content codes than interest groups. In addition, broadcasters concerned about a potential drop in advertising prices should be more willing to "underlabel" shows with higher advertising rates.

Both these hypotheses are confirmed by data from the early implementation of the TV Parental Guidelines. For all rated prime-time program episodes (except movies) on the six broadcast networks from January 25 through April 18, 1997 (N=1,039 shows), 22.9% were rated TV-G, 65.7% were rated TV-PG, and 11.4% were rated TV-14. The Parents Television Council rated these programs at the start of the 1996–97 television season into three categories: green ("family-friendly show promoting responsible themes and traditional values"); yellow ("series' adult-oriented themes and dialogue may be inappropriate for youngsters"); or red ("may include gratuitous sex, explicit dialogue, violent content, or obscene language, and is unsuitable for children").[27] The PTC ratings of these programs (N=904 episodes) at the start of the season placed 25.3% in the green category, 50.9% in the yellow, and 23.8% in the red. The interest group was much more willing than programmers to place programs in the most controversial rating classification.[28] From the perspective of the Parents Television Council ratings, the programs the industry "underlabeled" had higher advertising prices (as measured at the beginning of the season, before the rating system could effect prices).[29] For the programs rated by the PTC as red, the average 1996 fall ad price per 30-second commercial was $253,000 for those "red" programs the networks rated as TV-PG. The average 1996 fall ad price for the "red" programs that the networks were willing to rate as TV-14 was $198,000. The prospects for controversy and advertiser backlash may thus lead broadcast programmers to "underlabel" content in programs that earn higher advertising rates.

Though fears of advertiser reactions may drive broadcast programmers to resist content-based ratings, arguments about the costs of implementing program ratings that convey the specific presence of violence, sex, or adult language have also been offered as potential explanations for why the industry should not offer more information in program ratings. Several factors indicate, however, that the industry could provide low-cost content ratings. Since programmers need to establish viewer expectations about program content, shows are likely to contain similar content across weeks. In the January to April 1997 sample of 130 prime-time, regularly scheduled program series on the six broadcast networks, 11 had no ratings (because they were news programs), 89 had the same category ratings across episodes, and 30 had two different ratings depending on episode content during the sample period. I have found that based simply on the genre of a program, one can correctly predict 90 percent of the time whether a program contains a number of violent acts per hour greater than the average number for prime-time network broadcast shows.[30] A great deal of content information exists that is currently not made public to viewers. Advertisers may receive detailed information on prime-time network broadcast programming prior to its airing from AIS, a company that prescreens such programming and alerts advertisers to potential concerns they might have because of their customer demographics.

The notion that broadcasters would have to bear significant additional expenses to ascertain whether their programs contained violent or sexual content ignores the fact that these product attributes are explicitly used by the broadcast networks to build audiences. Consider table 1, reproduced from Hamilton, 1998. These results indicate that for movies shown on the four major broadcast networks from 1987 through 1993, overall, the networks strategically used certain types of violent content more often during sweeps months, when local ratings are measured and advertising rates thus established. Movies with murder themes, family crime themes, or a true crime focus were all aired more frequently during sweeps months than in nonsweeps months. Programmers explicitly analyzed their use of movies along these dimensions. Assessing the performance of films during the 1993–94 season, Ted Harbert, then the president of ABC Entertainment, said:

> . . . this season, ABC's best performance was with family crime. The domestic crisis movies that were nonviolent averaged a point lower than the true crime movies and two points lower than the family crime movies.[31]

Analysis of the scheduling of 11,000 films shown from 6:00 A.M. to midnight on 32 channels from February 1995 to March 1996 indicates that the strategic use of violence by broadcast and cable channels to build audiences still continues. In analyzing the use of films during this time period, I found:

> Channels specifically schedule particular types of violent programming at given days and times, so that viewers will have an expectation that violence will be used in that programming. At times this is a publicly announced marketing campaign, such as TNT's "Saturday Nitro" programming of violent films at 10 P.M. on Saturdays. In other cases it is a programming strategy pursued privately without fanfare, such as HBO's counterprogramming of violent films on Thursdays at 9 P.M. to compete with *Seinfeld* in 1995. The changes in the use of violence and sexual content during sweeps months when ratings are measured provide strong evidence that these movie characteristics are strategically chosen to develop audiences.[32]

During the 1995–96 sample period, I found that Fox increased its use of violent movies from 42.1% of films during nonsweeps months to 84.2% during sweeps periods. Similarly, the basic cable "superstation" WGN had violent films 70.1% of the time in nonsweeps periods and 88.7% during sweeps. Strategic decisions about whether and when to offer violent and sexual content thus indicate that programmers do possess information on program content they could summarize and provide to viewers.

TABLE 1

**Use of Violent Content in Prime-Time Broadcast Network Movies,
Sweeps vs. Non-Sweeps Months, 1987–1993**

	% of Films in		
	Sweeps Months (N=944)	Non-Sweeps Months (N=1,723)	Difference of Proportions Test (Z Statistic)
Murder Theme	32.7	28.9	2.1**
Family Crime Theme	6.5	3.3	3.8***
True Story	23.2	16.5	4.2***
True Murder	10.7	4.6	5.9***
True Family Crime	4.2	1.6	4.2***
TV Guide Ad Features Homicide	13.9	9.5	3.4***
TV Guide Ad Features Dead Body	0.9	0.3	2.0**
TV Guide Indicates Film is Particularly Violent	4.1	3.1	1.3
Warning Provided	2.8	3.3	-0.7
Murder Theme and Warning Provided	1.0	2.0	-2.0**

Note: ***=Statistically significant at 1% level
**=Statistically significant at 5% level

If broadcast networks chose a program ratings system based on the concerns of parents rather than advertisers, what might such a system look like? The rating format used by premium channels offers a natural contrast to the decisions of broadcast networks, since premium channels do not carry advertising and therefore are not constrained by advertiser concerns. The content advisory format used by HBO and Showtime includes, in addition to the provision of MPAA ratings for movies, the possible use of ten indicators: adult language (AL); graphic language (GL); mild violence (MV); violence (V); graphic violence (GV); nudity (N); brief nudity (BN); adult content (AC); strong sexual content (SC); and rape (RP).[33] This system demonstrates that it is possible to design and implement a content-based program ratings system that would convey to parents information on levels of different types of material they might want to shield their children from.

Faced with heavy criticism of the age-based ratings system, the developers of the TV Parental Guidelines announced in July 1997 that the original rating system would be amended so that content indicators would be added to program ratings. Children's programs in the TV-Y7 category could be supplemented with an FV indicator for shows "where fantasy violence may be more intense or more combative."[34] Shows in the TV-PG, TV-14, or TV-MA categories could also carry indicators for content, but the meaning of these indicators would vary with the program category. For shows classified as TV-PG, the programs could carry indicators for "moderate violence (V), some sexual situations (S), infrequent coarse language (L), or some suggestive dialogue (D)." For shows in the TV-14 category, the new indicators would be used to denote "intense violence (V), intense sexual situations (S), strong coarse language (L), or intensely suggestive dialogue (D)." For shows in the TV-MA category, the indicators denote "graphic violence (V), explicit sexual content (S), or crude indecent language (L)." The major broadcast networks, with the exception of NBC, announced that they would adopt these new categories.

The development and implementation of the revised ratings underscores the importance of economics to the willingness of broadcasters to provide program information. Although the industry committee agreed to provide content indicators, the same indicator (V) is used to convey different levels of violence. Though the combination of the age-based rating and content indicator will alert a viewer to the intensity of violence, the industry committee (cognizant of the concerns of broadcasters and advertisers) developed a scheme that avoided the use of premium channel indicators that directly convey content intensity (e.g., GV for graphic violence). The television industry committee agreed to the revised guidelines in part in exchange for assurances from advocacy groups and some legislators that they would not press for additional legislation directed at content. Potential losses from advertisers were thus balanced against potential losses from future legislative activity, including proposals dealing with an auction of the spectrum rights which broadcasters currently enjoy for free.[35] Describing the calculations that went into the revised guidelines, MPAA president Jack Valenti declared, "This is not what I would've done if I didn't think I had to. We went into these negotiations for one reason, and that was to shut the flow of legislation that we thought was inimical to our future and that may trespass on the First Amendment."[36]

When the revised guidelines were announced in July 1997, NBC issued a statement declaring, "The ultimate aim of the current system's critics is to dictate programming content. NBC is disappointed that the industry capitulated to political and special-interest pressure and did not look more seriously at the implications of the flawed process in which they engaged. Therefore, NBC will not be a part of the new agreement."[37] The network's resistance to adopting content indicators was hailed by some in the television industry as a principled defense of creative freedom. The network may also have had the most to lose in advertiser backlash, however, if program ratings were made more specific. Analysis of the PTC program ratings indicates that among the four major broadcast networks NBC had the highest mean 1996 ad price for episodes of shows rated as red by the PTC, a classification the group used for shows containing "gratuitous sex, explicit dialogue, violent content, or obscene language."[38] The network may have thus feared that more content indicators would result in higher backlashes among advertisers on its successful prime-time programs.

V. DIFFICULTIES IN APPLYING A COST-BENEFIT FRAMEWORK

Television violence represents a market failure, since programmers and advertisers may not consider the full costs to society of scheduling and sponsoring violent programs. They do not incorporate the increased likelihood of aggression, fear, and desensitization that may arise among some children from exposure to violent images in television programs. Parents who believe television violence is harmful may act to shield their children from such programming.[39] Since they do not calculate the broader benefits to society from protecting their children from violent programming, parents will not engage in the optimal amount of program monitoring from society's point of view.

This reasoning demonstrates that the actions of programmers and parents are likely to be inefficient. Programmers will offer more violent shows or shows with greater amounts of violence than they would if they considered the social damages arising from these programs. Parents will fail to monitor children's viewing sufficiently to protect them from violent programs. The existence of these market failures, however, does not guarantee the existence of a remedy to correct these problems. In correcting the negative externalities that arise from pollution, analysts often use cost-benefit analysis to examine whether there are net gains from the imposition of a particular policy. In analyzing whether a particular ratings system would pass a cost-benefit test, however, there are at least two major impediments to the answering this question—the imprecision of damage estimates and the special nature of values associated with free expression.

Extensive research exists on how the context of violent portrayals may influence viewer reactions to violent content. A key innovation of the National Television Violence Study (1996) is the development of a coding scheme to describe violent content that is based on research about media effects. The NTVS researchers identified a large set of contextual factors that laboratory experiments and other research indicate may influence learning of aggression, fear, and desensitization: attractive perpetrator; attractive target; justified violence; unjustified violence; presence of weapons; extensive/graphic violence; realistic violence; rewards; punishments; pain/harm cues; and humor.[40] These results may tell parents the types of programming they may wish to shield their children from. Yet the research is not developed enough to allow one to estimate the particular harms that will arise from the airing of a given program. Since many of the effects relating to stimulation of aggression or crime occur years after viewing, one cannot trace particular crimes to particular programs. The interactive effects of particular types of violent content have not been fully explored, so that one cannot know how the combination of the different harmful contexts identified by the NTVS researchers affects viewers. The research is sufficient to suggest that certain types of violent content are harmful, but the results are not developed enough to quantify the harms arising from particular programs. This quantification would be a key element in a cost-benefit analysis of a given rating system, for it would allow one to value the reduction in exposures of children to programming arising from the implementation of a rating system and the V-chip.

In the evaluation of environmental policies, "existence values" may play a prominent role in the analysis of the costs and benefits of a change in environmental outcomes. Consider, for example, the valuation of the preservation of the Grand Canyon. Some individuals will place a value on the preservation of this national park, even if they do not ever plan on visiting it. They may have a willingness to pay to preserve the park because they gain happiness from knowing it exists (i.e., an existence value) or because they wish to pass the park on to future generations (i.e., a bequest motive). Economists try to measure these values through the survey methodology of contingent valuation.[41] At least two types of existence values are evident in the debate over television violence. Some people involved in the debate may prefer a society without violence on television based on moral or ideological grounds, independent of any negative effects that violent content may have on behavior.

Others may place a value on free expression, independent of concerns about the negative outcomes that may arise from this expression. In a cost-benefit analysis of the particular form of program ratings, individuals who place a strong value on First Amendment freedoms may interpret a rating system as a product of government action. They may place a great value on the freedom of programmers to broadcast without placing ratings in their signals. In theory, the values placed on free expression would be measured through contingent valuation surveys, although here again the difficulties of empirical measurement could make this approach to incorporating First Amendment values into decision making extremely hard.

The imprecision of measuring damages from particular programs and the values placed on free expression mean that a cost-benefit analysis for a given rating system would be unlikely to yield empirical measures of costs or benefits. Another approach would assert that asking whether a rating system would pass a cost-benefit test is immaterial, since the First Amendment rules out rating systems because they are a product of state action.[42] This again parallels the treatment of some pollution problems, since the ability of regulators to consider the costs and benefits of particular instruments to control pollution will vary by the particulars of the specific environmental legislation setting up a program.[43]

VI. POLICY RECOMMENDATIONS

For an analyst judging policies by the standard of efficiency, the decisions about the optimal program rating system would involve consideration of the type of program information valued by parents, the accessibility and feasibility of using this information with the V-chip, and the transaction costs for the industry in designing and implementing the program. The industry letter from Valenti, Anstrom, and Fritts (1997) submitting the initial TV Parental Guidelines to the FCC makes clear that they believe that the Telecommunications Act of 1996 does not require the FCC to engage in such a search. They stress that the legislation's use of the word "acceptable" means that Congress "did not intend for the Commission to demand that an industry-developed system of guidelines conform to the Commission's own or anyone else's vision of an ideal program."[44]

The debate over the age-based system initially chosen by the industry and the content-based system supported by many educators and interest groups was often framed as a debate over what type of rating system would be "ideal" for parents. This essay has presented theoretical and empirical evidence on why the interests of parents and programmers may diverge in the design of a rating system. While content-based ratings could provide parents with more information to make viewing decisions, this information might also generate more backlash for advertisers. Consider, for example, the difference between the statement "Pepsico advertises on programs inappropriate for children under 14" and "Pepsico advertises on programs with graphic violence."[45] The latter statement might be more likely to damage the brand image of Pepsi and make the company a focus of interest group scrutiny. The revised guidelines announced in July 1997 represent a compromise between age-based and content-based systems, for they provide parents with some information on the intensity of violence or sexual content but do not make this information easily accessible as in the premium channel program rating system. How the FCC interprets whether the revised TV Parental Guidelines are "acceptable" may depend on the delegation doctrine invoked. Even if the agency were to reject the industry's system, the industry would be under no obligation to incorporate an alternative rating system in their broadcast signals. If Congress passed legislation requiring content-based ratings, this might increase the probability that the rating system would be found unconstitutional by the courts.

I believe that at least two policy lessons emerge from this analysis of the TV Parental Guidelines. The first is that the form of industry program ratings will be driven by profit maximization, just as the form of industry programming is. Broadcasters currently receive their licenses essentially for free, in return for a promise to broadcast in the "public interest, convenience, and necessity." Many analysts have interpreted the "public interest" requirement to be synonymous with profit maximization. Making this argument in the 1980s, FCC Chairman Mark Fowler declared that television is simply a "toaster with pictures," so that television programming should simply be left to the functioning of the free market.[46] With the backdrop of debates about a spectrum auction, industry participants often point to particular television practices (e.g., coverage of presidential debates, limited experiments with free time for presidential candidates) as evidence that networks will at times trade off profits for the "public interest." In the design of the rating system, the industry initially chose not to risk a reduction in profits for greater information for parents. After the threat of legislation that might impose additional costs on the industry, however, the industry committee adopted ratings that provided more content information. The reluctance of broadcast networks to provide more program content information than premium channels or some Internet sites does not stem from a greater distribution of altruism in these other media. The potential for advertiser backlash and the larger role that advertisers play in broadcast television means that networks have incentives to resist the provision of content-based information. Future debates about whether the broadcast spectrum should be auctioned should note whether the unwillingness of broadcasters to forego some profits affects the promised provision of content-based ratings by the broadcast networks.

A second policy lesson emerges from the prospect of the evolution of digital broadcasting and television technology. As the number of channels expands, television viewing may eventually involve software to aid viewer selections. In this world, software may include options to block out given types of programming (e.g., by genre), so that parents may be empowered to make choices at a low cost about what programs to shield their children from. The FCC may play a role in encouraging the use of more detailed ratings in its future rule making on the V-chip. The V-chip technology may already require some "reasoning," in the sense that the chip may have to differentiate between settings for children's shows (e.g. TV-Y, TV-Y7) and adult shows. Spitzer (1998) notes that the question exists about whether a program rated TV-Y7 will pass through a V-chip set for TV-PG. The FCC could, through its rule making on V-chip technology, encourage the adoption of technology capable of being used with multiple types of rating systems, so parents could choose to invoke one rating system or another through their use of the V-chip.

Questions about multiple ratings systems and V-chip technology have been debated in comments submitted during the FCC's consideration of the TV Parental Guidelines. The Consumer Electronics Manufacturers Association (1997, p. 2) argued for "the Commission's approval of a single consensus ratings system such as the Industry Proposal, with the understanding that, once established, the ratings system will not be changed in the foreseeable future." The association stressed that changes in a rating system made after technology had been placed in television sets could render some receivers obsolete. OKTV, a nonprofit developing its own program rating format based on research on program impacts on children, argued (1997a) for the development of a universal ratings format protocol that would facilitate the use of multiple rating systems. In its reply comments (1997b), OKTV, indicated that the FCC should adopt a "must-carry" policy so that television signals in line 21 of the vertical blanking interval will have to carry multiple program ratings. This would involve specification of a common ratings data structure, transmission protocol, and blocking technology, and would ultimately allow consumers to choose among different rating classifications carried in a signal. The Benton Foundation (1997) also proposed that alternative rating codes gain guaranteed rights of carriage in television signals. The American Medical Association (1997) urged the commission to adopt an "open" technological standard, so that if alternative ratings systems were developed in the future they would not be foreclosed by the design of the V-chip.

Currently television signals contain program identifiers that allow advertisers to more easily determine if ads have run during particular programs.[47] Programmers may be unwilling to include a rating other than the TV Parental Guideline indicator in a program's signal. In an era of digital broadcasting, however, a channel such as the local public broadcast station may be willing to transmit data on multiple program rating systems for shows on broadcast and cable channels in an area. Televisions could "download" this information, which would be used in conjunction with software and/or the V-chip to allow a viewer to draw on ratings from many different interest groups. If the FCC were dissatisfied with the TV Parental Guidelines submitted by the industry, the agency might still be able to encourage the proliferation and use of alternative rating systems through future decisions made about the design of the V-chip. Though broadcasters may be reluctant to provide viewers with detailed content information on programs, the possibilities for data transmission opened up by digital broadcasting mean that a single channel could transmit ratings information that could allow a television equipped with software to block programs based on detailed ratings. The FCC should investigate the degree that its decisions about the V-chip technology can ultimately encourage the use of multiple ratings systems.

Notes

1. Federal Communications Commission, 1997, p. 3.
2. For a discussion of congressional incentives and the delegation of decision-making power to agencies, see Arnold, 1990, and McCubbins, Noll, and Weingast, 1987.
3. See Valenti, Anstrom, and Fritts, 1997, p. 7. In their joint reply comments, the National Association of Broadcasters, National Cable Television Association, and Motion Picture Association of America stress that the issue before the FCC is only whether the TV Parental Guidelines are "acceptable." These organizations note (1997, p. 2): "Whether the Guidelines can or should be fine-tuned—or whether another system would also be 'acceptable'—is *not* the issue."
4. Valenti, Anstrom, and Fritts, 1997, p. 8.
5. See the reply comments of the Center for Media Education, et al., 1997, summary page 2.
6. See Markey, et al., 1997, p. 1.
7. See Sunstein, 1990, for a discussion of frameworks used to evaluate regulations. Landes and Posner (1987, p. 16) offer a simple definition of efficiency: "We use efficiency throughout this book in the Kaldor-Hicks (or potential Pareto superiority) sense, in which a policy change is said to be efficient if the winners from the change could compensate the losers, that is, if the winners gain more from the change than the losers lose, whether or not there is actual compensation."
8. For a more detailed discussion of the economics of television violence and empirical evidence for many of theories discussed here, see Hamilton, 1998. The incentives that broadcasters face to broadcast particular types of programming are also described in Hamilton, 1996.
9. Pollution and television violence are both examples of negative externalities, which are costs that are not incorporated into marketplace decisions. Economists define externalities by two conditions (Baumol and Oates, 1988, p. 17):

   > Condition 1: An externality is present whenever some individual's (say A's) *utility* or *production* relationships include real (that is, nonmonetary) variables, whose values are chosen by others (persons, corporations, governments) without particular attention to the effects on A's welfare. . . .

   > Condition 2: The decision maker, whose activity affects others' utility levels or enters their production functions, does not receive (pay) in compensation for this activity an amount equal in value to the resulting benefits (or costs) to others.

   A parallel between pollution and violence exists if violence on television generates negative impacts on society. The National Television Violence Study (1996) provides an excellent overview of the research demonstrating how violent programming may generate aggression, fear, and desensitization among some child and adult viewers. The NTVS emphasizes that the context of how violence is portrayed may increase or decrease the likelihood that the programming may have undesirable effects on some audiences. Though children are unintended audiences for violent programs aimed at adults, the second year research report by the National Television Violence Study researchers (1997) indicates that programming specifically aimed at children contains a high level of violence and uses violent portrayals that carry high risks for young viewers.
10. See Magat and Viscusi, 1992, for empirical evidence on the attributes of successful labeling efforts for hazardous chemical products. Ippolito and Mathios (1990) demonstrate how information provisions about the health effects of fiber caused consumers to alter their cereal purchases and led producers to engage in product innovation to respond to changes in consumer demand.
11. The parent survey (based on 679 completed questionnaires) by Cantor, Stutman, and Duran also focused on the impact of television on children's fright and risk-taking reactions. The results of the survey were presented to the industry committee developing the rating system, which initially chose an age-based rather than content-based system. Comments filed with the FCC by Cantor (1997) summarize the polling data on parents' views about the format of television program ratings.

12. Surveys may provide information that the "logic of collective action" (Olson, 1971) predicts might not be otherwise expressed by parents. Though industry participants suggest that they have not received many complaints about the age-based ratings from parents, economic theory would predict that if parents prefer content-based ratings to the age-based format, they would be unlikely to contact the networks to complain because they have such a low probability of influencing network decisions. Some parents may participate in the debate over ratings and contact the networks and the government because they believe this is the right thing to do. The FCC has radically lowered the costs to individuals of participating in the ratings inquiry by encouraging individuals to e-mail their comments to the agency. Reply comments from the Center for Media Education, et al. (1997, p. 3) stress that complaints about the ratings format may rise as the V-chip technology is implemented and more parents attempt to use the industry ratings.

13. The Yankelovich survey of 1,753 respondents included 1,001 parents with children living at home. This survey, released in March 1997, found "70% of those polled preferring a content-based system vs. 18% who prefer an age-based system." See Bash, 1997. The *New York Times* poll of 394 parents with children between age 2 and 17 conducted six weeks after the implementation of the TV Parental Guidelines found that "many parents also said they would prefer to see two separate rating labels, for violence and for sexual content, instead of the single, age-specific labels now in use." See Mifflin, 1997.

14. See Valenti, Anstrom, Fritts, 1997, p. 8.

15. For details of the Cantor and Krcmar study, see National Television Violence Study, 1996. Parents and children were offered program guides in a lab and asked to choose programs to watch. Shows in the viewing guides were randomly labeled with the parental discretion warning. The parent-child pairs were videotaped discussing their program selection decision.

16. National Television Violence Study, 1996, p. III-45.

17. National Television Violence Study, 1997, p. 321.

18. Hamilton, 1998, examined all movies shown on the four major broadcast networks during prime time from September 14, 1987 to September 26, 1993, a sample of 2,295 films. According to *TV Guide*, the networks placed viewer discretion warnings on approximately 2% of these films. Ratings regressions controlled for variables such as movie starting time, genre, network, and airing year. The regressions indicated that adult males had higher ratings for movies described by *TV Guide* as particularly violent, while adult females had higher ratings for family crime movies. The data also indicate that the networks were more likely to use movies with murder themes, family crimes, or true murder stories during sweeps months. Hamilton, 1998, discusses how violent content is often used strategically in broadcast and cable programming.

19. See Mifflin, 1997, p. 1–8.

20. Hatch, 1997, suggests that many daily newspapers do not carry the program ratings, in part because of higher printing costs associated with including this information on a daily basis. A survey by the U.S. House Committee on Energy and Commerce Subcommittee on Telecommunications and Finance similarly found in 1994 that newspapers did not often carry viewer discretion warnings in their television grids.

21. Note that the V-chip could allow parents to incorporate information on many different types of content (e.g., levels of violence, sex, or adult language) at a low cost. While industry participants initially argued in favor of age-based summary indicators on the basis that other suggested ratings systems are too "complex," the V-chip technology would allow parents to consider many different dimensions of programming simply by selecting particular levels of a given type of content (e.g., violence) to block out.

22. Hamilton, 1998, demonstrates that the estimated ad price for 30-second spots on *NYPD Blue* during November 1993 was $163,200, based on the demographic groups watching the program. The reported price for ads on the program, however, was only $89,800. I attribute the difference in ad prices to the controversy surrounding the program rather than to the specific wording of the warnings attached to the show, which generally focused on adult language or content. The American Family Association focused on the program's use of language and nudity rather than violence. The UCLA Center for Communication Policy monitoring report (1995, p. 59) indicated that "the show was never found to be irresponsible in its use of violence."

23. See Federman, 1996, p. 19.

24. Males and younger adults (e.g., those aged 18 to 34) are less likely to report in surveys that they believe television violence is offensive or has a negative impact on society. See Hamilton, 1998.

25. Hamilton, 1998, p. 5–4.

26. Viewers may have additional information about program content for movies previously released in theaters. Of the 357 prime-time movies scheduled to air on ABC, CBS, Fox, and NBC from May 1, 1995 through February 29, 1996, 36% were previously released in theaters (see Hamilton, 1998). One might

be tempted to argue that the MPAA ratings for these films, which are listed in *TV Guide*, provide viewers with indications of the prevalence of violence. I found for a sample of 1,210 movies released between 1982 and 1992 that in terms of the violent acts per hour measure used by the National Coalition on Television Violence, there was no statistical difference between the average number of violent acts per hour in a PG movie (20.1) and a PG-13 movie (19.8). There were clear differences between the average number of violent acts per hour in G (12.9) versus R (33.1) movies. Cantor, Harrison, and Nathanson (1997) make the point that it is hard to predict the particular combination of adult content, nudity, violence, and language that a PG or PG-13 movie will contain. They also note the importance of recognizing that the PG-13 rating was not used before 1984, so PG movies prior to that year may contain more potentially objectionable content than current PG films.

27. See Parents Television Council, 1996, for program evaluations.
28. In this analysis I compare the use of the TV-14 rating with the PTC red warning. None of the prime-time broadcast network series programs carried the TV-M or MA rating. The movie *Schindler's List*, broadcast on February 23, 1997 on NBC, did carry a TV-M rating. Note that the TV Parental Guidelines indicator for "Mature Audience Only" programs was eventually changed from an initial designation of TV-M to TV-MA.
29. See Hamilton, 1998, for a fuller comparison between the PTC and industry ratings.
30. For prime-time broadcast network programs between 1980 and 1991 examined by the National Coalition on Television Violence, the mean number of violent acts per hour calculated was 8.4. Of 534 programs classified as "nonviolent" based on genre, only 34 shows had counts of violent acts per hour greater than the sample mean of 8.4 (e.g., were false negatives). Of the 233 shows in violent genres, only 34 had violence counts lower than the sample mean (e.g., were false positives). Note that the ability to predict violent content from genre does not reduce the need for a ratings system, since the presence of indicators in signals will allow parents to use a V-chip to block programming more easily than they would in a world where they had to read program guides, determine genres, and then monitor viewing.
31. See Shales, 1994.
32. See Hamilton, 1998, p. 4–33.
33. See Rice and Brown, 1996.
34. For a detailed description of the revised TV Parental Guidelines, see PR Newswire Association, 1997 and Albiniak, 1997
35. See Albiniak, 1997 and Pottinger, 1997.
36. Pottinger, 1997.
37. Albiniak, 1997, p. 6.
38. Average 1996 prices for 30-second ads on episodes of programs rated as red by PTC were $239,000 for ABC, $223,000 for CBS, $178,000 for Fox, and $340,000 for NBC. For more information on the sample of programs and analysis, see Hamilton, 1998.
39. In analyzing survey responses from parents about whether they had switched channels during news broadcasts to shield their children from programming, I found that the estimated probability a parent had switched channels was .53. For a parent who reported being bothered by violence on television, the probability was higher by .18 than for a parent who was not bothered by television violence. See Hamilton, 1998.
40. See National Television Violence Study, 1996, p. I-17.
41. See the report released by the National Oceanic and Atmospheric Administration, 1993, for a description of and debate over the contingent valuation methodology.
42. Spitzer, 1998, demonstrates that the rating system would be likely to survive a court challenge, even though the courts would probably determine that the system was a product of state action.
43. Sunstein, 1990, contains an excellent discussion of rationales for regulation and the problems that may arise in the implementation of rules.
44. Valenti, Anstrom, and Fritts, 1997, p. 8.
45. In the sample of 251 movies on prime-time network broadcast television I examined from May 1995 through February 1996, Pepsico had the most ads on violent theatrical films that carried warnings and was the number three advertiser on violent theatrical films that did not carry warnings. See Hamilton, 1998, Appendix Table 5.6.
46. Hamilton, 1996, examines the economics of "public interest" programming.
47. See Federal Communications Commission, 1996, which indicates that signals have carried since 1989 Nielsen Automated Measurement of Lineup (AMOL) codes in line 22. These codes allow advertisers to monitor which programs carry their ads. Identification codes for programs also facilitate the ability of viewers to record programs with a VCR.

References

Albiniak, Paige. 1997. "Ratings Get Revamped: Networks, except for NBC, Agree to Add Content Labels." *Broadcasting and Cable*, July 14: 4–10.

American Medical Association. 1997. *Comments in CS Docket No. 97-55 Industry Proposal for Rating Video Programming*. April 8.

Arnold, R. Douglas. 1990. *The Logic of Congressional Action*. New Haven: Yale University Press.

Baumol, William J. and Wallace E. Oates. 1988. *The Theory of Environmental Policy*. New York: Cambridge University Press.

Bash, Alan. 1997. "Parents Crave a Clearer TV Ratings Code." *USA Today*, March 18:3D.

Benton Foundation. 1997. *Comments in CS Docket No. 97-55 Industry Proposal for Rating Video Programming*. April 8.

Cantor, Professor Joanne. 1997. *Comments in CS Docket No. 97-55 Industry Proposal for Rating Video Programming*. April 8.

Cantor, Joanne, Suzanne Stutman, and Victoria Duran. 1996. *What Parents Want in a Television Rating System: Results of a National Survey*. Madison, WI: University of Wisconsin Communication Arts.

Cantor, Joanne, Kristen Harrison, and Amy Nathanson. 1997. "Ratings and Advisories for Television Programming." In *National Television Violence Study Volume 2*, 267–322. Thousand Oaks, CA: Sage Publications.

Center for Media Education, et al. 1997. *Reply Comments in CS Docket No. 97-55 Industry Proposal for Rating Video Programming*. May 8.

Electronics Manufacturers Association. 1997. *Comments in CS Docket No. 97-55 Industry Proposal for Rating Video Programming*. April 8.

Eskridge, William N., Jr. 1988. "Politics without Romance: Implications of Public Choice Theory for Statutory Interpretation." *Virginia Law Review*, March: 275–338.

Farber, Daniel A., and Philip P. Frickey. 1991. *Law and Public Choice: A Critical Introduction*. Chicago: University of Chicago Press.

Federal Communications Commission. 1996. "Digital Transmission Within the Video Portion of TV Broadcast Station Transmissions." 61 *Federal Register* 36302. Washington, DC: U.S. Government Printing Office.

———. 1997. "Commission Seeks Comment on Industry Proposal for Rating Video Programming (CS Docket No. 97-55)." February 7. Washington, DC: Federal Communications Commission.

Federman, Joel. 1996. *Media Ratings: Design, Use and Consequences*. Studio City, CA: Mediascope, Inc.

Hamilton, James T. 1996. "Private Interests in 'Public Interest' Programming: An Economic Assessment of Broadcaster Incentives." *Duke Law Journal*, 45:1177.

———. 1998. *Channeling Violence: The Economic Market for Violent Television Programming*. Princeton: Princeton University Press.

Hatch, David. 1997. "In Some Papers, Ratings aren't Fit to Print." *Electronic Media*, March 10:4.

Ippolito, P.M. , and A.D. Mathios. 1990. "Information, Advertising, and Health Choices: A Study of the Cereal Market." *Rand Journal of Economics*, 21(3):459–80.

Landes, William M., and Richard A. Posner. 1987. *The Economic Structure of Tort Law*. Cambridge: Harvard University Press.

Magat, Wesley A., and W. Kip Viscusi. 1992. *Informational Approaches to Regulation*. Cambridge: MIT Press.

Markey, Rep. Edward J., et al. 1997. *Comments in CS Docket No. 97-55 Industry Proposal for Rating Video Programming*. April 8.

McCubbins, Matthew D., Roger G. Noll, and Barry R. Weingast. 1987. "Administrative Procedures as Instruments of Political Control." *Journal of Law, Economics, and Organization*, Fall: 243–78.

Mifflin, Laurie. 1997. "Parents Give TV Ratings Mixed Reviews." *The New York Times*, February 22:A8.

National Association of Broadcasters, National Cable Television Association, and Motion Picture Association of America. 1997. *Joint Reply Comments in CS Docket No. 97-55 Industry Proposal for Rating Video Programming*. May 8.

National Oceanic and Atmospheric Administration. 1993. "Panel on Contingent Valuation. Report." 58 *Federal Register* 4601. Washington, DC: U.S. Government Printing Office.

National Television Violence Study. 1996. *National Television Violence Study: Scientific Papers 1994–1995*. Studio City, CA: Mediascope, Inc.

_____. 1997. *National Television Violence Study, Volume 2*. Thousand Oaks, CA: Sage Publications.

OKTV. 1997a. *Comments in CS Docket No. 97-55 Industry Proposal for Rating Video Programming*. April 8.

_____. 1997b. *Reply Comments in CS Docket No. 97-55 Industry Proposal for Rating Video Programming*. May 8.

Olson, Mancur. 1971. *The Logic of Collective Action: Public Goods and the Theory of Groups*. Cambridge: Harvard University Press.

Parents Television Council. 1996. *1996–97 Family Guide to Prime Time Television*. Alexandria, VA: Media Research Center.

Pottinger, Matt. 1997. "Ratings Don't Satisfy Senators." *Hollywood Reporter*. July 11.

PR Newswire Association. 1997. "Joint Statement of Motion Picture Association of America, National Association of Broadcasters, National Cable Television Association." *PR Newswire*, July 10.

Rice, Lynette, and Rich Brown. 1996. "Networks Rolling Out TV Ratings; Broadcast and Cable Networks are Busy Assigning Ratings for Programs." *Broadcasting and Cable*, December 30:7.

Shales, Tom. 1994. "Sweeps Victory For the Violence-Weary." *The Washington Post*, May 2:B1.

Spitzer, Matthew L. 1998. "A First Glance at the Constitutionality of the V-Chip." Chapter 11 in James T. Hamilton (Ed.), *Television Violence and Public Policy*. Ann Arbor, MI: University of Michigan Press.

Sunstein, Cass R. 1990. *After the Rights Revolution*. Cambridge: Harvard University Press

UCLA Center for Communication Policy. 1995. *The UCLA Television Violence Monitoring Report*. Los Angeles: UCLA Center for Communication Policy.

———. 1996. *The UCLA Television Violence Report 1996*. Los Angeles: UCLA Center for Communication Policy.U.S. House Committee on Energy and Commerce. 1994. "Survey Finds Parents Not Routinely Receiving 'Violence Advisories' in Advance of Programs." Study Released January 14, 1994. Washington, DC: United States House Committee on Energy and Commerce, Subcommittee on Telecommunications and Finance.

Valenti, Jack, Decker Anstrom, and Eddie Fritts. 1997. Letter to William F. Caton, Secretary, Federal Communications Commission, January 17.

Media Content Labeling Systems:
Informational Advisories or Judgmental Restrictions?*

Donald F. Roberts

The past several years in the United States have witnessed a remarkable debate over whether and how to control media content. The discussion has included most of the media—film, television, popular music recordings, computer games and video games, and, of course, the Internet and the World Wide Web (traditional print media have been largely ignored)—and has ranged from arguments about whether controls are needed at all, to what kinds of controls best fit U.S. political and social needs. One recent upshot of this debate, although hardly the end of the discussion, has been Federal legislation mandating that a V-chip be installed in virtually every new television set sold in the U.S., the industry announcement of a companion TV rating system in January 1997, and a remarkable outpouring of public and government dissatisfaction with that system, leading to its modification less than a year later.

This paper considers why the content rating issue has gained such momentum, briefly reviews empirical research on current portrayals of violence on television and on consequences of exposure to such portrayals, and discusses what the V-chip is and how it works. It proceeds to argue that an informational content labeling system is preferable to a judgmental and restrictive rating system such as the one recently adopted, at least for the time being, by the U.S. television industry, and closes with a description of such an informational advisory system.

PROTECTING CHILDREN

Children are presumed, quite justifiably, to be different from adults—to be more vulnerable, less able to apply critical judgmental standards, more at risk (cf. Roberts, 1993, 1997). As a consequence, attempts to do anything about media content, whether to label it, to restrict access to it, or to censor it totally, are generally justified in terms of keeping children from harm.

Such arguments are not new. Consider these comments by a psychiatrist, Dr. Edward Podolsky, to a U.S. Senate Subcommittee on Juvenile Delinquency. He spoke following the committee's viewing of excerpts from several televised crime shows.

> Seeing constant brutality, viciousness and unsocial acts results in hardness, intense selfishness, even in mercilessness, proportionate to the amount of exposure and its play on the native temperament of the child. Some cease to show resentment to insults, to indignities, and even cruelty toward helpless old people, to women and other children. (in Starker, 1989, p. 137)

I selected that particular quote because it implicates several of the consequences I will be discussing in this essay, and because of its date—1954. I suspect the programs that committee viewed forty-four years ago would elicit smiles, or yawns, if they were held up as examples of television violence today.

Here is another statement about children and the mass media:

> The tendency of children to imitate the daring deeds seen upon the screen has been illustrated in nearly every court in the land. Train wrecks, robberies, murders, thefts, runaways, and other forms of juvenile delinquency have been traced to some particular film. The imitation is not confined to young boys and girls, but extends even through adolescents and to adults. (in Starker, 1989, p. 8)

That is taken from a now defunct periodical entitled *Education*, commenting on the new mass medium—film . . . in 1919.

I could continue moving back through history in hundred year chunks, reading similar expressions of concern about media content referring to each and every new medium, including print. But let me end with one final quote:

> Then shall we simply allow our children to listen to any story anyone happens to make up, and so receive into their minds ideas often the very opposite of those we shall think they ought to have when they are grown up?

The classicists may recognize that this is Plato, giving his justification for censorship as a necessary condition for building the ideal citizen to inhabit the Republic. My point is simply that fear of what the media may do to children is nothing new. Humans have always wrestled with the issue of what kinds of media content might be inappropriate for children—and what should be done about it.

Calls for Content Labeling

Responses to the question seem always to have ranged from "do nothing" at one extreme to "burn the books" (films/games/records—authors!) at the other. A middle ground, in the U.S. at least, has taken the form of calls for implementation of some kind of content labeling or rating system—that is, some means to identify the appropriateness of media content for children, and then to use that system either to empower parents, to control children's access, or some combination of the two. Most of us are familiar with motion picture ratings. In the U.S., they have been around since at least 1931, when the Hayes Production Code went into effect, and have been continued since 1968 in the form of the Motion Picture Association of America's (MPAA) movie classification and rating system (see Federman, 1996). So why the recent upsurge in concern and debate?

Why have ratings become such a social and political issue in the 1990s? There are probably many reasons that public concern with "doing something" about media content has reached such a crescendo in the past few years. In the case of the U.S., two of the more important factors are that several negative social trends began to peak at the same time that advances in communication technology enabled popular media to present content in new and more disturbing ways than ever before. Just when our society was experiencing dramatic (and unconscionable) increases in teenage violence and crime, in teenage pregnancies and venereal disease (Hechinger, 1992), and in just plain incivility, the media also began to portray violence, sex, and incivility in what seemed to be greater proportions (actually, levels of television violence have remained remarkably constant for over twenty years; see Gerbner & Signorelli, 1990; National Television Violence Study, 1997) and—more important—more graphically than ever before. (I suspect that increased graphicness feeds the perception of increases in amount of violence portrayed.) Film and television have now developed techniques to make bodies explode and blood spray right before—if not into—audiences' eyes; video games now reward kids for the number of on-screen enemies they can decapitate, with bonus points for extra blood and gore; some popular music lyrics, Web sites, and premium cable channel films make available—indeed, make almost commonplace—sexual content that, in the U.S. at least, once resided almost exclusively within "brown paper wrappers."

Given that adults have always worried that the messages media bring from "outside" may exert undue influence on children (Roberts, 1997), it is not surprising that the co-occurrence of these two trends led to a perception that the mass media are "obviously" having a negative impact on society, and, therefore, that controls or restrictions are needed. Given the complexity of devising regulation that satisfies the First Amendment guarantee of freedom of expression, one of the few viable options for exercising some kind of control seems to lie with a content labeling or rating system—*so long as it is not implemented by the government*. A *New York Times* poll published in July 1995, found that over 80% of all adult Americans and 91% of all parents favored the establishment of a rating system for television; 80% of parents believed that music recordings should be rated; 86% of parents thought videotapes and video games need ratings (Sex and power in popular culture, 1995).

RESEARCH ON MEDIA VIOLENCE

Before considering the kinds of rating systems that have been proposed and implemented in the U.S., I want to define some boundaries, make clear a premise or two, and briefly consider several of the issues that have been discussed in the ongoing debate about ratings, issues that I believe are central to understanding what a good content labeling system will look like. For the most part (albeit not exclusively), I will focus on television and television content—especially violent content—because that has been the most consistent subject of relevant scientific research. Nevertheless, and this is a basic premise that should be explicit: *a screen is a screen*. Viewers, especially children, do not respond differently to movie screens, television screens, and computer screens; what holds for one probably holds for the others. In other words, in terms of how members of the audience are affected, the issue is the nature of the content, not the channel by which the content is delivered. My second premise is that most of the psychological principles that guide human responses to screen portrayals of violence also guide responses to portrayals of any other kind of behavior, from sexual to altruistic to how to kick a football. The same kinds of things that increase the likelihood a child will learn a violent act from television also increase learning of an altruistic act, or any other kind of act. Obviously, there are some differences across media and across types of content, but on the whole the evidence indicates that the similarities are far more important than the differences.

It is also important to note at the outset that I distinguish between content labeling systems and content rating systems. The two terms are not interchangeable; they refer to quite different approaches to content advisories. Indeed, the distinction between the two is at the heart of this paper's argument. For me, the fundamental difference is one of providing information about content and allowing consumers to make decisions (good or bad) versus imposing restrictions or prohibitions on potential consumers based on someone else's evaluation of the information and judgment about the capabilities and/or vulnerabilities of potential consumers.

Given those caveats and assumptions, let us look at some of the issues in the debate over whether ratings are needed, and, if so, what form they should take. First, we need to spend a few minutes looking at what the research tells us about the impact of screen violence on children's beliefs, attitudes, and behavior, and about what is currently portrayed on U.S. television.

Most research on the consequences of exposure to media violence has focused on viewers' learning of aggressive behavior or attitudes through exposure to entertainment violence. Several exhaustive reviews of the hundreds of scientific studies conducted during the past forty years lead to the unequivocal conclusion *that exposure to mass media portrayals of violence contribute to aggressive attitudes and behavior in children, adolescents, and adults* (see, for example, Comstock with Paik, 1991; Huston, Donnerstein, Fairchild, Feshbach, et al., 1992; Paik & Comstock, 1994). Obviously, media violence is not the only cause of violent social behavior, but few social scientists any longer debate that it plays a contributory role. As long ago as 1982, a National Institute of Mental Health report on television and behavior concluded: "In magnitude, television violence is as strongly correlated with aggressive behavior as any other behavior variable that has been measured" (National Institute of Mental Health, 1982). Studies conducted in the intervening fifteen years have not altered that judgment (Comstock & Paik, 1991). More often than not, those who continue to claim that there is no evidence for such a causal connection tend to be associated with the media industry—and/or simply have not read (or choose to ignore) the scientific literature.

What the past decade and a half of research has added, however, is evidence that exposure to media violence can have negative consequences beyond increasing the likelihood of viewers' aggressive behavior. We now know that prolonged violence viewing can also lead to emotional *desensitization*, engendering callous attitudes toward real-world violence and decreasing the likelihood of helping real victims. In addition, a third consequence of violence viewing is increased *fear* of becoming a victim, which in turn leads to such things as mistrust in others and to increases in self-protective behavior. In short, research evidence confirms that excessive exposure to media violence can lead to learning aggressive behavior, to desensitization, and to fear, and that several of these outcomes might occur simultaneously (for reviews see Comstock & Paik, 1991; Wilson, Kunkel, Linz, Potter, Donnerstein, Smith, Blumenthal & Gray, 1996).

Given that such consequences of viewing violence are well documented, the more interesting research questions (particularly when faced with developing a content labeling system) concern identification of the contextual factors within media content that seem to make a difference. In other words, what are ways of portraying violence that increase or decrease the likelihood of a negative effect? Both intuitively and on the basis of scientific research, we know that some violent programs are more problematic than others, that some ways of displaying violence are likely to increase learning, fear, or desensitization, but that other depictions are quite likely to decrease these outcomes. It does not take a scientific background to sense that the consequences to viewers of the violence in a film like *Schindler's List* (in which a man saves numerous Jews from the Nazi concentration camps during World War II) are probably quite different than the consequences of the violence in a film like *Natural Born Killers* (in which young adults blast a bloody swath across the U.S.). Both films portray brutal violence, both show a number of killings, both are relatively graphic—yet one is generally thought of as an antiviolence statement while the other has been accused of celebrating violence. The interesting question is: Why? What are the differences in how each portrays violence that make the two films so different? If we are to design a content rating system that will differentiate between two such different media portrayals, such questions are critical. A simple body count will not do the job.

Fortunately, as part of a massive content analysis of violence on U.S. television (The National Television Violence Study, 1996, 1997), Barbara Wilson and her colleagues (1996) reviewed the experimental research on media violence with an eye to identifying contextual factors that make a significant difference in how viewers respond to violent content. Nine factors emerged from the experimental research literature: (1) the nature or qualities of the perpetrator; (2) the nature or qualities of the target or victim; (3) the reason for the violence—whether it is justified or unjustified; (4) the presence of weapons; (5) the extent and/or graphicness of the violence; (6) the degree of realism of the violence; (7) whether the violence is rewarded or punished; (8) the consequences of the violence as indicated by harm or pain cues; (9) whether humor is involved. Although the amount of research on each individual factor varies (i.e., we know a great deal about the role of rewards and punishments but not a great deal about the role of humor), Wilson and her associates contend that there is adequate evidence to safely conclude that each identified factor either *increases or decreases* the probability that a violent portrayal poses a risk to viewers on at least one of the three outcomes: learning, desensitization, or fear. When these contextual elements are mapped over the three outcomes, the matrix shown in table 1 results. The arrowheads show what experimental research says about how each contextual factor affects each outcome. Thus, for example, when violence is rewarded we expect an increase in both learning and fear; when violence is portrayed as unjustified, we expect a decrease in learning but an increase in fear; humor should increase both learning and desensitization; and so on. The spaces where no arrowhead occurs indicate a lack of adequate evidence concerning how that particular contextual factor affects that particular outcome. For example, no research examining how harm and pain cues affect either fear or desensitization was located.

Research on Television Content: The National Television Violence Study

The matrix in table 1 served to guide the content analysis component of the National Television Violence Study (NTVS), an ongoing, three-year study of violence and U.S. television. Although the overall study includes several different components, description of the work is limited here to its examination of the nature of violent television content.

Each year the NTVS researchers sample and analyze the content in a *representative week of U.S. entertainment television.* I include the italics to emphasize the magnitude of the task. For example, for the 1994–95 season, they sampled 23 channels of television available in the Los Angeles area, including broadcast networks, independent channels, public television, basic cable and premium cable channels. For each channel they randomly selected two daily, half-hour time slots between 6:00 A.M. and 11:00 P.M. over a period of 20 weeks, ultimately taping a total of 3,185 programs. After eliminating news programs, game shows, religious programs, sports, instructional programs and "infomercials" (none of which fell within their contracted definition of entertainment programming),[1] they were left with a sample of 2,693 programs—2,737 hours of programming. This resulted in a representative 7-day composite week of programming for each of the 23 channels, the largest and most representative sample of entertainment television content ever collected.

The coding scheme in this study is equally detailed and comprehensive. Violence is defined as:

> . . . any overt depiction of a credible threat of physical force or the actual use of such force intended to physically harm an animate being or a group of animate beings. Violence also includes certain depictions of physically harmful consequences against an animate being that occur as a result of unseen violent means. Thus there are three primary types of violent depictions: credible threats, behavioral acts and harmful consequences. (National Television Violence Study, Content Analysis Codebook, 1994–1995, p. 3)

But more important than the definition of violence per se, precise definitions have been developed for all of the contextual factors listed in table 1. That is, coding instructions were created to enable coders reliably to identify such content elements as harm, pain,

TABLE 1

**Predicted Impact of Contextual Factors
on Three Outcomes of Exposure to Media Violence**

OUTCOMES OF MEDIA VIOLENCE

CONTEXTUAL FACTORS	LEARNING AGGRESSION	FEAR	DESENSITIZATION
Attractive Perpetrator	↑		
Attractive Target		↑	
Justified Violence	↑		
Unjustified Violence	↓	↑	
Presence of Weapons	↑		
Extensive/Graphic Violence	↑	↑	↑
Realistic Violence	↑	↑	
Rewards	↑	↑	
Punishments	↓	↓	
Pain/Harm Cues	↓		
Humor	↑		↑

From the National Television Violence Study, 1996. Predicted effects are based on review of social science research on contextual features of violence. Spaces are used to indicate that there is inadequate research to make a prediction. Reprinted with permission.

↑ = likely to increase the outcome

↓ = likely to decrease the outcome

TABLE 2

Selected Findings from National Television Violence Study
Attributes of Television Content, 1994–95

58% OF ALL ENTERTAINMENT PROGRAMS CONTAINED VIOLENCE

Violent Programs

- 33% contained 9 or more violent interactions
- 51% portrayed violence in realistic settings
- 16% showed long-term consequences of violence
- 4% had an antiviolence theme

Scenes within Violent Programs

- 15% of violent scenes portray blood and gore
- 39% of violent scenes use humor
- 73% of violent scenes portray violence as unpunished

Interactions within Violent Scenes

- 25% of interactions employed a gun
- 35% of interactions depicted harm unrealistically
- 44% of interactions showed violence as justified
- 58% of interactions **did not** depict pain

Adapted from the National Television Violence Study, Executive Summary, 1996.
Reprinted with permission.

humor, justification for violence, attractiveness of the target of violence, and so forth. Thus, rather than simply counting how often violence occurs in current entertainment television programming, the NTVS analysis provides a detailed picture of the contextual features associated with portrayals of violence. Finally, the coding scheme operates at three distinct levels—that of the overall program, of the scene, and of the individual violent act (i.e., violent interaction), enabling independent inferences about the nature and context of violent acts, violent scenes, and violent programs. Such a multilevel approach is necessary if one is to be able to differentiate between programs that glorify violence and those that condemn violence. For example, although a program with an antiviolence theme may depict as many violent scenes as a program that glorifies violence, the more global antiviolence message may emerge only at the program level. If analysis were to be limited to individual acts or scenes, this point might be lost.

Obviously, a study of this magnitude produces results far too extensive to detail here. Nevertheless, a brief summary of a few of the findings will help form the foundation of my argument about what kind of content labeling system will best serve the television audience.

The first conclusion from the NTVS study is not surprising—there is a great deal of violence on U.S. entertainment television. Indeed, in 1994–95 more than half of all entertainment programs—58%—contained violence (the comparable number for 1995–96 was 61%). More interesting than the total amount of violence, however, is its nature—that is, the context in which it is portrayed and the attributes with which it is associated. Table 2 summarizes a few of the contextual results.

For the most part, the table speaks for itself. Although a substantial proportion of U.S. entertainment television contains no violent content whatsoever, over half of the programs do portray violence. Moreover, when violence does occur it is often portrayed in ways that are more likely than not to increase the chances of some kind of negative effect on viewers. Violence often goes unpunished, seldom results in either immediate pain or negative long-term consequences, and is often portrayed as something to laugh about. Over a third of violent interactions depict harm unrealistically, almost 45% portray violent acts as justified, and well over half fail to depict any associated pain. These are all factors that have been shown to increase the likelihood of viewers learning to be more aggressive, or becoming more fearful, or becoming more desensitized. In other words, the contextual factors characteristic of much (not all, but much) U.S. television programming are just those that *increase* the likelihood of negative consequences among youthful viewers. Indeed, the results of the NTVS content analysis read like a primer on how *not* to produce programming for children.

THE V-CHIP

In February 1996, President Bill Clinton signed into law the Telecommunications Act of 1996, a far-reaching piece of legislation that is destined to change the face of the U.S. telecommunications. One small part of that legislation was intended to empower parents by providing a way for them to control the television content to which their children can have access. This was accomplished by mandating that within two years of the signing of the bill (February 1998), all new television sets sold in the U.S. must contain a V-chip, and that within one year (February 1997) the television industry must have developed a system to implement V-chip capabilities (otherwise, the Federal Communications Commission would appoint an independent committee to do it for them). Now what does this mean? What is the V-chip, and what is the system designed to implement it?

Briefly, a V-chip is simply a piece of hardware, a very tiny piece of hardware, that will be included in the electronics of new TV sets (or added to existing TV sets). It allows consumers to block programs depending on how their content is labeled or rated. The chip reads a signal that is not visible to viewers (it is embedded in the vertical blanking interval, the portion of the television signal that currently carries closed caption services for the hearing impaired). That signal, which is to be included within every television program, will carry information about the content of the program. The consumer can program the chip to recognize and respond to any particular rating or level of intensity or other kind of information embedded in the signal. Programs that fail to meet the selected criteria, whatever they might be, are blocked. Thus, for example, a show might be labeled somewhere between V-0 (for no violence) to V-4 (for a great deal of violence). Or, using the television rating system employed from December 1996 through September 1997, it might be rated anywhere from TV-G (General Audience), through TV-PG (Parental Guidance Suggested) or TV-14 (Parents Strongly Cautioned), to TV-M (Mature Audience Only). On the basis of such a label or rating, parents decide what kinds of shows are to be allowed in their home and set the V-chip to block anything in excess of, or not conforming to, the selected criteria. Once that selection is made, the chip automatically decodes the signal embedded in each program and acts in accordance with parental (or other consumer) decisions. If the program exceeds the rating, the V-chip picks up the signal and the screen simply goes blank. In short, the chip is simply a device that enables consumers to decide what kinds of television content they want to allow into their homes at any given time, and to block out any content that does not meet their standards.

Several other things about this technology are important to note: (1) the V-chip is capable of accommodating any one of a number of different labeling or rating systems; (2) the chip can accommodate several different systems simultaneously (there is no requirement to settle on a single approach); (3) a single program can have independent ratings for different kinds of content; that is, there can be one rating for violence, another for sex, and another for language, all pertaining to the same program; and (4) the chip can be turned on or off, or reprogrammed, at any time. For all these reasons, I believe the chip has been misnamed. Initially the "V" was appended to indicate violence chip, but since it can do much more than respond to violence levels, I think a more appropriate name would be C-chip, standing for "Choice Chip." To make it a real choice chip, however, requires giving consumers the necessary information to make reasoned choices—what I call an informational content advisory.

Informational vs. Judgmental Systems

An informational content labeling system posits that information contained in an advisory helps consumers direct their behavior by telling them what is in "the package"— that is, what is contained in the program, film, or game they are considering. The usefulness of the information depends on how clear, specific, and relevant it is to a given consumer. For example, assume one wishes to avoid—or select—content depicting violent or sexual behavior. In this case, a label explicitly describing the kind and amount of either behavior is more helpful than content-free proscriptions that simply warn the content may be problematic but do not state why (e.g., TV-14). In other words, informational systems assume that the primary function of content advisories is to inform viewers about what to expect, and that the more fully they do this, the better. An informational system leaves open both the question of appropriateness and the selection decision.

Judgmental approaches—for example, the MPAA Film Classification System— generally do not provide much descriptive information. Rather, they make judgments about what is or is not judged to be appropriate for particular audiences—specifically, for different age groups of children. Thus, a TV-14 rating tells consumers that somebody has made a judgment that something about the content is inappropriate for children younger than fourteen, but says little or nothing about what that content is (e.g., violence, sex, inappropriate language, etc.). In the most extreme cases, such judgments become proscriptions. For example, in the U. S., youngsters under seventeen years old are prohibited from attending an R-rated film unless accompanied by an adult. In other words, judgmental approaches hand over to someone other than the consumer the question of what is appropriate, and in some cases, the selection decision. Usually the judgment is made by some relatively anonymous ratings board (Federman, 1996).

Typically, two rationales are offered for adopting a judgmental as opposed to an informational approach. First, it is argued that given the thousands of hours of media content produced each year, there is no way to develop a descriptive system complex enough to identify the kinds of content differences that proponents of informational systems would like to describe, but still simple enough to be employed by whomever is charged with the task of labeling. Second, even if an informational system could be developed, proponents of judgmental systems say that it would be far too complex for most consumers to use. Rather, they argue, parents are more likely to use a system that only requires them to make a single, simple, age-based choice.

By now it should be clear that I favor informational content labeling systems over judgmental systems. There is, of course, the possibility of combining the two approaches—of both telling the consumer what is in the package *and* providing judgments about its age-appropriateness. But even that, I think, is a mistake. Not only do judgmental systems take fundamental decision-making power away from parents, but they also increase the risk of attracting children to the very kinds of content from which we would like to protect them. Even though content advisories are intended to help parents monitor and guide their children's media consumption, we cannot lose sight of the fact that youngsters also see and respond to these ratings. Nor can we ignore that content decisions are under control of at least some children most of the time and of most children at least some of the time. It follows that how content advisories affect children also warrants careful consideration.

BOOMERANG EFFECTS

Unfortunately, there is mounting evidence that advisory labels can boomerang, attracting youngsters to inappropriate content—a kind of "forbidden fruit" effect (Christenson, 1992). And although both informational and judgmental advisories have been found to boomerang sometimes, the effect is more general and more consistent with judgmental ratings (see Bushman & Stack, 1996; Cantor & Harrison, 1996; Cantor, Harrison & Nathanson, 1997; Christenson, 1997; Morkes, Chen & Roberts, 1997).

To the extent that informational systems attract children to "forbidden fruit," they do so because they identify content that youngsters seek because of some need or interest independent of the labeled content. For example, youngsters interested in sex or violence for whatever reason will read the advisory to determine whether a given program can satisfy their interest, and act accordingly. Children not interested in these topics may either ignore or actively avoid the program, also depending on the information in the advisory. It is no different than when people who are interested in gardening read program listings to locate programs about gardening. For better or worse, information is used to guide choices; not approving of the choice a person might make on the basis of information is not a legitimate reason to withhold information.

The boomerang effect associated with judgmental ratings, on the other hand, is not primarily a function of fulfilling a child's information needs; judgmental ratings provide little information. Rather, when children are drawn to content rated as inappropriate by a judgmental system (e.g., when a twelve-year-old chooses a TV-14 program), it is primarily because they are reacting against what they perceive to be someone attempting to control their media choices; such a reaction is quite independent of what the content may be. Reactance theory (Brehm, 1972) posits that a perceived threat to individual freedom motivates humans to restore freedom by actively seeking to engage in the proscribed behavior. Thus, to the extent that children perceive content advisories as attempts by some "authority" to limit their access to content or otherwise impose control or censorship, the theory predicts that they will strive to consume the proscribed material *regardless of the nature of the content*. Several studies indicate that youngsters perceive labels proscribing content on the basis of age or appearing to put control in the hands of others—particularly parents (e.g., an advisory such as "Parental Discretion Advised")— as highly restrictive, and that they react strongly against them. At least three experiments have shown that the MPAA Film Classification system is particularly likely to engender reactance and a boomerang effect among children (Cantor & Harrison, 1996; Cantor, Harrison & Nathanson, 1997; Morkes, Chen & Roberts, 1997; also see Bushman & Stack, 1996).

Of course, the informational and the judgmental models are not entirely independent. Simply the fact that any rating is assigned—whether a single letter icon (e.g., "R") or a descriptive phrase (e.g., "Humans killed; blood and gore")—indicates that someone hopes to control at least some consumers' access to the content, thus creating some potential for reactance. Similarly, even the most "content free" label usually elicits consumer inferences about the nature of the proscribed material. For example, when asked what an MPAA "R" stands for, most young adolescents in the U.S. will refer to sex and/or violence. Moreover, both mechanisms may operate simultaneously. A twelve-year-old boy might seek out an R-rated film both because he has been told he can't see it (reactance) and because he believes it may portray activity about which he is curious (information seeking). Whether a particular rating or advisory provides information or elicits reactance, then, is a matter of degree. When concerned with children's responses to ratings from a practical point of view, the question is better phrased in terms of which systems are less likely to cause reactance and more likely to provide useful information.

THE RSAC CONTENT LABELING SYSTEM

Let me turn, then, to the issue of whether it is possible to design an informational system complex enough to give relatively fine-grained information about a program but still simple enough for both labelers and parents to use. I shall describe a content advisory system I helped devise a few years ago and start by describing some questions we addressed from the beginning of the project.

First, consider how satisfied a parent would be with a system that rated programs with either a simple G (good for children) or NG (not good for children). Prior to viewing, that's all one would know about the program—either its G or NG. Would the situation be better if there were four or five ratings levels—say from 0 to 5, or from TV-G through TV-PG, and TV-14 to TV-M (the TV Parental Guidelines)? My experience has been that most parents would prefer either of the latter options to the simple G or NG. But is that enough? Wouldn't the "parent" want to know what the ratings mean by "children?" That is, would it help to know if G - NG referred to seven-year-olds, ten-year-olds, or fourteen-year-olds? Would your answer to the questions change depending on *who* gave the rating, on whether, for example, the G (for "good") or NG (for "no good") was assigned by a leader in your public educational system or by a youthful college dropout marking time as a television content rater while awaiting a "real" job? What if the rating was always assigned by one of two educators, one of whom was obsessed with keeping violence off television while the other made keeping children safe from nudity his life's work—but you never knew which gave a particular rating? Would it make a difference which one assigned the rating? Are you more concerned with portrayals of violence than with portrayals of sex? Do you have different feelings about depictions of nudity? Of vulgar language? And even if you decide which kind of content concerns you most, are you certain about how any particular portrayal should be rated? Perhaps what you see as brutal violence someone else will judge to be little more than a friendly tussle. Indeed, consider the wide range of answers the preceding questions are likely to elicit from a large, diverse group of parents.

The importance of such questions began to emerge for me when I was asked by the U.S. Software Publishers Association to help develop a parental advisory system for computer games.[2] In 1994, in response to the release of several particularly violent and bloody video games, some members of the U.S. Congress brought pressure to bear on both the video game and computer game industries to develop some kind of parental advisory label to be placed on game packages (see Federman, 1996). At minimum, the argument went, parents should have some indication of what is in a game before they purchase it for their children. I won't detail the history of that particular debate, except to note that in order to preclude threatened government action, each of the two industries (video games and computer games) developed its own system, and the one produced for computer games took an informational approach. Ultimately, when the computer game content labeling system was completed, it was turned over to a nonprofit advisory board independent of the computer game industry, the Recreational Software Advisory Council (RSAC), and became known as the RSAC system. Over the past two years a slightly revised version of the system, called the RSACi system ("i" for Internet) has gone into effect on the World Wide Web, and over 60,000 Web sites currently use it to label content.

Several factors influenced the shape of the RSAC content labeling system. Most important was the issue of whether an advisory should be judgmental or informational—(evaluative or descriptive). That is, should a content advisory make an evaluative judgment about what a child should see, or should it provide descriptive information about what is in the game, allowing parents to make the evaluative judgments appropriate to their personal beliefs and value systems? Is it better to label a program as "inappropriate for children under thirteen years," or to say "this game depicts violence that goes unpunished and that results in injury to humans," asking parents to decide whether their children should play? When I talked to parents about the Motion Picture Film Classification System, I found that many objected to age-based, judgmental ratings because they believed that often such ratings were not appropriate for their own children. Some felt their ten-year-olds were perfectly capable of handling some kinds of content likely to get a PG-13 rating, but not other kinds; some felt that their fourteen-year-olds should not see a PG-13 movie, but had a great deal of trouble defending their position in the face of such "expert" ratings; most complained that the simple lettering system simply did not tell them enough to enable them to exercise informed judgment. They believe that a PG-13 rating can be assigned to a film on the basis of violence, or sex, or language, but they often are uncertain about what particular kind of content is at issue in any given film—sometime even after they have seen the film. Many parents indicate that all they really know when faced with a PG-13 rating is that someone has made an evaluative judgment that the content is "inappropriate" for younger children.

Of course, to the extent that an advisory provides both descriptive information and an age-based judgment, parents can make a decision based on descriptive information combined with the additional knowledge of someone else's evaluative judgment about appropriate age levels. That evaluative judgment, however, is or is not valuable to the parent depending on who that someone else is and what the criteria underlying the judgment were—information that is not currently available for the MPAA system (Federman, 1996). Moreover, in some circumstances that judgment can override a parental decision; that is, parents cannot decide to have their sixteen-year-old attend an R-rated film absent the company of an adult.

In any case, given: (a) parents' expressed desire for more information, (b) game developers' antipathy toward others making evaluative judgments about their products, and (c) reactance theory's prediction that age-based content restrictions are likely to boomerang, we opted for informational content labeling as opposed to judgmental ratings. Ultimately, we took as our model the U.S. food labeling system, which requires food packagers to list the ingredients in the package. Consumers are not told what they should or should not eat; rather, they are given adequate information and the consumption decision is left to them. The RSAC content labeling system used the same principles.

Another important factor that shaped the final form of the RSAC system was logistical. The nature of computer games makes it very difficult to require that they be screened by independent raters. Unlike films or videotapes, which can be viewed in ninety minutes or so, it can take upwards of one hundred hours to review a computer game (make that two hundred hours if you are over forty years old). Given the hundreds of games that need to be labeled each year, it would be extremely expensive and impractical to require independent coders to describe or rate each game. We decided, therefore, to develop a self-rating system—that is, a system whereby the game developers themselves rate their own games. This, of course, created a new problem. To ask a game developer to label his or her own game, particularly when many developers tend to believe that labels or ratings indicating higher levels of violence (or sex, or vulgar language) may decrease sales, is like asking the fox to guard the henhouse. It would seem to invite the developers to bend the rules. Thus, we had to find a way to keep game developers accurate and honest as they labeled their own games, and equally important, a way that would also assure the public that such self-administered ratings are, in fact, accurate and honest. Ultimately, the solution turned out to be quite simple. We took the norms and canons of science and moved them into the public arena. That is, we developed a content labeling system that is *reliable* and *public*, and those two attributes largely solved the problem.

A reliable system means that any two individuals using the coding procedures correctly will describe or rate a game identically. This requires very concrete, very detailed definitions of everything to be described, and a set of questions about the content based on those definitions that ask for nothing other than yes/no responses. The idea is that no matter how different the individuals, if they use the same objective definitions correctly, and answer the questions honestly, they cannot help but assign the same label or rating to a game.

A public system means open to public oversight; that is, anyone and everyone has access to the system, its definitions, and its procedures. To the extent that open access to a reliable system is guaranteed, then anyone should be able to check the label or rating given to any game at any time. The idea underlying this requirement is that if it is easy for anyone in the public to raise questions or objections in those instances when they do not agree on the rating (using, of course, the same rating system), the threat of such checks keeps game developers honest. If the game developers misuse the system, they face loss of their rating (which can cost them access to retail outlets) and heavy fines. (A public system can also provide increased flexibility in that, over time, public input can be used to sharpen or modify questions and/or definitions, keeping the system in step with cultural norms.)

Finally, there remained the question of what to label and how to label it. Both public opinion and prodding from Congress dictated advisories addressing each of four content dimensions—violence, sex, nudity, and language (ultimately, the labels combine sex and nudity, but the two kinds of content are still rated separately). Here, however, I will focus on violence.

We decided that there would be five levels of intensity for each content area—that is, from 0 for no violence to 4 for the most potentially harmful portrayals of violence. We reviewed the research literature on the effects of media violence, identifying content dimensions—what Wilson et al. (1996) called contextual factors—that were most likely to increase negative effects and that seemed most appropriate to the *content of games*. (Since games do not have the kinds of story lines found in dramatic narratives, their content labels focus on slightly different dimensions than might be the case for television programs.) By this procedure we settled on five primary features that would make a difference in the level of the advisory:

1. the nature of the target (victim)—i.e., is the target humanlike, nonhuman, or an object?;
2. the stance of the target (victim)—i.e., is the target threatening or nonthreatening?;

3. consequences to the target (victim)—i.e., death v. injury v. disappearance v. no consequences;
4. depiction of blood and gore;
5. consequences to the player—i.e., is the player rewarded or not rewarded for aggressive behavior?

To the extent that one or more of these attributes occur within a computer game, the advisory of the level of violence increases. For example, if the game portrays a threatening human attacked but not injured, the game gets a 1 for violence; if the threatening human is injured, it gets a 2, and so on. Combinations of these various dimensions result in the logic chart shown in table 3, which illustrates the various attributes in a computer game that result in different violence advisories.

Of course, the person judging the content is not required to make his or her way through that chart. Rather, there is a set of highly concrete, highly objective definitions for every term used in the chart, and a parallel set of yes/no questions employing those definitions. For example, one question asks: "Does the software title depict blood and gore of sentient beings?" That question results in a straightforward "yes" or "no" response from the person doing the labeling because the terms "depict," "blood and gore," and "sentient beings" are each explicitly and extensively defined. (Terms such as "sentient beings" would never be used in a descriptive label, but are included in the definitions in order to cover the wide array of creatures inhabiting the world of computer games—from realistic humans, to animated space aliens, to killer frogs.) Here, for example, is part of the definition of "blood and gore":

> Blood & Gore: Visual Depiction of a great quantity of a Sentient Being's blood or what a reasonable person would consider as vital body fluids, OR a visual Depiction of innards, and/or dismembered body parts showing tendons, veins, bones, muscles, etc., and/or organs, and/or detailed insides, and/or fractured bones and skulls.
>
> The depiction of blood or vital body fluids must be shown as what a reasonable person would classify as flowing, spurting, flying, collecting or having collected in large amounts or pools, or the results of what a reasonable person would consider as a large loss of the fluid such as a body covered in blood or a floor smeared with the fluid . . . etc.

There are literally dozens of pages of such definitions and associated examples, one for every important term in each of the questions.

The questions are arranged in a branching format and are typically administered on a computer. Depending on the response to any given question, the system either gives an appropriate content label or determines what the next question should be. Depending on the amount and nature of violence in a given game, whoever does the labeling may respond to as few as two or as many as fifteen questions. The same procedure is followed for sex/nudity and for language. Finally, depending on how the questions have been answered, the program determines what the advisory icon should be (see figure 1) and

TABLE 3

RSAC Methodology Logic Chart

	All	1	2	3	4
Maximum Violence					
Rape					X
Wanton and Gratuitous Violence					X
Blood/Gore				X	
Human Threatening Victims					
No Apparent Damage/No Death		X			
Damage with or without Death			X		
Death/No Damage			X		
Human Non-Threatening Victims					
Damage/No Death					
Player Not Rewarded (unintentional act)			X		
Player Rewarded				X	
Death With or Without Damage					
Player Not Rewarded (unintentional act)			X		
Player Rewarded (gratuitous violence)					X
Non-Human Threatening Victims					
No Apparent Damage/No Death		X			
Damage With or Without Death		X			
Death/No Damage		X			
Non-Human Non-Threatening Victims					
Damage/No Death					
Player Not Rewarded (accidental)		X			
Player Rewarded (intentional)			X		
Death With or Without Damage					
Player Not Rewarded (accidental)		X			
Player Rewarded (intentional)				X	
Natural/Accidental Violence					
Damage/Death-Human Victims			X		
Damage/Death Non-Human Victims		X			
Blood/Gore (humans and non-humans)				X	
Objects (Aggressive & Accidental Violence)					
Damage and/or Destruction of Symbolic Objects	X				
Realistic Objects					
Disappear w/o Damage or Implied Social Presence	X				
Disappear w/o Damage with Implied Social Presence		X			
Damage With or Without Destruction		X			

Reprinted with permission.

FIG. 1. Example of two RSAC Advisory labels for hypothetical computer games: one with no instances of Violence, Nudity/Sex, or Language requiring a label (i.e., Suitable for All), and one with level 2 Violence and Language and level 3 Nudity/Sex.

what information is to be used to explain that icon. In other words, the final label consists of both an icon and associated number (from 0 to 4) indicating the level of violence, and a descriptive phrase explaining why that number was assigned. As shown in the logic chart in table 3, the content description associated with any given level may vary. For example, there are six different reasons a game can receive a violence score of 2 and four different reasons it could earn a violence score of 3. In all cases, the advisory informs the consumer about the specific kind of content underlying each specific level of violence assigned. Note, for instance, the descriptive information in the violence section of the RSAC advisory label displayed in figure 1. The hypothetical game described by that label received 2 for violence level because it "rewards injuring non-threatening creatures" (e.g., the player scored points for shooting living creatures that posed no threat to other figures in the game). Another descriptive phrase paired with a level 2 violence advisory might have been simply: "Humans injured."

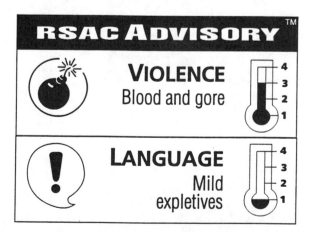

FIG. 2. Example of RSAC Advisory label attached to a particular computer game: "Doom."

Finally, figure 2 shows an advisory label assigned to one of the more violent games available in the U.S. a year or so ago (even more violent games have since reached market), a game called "Doom." As you can see, the game received the next to highest advisory for violence—in this case because it portrayed blood and gore—and a very mild rating for language (mild expletives). There were no instances of either sex or nudity in the game.

CONTENT LABELING AND TELEVISION

Now, how might something such as the RSAC content labeling system relate to a TV content labeling system to implement the V-chip? Clearly, some modifications would have to be made in the dimensions employed and in some of the questions required to assign a label. (The contextual features identified in the NCTV study would be a good place to begin developing the appropriate dimensions for television content). But for the most part, such an informational approach seems ideal for the new V-chip technology. It would be inexpensive and quick, because the producers/writers of each television show would rate their own product with the understanding that the rating procedure is public. More important, it would serve the consumer well because it has the advantage of being descriptive and informational rather than judgmental.

Joel Federman (1996) concluded his recent book on media ratings with the recommendation that whatever rating system is adopted, it should make every effort to maximize information and minimize judgment. Of course, "informational" and "judgmental" are relative terms. Since even the act of choosing to label content implies evaluation, no rating system can be purely informational. Nevertheless, because something like the RSAC content labeling system leans far more in the direction of description than evaluation, it has several valuable advantages over evaluative systems. First, and most important, it puts the decision-making power in the hands of the parents rather than some outside agency with which the parent may or may not agree. It presumes that children are different from each other and that parents know the needs and capabilities of their own children far better than anyone else can. Second, it has the advantage of consistency because the criteria for labeling any content are objective, concrete, and public. And this, in turn, means that it can be used in highly flexible ways. Parents whose primary concern might be media violence and parents whose primary concern might be language or sexuality can all use the system with confidence, adapting it to fit each of their different needs.

There is probably no such thing as a perfect solution to the problem of protecting a highly vulnerable audience such as children while simultaneously protecting people's right to say/write/film/program freely. Nevertheless, providing parents with descriptive information on which they can base informed decisions would be a big step in the right direction—a step that attempts to respond to the needs and right of all concerned parties.

Notes

*   Earlier versions of this paper were delivered as The Wally Langenschmidt Memorial Lecture at the South African Broadcasting Corporation in Johannesburg, Republic of South Africa, August 28, 1996, and as an invited address to the Korean Broadcasting Commission, Seoul, Korea, June 3, 1997.

1.   The National Cable Television Association, which funded the study, determined which kinds of programming would be included in the content analysis.
2.   The design team consisted of Mr. Glenn Ochsnreiter of the Software Publisher's Association (Washington, DC), Mr. Jim Green of Shareware Testing Laboratories (Indianapolis, IN), and myself.

References

Brehm, J. W. (1972). *Responses to loss of freedom: A theory of psychological reactance.* Morristown, NJ: General Learning Press.

Bushman, B. J., & Stack, A. D. (1996). Forbidden fruit versus tainted fruit: Effects of warning labels on attraction to television violence. *Journal of Experimental Psychology: Applied, 2,* 202–36.

Cantor, J. & Harrison, K. (1996). Ratings and advisories for television programming. In *National television violence study, 1995–1996: Scientific papers* (pp. III.1–III.50). Studio City, CA: Mediascope.

Cantor, J., Harrison, K., & Nathanson, A. (1997). Ratings and advisories for television programming: University of Wisconsin study. In *National television violence study 2* (pp. 267–322). Thousand Oaks, CA: Sage.

Christenson, P. G. (1992). The effects of parental advisory labels on adolescent music preferences. *Journal of Communication, 42*(1), 106–13.

Christenson, P .G. (1997, May). *The effect of videogame ratings: Is there a boomerang effect?* Paper presented at the annual meetings of the International Communication Association, Montreal, Canada.

Comstock, George, with Paik, Haejung (1991). *Television and the American child.* San Diego, CA: Academic Press.

Federman, Joel (1996). *Media ratings: Design, use and consequences.* Studio City, CA: Mediascope.

Gerbner, G., & Signorelli, N. (1990). *Violence profile, 1967 through 1988–89: Enduring patterns.* Unpublished manuscript, University of Pennsylvania, Annenberg School of Communications.

Hechinger, F. M. (1992, April). *Fateful choices: Healthy youth for the 21st century— Executive summary.* New York: Carnegie Council on Adolescent Development, Carnegie Corporation of New York.

Huston, A. C., Donnerstein, E., Fairchild, H., Feshbach, N. D., Katz, P. A., Murray, J. P., Rubinstein, E.A., Wilcox, B.L., & Zuckerman, D. (1992). *Big world, small screen: The role of television in American society.* Lincoln, NB: University of Nebraska Press.

Morkes, J., Chen, H. L., & Roberts, D. F. (1997, May). *Adolescents' responses to movie, television and computer game ratings and advisories.* Paper presented at the annual meeting of the International Communication Association, Montreal, Canada.

National Institute of Mental Health (1982). *Television and behavior: Ten years of scientific progress and implications for the eighties, Vol. 1, Summary report.* Washington, DC: U.S. Government Printing Office.

National Television Violence Study (1996). Studio City, CA: Mediascope.

Executive Summary: 1994–95
Scientific Papers: 1994–1995
Content Analysis Codebooks: 1994–1995.
National Television Violence Study, Volume 2: Executive Summary. (1997). Santa Barbara, CA: University of California at Santa Barbara.
Paik, H., & Comstock, G. (1994). The effects of television violence in antisocial behavior. *Communication Research, 21,* 516–46.
Roberts, D. F. (1993). Adolescents and the mass media: From "Leave it to Beaver" to "Beverly Hills 90210." *Teachers College Record, 94,* 629–43.
Roberts, D. F. (1997, in press). From Plato's republic to Hillary's village: Children and the changing media environment. In R.P. Weissberg, C.B. Kuster, O. Reyes, & H.J. Walberg (Eds). *Trends in the well-being of children and youth.* Thousand Oaks, CA: Sage.
Sex and violence in popular culture (1995). *New York Times,* July 23–26, p. 6.
Starker, Steven (1989). *Evil influences: Crusades against the mass media.* New Brunswick, NJ: Transaction Publishers.
Wilson, Barbara J., Donnerstein, Ed, Linz, Dan, Kunkel, Dale, Potter, James, Smith, Stacy L., Blumenthal, Eva, & Gray, Tim (1996). Content analysis of entertainment television: The importance of context. Paper presented to the Duke University Conference on Media Violence and Public Policy, June 28–29, Raleigh-Durham, North Carolina.
Wilson, B. J., Kunkel, D., Linz, D., Potter, J., Donnerstein, E., Smith, S., Blumenthal, E., & Gray, T. (1996). Television violence and its context: University of California, Santa Barbara study. *National Television Violence Study, Scientific Papers* (pp. 5–268). Studio City, CA: Mediascope.

CHAPTER NINE

An Alternative to Government Regulation and Censorship: Content Advisory Systems for Interactive Media

C. Dianne Martin

BACKGROUND

The RSACi system was developed to provide parents and consumers with objective, descriptive information about the content of an Internet site, allowing them to make informed decisions regarding site access for themselves and their children. (RSAC home page)

There are now over one million online users below the age of eighteen. A recently pronounced goal in the United States for the National Information Infrastructure (NII) is to enable it to provide a level of education to all students that surpasses the highest levels of education available today. Throughout the history of the NII, education and research were key motivations for the development of the technology, first as the ARPANET, then the Internet, the NREN, the NII, and as part of the United States Department of Education project GOALS2000. Many recent initiatives have focused on the educational capabilities of these networks for K–12 students. In addition, a significant reason for the presence of young people on the Internet has been the explosive growth of online services and Internet access, especially through services such as America Online (AOL), CompuServe, and Prodigy. Ironically, this surge of new users has also brought an increase in the availability of adult-oriented content and services, much of which is considered inappropriate for young people.

In addition, the rapid adoption of the World Wide Web (WWW) as the most popular Internet browsing platform has meant that the types of material available on the Internet have expanded from a primarily text medium to a whole range of media including graphics, sound, animation, and full-motion video. Thus, the potential impact of the Internet, both positive and negative, has dramatically increased. For those who find this alarming, the situation is further complicated by other Internet controversies involving censorship, anonymity, and government control; the decentralized nature of the Internet; and ill-informed media attention. Hence, those who are sincere about preventing censorship on the one hand, and providing appropriate child protection measures on the other hand, are left in a difficult position. One solution that has been proposed that will meet the dual goal of noncensorious content selection and screening has been content labeling. Several different labeling schemes now available allow Internet content providers to either self-label or to be labeled by third parties with respect to any number of attributes. The areas of greatest concern relate to attributes such as sex, violence, nudity, and language.

The saga of content labeling on the Internet actually started in the murky realm of computer games. In 1994, Senators Joseph Lieberman (D-Conn.) and Herbert Kohl (D-Wisc.) chaired a number of Senate hearings with senior executives of the computer and video game industry regarding the increasing levels of violence in computer games. Legislation in the form of the Video Game Ratings Act of 1994 was drafted and held as a potent threat over the heads of the industry to get their houses in order. As with the recent V-chip legislation, there was a clause that allowed the industry a one-year period to create a self-regulated rating system for computer games and be spared from the new law. Otherwise, Congress would create and administer a rating system itself. Further, Senator Lieberman laid out three aspects that were essential for a self-regulated ratings system to be seen as credible: it must be subject to sanctions; it must provide as much information about the reason for the rating as possible; and it must have "tough, conservative standards" (Balkam, 1997).

To address these concerns and to deflect possible government regulation of this media, two major content classification systems for interactive electronic entertainment were developed in the United States. These are known as the Recreational Software Advisory Council (RSAC), developed by a coalition of over twenty-five organizations led by the Software Publishers Association (SPA), and the Entertainment Software Rating Board (ESRB), sponsored by the Interactive Digital Software Association (IDSA). Both were established in 1994 as independent, nonprofit organizations, but the two content advisory systems are fundamentally different from each other. The RSAC system is a content-based advisory system based upon self-disclosure using an interactive ratings package. The ESRB system is an age-based advisory system based upon the decisions of a rating board. The RSAC system has been used mainly by manufacturers of computer games, while the ESRB system has been used for both video platform games, such as Sega and Nintendo, and computer games.

THE RSAC COMPUTER GAME RATING SYSTEM

The RSAC system, developed by the industry-based Computer Game Ratings Working Party, was based upon the following criteria established for a "good" rating board: (1) be independent; (2) have members who reflect the interest of the public, not the industry; (3) have the power to penalize wrongdoers; (4) be able to keep pace with technological advances; and (5) be able to advertise the ratings so that they become as well known to consumers as movie ratings are today. These ambitious goals were later transformed into the nonprofit organization now known as RSAC, which administers a new kind of rating system based upon content descriptions rather than age appropriateness.

To fully understand the RSAC labeling system, it is first necessary to understand content advisory systems in general. The basis of any rating system is the way in which it classifies content. Federman (1996) has used the terms "descriptive" versus "evaluative" to characterize content labeling methodologies. In addition, Reagle et al. (1996) used the terms "deterministic" versus "nondeterministic" to characterize the labeling process itself. They also introduce the dimension of voluntary versus mandatory to the rating process. These terms can be defined as follows:

> *descriptive*—a rating system that provides a description of the content of the labeled media and can provide a set of indicators about different content categories;
>
> *evaluative*—a rating system that makes a judgment about content using a standard of harmfulness and typically provides a single rating indicator, usually based upon age;
>
> *deterministic*—a rating process based upon some objective methodology in which the final rating is the result of following the methodology;
>
> *nondeterministic*—a rating process based upon the opinions of a rating body;
>
> *voluntary*—the content producer is free to choose to rate or have product rated;
>
> *mandatory*—the content producer is required to rate or to have product rated by some other agency.

No rating system is purely descriptive or deterministic. Rather, each system varies with respect to where it falls between extremes. Our usage of these terms is with the understanding that no system is completely without bias or arbitrariness. Most people are familiar with the Motion Picture Association of America (MPAA) rating system in which a board of reviewers examines the content of a movie and then issues an evaluative, nondeterministic rating. The process is nondeterministic because while general rules of thumb may guide reviewer decisions, the process itself is opaque and the results are sometimes at odds with other ratings. It is evaluative because the ratings do not describe the content of the film but what age group may see the film.

Unlike a motion picture, which averages just over two hours to view, a typical computer game can take up to one hundred hours of playing before all the material has been uncovered. This fact alone posed an enormous challenge to the Working Party when they began to design a rating system for interactive CD-ROMs. In addition, there has a growing dissatisfaction with the MPAA system for being too subjective, secretive in its criteria and decision-making process, lenient on violence and unduly tough on sex, and providing ratings that were too broad to allow members of the public to appropriately discriminate among films based upon personal values.

In contrast to the MPAA, the RSAC system is based upon specific deterministic criteria by which content is rated in a descriptive manner. Content producers, such as video game makers, answer a detailed questionnaire (either in paper or electronic format) about their content with respect to the three categories of violence, sex/nudity, and language. RSAC then processes the questionnaire, registers and returns the consequent rating to the company. The company is able to use that label in advertising or on their product. The label consists of a number, between 0 and 4, for each of the three categories. A rating of All 0 means that the content has no objectionable material in any category. The system is represented in graphical form by a thermometer. The number, or the temperature of the thermometer, informs the customer about the level of the content in question followed by a brief descriptor to indicate the specific type of content causing the rating. Examples of the levels and descriptors are shown below in the RSAC advisories for violence:

RSAC Advisories on Violence

- **0:**   Harmless conflict; some damage to objects
- **1:**   Creatures injured or killed; damage to objects; fighting
- **2:**   Humans injured or killed with small amount of blood
- **3:**   Humans injured or killed; blood and gore
- **4:**   Wanton and gratuitous violence, torture, and/or rape

The RSAC system does not say for whom the content is appropriate; instead it describes the content with respect to characteristics that may be of concern to parents. Since content providers fill out the questionnaire, it is a self-labeling and voluntary system. To ensure public confidence in the RSAC system, the content producer is contractually obligated to rate the content accurately and fairly. Every month a number of registered titles are randomly sampled. Producers who have willfully misrepresented the nature of their content may be fined up to $10,000 and may be required to recall their product from the shelves. Using this system, RSAC has rated over five hundred game titles including the popular "Myst" by Broderbund, "Doom II" by id Software, and "Dark Forces" by LucasArts. Only two companies have ever requested an appeal, and so far no suits have been filed for misrepresentation. A key part to making the computer game rating systems effective was the active involvement of major retailers such as Wal*Mart and Toys R Us. In early 1995 they announced that they would no longer offer unrated titles for sale in their stores. Other major retailers soon followed suit (Balkam, 1995).

CONTENT REGULATION ON THE INTERNET

In July 1995, Sen. Grassley (D-Iowa) chaired a Senate Judiciary Hearing on the issue of pornography on the Internet. These hearings were "held in an atmosphere of near hysteria following the cover article in *Time* magazine on the Rimm report suggesting that pedophiles and pornography peddlers roamed the Internet unchecked and that merely switching on your computer would expose you and your children to an avalanche of smut, porn, and bestiality" (Balkam, 1997, p. 5). As a result of those hearings, an amendment, called the Communications Decency Act (CDA), was attached to the Telecommunications Act moving through both houses of Congress to make transmission of indecent material over the Internet a criminal offense. Further, it held Internet Service Providers (ISP) such as AOL or CompuServe responsible for material that passed through their services. It stated that the display or transmission of indecent or patently offensive material in a manner available to minors would result in fines up to $250,000 and two years in prison. In spite of the outcry over censorship of free speech, the CDA passed along with the rest of the Telecommunications Act at the end of 1995.

The president signed the bill with the CDA into law in early 1996, but recognizing the impending constitutional challenge to the CDA, he instructed the Justice Department not to start enforcing it. A broad coalition of organizations, including the American Library Association, the American Civil Liberties Union, and the Electronic Freedom Foundation, immediately challenged the constitutionality of the CDA based upon the First Amendment protection of free speech. During the first round in the district court in spring 1996, a preliminary injunction against the CDA was upheld by a three-judge panel. In throwing out the CDA as "unconstitutional on its face," Judge Stewart Dalzell emphasized the unique nature of the Internet:

> It is no exaggeration to conclude that the Internet has achieved and continues to achieve, the most participatory marketplace of mass speech that this country—and indeed the world—has yet seen. ... My examination of the especial characteristics of the Internet communication, and review of the Supreme Court's medium specific First Amendment jurisprudence, lead me to conclude that the Internet deserves the broadest possible protection from government-imposed, content-based regulation. (Sieger, p. 14)

Thus, the Internet was ruled to be more analogous to print media than broadcast media, which does not enjoy the same protection of free speech. It was recognized that material on the Internet is not broadcast by content providers, but accessed by interested parties seeking specific material. The finding was unanimously upheld by the Supreme Court, which handed down its ruling in June 1997, that the CDA as written was unconstitutional.

PICS-Based Content Labeling Systems for the Internet

In the meantime, the major players in the Internet industry organized to consider the development of a voluntary, self-regulatory system to provide workable child protection features to obviate the need for government regulation. Such a system would have to provide both content labeling and the ability to use the labels to block objectionable content from being accessed, like a virtual version of the V-chip for television. During the year leading up to the passage of the CDA, a number of Internet specific labeling activities had occurred related to the development of technical solutions and standards:

1. The Information Highway Parental Empowerment Group (IHPEG), a coalition of three companies (Microsoft Corporation, Netscape Communications, and Progressive Networks), was formed to develop standards for empowering parents to screen inappropriate network content.
2. A number of standards for content labeling were proposed including Borenstein and New's Internet Draft "KidCode" (June 1995).
3. A number of services and products for blocking inappropriate content were announced, including Cyber Patrol, CyberSitter, Internet Filter, NetNanny, SurfWatch, and WebTrack.

By August 1995, much of the standards activity was consolidated under the auspices of the World Wide Web Consortium (W3C) when the W3C, IHPEG, and twenty other organizations agreed to merge their efforts and resources to develop a standard for content selection. The result of the agreement is the Platform for Internet Content Selection (PICS) standard that allows organizations to easily define content rating systems and enable users to selectively block (or seek) information. It is important to stress that the standard is not a rating system like MPAA or RSAC, but an encoding method for carrying the ratings of those systems. Those encoded ratings can then be distributed with documents or through third-party label bureaus.

To alleviate the necessity of a content provider going through the onerous task of rating each individual page of large sites separately, labels may apply to whole directory structures (hierarchies) of a Web site if the label is appropriate to all the content. Labels can also be put on individual Web pages or individual assets on a Web page. This flexibility to rate at different levels is referred to as the *granularity* of a particular rating. The following example demonstrates an RSAC label that describes language (l=3), sex (s=2), nudity (n=2), and violence (v=0):

(PICS-1.0 "http://www.rsac.org/v1.0/" labels
on "1994.11.05T08:15-0500" until "1995.12.31T23:59-0000"
for "http://www.gcf.org/stuff.html"
by "John Doe" ratings (l 3 s 2 n 2 v 0))

The PICS encoding specifies the rating service, version number, the creation and expiration date, the page, the rater, and the ratings themselves (other options may be specified but are not shown). Multiple labels can exist for any page. That is, the PICS labels can be used to describe content on one or more dimensions. It is the selection software, not the labels themselves, that determines whether access will be permitted or prohibited. Thus, "parents have the choice of prohibiting access to any unlabeled documents, [thereby] confining children to a zone known to be acceptable, or they can allow access to any document that is not explicitly prohibited" (Resnick and Miller, p. 89). PICS was designed to enable the labels to be handled in several ways. They can be included in html documents within the metatag, they can be fetched from the http server using the http "get" command, or they can be fetched from label bureaus. Hence, the author of a homepage could include a variety of labels on the page itself (i.e., the RSAC, MPAA, or Golf-Fan systems). The http server on which the page resides could have a label or labels for that particular page, and a third-party label bureau like the Good Housekeeping Seal of the Web could be queried for its opinion of the quality of the Web page.

The multiple distribution methods lead the authors of PICS to stress the difference between rating systems and rating services. A rating service provides content labels for information on the Internet. A rating service uses a rating system to describe the content. For instance, the Unitarian rating service and Christian Coalition rating service could both use the MPAA rating system to describe what each thought was the appropriate age for viewing the information.

In the rapidly evolving market of the Internet, label systems and services have a significant stake in maintaining the public confidence in the authenticity of their ratings. Malicious users who falsely label content could damage the reputation of a service, a rating system, or PICS in general. To prevent the manipulation of labels or the content to which they apply, PICS includes the capability to ensure the integrity of a label using message integrity checks (MICS) and its authenticity using digital signatures. In this way, compliant browsers can ensure that a document has not changed or been manipulated since the labeling of the document and that the label is genuine. An important part of PICS compliance is the requirement that PICS-compatible clients read any label system definition from a user accessible configuration file.

The PICS standard has already been adopted by major software vendors. By early 1996, IBM, Microsoft, Microsystems, Netscape, NewView, and other software vendors had announced PICS-compatible products. In addition, major ISPs such as AOL, AT&T, WorldNet, Compuserve, MSN, and Prodigy have promised to develop free blocking software to their customers that is PICS-compliant (Resnick and Miller, 1996).

RSACi on the Internet

In April 1996, the RSAC computer game rating system was adapted for rating Internet content under the name RSACi using the PICS encoding standard. The RSACi system is a Web-based questionnaire that queries the user about the content of a Web page or directory tree based upon the content categories shown in figure 1. Upon completion of the questionnaire, a PICS metatag similar to the one shown previously is returned to the user to be placed in the file header. There is also the option to place the RSACi symbol on the Web page.

Use of the RSACi system is free to anyone interested in labeling the contents of a Web site. In the eighteen months after its introduction in April 1996, over 40,000 sites had rated with RSACi with the number increasing by 150 per day. A new streamlined rating process, developed to address concerns about the slow speed of the first RSACi system, was brought online in April 1997. Although the service does not currently provide message integrity checks or digital signatures, by using a Web crawler program, RSAC has instituted a procedure to sample sites for labeling veracity and compliance with the terms of service that a user agrees to before receiving the label.

PICS-Based Blocking Mechanisms

Providing labels on Internet content is only half of the content control problem. Internet users must have the capability to use the labeling data to make decisions about what content they want to be able to access from their computers. For this reason the efforts of IBM, Microsoft, Microsystems, Netscape, NewView, AOL, AT&T, WorldNet, Compuserve, MSN, and Prodigy to develop PICS-enabled browsers is laudable. A PICS-enabled browser is able to detect a PICS label on a Web site being accessed and to decode it. It is also able to block that site from being accessed if it has a label that has been designated inaccessible to the requesting computer. This mechanism is established by activating the blocking feature of the browser.

LEVEL 0	LEVEL 1	LEVEL 2	LEVEL 3	LEVEL 4
VIOLENCE: content may include				
Harmless conflict; some damage to objects	Creatures injured or killed; damage to objects; fighting	Humans injured or killed with small amount of blood	Humans injured or killed; blood and gore	Wanton and gratuitous violence; torture; rape
NUDITY: content may include				
No nudity or revealing attire	Revealing attire	Partial nudity	Non-sexual frontal nudity	Provocative frontal nudity
SEX: content may include				
Romance; no sex	Passionate kissing	Clothed sexual touching	Non-explicit sexual activity	Explicit sexual activity; sex crimes
LANGUAGE: content may include				
Inoffensive slang; no profanity	Mild expletives	Expletives; non-sexual anatomical references	Strong, vulgar, or hate language; obscene gestures	Crude, explicit sexual references; extreme hate language

FIG. 1. RSACi Content Advisory Categories

For example, in Microsoft Internet Explorer 3.0 under the Security options, there exists an option called Content Advisor. When a parent enters that option, he or she is presented with the RSACi content labeling system. A parent can use a slider to set the level from 0 to 4 for each of the four content areas of nudity, sex, violence, or language. He or she can also decide whether to block all unrated sites or not. The feature is then enabled with a password known (hopefully!) only to the parent who can disable or enable the feature with the password. After activating the blocking capability, the computer will not allow any sites with a higher rating to be accessed on that machine. Instead a message that states that the "site is inaccessible to this machine" will appear on the screen if such a site is requested by the user.

IMPACT OF LABELING SYSTEMS ON THE INTERNET

The potential impact of labeling systems on Internet content is complex. Just as the production and distribution of Internet content is more than a matter of placing an html document on a server, RSACi and other PICS-compliant rating systems are more than the voluntary insertion of labels into documents by their creators. This simple act is only the first step in a complex flow of information from origin to destination. This section presents an analysis of the relationship of a labeling system like RSACi to the production and distribution of content on the Internet.

The production and flow of content is neither a vertically integrated production chain—the same people who create the content do not necessarily provide the conduit and browser—nor is it a purely distributed and segmented market. Although this market is highly compartmentalized, the need for market efficiencies will drive the creation of strategic alliances and standards between functional domains (such as online companies and browsers). This consequently affects the delivery paths and quality of content. Included in this rapidly evolving market are content producers, content hosts, other rating services, bots, search engines, directories, filters, Internet Service Providers (ISPs), online services, protocol developers, and browser/software companies (Reagle et al. 1996) (see figure 2).

Content Producers. Commercial and noncommercial developers of Internet information and Web sites; they can range from single individuals to huge multinational corporations. They may or may not have incentives on their own to provide content advisories with the information they produce. Sites that want access to homes with young children, such as the Disney site, would have the greatest incentive to rate their content.

Web Farms/Content Hosts. Web farms and content hosts provide server services to individuals and organizations that lack the means or interest to support their own server. As a defense against charges of harboring objectionable material without proper safeguards, these entities may encourage or require content developers to self-label. For example, CompuServe has endorsed the RSACi system through an implementation with CyberPatrol and has encouraged individual and institutional content developers on its systems to employ the RSACi system.

Search Engines and Agents. Search engines and agents lay outside of the direct path of content flow—one does not need a search engine. However, they often provide an important value-added service in channeling and selecting information. As such, search engines may gain from being compatible to PICS because label information may improve searching and indexing capabilities. This may provide more incentive to adopt PICS-based rating systems like RSACi.

Bots. Bots travel from site to site retrieving information of interest to their owners. Since bots are personal, discriminatory spiders, their ability to search and retrieve content with content labels has implications similar to that of search engines As they gain the ability to communicate with each other (one could now call them "agents"), PICS-compliant labels could become the language for communicating about the preferences of their owners.

Internet Service Providers (ISPs). Internet Service Providers provide the means for connectivity from one point on the Internet to another. They have been viewed by governments as convenient points of control. Legislators have been eager to make ISPs legally responsible for the material they carry. Since ISPs have been a focus of much of the controversy, they have been very interested in adopting or supporting content labeling systems such as RSACi.

Browsers. Browsers are used to access information on the World Wide Web. For example, Microsoft has incorporated the RSACi PICS implementation into its most recent browser product, the Microsoft Internet Explorer 3.0. The value of such an agreement for browser companies is that it addresses parental and institutional concerns about restricting

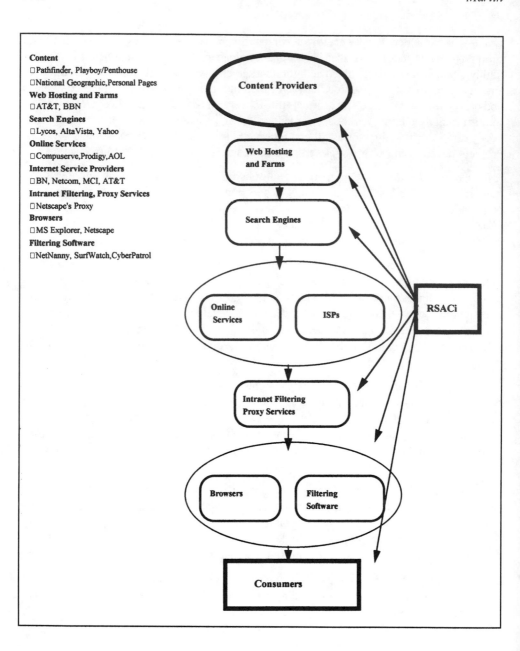

FIG. 2. Structure of Content Flow on the Internet

access to inappropriate material. One point of particular interest is that while many of the PICS recommendations will be implemented by these and other browsers, the companies have thus far declined to implement signature verification of the labels, an omission that may put the trustworthiness of RSACi and other PICS-compliant systems at risk.

Online Services, Firewalls, Proxies, and Intranets. These categories include both publicly accessible (AOL, CompuServe, Prodigy) and private/corporate networks. This market has been particularly concerned with inappropriate material. While ISPs have argued for common carrier status, online services have invested significantly in the creation of a family-oriented image. Hence, they have been the quickest adopters of content selection and screen software, such as SurfWatch and CyberPatrol. Corporations are also concerned about the inappropriate activity on their networks, and some are seeking the ability to monitor or screen the activities of their employees using systems like NetShepard. Network services such as Intranet servers, firewalls, and proxies are also points of control for the dissemination of information to an organization.

The relationships between all of these entities is analogous to a plumbing system made of reservoirs (containing a variety of liquids), conduits (with a variety of delivery capacities, operating pressures, and flow rates), and control systems (upstream versus downstream regulation), with filtering mechanisms interposed at various points in the plumbing. At each step, information may be redirected, collected, or amplified by a value-added service (Reagle et al. 1996).

Non-RSAC Rating Mechanisms

Some browser filtering systems have similarities with the RSACi system in that they are PICS compliant and content descriptive, but they may differ in significant ways. In the case of SafeSurf, it's rating system provides an example of a PICS compliant system that is more evaluative than the RSACi system: (1) it includes an appropriateness rating with regard to age; (2) it provides descriptive labels that have highly judgmental definitions and descriptions.

Other methods for content filtering include mechanisms like SurfWatch, which maintains lists of URLs with objectionable content. NetNanny has filters that block objectionable material (such as curse words) in real time. Although non-RSAC filtering mechanisms may be synergistic in some cases (meaning they may be able to cooperate at some levels), these blocking technologies are different from the RSACi system because they: (1) require proprietary software; (2) are labor-intensive; (3) are not extendible to other areas of concern or interest; (4) realize no economies of scale as the volume of content grows; (5) employ standards that are obscure, somewhat arbitrary, and ultimately restrictive.

CONCERNS

In spite of what appears to be a technically elegant solution to the issue of content control for the Internet, there are still a number of concerns related to the nature of the Internet, the rapidly changing technology platforms upon which it is based, and the efficacy of systems such as RSACi.

Who's In Charge? The implicit assumption with the PICS-compatible labeling and blocking systems described in this paper is that the parents are in control of and responsible for setting the system options on their home computers. Many naysayers have stated that this is actually not the case in many homes; instead, it is the children who are more computer savvy than the parents, and they would be able to circumvent any security features that the parents try to institute. This problem can be best addressed with a vigorous public education campaign to help inform parents how to activate the new features now available in their browsers. It can also be addressed by the browser developers making the feature very easy for parents to use.

Content Context. One of the major criticisms of the RSACi system so far is the one-dimensionality of its ratings. Whether the content is a work of art, an educational encyclopedia, a NASA site, a news site, or an online adult bookstore, it is all rated by the same standards. This means that a picture of the famous statue of David would be rated at the 3 level for nudity (full-frontal nudity) and a work of Shakespeare might receive a 2 level for bawdy language. The dilemma faced by organizations such as RSAC as well as the PICS standards group is the trade-off between complexity and context.

In order to take the context of the content into account, the system would have added complexity at both ends. The content provider doing the labeling would have to answer additional questions so that additional tags such as education, art, and news could be incorporated into the tag. A more difficult problem, however, is the change to the PICS standards and to the browsers that are needed to allow for a multidimensional blocking capability. And this would translate into added complexity for the parent to activate the blocking capability. For example, a parent might select nudity=2, sex=1, language=1, and violence=2 for regular content; but choose nudity=3, sex=2, language=2, and violence=2 for educational or art material; and nudity=2, sex=1, language=1, and violence=4 for news. Each new context adds another dimension to the rating process.

Several major news organizations have objected to the fact that they will have to rate their content on a daily basis since their sites typically contain hundreds of new stories each day. Right now they have the choice of rating each story separately or rating their entire site at the highest level of content contained in any story. Additionally, since they have been exempted from having to rate their television content, they object to having to rate their Internet content. They view news as a special kind of content, protected speech that is above any kind of rating system.

The obvious answer to this issue is for news sites not to rate at all (after all, the rating process is voluntary). However, they further object to the browser feature that enables the blocking of all unrated sites and claim that it is a form of censorship of the news. Again, the response to that complaint is that the blocking of unrated sites is not automatic but must be activated by parents exercising their parental discretion. In fact, a number of the studies about the harmful effects of violence on children have shown that real violence as shown in news is actually more disturbing to children than fantasy violence. The issues related to content context are still being resolved as the PICS standards and labeling systems continue to evolve on the Internet.

Digital Signatures and Label Integrity. Elsewhere we discuss digital signatures with respect to the PICS standard. To engender public trust in labeling systems, any organization like RSAC must ensure that its labels correspond to the content, and that no unauthorized content developers use their labels and their respective icons. On the Internet the important "content" with respect to selection software will be the validity of the rating that is accessed by the content seeker. How easily can this text be misappropriated? If a digital signature is provided by RSAC and checked by the browsers for authenticity, it is very difficult. If digital signatures are not incorporated, it can be misused very easily. One could create such a label for an adult Internet service without consulting the RSAC questionnaire, and one may do so with malicious intent. Hence, simple encryption technologies would seem to provide the only protection to widely used labeling systems.

Instability. The process of content screening and selection will continue to be highly unstable for the near future. One must remember that it is only within the past year that many of these standards and services became available to users of the Internet. As an example of the tremendous pace of events, consider the case of CompuServe. CompuServe has offered SurfWatch as part of its Internet in a Box, a suite of Internet access applications including software from Spry. A competitor of Spry, SpyGlass, has now bought SurfWatch!

International Issues. The threat of governmental censorship of electronic media provided the main impetus for the formation of RSAC and the development of PICS. "What began as a response to threatened legislation in the U.S. has, unwittingly, become a major factor in discussions regarding content on the Internet with governments around the world. In virtually every case, governments are struggling with the issue of whether to wade in with draft legislation, or to encourage, or even coerce, the Internet industry to regulate itself" (Balkam, 1997, p. 7). In each case they must first deal with the issue of the fundamental nature of the Internet. Should it be dealt with like print, broadcast, or some hybrid media? The response to that issue by particular governments seems to determine their attitude toward regulation or nonregulation of the Internet within their borders.

An often-cited characteristic of the Internet is its global, and some would say therefore ungovernable, scope. This global scope increases the difficulty of developing an international content labeling system because the cultural norms of violence, language, sexuality, and political freedoms differ across the globe. Hence, content that may be considered appropriate within one culture may be considered inappropriate to others. A number of governments, such as the government of Singapore, have been attempting to legislate technical infrastructure requirements to address their specific cultural concerns. Even though there may be no national borders in cyberspace, local cultural sensitivities are still very real.

An immediate difficulty with evaluative labeling systems is that what may be appropriate for one culture may be highly inappropriate for another. Fortunately, the PICS system allows for multiple rating systems, services, and label bureaus. As an example of a potential problem, consider the aversion for Nazi propaganda by the German government. Without requiring draconian regulation of infrastructure or ISPs, Germany could require that all browsers and ISPs use a labeling system and label bureau for filtering information pertaining to Nazism. All PICS-compliant browsers must be able to read label system definitions from a configuration file, and the government could be responsible for developing the appropriate rating and labeling services. However, this technique can also be extended to filter sensitive information even further by totalitarian nations such as China. There the government could require that the only Internet access into the country would be through gateways that employ officially sanctioned filtering software.

Regardless, RSACi has an advantage in the international market because systems that use straightforward content description rather than age appropriate evaluations will have greater applicability and adaptability across multiple cultures. While there is some cultural bias within the RSAC system, efforts to extend the system while keeping it content-based would allow it to have international scope. Some countries may associate different icons or names with the ratings, but the numeric value of a descriptive rating would stay the same. Potentially, this would extend usage of the RSACi system beyond the United States, and it would become accepted as an international content labeling standard.

TELEVISION RATINGS AND THE V-CHIP

Running parallel to the development of a self-regulatory system for both computer games and the Internet has been another highly politically charged debate over rating content on television. Rep. Markey (D-Mass.) and Sen. Conrad (D-S.Dak.) successfully steered the V-chip amendment through Congress as part of the Telecommunications Act of 1996. The amendment contained a mandate to the TV industry to develop a content rating system for television within a year or have one legislated by Congress. It also mandated that television set manufacturers would be required to include the V-chip in all new TV sets built starting in 1998. Thus, the wheels were set in motion to implement a technology-based solution for television similar to the content labeling and blocking mechanism being developed for the Internet. The TV V-chip would block television material based upon labeling information carried in the TV signal, much the same way that an Internet browser can block the access to Internet content based upon the labeling information carried in the file headers.

Throughout 1996 a television industry steering committee headed by Jack Valenti deliberated on what such a TV rating system should look like. Groups such as RSAC, the National PTA organization, Children Now, medical organizations, and academic institutions that have done research on the effects of violence on children participated in the discussions. Recommendations from those groups suggested that a TV rating system should be content descriptive, not age-based, and overseen by an independent body with representatives outside of the TV industry to include child experts, psychologists, and children advocates.

However, the Valenti-led group took a very different stand. Their new ratings system, unveiled in January 1997, will be completely controlled by the industry with no outside involvement. In spite of a unanimous call from virtually all interested parties for a content-based, descriptive rating system to be tied in with the V-chip, the industry group chose an age-based system that mirrors the one used by the movie industry. The proposed system contains very broad categories: TV-Y (suitable for all children), TV-Y7 (recommended for children seven years and older), TV-G (recommended for general audiences), TV-PG (parental guidance urged), TV-14 (not recommended for children under fourteen), and TV-M (mature audiences only). Since the categories contain no content descriptors to enable parents to make informed decisions, they have been universally condemned as self-serving to the industry and essentially uninformative to the television consumer.

Several groups monitoring the experimental use of the new system have noted that 75% of all television shows are getting a rating of TV-PG, suggesting that the system is not an effective discriminator of television content. As a result of what has been construed as a lack of good faith on the part of television industry to be socially responsible, Congress is once again threatening to legislate a rating system for television. Industry leaders have now backed down from the original position taken by the Valenti-led group that any attempt to do content labeling of television would be immediately challenged in court as censorship of free speech. The TV rating system now proposed will be a combination of content- and age-based advisories.

Many child advocate groups as well as major newspapers around the country have commented upon the opportunity this debate provides for the whole issue of both television and movie content ratings to be examined critically to put pressure on both industries to develop informative, content-based ratings systems that will address the concerns related to child protection and disparate family values as well as to protect free speech and artistic expression. In the meantime, the 1998 deadline for implementation of the V-chip in television sets continues to loom over the television industry, and the technical specifications for that chip remain in limbo until a rating system is adopted.

CONCLUSIONS

A common saying among those that study the Internet is that, "three months are one Web year." There are a number of observations one can make about content labeling today. One observation is that this market is extraordinarily dynamic. Many of the entities discussed in this chapter are only one to three years old. Some of the companies will likely go out of business or be purchased or bought by larger content or infrastructure organizations— as has happened with SurfWatch. The dynamic nature of the Internet leads one to realize the importance of cooperation between the entities discussed. It is imperative that with the chaotic development and flow of information on the Internet, standards such as PICS be adopted at each level of information delivery to bring some sense of order and control to concerned users. It is in this spirit of cooperation that disparate organizations such as RSAC and Microsoft have worked together to use the PICS encoding system to develop a content labeling and blocking mechanism and to make the system available as widely as possible. The ultimate goal of content advisory systems is to provide a technical alternative to government regulation and censorship of the Internet and to empower members of the public to make informed decisions based upon their own value systems about the appropriateness of content accessible on the Internet.

Based upon the activity that has occurred in the three related industries discussed in this paper—computer games, the Internet, and television—it appears that it is rare for a group of companies within an industry, who are usually fierce competitors with each other, to voluntarily set up a rigorous self-policing system that will cost its members time and money to administer, promote, and develop. In fact, "this would run counter to the mission of most trade associations *unless* there was a very real and potent threat of similar if not worse legislation coming from government. Only then can an industry association legitimately spend its member dues on rallying behind a self-regulatory regime" (Balkam, 1997, p. 9).

On the other hand, it is the role of government to reflect the legitimate concerns of the public and to bring these issues to a wider audience through hearings, press conferences, and possibly draft legislation. Thus, it is often that government uses its power to "embarrass, criticize, or even humiliate an industry into recognizing its shortcomings" (Balkam, 1997, p. 9), in short, to browbeat them into compliance with socially responsible goals. With the right oversight and controls, self-regulation is far more attractive than government regulation, but it takes time, money, and resources to make it work. It also requires a healthy partnership between industry, government, and the general public for it to succeed.

References

Balkam, Stephen. "Content Ratings for the Internet and Recreational Software." Submission to the National Telecommunications and Information Administration report on Privacy and Self Regulation, January 1997.

Balkam, Stephen. "Testimony Regarding the Protection of Children from Computer Pornography Act of 1995. Submission to U.S. Senate Judiciary Committee Hearings, July 1995.

Center for Technology and Democracy Homepage, <http://ctd.org, 1997>.

Federman, Joel. *Media Ratings: Design, Use and Consequences.* Mediascope, Inc. Studio City, CA. 1996.

Reagle, J. M., Evans, M., and Shareck, P. "RSACi Case Study." Electronic Commerce and Marketing Course, MIT's Sloan's School of Business Management, Boston, Mass., 1996.

Resnick, Paul, and Miller, James. "PICS: Internet Access Controls without Censorship." *Communications of the ACM* (vol. 39, no. 10, p. 87–93), October 1996.

RSAC Homepage, <http://www.rsac.org>, 1997.

Sieger, Jonah. "from Washington: Communications Decency Act is Defeated: Landmark Victory for Netizens." *Communications of the ACM* (vol. 39, no. 8, p. 13–15), August 1996.

Acknowledgment

Much of the background information in this article was developed as part of a case study on RSACi during an internship at RSAC by Joseph M. Reagle, Jr., Michael Evans, and Patrick Shareck for an Electronic Commerce and Marketing Course at MIT's Sloan's School of Business Management, Boston, Massachusetts during the spring of 1996.

CHAPTER TEN

Motion Picture Ratings in the United States

Richard M. Mosk

INTRODUCTION

The motion picture is a major art form and a significant United States industry. Millions of Americans go to motion picture theaters regularly. Motion pictures are also seen on television and on videocassettes. They are one of America's major exports and are regarded as portraying, and even having an influence on, culture, morals, and behavior. As a result, motion pictures are widely discussed and critiqued.

The voluntary system of rating motion pictures for the benefit of American parents has become a widely used component of the American movie scene. Nevertheless, it engenders criticism in certain academic and entertainment circles.[1] As chairman of the Classification and Rating Administration (CARA),[2] which administers the motion picture ratings, I believe that much of this criticism is unjustified. Although the system is not perfect—what is?—it is far preferable to the alternatives. I shall briefly discuss the origins and operation of the ratings system and address some of the issues concerning it.[3]

HISTORY

From as early as 1911, city and state governments had established censorship boards. By the 1960s there were many such boards, each applying its own set of standards. There were also private evaluators, such as religious groups, that recommended that certain pictures not be viewed due to content.[4] Thus, it was difficult for the motion picture creator to determine if the film would meet all of the various criteria for acceptability. In addition, many of the boards imposed significant economic burdens on the industry by ordering cuts in motion pictures.

In the early years, to deal with these problems and to provide guidance to motion picture makers, the motion picture industry published a list of scenes ordered by censor boards to be deleted. The Motion Picture Producers and Distributors Association—formed in 1922 and now called the Motion Picture Association of America (MPAA)—promulgated a "production code," which set forth forbidden elements. Only in the absence of the forbidden elements would a movie obtain a production code seal of approval. For several decades, motion pictures produced by major studios were not exhibited in theaters in the United States without a seal. The code was known as the Hays Office Production Code— named after Will Hays, the first president of the MPAA. The code was influential because the MPAA member studios produced and exhibited many motion pictures. Many thought that the code stifled creativity.[5]

In 1966, Jack Valenti, a highly regarded assistant to President Lyndon Johnson, became the third president of the MPAA and recognized that adherence to the Production Code was disintegrating. Motion picture makers began circumventing the code. Theaters were no longer controlled by the moviemakers. Social and cultural mores were changing, and motion pictures had to compete against other forms of entertainment, such as television. Consequently, in 1967, Mr. Valenti essentially eliminated the Hays Office Production Code.

After numerous meetings with producers, distributors, theater owners, religious leaders, and other members of the public, Mr. Valenti began to formulate a voluntary film rating system. The concept was not to approve or disapprove a motion picture based on content, but to give advance guidance to parents so that they could make an informed decision about the movie viewing of their children.[6]

As a result, in November 1968 the MPAA, the National Association of Theatre Owners ("NATO"), and the International Film Importers and Distributors of America (IFIDA), announced the creation of a new voluntary film rating system. This new system led to the breakdown of the former censorship board system, and eventually, the last local censorship board disbanded. Other private systems either disappeared or became less significant.

THE RATING SYSTEM

Under the voluntary rating system, a submitted film would receive a rating based on a determination of what most American parents would consider appropriate for viewing by children.[7] The factors to be considered included theme, language, nudity and sex, violence, and drugs. Initially, the ratings used were G for all ages; M for parental guidance suggested; R for children under a certain age not admitted without an accompanying parent or adult guardian; and X for no one under seventeen admitted.

The current system has modified the earlier symbols. The present rating symbols are the following:

G   General Audiences—all ages admitted. Nothing that would offend
        parents for viewing by children.

PG   Parental Guidance Suggested. Some material may not be suitable for children. Parents urged to give "parental guidance." May contain some material parents might not like for their young children.

PG-13 Parents Strongly Cautioned. Some material may be inappropriate for children under 13. Parents are urged to be cautious. Some material may be inappropriate for pre-teenagers.

R   Restricted. Under 17 requires accompanying parent or adult guardian. Contains some adult material. Parents are urged to learn more about the film before taking their young children with them.

NC-17 No one 17 and under admitted. Patently adult. Children are not admitted.

The rating symbols are trademarked. The X designation is not trademarked. Pictures that are labeled X no longer receive that rating from the MPAA. Rather, an X rating is now self-imposed. Generally, X pictures are not submitted for rating.[8]

For all submitted films, the ratings appear on all advertising, videocassette packages and the cassettes themselves, and at the theaters. The ratings are generally included in newspaper reviews and listings. When a rating is given, it is accompanied by a short explanation for the rating; the explanation is not generally used in advertising. Nevertheless, the reasons for the ratings are often reported by the media and available to the public from various sources, including theaters, Moviefone, and the Internet.[9]

Motion picture makers can choose whether or not to submit their films for rating. Member companies of the MPAA have pledged to submit all of their films for classification; other distributors and producers are free to submit their films, but motion pictures can be, and are, released without ratings. Movie theaters may decline to comply with the rating system, but the majority of the theaters—approximately 85%—do utilize the ratings for information and admission policies.[10]

A movie's rating is decided by a rating board located in Los Angeles. The members of the board work for CARA, which is funded by fees charged to the producers/distributors for the rating of their films. The MPAA president, after consultation with NATO and others, designates the chairman of the Rating Board.

The board is currently composed of a group of twelve people,[11] each with parenting experience and many of whom serve full-time. For most of the raters, the rating position is not a long-term career or job. Most of them have other careers, and their service is generally for a limited period. The current board includes a cabinetmaker, a homemaker, a teacher, a postal worker, a microbiologist, a hairdresser, a store owner, and a restaurant manager. Some have college degrees and some do not, and they come from various parts of the country. Considering all characteristics, they are a diverse group of people.

If dissatisfied with a rating, a producer/distributor may appeal the rating to the Rating Appeals Board, which is composed of fourteen to eighteen members designated by the MPAA, NATO, and the American Film Marketing Association (a group of independent movie producers and distributors). A rating can be changed only by a two-thirds vote of those Appeals Board members present at an appeal. The Appeals Board members vote to change a CARA rating only if they believe that the rating was "clearly erroneous." Reversals are not common. Aside from appealing the rating or editing the motion picture, there are no means to change a rating. There is also a Policy Review Committee, comprised of members of the MPAA and NATO. The Policy Review Committee can revise the basic rules and regulations administered by CARA and promulgate new regulations.

Advertisement of films is also part of the film industry's self-regulatory mechanism. Advertising for all media is submitted to the Advertising Administration (not part of CARA, but within the MPAA) for approval with respect to rated motion pictures. For example, when trailers are approved for "all audiences" that means they may be shown with all feature films. Trailers rated for "restricted audiences" can only be shown with films rated R or NC-17.

OPERATION OF CARA

CARA board members view a submitted film and fill out preliminary ballots to record their impressions as to what most parents would consider the appropriate rating. After further reflection and discussion, the members complete a more detailed rating form to indicate the basis for their formal votes. The board members also discuss and formulate the reasons for the rating. The rating is communicated to the producer/distributor of the submitted film, and the producer/distributor can accept the rating or edit the film and resubmit it for a new round of viewing and rating. The producer/distributor can continue the editing and submittal process, but release commitments usually deter endless resubmissions. If the producer/distributor is still dissatisfied, it may appeal as described above.

COMPARISON WITH OTHER SYSTEMS

In most other countries, there are government classification authorities or "censors"[12]— just as there once were in this country. Their edicts have the force of law. The premise of those systems is that the classifiers are qualified by training and education to determine what is appropriate for children to see at various age levels.[13]

The CARA system has an entirely different focus. CARA does not purport to determine what is or is not appropriate for children. Rather, CARA seeks to determine how parents would consider the picture and what they would want to know about the picture. CARA informs parents of the rating, leaving it up to the parents to determine whether their children should see the picture. Thus, CARA raters are not trained to determine what is best for, or potentially harmful to, children. The system assumes that parents, given a certain indication as to the nature of the picture, will seek to learn more about the picture before deciding whether to take their children to see it.

Many aspects of our legal system are premised on the principle that parents have certain responsibilities toward their children.[14] Thus, it is not unreasonable to assume that parents will exercise this responsibility in connection with their children's movie viewing. If we do not recognize and act upon what we consider parental responsibility, we risk erosion of parental accountability.

NO INFLUENCES ON CARA

The chairman of CARA oversees the rating system and ensures that no outside or improper sources influence the CARA board. The CARA rating system is not subject to outside pressures or influences. There is no favoritism of MPAA members or studios over independent producers. Aside from the appeal process, no one outside of CARA has any power to affect CARA Rating Board decisions. Except for senior raters, who communicate ratings to the producer/distributor, members of the CARA board are anonymous. This anonymity, which is sometimes criticized,[15] immunizes the board from attempts to influence its members.[16]

While CARA board members are paid by the MPAA, there are no incentives for a board member to favor any particular producer or distributor. No member of the board has any connection with the motion picture industry. Neither the status nor the future of a board member can be affected by any particular producer/distributor, any class of producers/distributors, or by how the rater votes.

I have never felt or observed any pressure to favor MPAA members or larger producers/distributors over independent or smaller producers/distributors. The industry itself has an incentive to maintain a rating system with probity. The last thing any studio would want is multiple rating systems or a reversion to government censors.[17]

Everything possible has been, and is being done by CARA to ensure fair and equal treatment to every person or entity that submits a film for classification by it. Although there are bound to be disagreements over ratings, the process is conducted in good faith and with integrity. The fact that some producers/distributors are able to edit to achieve a desired rating, while others may lack the time, inclination, or ability to undertake the editing process, has nothing to do with the integrity or fairness of the rating system.

NOT CENSORSHIP

Some have contended that the rating system contains elements of censorship.[18] Such a position relates in large part to the NC-17 rating because that classification, if enforced by theaters, would preclude minors from seeing a motion picture.

It has been suggested that there are impediments to the exhibition of a picture with an NC-17 rating, and, in effect, an NC-17 label is tantamount to a prior restraint.[19] It may be true that NC-17 movies face some hurdles in obtaining places of exhibition and advertising.[20] That, however, is generally based on the choice made by the theaters and advertisers. Some theaters will not even show movies rated R,[21] while some theaters will generally show so-called art pictures and foreign films—often unrated.[22] Thus, what is shown and by whom remains a matter of freedom of choice. A moviemaker that creates a patently adult motion picture should expect that the audiences will be composed of adults. The moviemaker has a choice of what type of picture it will make and for which audiences.

It is important to recognize that an NC-17 rating does not suggest that the picture is obscene or pornographic in the legal sense.[23] It simply means that most parents would consider the film off-limits for viewing by their children.[24] While the United States Supreme Court, invoking the First Amendment of the Constitution, restricted government censorship of motion pictures,[25] it also provided more leeway for classifying films as suitable or unsuitable for minors.[26] In 1968, the Court upheld the constitutional power of states and cities to preclude minors from access to books and films that could not be denied adults.[27]

An NC-17 rating should only be considered as indicating that the picture is not appropriate for minors. A number of pictures with NC-17 ratings have achieved financial and critical success.[28] Also, it must be remembered that aside from MPAA members, producers and distributors are not required to submit a picture for rating. They are free to distribute a film without any rating.

FACTORS IN RATINGS

Ratings do not purport to be judgments or evaluations of the merits of films.[29] Ratings deal only with certain elements that would affect parental decisions concerning children's movie viewing. These elements continue to include theme, language, nudity, violence, sex, drugs, and other relevant matters.

There are generally no hard and fast rules for ratings. The exception is that certain numbers of usages of the harder sexually derived words require certain ratings, unless the Rating Board, by a two-thirds vote, decides that a less restrictive rating would more likely reflect the opinion of American parents. The Policy Committee promulgated this explicit rule concerning language because language has always seemed to be of great concern to American parents.[30]

Some people, comparing the ratings of different pictures, have criticized one picture's rating as being inconsistent with a rating for another picture.[31] There is often the criticism that CARA is more strict about sex than violence,[32] or more concerned with male nudity than female nudity.[33] These observations and comparisons are not accurate.

Films change from period to period, as does the social milieu in which they are seen. Ratings adapt and evolve in response to parental attitudes and concerns. Although consistency is a factor, context is also important. No two films are identical. For example, some violence may be more acceptable in one setting than in another. The rating must be based on the entire film, even if one scene may appear to be decisive. Every rating is a matter of discretion and judgment. But it is important to recognize that a number of raters see each film, observe it carefully, take notes, have discussions, and fill out extensive forms. Thus, the ratings are chosen carefully and methodically. The raters, as a diverse group of Americans having parenting experience, are as capable as anyone of predicting the views of parents throughout America—not just those from Los Angeles and New York.

Although there is no binding precedent or *stare decisis* in rating pictures,[34] patterns and consistencies in ratings can be discerned. Moreover, ratings reflect common sense. The published factors and years of ratings do provide adequate notice to moviemakers. Indeed, moviemakers who call CARA are provided help and guidance on ratings. A particular rating should rarely surprise a producer/distributor.

Violence is a difficult area to rate because there is an infinite number of variations in type and intensity of such violence, but generally, films with significant violence receive restricted ratings.[35] A picture may receive a strict rating for violence and then be edited to obtain a less severe rating. The public is not aware of rating decisions that precede editing and the final rating. Some people complain about violence in restricted pictures.[36] But once a picture is restricted, it is then up to parents to determine if the film is appropriate or inappropriate for their children. While people may deplore violence in films, that does not mean that films are not rated properly.

Of course, as long as the public continues to pay to see pictures containing significant amounts of sex and violence, Hollywood will continue to make them. But it should be noted that the highest grossing and most successful films generally have been unrestricted and so-called family films.[37]

CHANGE IN THE RATING SYSTEM

The ratings have changed over the years to meet new circumstances. Not only have the classifications changed, but rating reasons have been added. Efforts are made to disseminate the ratings and reasons as widely as possible.

CARA invites and welcomes comments and suggestions. I have met, and am willing to meet, with religious, educational, and industry groups about the rating process. For example, Dr. James Wall, president of the Christian Century Foundation, and Henry Herx, a director of the United States Catholic Conference Department of Communications, have long provided invaluable input. Jack Valenti and William Kartozian, president of NATO, often publicly discuss the rating system and receive input. They continue to consider suggestions for improvement in the system in order to provide better service to parents and to promote creativity on the screen. Mr. Valenti, as father of the rating system, has the historical perspective that is particularly helpful in the evaluation of proposals for changes in the system.

While some may suggest additional rating classifications, it must be remembered that if the ratings become too complicated or confusing, they will be less useful. If the system is working, there is an understandable reluctance to tamper with it.

THE IMPACT OF THE RATINGS SYSTEM

If there were no rating system, there would still be some other mechanism, and that mechanism would likely include censors or censorship boards. The creation of the rating system has fostered creativity in the movie industry, while assuring that parents are receiving information to guide them in supervising what their children see at the theaters or on videos.

Public opinion polls demonstrate overwhelming public use and acceptance of the rating system.[38] Many have pointed to the CARA rating system as an example to be emulated by the television industry.[39]

Every year, CARA rates more and more pictures. This reflects increases in production and made-for-video pictures. In addition, pictures made for television are sometimes submitted for rating, not only for television exhibition, but also for release on video. The rating symbols are widely known and accepted as a part of the American lexicon. The system has prevailed whenever there has been a legal challenge.[40]

The CARA rating system appears to be performing the function for which it was designed. It is occasionally criticized by those in the motion picture industry unhappy with a rating or ratings, by certain commentators who deplore any perceived restrictions and who can find fault with a particular aspect of the rating system or a specific rating, and by those who demand more restrictions and even censorship. CARA generally lets the ratings speak for themselves and does not publicly attempt to defend any specific rating.

The rating system has survived for almost thirty years and continues to be widely used. Few institutions would have such longevity unless they provided a valuable public service. The rating system does.

Notes

1.   *See* Jane M. Friedman, *The Motion Picture Rating System of 1968: A Constitutional Analysis of Self-Regulation by the Film Industry*, 73 COLUM. L. REV. 185 (1973); *see also* Bill Broadway, *Hollywood as Babylon: Not Satisfied with Movie Industry's Rating System, Christian Groups Offer Their Own Warning Guides For Parents*, WASH. POST, Aug. 24, 1996, at D6; Timothy M. Gray, *The Movie Ratings Codes: Grade it C for Confusing*, CHI. SUN-TIMES, Jan. 23, 1994, at 1NC; Joanna Connors, *Industry's Movie Rating Is Labeled a Farce*, PLAIN DEALER, Aug. 18, 1990, at 1E.

2.   The Classification and Rating Administration ("CARA") is a part of the Motion Picture Association of America.

3.   For a detailed description of the history and workings of the ratings system, see JACK VALENTI, MOTION PICTURE ASSOCIATION OF AMERICA, THE VOLUNTARY MOVIE RATING SYSTEM, HOW IT BEGAN; ITS PURPOSE; THE PUBLIC REACTION (1996).

4.   *See generally* F. WALSH, SIN AND CENSORSHIP: THE CATHOLIC CHURCH AND THE MOTION PICTURE INDUSTRY (1996).

5.   *See, e.g.*, Alexandra Marks, *Who Should Rate TV Shows, Laymen v. Experts*, CHRISTIAN SCI. MONITOR, Mar. 13, 1996, at 1.

6.   VALENTI, *supra* note 3, at 4–5.

7.   VALENTI, *supra* note 3, at 11.

8.   *Id.* at 3.

9.   The Internet address is <http://www.mpaa.org>.

10. VALENTI, *supra* note 3, at 11.

11. The number of board members can range from eight to thirteen.

12. *See generally* JONATHON GREEN, THE ENCYCLOPEDIA OF CENSORSHIP (1990) (detailing government censorship in many countries).

13. *Id.*

14. *See* 3 J.D. LEE & BARRY A. LINDAHL, MODERN TORT LAW LIABILITY & LITIGATION §§ 29.35, 29.39 (rev. ed. 1996) (discussing parental liability for a child's torts and parental obligation to control a child).

15. *See* Hal Hinson, *Twenty Years of G and R Ratings; Plus X, PG, PG-13, and Don't Forget M*, CHI. SUN-TIMES, Nov. 27, 1988, at G01; *see also* Jonathan Wacks, *Just Who Are the People Who Censor Our Films?*, L.A. TIMES, Oct. 7, 1991, at F3.

16. *See* Marks, *supra* note 5.

17. *See* Friedman, *supra* note 1, at 199.

18. *See, e.g.*, Mark Caro, *The Heat is On: Will NC-17 Go Legit*, CHI. TRIB., Sept. 10, 1995, at C1; Hal Hinson, *Smash the Ratings System!; If This Isn't Censorship, Then Why Does It Feel Like It?*, WASH. POST, Apr. 21, 1990, at G1, G19.

19. *See* Bob Strauss, *Debate on "Basic Instinct"; Film Thriller's Trials Illustrate Problems of NC-17 Rating*, CHI. SUN-TIMES, Feb. 23, 1992, at Show-5.

20. *Id.*

21. *See* Jack Mathews, *A System Rated NC-17*, NEWSDAY, Nov. 22, 1992, at Fanfare-5.

22. *See* Stephen Schaefer, *Explicit "Kids" to Hit Screen Unrated*, BOSTON HERALD, July 24, 1995, at Entertainment-27.

23. For a discussion of court cases dealing with obscenity in movies, see Friedman, *supra* note 1, at 206–21.

24. VALENTI, *supra* note 3, at 9.

25. See, e.g., Erzonik v. City of Jacksonville, 422 U.S. 205 (1975) (invalidating local ordinance that forbade the showing at drive-in theaters of movies that included nudity).
26. Ginsberg v. New York, 390 U.S. 629 (1968); *see* Friedman, *supra* note 1, at 190.
27. *Ginsberg*, 390 U.S. 629.
28. *See* John Hartl, *NC-17 Ratings Can Stir Up Controversy—As Well as the Box Office*, SEATTLE TIMES, Jan. 17, 1993, at L4.
29. VALENTI, *supra* note 3, at 4–5.
30. *See, e.g.*, Kathy Boccella, *Too Foul for Words/Adults are Fed Up with Crass Language from the Mouths of Teens*, BUFF. NEWS, Aug. 23, 1995, at B9; Harriet Webster, *Experts Swear by Clean Language/Parents Can Control, Not Eliminate, Kids' Bad Words*, ARIZ. REPUBLIC, June 16, 1996, at A2.
31. *See, e.g.*, Connors, *supra* note 1; Wacks, *supra* note 15.
32. *See, e.g.*, Gray, *supra* note 1.
33. *See* Mathews, *supra* note 21.
34. *See* Friedman, *supra* note 1, at 195.
35. *See* VALENTI, *supra* note 3, at 5.
36. *See* Connors, *supra* note 1.
37. *See* Joyce Price, *Clean Movies Cleaned Up at the Box Office in 1995; Some See "Sleaze Doesn't Sell" Trend*, WASH. TIMES, Dec. 29, 1995, at A2.
38. *See* VALENTI, *supra* note 3, at 11 (explaining that there is 76% approval of the current rating system among parents with children under 13 years of age). The most recent poll released by the MPAA on November 14, 1996 shows that 80% of parents with children under the age of 17 found the rating system useful.
39. *See, e.g.*, 139 CONG. REC. E 1847 (1993) ("The federal government could attempt to regulate violence on TV programs the way it regulates indecency, with fines and revocation of licenses. . . . Or networks could impose stronger standards. Such measures might include showing violent programs at later hours, perhaps after 10 pm, or establishing a ratings system for TV shows similar to that used for the movie industry.").
40. *See, e.g.*, Miramax Films Corp. v. Motion Picture Ass'n of America, 560 N.Y.S.2d 730 (Sup. Ct. 1990) (dismissing Article 78 proceeding that challenged "X" rating system as discriminatory and arbitrary); Tropic Film Corp. v. Paramount Pictures Corp., 319 F. Supp. 1247 (S.D.N.Y. 1970) (rejecting antitrust challenge to rating system).

PART THREE

THE INTERNET DEBATE

Yelling "Filter" on the Crowded Net: The Implications of User Control Technologies

Daniel J. Weitzner

I. INTRODUCTION

Alongside the debate over the V-chip and rating schemes for television smolders burning questions about the impact of blocking, filtering, and other user empowerment tools for the Internet. User empowerment technologies that give users and parents more control over information available online to their children have emerged as critical elements of protecting children from inappropriate content and as a leading alternative to government censorship of content on the Internet.[1] During the constitutional litigation that led to the demise of the Communications Decency Act, a broad cross section of the Internet and civil liberties community—from the ACLU to America Online, Microsoft to the American Library Association, and over 50,000 individual Internet users—enthusiastically supported user empowerment tools as an alternative to censorship. Indeed, in striking down the CDA, the U.S. Supreme Court found the fact that parents can shield their children from material judged inappropriate as a significant alternative to government censorship laws enacted for the purpose of protecting those same children.[2]

With the first battle over the CDA won, however, serious concerns have been raised about the impact of user empowerment tools on the free flow of information. Civil liberties advocates raise significant questions: Will blocking and filtering tools squelch the free flow of information that the Supreme Court sought to protect? Will these technologies become dominated by "mainstream" speakers and publishers, crowding out alternative, noncommercial speech? How will filters account for controversial, yet important speech such as news and public affairs? Will Internet technologies designed to enable parents to protect their children ultimately be used by repressive governments whose goal is to censor the speech of their citizens, adult and child alike?

Supporters of the CDA, on the other hand, maintain that parental empowerment alone is not sufficient to protect children, and they worry that user empowerment tools will not develop to be truly effective tools. Are the tools developing today sufficient to protect children? On what basis should parents trust commercially available filters? How should parents choose among the various offerings currently on the market? Can third-party filtering alone be effective, or is a uniform, universal self-rating approach necessary? Will Internet market forces provide all that families need to protect their children or is some government intervention necessary?

The challenge before the Internet community today is to deploy user empowerment technologies in a way that maximizes the goals of protecting children and at the same time, protects bedrock freedom of expression principles. It must also do so in a way that is sustainable over the long run in the new online environment, recognizing the unique nature and potential of the Internet—its decentralized structure, its potential for promoting access to information, and its global scope.

This is no abstract debate, however, for today the Internet market is offering users a wide variety of software tools and services that either block out content judged inappropriate for children or limit children's access to only that content which has been approved for children. Unlike the V-chip, which will only come into existence as a result of a legislative mandate, the entrepreneurial energy of the Internet is producing a growing range of software and services to give users control over content through blocking, filtering, rating, and labeling mechanisms. The ways in which these tools are deployed in the Internet environment will have a major impact on both the propensity of policymakers to impose government censorship on Internet speech and on the very character of the Net as a platform for speech. This paper begins with a review of the technology landscape and will then consider the various policy positions regarding the appropriate technological and legal outcomes.

II. INTERNET BLOCKING, FILTERING, RATING, AND POSITIVE GUIDANCE TOOLS AND SERVICES

There are a growing number of parental empowerment options available to families online. These options range from services that are part of commercial online services to stand-alone software to Web-based labeling services and filtering software. Today it is safe to say that every family using the Internet has ready access to filtering sufficient to shield themselves and their children from unwanted content. In the future, we can expect even more developments in several areas: direct access to a diversity of rating services through major Web browsers, creation of additional third-party labeling services, broader use of self-labeling options, and increased availability of positive guidance services to help families find appropriate Internet content. Tools and services that filter out certain materials when accessing the Internet fall into three distinct categories:

1.   *Stand-Alone Filtering Software.* Software that runs on personal computers

together with an Internet access program and blocks access to whatever type of content the parent believes inappropriate for their child. In this category are products such as SurfWatch and Cyber Patrol, as well as Cybersitter, NetNanny, and over ten others.

2. *Commercial Online Service Blocking Features.* Several major commercial online services offer blocking features integrated into their access software. These features are easy to use and part of the regular menu of options offered to users.

3. *Web-Based PICS Filtering.* An integral part of major Web browsing software gives parents the ability to set up their Web software to block access to certain material on the World Wide Web through both self-rating systems such as RSACi and SafeSurf or independent third party systems such as Net Shepherd.

A. Stand-Alone Filtering Software

Since the introduction of the first Internet filtering software in May 1995, a wide variety of software products have been offered that gives parents (or other users) the ability to block access to various categories of objectionable content. This software is easy to use and available today to 100% of Internet-connected households, often at no charge.

A variety of stand-alone, inexpensive, and easy-to-install software blocks access to material judged inappropriate for children. Most packages give parents the option of choosing what kinds of material to block such as sexually explicit material, violence, advertising, or extremist views. Each filtering software offers different choices of content categories to be filtered. For example, one product, SurfWatch, offers users the following filtering choices:

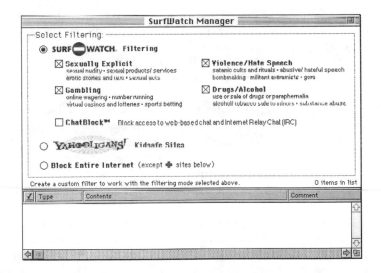

FIG. 1. SurfWatch Setup Screen

Different software also offers additional features such as the ability to selectively unblock blocked sites, track e-mail sent and received by particular children in the household, and even monitor the amount of time spent online.

The product Cyber Patrol offers the parent this choice:

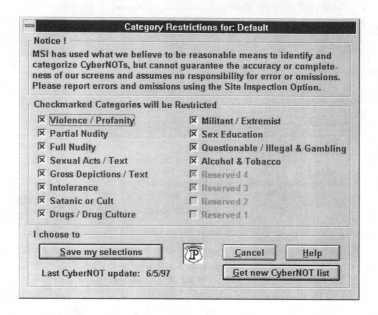

FIG. 2. Cyber Patrol Setup Screen

In addition to the two software products described above, over fifteen such filtering software packages exist, blocking material based on a diversity of editorial standards of the software's developers.

Many households have easy access to filtering software because it has been pre-installed on the computer they have purchased. PCs purchased through retail outlets or by mail order often come "bundled" with a variety of software products. Many consumers who have purchased a PC recently will find that it includes not only software to allow immediate Internet access, but also some form of filtering software. This is especially true of PCs sold with internal modems. Since bundled software is already loaded onto the computer's hard drive, no complicated installation is necessary and even parents who need their child's help to load software can employ blocking software as they judge necessary. Through these arrangements many millions of users around the country have ready access to filtering mechanisms.

Most filtering software vendors claim to filter based on objective criteria, but the blocking options do span the political spectrum. General interest software, such as Cyber Patrol and SurfWatch, exists along with software affiliated with conservative Christian groups such as CyberSitter, which has been endorsed and funded by Focus on the Family. Though many filtering vendors disclose their general filtering criteria, they do not reveal the actual lists of blocked sites. This lack of transparency in blocking software is a deficiency of this approach. During the relatively short lifetime of these products there have been occasions where sites are blocked inappropriately (i.e., the Center for Democracy and Technology's Web site was blocked for our discussion of bomb-making information and counterterrorism policy). For the most part, the filtering software vendors have been responsive to complaints and corrected their blocking lists based on such mistakes. However, the critical issue is that consumers be aware of such possibilities. More difficult and troublesome are situations in which filtering software publishers have blocked access to sites with information on homosexuality, feminism, or safe sex.

B. Built-In Online Service Parental Controls

Major commercial online services also offer a variety of parental controls that include site blocking, limitation on receipt of e-mail, and restriction of children's accounts to limited areas of the online service's own content. These controls are available at no cost and are easy to configure as part of establishing accounts for children.

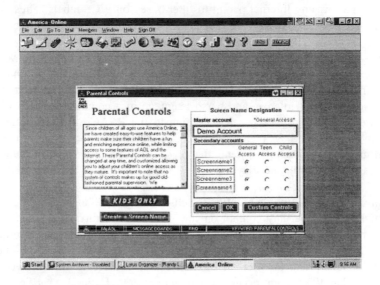

FIG. 3.   AOL Parental Control Screen

Taken together with the filtering options offered by other online services, over 14,000,000 Internet households today already have easy access to filtering capability.

C. Web-Based PICS Filtering for a Diversity of Third-Party Rating

In response to a perceived need on the part of Internet parents to control children's access to inappropriate material, the Internet community undertook the development of technical standards to facilitate the growth of an unlimited variety of rating and filtering systems for the Internet. In less than two years the result is that today there are three well-established, independent rating systems accessible at no charge to all Internet families, plus a platform on which any interested party can create additional rating systems to meet the needs and values of its own community.

These three rating systems have been created using the technical tools made available by the Platform for Internet Content Selection (PICS), created through the efforts of the World Wide Web Consortium and a number of leaders in the Internet development community.[3] Since the creation of PICS and the launch of these three labeling systems, virtually all leading Internet hardware, software, and service vendors have cooperated to give families the ability to block and filter content based on PICS-formatted labels. Anyone on the Web can create third-party labels, self-label their own content, and use the labels that exist to filter Web access. Since 1996, Microsoft's Web browser, Internet Explorer, has enabled parental control through any PICS-formatted labeling service. With roughly 30% of the browser market, a substantial number of users have PICS access today. Netscape has also recently announced its commitment to implement PICS. In addition to PICS-compatible browsers, a number of stand-alone filtering products such as Cyber Patrol allow any Internet parent to filter based on PICS labels. Thus, today 100% of Internet-connected families have easy access to all PICS labeling services.

Self-Labeling. The PICS platform allows Web publishers to label their own content. Leading examples of this approach include RSACi and SafeSurf. Both RSACi and SafeSurf include standard rating vocabularies that allow Web publishers to describe the levels of sex, nudity, violence, and harsh language in a common format. To date, over 35,000 sites have rated their pages according to the RSACi labeling system and over 50,000 have rated their pages with SafeSurf. A number of major online content providers are working with RSACi to extend the reach of RSACi's ratings around the Web, including Disney, ESPN, and Playboy.

Third-Party Labeling. In addition to self-labeling, PICS also enables any individual or organization to label any content on the Web. This feature supports the creation of multiple, diverse, independent labeling on content. Recently, a Canadian group called Net Shepherd created independent labels for over 300,000 Web sites. Net Shepherd has teamed with Alta Vista to offer an Internet search service to find materials that Net Shepherd has labeled as appropriate for younger children. Using this service, children can search the Web and have returned results that include only those sites that meet rating criteria specified by parents.

III. EVALUATING THE FREEDOM OF EXPRESSION
IMPLICATIONS OF VARIOUS
USER EMPOWERMENT APPROACHES

Soon after the emergence of blocking and filtering technologies for the Internet, a debate ensued over the wisdom of bringing such capability to the Net. In order to assess the implications of various approaches for the Net, we can evaluate three broad categories of approaches characterizing the evolving area of user empowerment:

No Filtering—Work Toward an Unfiltered Net. This approach assumes that the evils of filtering and harmful uses of the technology outweigh any possible positive effects. In the filter-free future there may or may not be laws that censor content online.

Ubiquitous, Uniform Self-Labeling. Move toward a universal, ubiquitous content rating system: full and effective user empowerment will only come with uniform content labels that users around the world can filter based on their own values. Assuming that such labeling were to be created, it could be legally compelled, left purely voluntary for content creators, or be compelled by pressure from browsers that may block all unlabeled content and search engines that may refuse to search unrated sites.

Multiple, Third-Party Filtering. Support a diversity of third-party labeling and filtering systems as a means to provide families online with the ability to block, filter based on filters, ratings, and labels assigned by other individuals or organizations that the family chooses to trust.

This paper will judge such approaches with the following goals in mind:

Diversity. The great promise of the Internet for democracy, freedom, cultural development, and economic participation lies in its low barriers to entry for speakers, publishers, and listeners. Any solution designed to protect children must also support this fundamental value.

Trust. As a global, general purpose information and communication platform designed to serve users from different cultures and backgrounds, any approach must be an effective and trusted means of assisting parents in guiding their children's online experience.

Sustainability. Any approach must take into account the unique nature of the Internet, both as a set of technologies and a new forum for speech and market for information. While the Internet is not, and ought not be, a lawless environment, policymakers must take into account the limits of law for imposing solutions on the Internet environment.

Minimize Government Censorship of Protected Expression. Censorship of speech on the Internet is both a trespass on national free speech rights and the international right to freedom of expression and association. Solutions to the problem of children's access to inappropriate content must not result in limitations on adult's freedom of expression.

Preserving the Free Flow of Information on the Net. Finally, any approach adopted must support the free flow of information globally and enhance, or at least not harm, the democratic potential of the Internet both in the United States and around the world.

A. Option 1: The Unfiltered Net

Following the U.S. Supreme Court CDA decision, critics of Internet blocking and filtering technologies stepped up their effort to smoke out the evils of blocking and filtering technologies. Taking these concerns seriously, we must consider that the alternative to having blocking and filtering technologies is the absence of these tools. Therefore, following a look at the free expression concerns raised by these technologies, we will consider the option of working toward a wholly unfiltered Internet environment. The ACLU, one of the leading organizations to oppose the CDA in the courts, issued a strongly worded report arguing that "the dense smoke of the many rating and blocking schemes"[4] on the Net put at risk the very free speech rights won in the CDA case. Leading commentators on Internet law issues have also raised concerns about the availability of labeling, filtering, and blocking features in the Internet infrastructure. Writing in *Wired* magazine, Professor Larry Lessig declared "PICS is the devil. . . . As part of the Web's infrastructure, PICS will be an extremely versatile and robust censorship tool."[5]

While the rhetorical temperature of some filtering critics is often quite high, there are a number of substantial reasons to have concern about the impact of filtering technologies on freedom of expression. The concerns of the filtering critics include:

1. Filtering will disadvantage unpopular and controversial speech: third-party raters are more likely to filter out what the ACLU characterizes as "quirky and idiosyncratic speech" and allow only "mainstream" and commercial speech through the filters. In self-rating scenarios, the burden of rating one's own content will be high for noncommercial speakers on the Net.

2. Filtering technologies will make censorship easier for national governments: building filtering tools such as PICS into the Internet infrastructure will make it that much easier for countries who are inclined to censor the Internet.

3. Numerous problems exist with self-rating systems: aside from those already discussed, conversation and chat is hard to rate and the pressure to rate will lead speakers to homogenize their speech.

4. Third-party rating systems are not a viable alternative: the ACLU believes that the lack of development of third-party rating systems indicates that this is not a real option for the future. Without explaining why, they do not consider the over fifteen filtering software products on the market and two PICS-based third-party rating systems substantial services. Thus, the ACLU report expresses concern that third-party raters will only consider mainstream sites for rating.

5. Current rating systems fail to disclose their criteria for blocking: the ACLU and a number of other critics of filtering point out that potential users and consumers of most of the filtering products available today have a difficult time selecting among filtering options because rating and filtering criteria are not always well disclosed, nor do users have an adequate basis for deciding which filtering services to trust.

Assessment of the Unfiltered Net

Taken together, we may reasonably conclude that the filtering critics would rather see an Internet environment without filtering altogether.[6] We must now ask whether this is a desirable, viable option.

1. Effective and Trusted Solution? By definition, the unfiltered Net leaves users, including parents, with less control over the content that comes into their homes than they have today. Advocates of less filtering, or a total absence of filtering, clearly believe that families ought to rely on nontechnical means of guiding their children's Internet usage. There is general agreement that healthy, constructive use the of the Internet by children begins with parental involvement and responsibility. Yet, an unfiltered Net may leave the many parents who have chosen to use some form of filtering feeling less secure and trusting.

2. Diversity of Voices and Editorial Choices. Decreasing filtering options will reduce, not enhance, the diversity of voices online. First, both the choice to access the Net through a filter of any kind, and the act of creating a list of sites to be included or excluded in any view of the Net are each, in and of themselves, First Amendment protected activity. Second, no amount of policy debate is likely to eliminate filtering products and services from the market. Thus, those concerned about freedom of expression and diversity must work to make sure that such services serve those goals, rather than seek to eliminate them.

Creation and dissemination of blocking, filtering, and other content evaluation tools constitute important expression of editorial and critical judgments that increase the information available online. Moreover, any steps to decrease access to the tools necessary for large and small, commercial and noncommercial speakers to develop and distribute their own filtering judgments might seriously disadvantage the editorial expression of these groups, leaving only large, commercial, well-financed groups and individuals in the filtering arena.

Perhaps the technical nature of blocking, filtering, and labeling tools online lead us to forget that filtering entails important positive expression in the form of editorial judgments about other content. Even though they take a different form than in traditional media, the editorial decisions of a private entity—individual or organization—as to which content to filter in or out is a First Amendment protected activity every bit as much as is a newspaper editor's regarding which news stories to run and which letters to print or a movie reviewer's expression of opinion about a new movie.[7] The great opportunity offered by filtering in general and open specifications such as PICS is to increase the diversity of information on line. This is not an increase in primary information but in information about information, much as book reviews, movie reviews, and TV listings are not primary information yet they make important contributions to the free flow of information and ideas.

Content categorization and filtering has always been part of the Internet infrastructure and blocking software and services are unlikely to disappear. To advocate or rely on a position that hopes to eliminate blocking and filtering capabilities is to ignore key facts about the technical and market development of the Internet and online services. Filtering products and services have been in use since well before the Communications Decency Act debate. These products and services exist because at least some online users appear to want them and market forces have built upon basic open standards of the Net to provide them. To expect that these capabilities will disappear, or can be eliminated, is simply not supported by the facts of the development of the Net.

Filtering and blocking tools are based on the fundamental building blocks of the

Internet infrastructure and do not, in fact, depend on new technology specifications such as PICS. User empowerment tools, beginning with America Online's Parental Controls and products like SurfWatch and CyberPatrol, are able to block online content simply by using basic Internet addressing features—domain names, Web addresses known as URLs, numeric IP addresses that are assigned to every computer on the Internet, and newsgroup names. Specifications like PICS are important tools for making filtering easier to deploy, but blocking and filtering tools have been successfully deployed without PICS. In fact, the only foreseeable means of eliminating filtering tools would be to make them illegal. Absent such a step, which would itself raise serious freedom of expression concerns, the Internet marketplace can be expected to continue to provide user empowerment tools in response to user demand.

Shunning filtering on the Net, then, is not only an unsustainable policy option from the standpoint of the development of the Net (as described above), but it is also contrary to core First Amendment values. Blocking, filtering, and labeling tools are enabling technologies for increasing the diversity of editorial opinion on the Net. While in traditional media, the power to review a book or movie is limited to the media elite who often represent only mainstream opinion, the power to do so online can be distributed among all Internet users, thereby increasing and enriching the diversity of voices online. Since filtering is almost certain to remain part of the Internet, resisting its progress will only serve to limit its power to voices that are already powerful, a grave disservice to First Amendment values.

3. Invites Censorship: No user control invites government censorship. Decreasing the degree of user and parental control online will increase both the pressure and justification for governments to censor the Internet. For both political and legal reasons, the availability of user control is a bulwark against censorship. The United States Supreme Court decision overturning the Communications Decency Act was, without doubt, a landmark decision for freedom of expression on the Internet, inasmuch as it declared that speech online is entitled to the highest degree of First Amendment protection. The decision to overturn the statute turned on two critical factual findings: first, that the burden on speakers to limit access to minors is so great that it amounts to a total ban on speech, and second, that less restrictive alternatives such as user empowerment technologies are available to parents, so the government need not step in to protect children. From all sides of the political spectrum, policymakers agree that if parents have options that enable them to shield their own children from material they judge inappropriate based on their own family values, then the government need not step in to make the decision for the parents. All plaintiffs in the CDA challenge presented evidence and made legal arguments stressing the availability of these technologies.

Contrary to the concern that a decline in filtering will increase the call for censorship, critics of filtering worry that the availability of filtering tools will actually encourage government censorship. With such tools at hand, the reasoning goes, governments will be emboldened to act. The recent history of Internet censorship suggests, however, that the cause and effect is actually the reverse. Countries with a political tradition of censorship and repression like Singapore[8] and China began Internet censorship programs long before

PICS and other filtering options were available. Even more liberal countries, such as Australia, that are calling for the use of the PICS-based RSACi system have a long tradition of censoring film and TV. Germany, which has sought to prosecute Internet Service Providers for providing access to illegal political materials (racist and xenophobic statements), rejected proposals to employ user empowerment tools. So, countries that seek to censor the Net appear to feel able to do so without the help of blocking, filtering, and labeling tools, and are not even satisfied when such tools are offered.

Any effort that results in an actual decline in these empowerment tools would only strengthen the hand of those who would re-invoke government censorship and could even lead the courts to reevaluate their understanding of the Net. Censorship is a political decision, based on repressive impulses that extend far deeper that what is merely technically possible. The absence or presence of user empowerment tools are not likely to sway the determined censor in either direction, but they do offer many countries that option of enabling parents to protect children from what they believe to be inappropriate, without sweeping restrictions on the freedom of expression.

B. Option Two: Ubiquitous, Universal Labeling

At the other end of the policy spectrum from the unfiltered Net is the completely labeled or rated Net. Several self-labeling systems—most notably RSACi but also SafeSurf—propose to have all content on the Internet labeled by its creator according to a uniform, objective rating vocabulary. With all content thus labeled, users would be able to block access to that content that fails to meet their individual criteria. The proponents of this self-rating approach have been quite aggressive, both in the United States and around the world, in advocating their version of blocking and filtering. The Recreational Software Advisory Council has support from some of the major Internet companies in the U.S. A new International Working Group for Content Rating met with supporters in London in early October to plan a "coded means of describing Internet content, which can be used worldwide."[9] And in a recent speech, the chairman of the Australia Broadcasting Authority endorsed RSAC's self-rating approach as the best substitute for his country's traditional "subjective, state-managed classification" system, which works in traditional mass media but, according to him, will not be viable online.[10] Ubiquitous, uniform self-rating may appeal to mass media regulators, but whether it will work on the global Internet is an unanswered question. Based on the criteria used in this paper, it has several serious shortcomings.[11]

1. Limited Effectiveness and Questionable Trust: Self-rating has yet to prove effective and fails to inspire trust. The effectiveness of any objective, self-rating system turns on the feasibility of creating a single, uniform rating vocabulary that is sophisticated enough to express adequate information about Internet content to enable families around the world to make filtering decisions, while being easy enough to use and understand that Internet content creators, including individual users, can easily label their content on a real-time basis. In addition to being effective, the system must be trusted. PICS technology provides the basis to protect against fraudulent alteration of labels by unauthorized users, but will parents filtering based on labels applied by the creator of the content trust that the label is accurate?

The problems of developing an effective, objective uniform self-rating vocabulary have shown themselves most directly in the difficulty RSAC recently experienced in applying its ratings to online news sources. The RSAC system allows content providers to rate their content with numeric scores representing various levels of sex, violence, nudity, or harsh language. This classification system is in keeping with its goal of helping parents avoid online content that contains, in the parent's judgment, unacceptable levels of such material. Applying these ratings may be relatively straightforward for clearly erotic content such as pictorials from the Playboy Web site, or for obviously inoffensive material such as a geography site, however, what about the MSNBC or *Time* magazine Web site? On any given day these sites may contain reports on grisly airplane accidents or murders, discussion of sexual abuse, or reports that contain, for some reason, harsh language. Should a news story on a earthquake describing death and dismemberment receive the same rating as the Jean-Claude Van Dam fan club Web site? In a purely objective classification of the content, the answer would have to be yes, but surely many parents would want to allow access to the former but not the latter.

In reaction to the difficulty in applying RSAC's rating system to news, the organization proposed a special "news" label. This, too, produced a furor, as the debate over who is a bona fide news organization and who decides the bona fides, went public. In the end, most of the major news organizations announced that they would not self-rate their sites and RSAC put its "news" label plan on hold indefinitely.[12]

Why should parents trust the rating that content providers attach to their own material online? What incentive is there to rate honestly, rather than to rate in a way that attracts the desired surfers? RSAC's system deals with this question by providing contractual penalties for anyone who misrates using the RSAC label. Some have also proposed legislation that would provide penalties for improper or fraudulent labeling of content. It may even be that in the United States the Federal Trade Commission has the power to punish fraudulent labels under it "unfair and deceptive practices" jurisdiction. Whether enforcement is by private contract, statute, or regulation, the task of auditing labels for the thirty-five million Web pages that exist only today is certainly daunting and leaves some doubt as to whether parents can trust the labels attached by all content providers from the most scrupulous publishers to the shadiest providers of illicit material.

2. Squelching Diversity of Online Content: Uniform rating vocabulary will necessarily limit range of speech online. The limits inherent in any single ratings vocabulary go far beyond application to news and public affairs. Can a single vocabulary be developed that captures the concerns of all communities and cultures that participate in the Net, now and in the future? Keyed to Western tastes and values, the RSAC system provides tags for sex, nudity, violence, and harsh language. But what about blasphemy, racism, political extremism, excessively democratic discourse? All of these are categories of speech that some individuals or governments wish to avoid by blocking and filtering. Even if it were possible to develop a sufficiently comprehensive vocabulary, could it at the same time be made simple enough to be used by the millions of content providers (speakers) online?

Inevitably some compromises would be made to balance ease of use for publishers and those who seek to use the ratings to filter. But in these compromises will be lost the great diversity of speech that already exists on the Net today and grows daily. The result of these necessary compromises is either to limit that range of speech allowed on the Net (because unratable speech would not be permitted), or to render filtering useless for certain cultures and communities. In either case, the result is reduced diversity and homogenization of online discourse.

3. Unsustainable: Limited incentives for self-rating cast sustainability in doubt absent Internet-distorting coercion. Perhaps it is possible to design a self-rating system trusted by users and sufficiently complete to encompass all varieties of information online. Is such a system sustainable? The critical stumbling block for self-rating is that content providers, all the tens of millions of speakers who contribute content to the Internet, have no apparent reason to self-rate their sites. In the two years since RSAC was launched, roughly 43,000 sites have been rated, or 2–4% of all the million to 1,500,000 sites estimated to be on the Net today. For self-rating to work, nearly all sites must rate themselves. Proponents of self-rating have been relatively silent on how to bridge the gap from 2–4% to 100% coverage. Two options, however, have emerged: one set of infrastructure distortions, and the possibility of legal requirements to force self-rating.

First, RSAC supporters and others have suggested that critical points in the Internet infrastructure could be altered in order to force sites to rate themselves or become nearly invisible to users. Several proposals emerged that would cut off the flow of all unrated content to most users. This threat is designed to force content providers, who want their content read as widely as possible, to rate using the RSAC system. This summer, calls came for Web browsers to be configured to block access to all unrated sites. RSAC supporters even suggested that the next version of Microsoft's Internet Explorer Web browser would be shipped to customers with the default configuration set to block all sites that had not rated with RSAC. This suggestion was quickly refuted by Microsoft. At the same time, similar comments claimed that major search engines would refuse to search sites that did not have RSAC ratings. Again, the search engine operators quickly denied that such plans ever existed.

The need to distort the Internet infrastructure in order to create "incentives" for self rating shows that this approach is entirely unsustainable and goes against the grain of the Net. Such coercive approaches would lock users into a single rating system that is quite possibly inadequate for many needs, and would force all who speak online to choose between rating every item published online or relegating their speech into certain oblivion.

4. Self-Rating Invites Censorship: Lack of incentive to rate suggests government mandates will be required. Reliance on self-rating can only be effective with legal mandates that require all content to be rated. If the above infrastructure distortions are not achieved, or not successful at forcing 100% of Internet content to be rated, the only other alternative is to make self-rating a legal requirement. In the United States, such a law would likely run afoul of First Amendment protections against "compelled speech." First Amendment doctrine holds that the government forcing someone to speak—in this case to label his or her content—is every bit as much a violation of the First Amendment as a government action that prohibits speech.[13]

U.S. legislative action alone, however, would not be sufficient. For self-rating to be an effective user empowerment strategy, nearly 100% of all content on the Internet would have to be rated, requiring an international agreement to compel self-rating according to a common ratings system. An international requirement to rate according to a single ratings code is sure to stifle the freedom of expression of users around the world, and, as was argued in point B above, unlikely to serve the needs of all the disparate cultures on the Net. Perhaps the only consolation to advocates of the free flow of information is that such a agreement is far off in the future, at best.

C. Option 3: A diversity of third-party rating services

Encouraging easy access to a multiplicity of third-party filtering systems is most likely to support the free flow of information, a diversity of ideas, and empower parents to protect their children from unwanted material online. In the last few years, over fifteen independent third-party filtering products and services have come to market. More commercial products come to market every month. The platform for third-party ratings afforded by PICS may enable the creation of an even greater diversity of third-party rating services, but this process is slow and has yet to yield encouraging results. Still, third-party services show the most promise for helping to preserve the Internet as an environment that supports the free flow of information and make it a place where parents feel empowered to protect their children as they see fit.

1. Third-Party Filtering Products Are the Most Effective Tools Available Today and Have the Potential To Build Trust Among Users. By far the most effective user empowerment tools today are the third-party blocking and filtering services for sale as stand-alone software or packaged as part of commercial online services. All of the products on the market work by creating lists of sites that are deemed inappropriate for access by children.[14] The producers of these products are continually updating these site lists so that even newly launched sites will be blocked if they meet the filtering criteria. None of the products claim to block 100% of what should be blocked, but they do claim to cover the vast majority of sites. However, because there is an active, competitive market for these tools, and because computer and consumer magazines have begun to test the relative performance of various products, market pressures are forcing competing products to do a better and better job of finding sites that should be blocked.

Not surprisingly, user empowerment technology has progressed faster than has consumer and community trust in these tools. Since trust is harder to build than software, creating trusted empowerment tools will take time. The software industry has shown that these tools are possible to develop; now trusted institutions in the community—newspapers, parent-teacher groups, librarians, religious organizations, Boy Scouts, etc.—must become involved in developing user empowerment tools that meet the needs of their constituencies and carry with them the values and trust associated with those institutions.

Rating the Net*

Jonathan Weinberg

I. INTRODUCTION

Internet filtering software is hot. Plaintiffs in *ACLU v. Reno*[1] relied heavily on the existence and capabilities of filtering software (also known as blocking software) in arguing that the Communications Decency Act was unconstitutional.[2] President Clinton has pledged to "vigorously support" the development and widespread availability of filtering software.[3] Some free speech activists see this software as the answer to the dilemma of indecency regulation, making it possible "to reconcile free express of ideas and appropriate protection for kids."[4] Indeed, some of the strongest supporters of such software are First Amendment activists who sharply oppose direct government censorship of the Net.[5]

Internet filtering software, further, is here. As of this writing, the Platform for Internet Content Selection (PICS) working group has developed a common language for Internet rating systems, making it much easier to create and market such ratings.[6] Already, two heavily promoted ratings systems (SafeSurf and RSACi) allow content providers to rate their own World Wide Web sites in a sophisticated manner. Microsoft's World Wide Web browser incorporates a feature called Content Advisor that will block Web sites in accordance with the rules of any PICS-compliant ratings system, including SafeSurf and RSACi.[7] Stand-alone blocking software—marketed under such trademarks as SurfWatch, Cyber Patrol, CYBERSitter, KinderGuard, Net Nanny, and Parental Guidance—is gaining increasing sophistication and popularity.

It is easy to understand the acclaim for filtering software. This software can do an impressive job at blocking access to sexually explicit material that a parent does not wish his or her child to see. The PICS standard for describing ratings systems is an important technical achievement, allowing the development and easy use of a variety of sophisticated ratings schemes. In the midst of the general enthusiasm for Internet filtering software, it is worth trying to locate filtering technology's limitations and drawbacks. Blocking software is a huge step forward in solving the dilemma of sexually explicit speech on the Net, but it does have costs. People whose image of the Net is mediated through blocking software may miss out on worthwhile speech through deliberate exclusion, through inaccuracies in labeling inherent to the filtering process, and through the restriction of unrated sites.

II. BACKGROUND

Internet rating services respond to parents' and governments' concerns about children's access to sexually explicit material, and other adult content, available on the Net. The services focus greatest attention on children's access to the World Wide Web (Web). The Web consists of a vast collection of documents, each residing on a computer linked to the Internet. These documents may contain text, pictures, sound, and/or video. Any Web document may contain links to other Web documents or other Internet resources, so that a user with a Web browser can jump from one document to another with a single mouse click. It is easy for users without sophisticated equipment or expensive Internet connections to create Web pages that are then accessible to any other user with access to the Web.

Rating services have also paid special attention to Usenet newsgroups. Usenet newsgroups allow any user to post text, pictures, sound, or video to one of more than 15,000 different open forums, each devoted to a different topic. About 200,000 computer networks worldwide participate in the Usenet news system. A small number of Usenet newsgroups are devoted to sexually explicit material.

It is fairly easy for software to screen access to Usenet news. Because each newsgroup has a name describing its particular topic (such as rec.music.folk, soc.culture.peru, or alt.tv.x-files), software writers can do a reasonably effective job of blocking access to sexually explicit material by simply blocking access to those newsgroups (such as alt.sex.stories) whose names indicate that they include sexually explicit material.

Blocking access to sexually explicit material on the Web is much more difficult. There are millions of individual pages on the Web, and the number is increasing every day. An astonishingly small fraction of those pages contain sexually explicit material.[8] Every Web page (indeed, every document accessible over the Internet) has a unique address, or "URL,"[9] and the URLs of some Web pages do contain clues as to their subject matter. Because nothing in the structure or syntax of the Web *requires* Web pages to include labels advertising their content, though, identifying pages with sexually explicit material is not an easy task.

First-generation blocking software compiled lists of off-limits Web pages through two methods. First, the rating services hired raters to work through individual Web pages by hand, following links to sexually explicit sites and compiling lists of URLs to be deemed off-limits to children. Second, they used string-recognition software to automatically proscribe any Web page that contained a forbidden word (such as "sex" or "xxx") in its URL.[10]

The PICS specifications contemplate that a ratings system can be more sophisticated.

A rating service may rate a document along multiple dimensions. Instead of merely rating a document as "adult" or "child-safe," it might give it separate ratings for violence, sex, nudity, and adult language. Further, along any given dimension, the rating service may choose from any number of values. Instead of simply rating a site "block" or "no-block" for violence, a rating service might assign it a rating of between 1 and 10 for increasing amounts of violent content. These features are important because they allow the creation of filtering software that is customizable by parents. A parent subscribing to such a rating service, for example, might seek to block only sites rated over 3 for violence and 8 for sex. Finally, the PICS documents note that ratings need not be assigned by the authors of filtering software.[11] They can be assigned by the content creators themselves or by third parties. One of the consequences of the PICS specifications is that varying groups—the Christian Coalition, say, or the Boy Scouts—can seek to establish rating services reflecting their own values, and these ratings can be implemented by off-the-shelf blocking software.[12]

Most rating services today follow the PICS specifications. Their particular approaches, however, differ. The Recreational Software Advisory Council (RSAC) has developed an Internet rating system called RSACi.[13] Participating content providers rate their own sites along a scale of 0 through 4 on four dimensions: violence, nudity, sex, and language. RSAC does not itself market blocking software; instead, it licenses its service to software developers. SafeSurf is another system in which content providers rate their own speech.[14] In that system, content providers choose from nine values in each of nine categories, from "profanity" through "gambling."[15]

Rating services associated with individual manufacturers of blocking software include Cyber Patrol, Specs for Kids, and CYBERSitter. Cyber Patrol rates sites along fifteen dimensions, from "violence/profanity" to "alcohol & tobacco," but assigns only two values within each of those categories: CyberNOT and CyberYES.[16] Specs for Kids rates documents along eleven dimensions, including "advertising," "alternative lifestyles," "politics," and "religion," and assigns up to five values (including "no rating") in each of those categories.[17] CYBERSitter, by contrast, maintains a single list of objectionable sites; it affords users no opportunity to block only portions of the list.[18]

III. ACCURACY

Since blocking software first came on the market, individual content providers have complained about the ratings given to their sites. Not all of those complaints relate to problems inherent to filtering software. For example, some programs tend to block entire directories of Web pages simply because they contain a single "adult" file. That means that large numbers of innocuous Web pages are blocked merely because they are located near some *other* page with adult content.[19] Some programs block entire domains, including all of the sites hosted by particular Internet service providers.[20] This may be a temporary glitch, though; over time, it is possible that the most successful rating services will—properly—label each document separately.[21]

Other problems arise from the wacky antics of string-recognition software. America Online's software, ever alert for four-letter words embedded in text, refused to let users register from the British town of "Scunthorpe."[22] The University of Kansas Medical

Center installed SurfWatch in its Internet kiosk and discovered that users could not see the Web page of their own Archie R. Dykes Medical Library.[23] For sheer wackiness, nothing can match a CYBERSitter feature that causes Web browsers to white out selected *words* but display the rest of the page (so that the sentence "President Clinton opposes homosexual marriage" would be rendered "President Clinton opposes marriage").[24] These problems too, though, may be addressed through proper software design.

Controversies over sites actually rated by humans are less amenable to technological solution. One dispute arose when Cyber Patrol blocked animal-rights Web pages because of images of animal abuse, including syphilis-infected monkeys; Cyber Patrol classed those as "gross depiction" CyberNOTs.[25] The situation was aggravated because Cyber Patrol, following the entire-directory approach described above, blocked *all* of the hundred or so animal welfare, animal rights, and vegetarian pages hosted at the Animal Rights Resource Site.[26] An officer of Envirolink, which had provided the Web space, responded: "Animal rights is usually the first step that children take in being involved in the environment. Ignoring companies like Mary Kay that do these things to animals and allowing them to promote themselves like good corporate citizens is a 'gross depiction.'"[27]

Sites discussing gay and lesbian issues are commonly blocked, even if they contain no references to sex. SurfWatch, in its initial distribution, blocked a variety of sites including the Queer Resources Directory, an archive of material on homosexuality in America,[28] and the International Association of Gay Square Dance Clubs. SurfWatch responded to protests by unblocking most of the contested sites.[29] Other blocking programs, on the other hand, still exclude them: Cyber Patrol blocks a mirror of the Queer Resources Directory, along with Usenet newsgroups including clari.news.gays (which carries AP and Reuters dispatches) and alt.journalism.gay-press.[30] CYBERSitter is perhaps the most likely to block any reference to sexual orientation, forbidding such newsgroups as alt.politics.homosexual. In the words of a CYBERSitter representative: "I wouldn't even care to debate the issues if gay and lesbian issues are suitable for teenagers. . . . We filter anything that has to do with sex. Sexual orientation [is about sex] by virtue of the fact that it has sex in the name."[31]

The list of blocked sites is sometimes both surprising and alarming. Cyber Patrol blocks Usenet newsgroups including alt.feminism, soc.feminism, clari.news.women, soc.support.pregnancy.loss, and alt.support.fat-acceptance.[32] It blocks gun and Second Amendment Web pages (including one belonging to the NRA Members' Council of Silicon Valley). It blocks the Web site of the League for Programming Freedom (a group opposing software patents). It blocked the Electronic Frontier Foundation's censorship archive.[33] It blocked a site maintained by the U.S. Naval Academy Weapon Systems Engineering Department.[34] CYBERSitter blocks the National Organization of Women Web site.[35] It blocks the Penal Lexicon, an encyclopedic British site concerned with prisons and penal affairs.[36] It blocks some Web pages that criticize its blocking decisions,[37] and at one point demanded that a critic's Internet service provider terminate the critic's account or see all of the sites on its server blocked.[38] After the *Netly News*—a component of Time Warner Pathfinder—posted a search engine allowing viewers to find out whether the software blocked particular sites, CYBERSitter blocked the more than 150,000 pages on pathfinder.com.[39]

One might think that a better answer lies in rating systems, such as RSACi and SafeSurf, in which content providers evaluate their own sites. An author, one might assume, could hardly disagree with a rating he chose himself. The matter, though, is not so clear. When an author evaluates his site in order to gain a rating from any PICS-compliant rating service, he must follow the algorithms and rules of that service. Jonathan Wallace, thus, in an article called *Why I Will Not Rate My Site*, asks how he is to rate "An Auschwitz Alphabet,"[40] his powerful and deeply chilling work of reportage on the Holocaust.[41] The work contains descriptions of violence done to camp inmates' sexual organs. A self-rating system, Wallace fears, would likely force him to choose between the unsatisfactory alternatives of labeling the work as suitable for all ages, on the one hand, or "lump[ing it] together with the Hot Nude Women page" on the other.[42]

IV. RULES AND STANDARDS

At least some of the rating services' problems in assigning ratings to individual documents are inherent. It is the nature of the process that no ratings system can classify documents in a perfectly satisfactory manner. Consider first how a ratings system designer might construct a ratings algorithm. She might provide an algorithm made up entirely of simple, focused questions, in which each question has a relatively easily ascertainable "yes" or "no" answer. (Example: "Does the file contain a photographic image depicting exposed male or female genitalia?") Alternatively, she might seek to afford evaluators more freedom to apply broad, informal, situationally sensitive guidelines so as to capture the overall feel of each site. (Example: "Is the site suitable for a child below the age of 13?")[43]

In jurisprudential terms, the first approach relies on "rules" and the second on "standards."[44] The RSACi system attempts to be rule based. In coding its violence levels, for example, to include "harmless conflict; some damage to objects"; "creatures injured or killed; damage to objects, fighting"; "humans injured or killed with small amount of blood"; "humans injured or killed; blood and gore"; and "wanton and gratuitous violence; torture; rape," its designers have striven to devise simple, hard-edged rules, with results turning mechanically on a limited number of facts.[45] Not all RSAC categories are hard edged—the "revealing attire" nudity level requires a rater to decide whether a "reasonable person" would consider particular clothing sexually suggestive and alluring[46]—but the system overall aims for rules.

Other rating systems rely more heavily on standards. The SafeSurf questionnaire, for example, requires the self-rater to determine whether nudity is "artistic" (levels 4 through 6), "erotic" (level 7), "pornographic" (level 8), or "explicit and crude" pornographic (level 9).[47] The Voluntary Content Rating self-rating system promoted by CYBERSitter is almost the model of a standards-based regime: it offers as its only guidance the instructions that self-raters should determine whether their sites are "not suitable for children under the age of 13," and whether they include material "intended for an audience 18 years of age or older."[48] Specs for Kids raters are instructed to distinguish between sites that: (1) refer to homosexuality "[i]mpartial[ly]"; (2) discuss it with "acceptance or approval"; or (3) "[a]ctive[ly] promot[e]" it or "attempt[] to recruit the viewer."[49] Each of these classifications requires more judgment on the part of the evaluator, and is not so hard edged as the

RSACi categories. Individuals with different perspectives and values may disagree as to where the lines fall.[50] With respect to the Specs treatment of references to homosexuality, individuals disagree as to whether the categories are even coherent.[51] These categories work only within a community of shared values, so that evaluators can draw on the same norms and assumptions in applying the value judgments embedded in the standards.

This distinction follows the more general rules-standards dichotomy in law, which focuses on the instructions lawmakers give to law-appliers in a variety of contexts.[52] Legal thought teaches that rules and standards each have disadvantages. A problem with standards is that they are less constraining; relatively speaking, a standards-based system will lack consistency and predictability.[53] Rules become increasingly necessary as the universe of law-appliers becomes larger, less able to rely on shared culture and values as a guide to applying standards in a relatively consistent and coherent way.[54] One can see a parallel in problems the Yahoo! indexing service faces in seeking to classify the increasing number of Web sites. Yahoo!'s taxonomy embodies editorial judgments; the job is not amenable to resolution simply through rules. Consistent application of the taxonomy "comes from having the same 20 people classify every site, and by having those people crammed together in the same building where they are constantly engaged in a discussion of what belongs where."[55] As a result,

> Yahoo! is faced with an unforgiving trade-off between the size and the quality of its directory. If Yahoo! hires another 50 or 60 classifiers to examine every last site on the Web, the catalog will become less consistent. ... On the other hand, if Yahoo! stays with a small number of classifiers, the percentage of sites Yahoo! knows about will continue to shrink.[56]

For this reason, the designers of RSACi attempted to be rule-like. They contemplate that the universe of ratings evaluators will include every content provider on the Web; that group can claim no shared values and culture. To accommodate that heterogeneous group, RSAC offers a rules-based questionnaire that (it hopes) all can understand in a similar manner. This, RSAC explains, will "provide[] fair and consistent ratings by eliminating most of the subjectivity inherent in alternative rating systems."[57] It seems plain that with a relatively large universe of evaluators—and it is hard to see how one could seek to map the entire Net without one—a ratings system relying too heavily on standards just won't work. The dangers of arbitrariness and inconsistency will be too great.[58]

Rules, though, have their own problems. They direct law-appliers to treat complex and multifaceted reality according to an oversimplified schematic.[59] The point of rules, after all, is that by simplifying an otherwise complex inquiry, they "screen[] off from a decisionmaker factors that a sensitive decisionmaker would otherwise take into account."[60] They may thus generate results ill-serving the policies behind the rules.[61] Consider the task of deciding which citizens are mature enough to vote. A rule that any person can vote if he or she has reached the age of eighteen has the advantage of administrability and avoids biased enforcement. Few of us would welcome a system in which a government bureaucrat examined each of us individually to determine whether we were mature enough to vote. Because the rule is much simpler than the reality it seeks to govern, though, it is both over- and underinclusive: it bars from the franchise some people under eighteen who are mature, and grants the franchise to some people over eighteen who are not. Rules thus give rise to their own arbitrariness.[62] At best, a rules-based filtering system will miss nuances; at worst, it will generate absurd results—as when America Online, enforcing a rule forbidding certain words in personal member profiles, barred subscribers from identifying themselves as "breast" cancer survivors.[63]

V. RSACI AND ITS LIMITATIONS

Given this theoretical critique, one might think that the challenge facing ratings system designers is to devise really good rules-based systems, ones that track reality as well as possible, minimizing the difficulties noted above. That is what RSAC claims to have done in RSACi.[64] I think the product of any such effort, though, necessarily will be flawed.

Let's return to the choices facing a ratings system designer as she constructs blocking software. So far, this article has not addressed the most basic question confronting her: What sort of material should trigger ratings consequences? Should children have access to material about weapons making?[65] How about hate speech?[66] Or artistic depictions of nudity?[67] Again, she can take two different approaches. First, she can decide all such questions herself, so that the home user need only turn the system on and all choices as to what is blocked are already made. CYBERSitter adopts this approach.[68] This has the benefit of simplicity, but seems appropriate only if members of the target audience are in basic agreement with the rating service (and each other) respecting what sort of speech should and should not be blocked.[69]

Alternatively, she can leave those questions for the user to answer. The ratings system designer need not decide whether to block Web sites featuring bomb-making recipes or hate speech. She can instead design the system so that the user has the power to block those sites if he chooses. Microsoft's implementation of the RSACi labels allows parents to select the levels of adult language, nudity, sex, and violence that the browser will let through.[70] Cyber Patrol allows parents to select which of the twelve CyberNOT categories to block.

Either approach, though, imposes restrictions on the categories chosen by the ratings system designer. If the system designer wishes to leave substantive choices to parents, she must create categories that correspond to the different sides of the relevant substantive questions. That is, if the designer wishes to leave users the choice whether to block sites featuring hate speech, she must break out sites featuring hate speech into a separate category or categories. If she wishes to leave the user the choice whether to block sites that depict explicit sexual behavior but nonetheless have artistic value, she must categorize those sites differently from those that do not have artistic value.[71] On the other hand, if the system designer makes those substantive decisions herself, making her own value choices as to what material should and should not be blocked, she must create categories that correspond to those value choices.

The problem is that many of these questions cleave on lines defined by standards. Many users, for example, might like to block "pornography," but allow other, more worthy speech, even if it is sexually explicit. SafeSurf responds to that desire when it requires self-raters to determine whether nudity is "artistic," "erotic," "pornographic," or "explicit and crude." It gets high marks for attempting to conform its system to user intuitions, but its lack of rulishness means problems in application.[72] Similarly, Specs's distinction between "impartial reference," "acceptance or approval," and "active promotion" of homosexuality may well correspond to the intuitions of much of its target audience but will hardly be straightforward in actual application. The problem increases with the heterogeneity of the service's audience: the more heterogeneous the audience, the more categories a rating system must include to accommodate different user preferences.

With this perspective, one can better appreciate the limitations of RSAC's attempt to be rule-bound. RSACi ignores much content that some other ratings systems classify as potentially unsuitable, including speech relating to drug use, alcohol, tobacco, gambling, scatology, computer hacking and software piracy, devil worship, religious cults, militant or extremist groups, weapon making, tattooing and body piercing, and speech "grossly deficient in civility or behavior."[73] For many observers (myself included), RSACi's narrow scope is good news because it limits the ability to block access to controversial political speech. My point, though, is that RSACi *had to* confine its reach if it was to maintain its rule-bounded nature.

The problem appears as well in connection with the categories RSACi *does* address. Consider RSACi's treatment of sex. It divides up sexual depictions into "romance, no sex," "passionate kissing," "clothed sexual touching," "non-explicit sexual activity," and "explicit sexual activity; sex crimes."[74] But RSACi, in contrast to some other ratings systems, does not seek to distinguish educational, artistic, or crude depictions from others. There is no way, consistent with rulishness, that it can seek to distinguish the serious or artistic from the titillating. It achieves rule-boundedness and ease of administration, at the expense of nuance; it achieves consistent labeling but in categories that do not correspond to the ones many people want.

In sum, rating system designers face a dilemma. If a rating service seeks to map the Web in a relatively comprehensive manner, it must rely on a relatively large group of evaluators. Such a group of evaluators can achieve fairness and consistency only if the ratings system uses simple, hard-edged categories relying on a few, easily ascertainable characteristics of each site. Such categories, though, will not categorize the Net along the lines that home users will find most useful, and will not empower those users to heed their own values in deciding what speech should and should not be blocked. To the extent that ratings system designers allow evaluators to consider more factors in a more situationally specific manner to capture the essence of each site, they will ensure inconsistency and hidden value choices as the system is applied.

VI. UNRATED SITES

Blocking software can work perfectly only if all sites are rated. Otherwise, the software must either exclude all unrated sites, barring innocuous speech, or allow unrated sites, letting in speech that the user would prefer to exclude.[75] What are the prospects that a rating service will be able to label even a large percentage of the millions of pages on the Web? What are the consequences if it cannot?

First, consider rating services associated with individual manufacturers of blocking software, such as CYBERSitter and Cyber Patrol. These services hire raters to label the entire Web, site by site. The limits on their ability to do so are obvious. As the services get bigger, hiring more and more employees to rate sites, their consistency will degrade; that was one of the lessons of Part III of this article. Moreover, no service could be big enough to rate the entire Web. Too many new pages come online every day. The content associated with any given page is constantly changing.[76] Further, some of the sites most likely to be ephemeral are also among the most likely to carry sexually explicit material. A ratings service simply cannot keep tabs on every college freshman who gets to school and puts up a Web page, notwithstanding that college freshmen are of an age to be more interested in dirty pictures than most. A ratings service certainly cannot keep tabs on every Web page put up by a college freshman in Osaka, say, or in Amsterdam. So any such rating service must take for granted that there will be a huge number of unrated sites.

As a practical matter, providing access to all unrated sites is not an option for these rating services; it would let through too much for them to be able to market themselves as reliable screeners. Instead, they must offer users other options, dealing with unrated sites in one of two ways. First, they can seek to catch questionable content through string-recognition software. CYBERSitter, for example, offers this option. The problem with this approach, though, is that at least under current technology, string-recognition software simply doesn't work very well. This article has already mentioned America Online's travails with the town of Scunthorpe and the word "breast"; other examples are easy to find. SurfWatch, for example, blocked a page on the White House Web site because its URL contains the forbidden word "couples" (http://www.whitehouse.gov/ WH/kids/html/couples.html).[77] The second option is for the rating services simply to block all unrated sites. Industry members seem to contemplate this as the necessary solution. Microsoft, for example, cautions Internet content providers that "[f]or a rating system to be useful, the browser application must deny access to sites that are unrated."[78] Other observers reach the same result.[79]

What about self-rating approaches, like those of SafeSurf and RSACi? These services have the potential for near-universal reach, since they can draw on the services of an effectively unlimited number of evaluators. While the evaluators will be a diverse group (to say the least), rating service designers can try to cope with that diversity by constructing rule-bound questionnaires. While some evaluators may misrepresent their sites, rating services can try to devise enforcement mechanisms to cope with that as well. On the other hand, self-rating services will not achieve their potential unless content providers have a sufficient incentive to participate in the ratings process in the first place.[80]

That incentive is highly uneven. Mass-market commercial providers seeking to maximize their audience reach will participate in any significant self-rating system, so as not to be shut out of homes in which parents have configured their browsers to reject all unrated sites.[81] Many noncommercial site owners, though, may not participate. They may be indifferent to their under-eighteen visitors and may not wish to incur the costs of self-rating. It is still early to predict what those costs may be. For the owner of a large site containing many documents, supplying a rating for each page may be a time-consuming pain in the neck.[82]

RSAC appears to have abandoned plans to charge Web sites for using its ratings,[83] but there may be other disincentives. Some content providers may not self-rate because they are philosophically opposed to the censorship a rating system enables[84] or are dissatisfied with the choices a rating system provides. More generally, why should a college or graduate student with a Web page bother to self-rate? He's not necessarily writing for people concerned about ratings, and if those people exclude him, the author may not much care.

VII. COMPULSORY SELF-RATING

It may be that the only way to ensure participation in a self-rating system even in a single country (let alone internationally) would be for the government to compel content providers to self-rate (or to compel Internet access providers to require their customers to do so). It is not obvious how such a requirement would work. The drafters of such a law would face the choice of forcing content providers to score their sites with reference to a particular rating system specified in the law, or allowing them leeway to choose one of a variety of PICS-compliant ratings systems. Neither approach seems satisfactory. The first, mandating use of a particular rating system, would freeze technological development by eliminating competitive pressures leading to the introduction and improvement of new searching, filtering, and organizing techniques. It would leave consumers unable to choose the rating system that best serve their needs. The second would be little better. Some government organ would have to assume the task of certifying particular self-rating systems as adequately singling out material unsuitable for children. It is hard to imagine how that agency could ensure that every approved system yielded ratings useful to most parents, while nonetheless maintaining a healthy market and allowing innovation.

In any event, a mandatory self-rating requirement would likely be held unconstitutional. In *Riley v. National Federation of the Blind*,[85] the Court considered a requirement that professional fundraisers disclose to potential donors the percentage of charitable contributions collected over the previous twelve months that were actually turned over to charity. The Court explained that "mandating speech that a speaker would not otherwise make" necessarily alters the content of the speech and thus amounts to content-based regulation.[86] Even when a compelled statement is purely factual, the compulsion burdens protected speech and is subject to "exacting" scrutiny, subject to the rule that government cannot "dictate the content of speech absent compelling necessity, and then, only by means precisely tailored."[87]

The Court repeated that analysis in *McIntyre v. Ohio Elections Commission*,[88] striking down a requirement that persons distributing election materials state their names and addresses in those materials. The Court explained that the requirement was a "direct regulation of the content of speech" subject to "exacting" scrutiny.[89] Even though the compelled disclosure was useful to voters and uncontroversially factual, the state was requiring "that a writer make statements or disclosures she would otherwise omit"; the restriction, accordingly, could not stand unless narrowly tailored to serve an overriding state interest.[90]

A requirement that Internet content providers provide ratings of their speech falls straightforwardly under the rule of those cases.[91] Even if the characterization of speech according to the taxonomy of a particular rating system were deemed factual and value-neutral, requiring a speaker to characterize her speech in that manner would require her to incorporate into her speech a "statement[] . . . she would otherwise omit." Such a requirement must surmount exacting scrutiny.[92]

In fact, mandatory self-rating is even more problematic. The Court has repeatedly recognized the impermissibility of requiring a speaker to associate herself with particular ideas she disagrees with.[93] Requiring self-rating does that, because rating is *not* factual and value-neutral. Mandatory self-rating compels the speaker to associate herself with the values and worldview embodied in the rating taxonomy. The drafters of RSACi, or SafeSurf, may view—and hence compartmentalize—the universe of speech in a way I reject. RSACi, for example, classifies sexually explicit speech without regard to its educational value or its crass commercialism; that choice is inconsistent with the values of many. Some taxonomies make the conflict more obvious than others; it would surely be offensive for many to be required to characterize their speech using Specs for Kids criteria, under which a message that expresses "acceptance" of homosexuality is by definition not "impartial." But any taxonomy incorporates editorial and value judgments.

Moreover, a self-rating requirement may otherwise chill protected speech. To the extent that rating criteria are less than wholly rule-like, their vagueness will lead Internet content providers to self-censor. Content providers will "steer far wider of the unlawful zone"[94] in order to avoid sanctions for misrating. "Vagueness and the attendant evils . . . are not rendered less objectionable because the regulation of expression is one of classification rather than direct suppression."[95]

I am doubtful that a self-rating requirement could survive exacting scrutiny. Even without a self-rating requirement, parents can restrict their children's access to sexually explicit sites by using blocking programs, and instructing the software to block all unrated sites. Indeed, the wave of the future may well be Web browser add-ons, marketed by entities such as Disney, that collect a few tens of thousands of Web sites specifically chosen to be kid-friendly and block access to all others. A self-rating requirement would be helpful to parents only in that it would enable them to limit their children's access in such a way that the kids could also view an uncertain number of *additional* sites, not containing sexually explicit material, whose providers would not otherwise choose to self-rate. In light of the First Amendment damage done by a compelled self-rating requirement, accomplishing that goal does not seem to be a compelling or overriding state interest.[96]

The result, though, is that child-configured lenses will show only a limited, flattened view of the Internet. If many Internet content providers decline to self-rate, the only "safe" response may be to configure blocking software to exclude unrated sites. The plausible result? A typical home user, running Microsoft Internet Explorer set to filter using RSACi tags will have a browser configured to accept duly rated mass-market speech from large entertainment corporations, but to block out a substantial amount of quirky, vibrant individual speech from unrated (but child-suitable) sites. This prospect is disturbing.

The Internet is justly celebrated as "the most participatory form of mass speech yet developed."[97] A person or organization with an Internet hookup can easily disseminate speech across the entire medium at low cost; the resulting "worldwide conversation"[98] features an immense number of speakers and "astoundingly diverse content."[99] As Judge Dalzell noted in *ACLU v. Reno*, the Internet vindicates the First Amendment's protection of "the 'individual dignity and choice' that arises from 'putting the decision as to what views shall be voiced largely into the hands of each of us,'" because "every minute [Internet communication] allows individual citizens actually to make those decisions."[100] But this prospect is threatened if widespread adoption of blocking software ends up removing much of the speech of ordinary citizens, leaving the viewer little to surf but mass-market commercial programming. One hardly needs the Internet for that; we get it already from the conventional media.

In sum, blocking software could end up blocking access to a significant amount of the individual, idiosyncratic speech that makes the Internet a unique medium of mass communication. Filtering software, touted as a speech-protective technology, may instead contribute to the flattening of speech on the Internet.

VIII. CHILDREN, ADULTS, AND BLOCKING SOFTWARE

You may protest that I am making much of little here. After all, blocking software is intended to restrict *children's* access to questionable sites. It won't affect what adults can see on the Internet—or will it? It seems to me that, in important respects, it will. The desire to restrict children's access has spurred the recent development of filtering technology. Widespread adoption of that software, though, will not likely leave adults unaffected.

In a variety of contexts, we can expect to see adults reaching the Internet through approaches monitored by blocking software. In the home, parents may set up filters at levels appropriate for their children and not disable them for their own use.[101] They may subscribe to an Internet access provider that filters out material at the server level, so that nobody in the household can see "objectionable" sites except by establishing an Internet access account with a new provider.[102] If, as seems likely, future versions of the PICS specifications support the transmission of filtering criteria to search engines, then users running Internet searches will not even know which sites otherwise meeting their criteria were censored by the blocking software.[103]

Other people get their Internet connections through libraries; indeed, some policy-makers tout libraries and other community institutions as the most promising vehicle for ensuring universal access to the Internet.[104] The American Library Association takes the position that libraries should provide unrestricted access to information resources; it characterizes the use of blocking programs as censorship.[105] This policy, however, is not binding on member libraries. It is likely that a substantial number of public libraries will install blocking software on their public-access terminals, including terminals intended for use by adults; indeed, some have already done so.[106] As one software vendor warns:

> Unlimited Web Access is a Political Nightmare. Your library may spend tens
> of thousands of dollars on Internet hardware/training and then be closed down
> by an angry parent willing to go to the press and the town council because
> their child saw pornographic materials in the library.[107]

Still other people get Internet access through their employers. Corporations too, wary of risk and wasted work time, may put stringent filters in place. Some large companies worry about the possibility of being cited for sexual harassment by virtue of material that came into the office via the Internet.[108] Even more are concerned about sports and leisure information they feel may detract from business productivity. One consultant sums up the corporate mood: "My kids went out on the Web to a museum and saw great artwork, but I don't want my employees hanging out at the Louvre all day on my nickel."[109]

In sum, we may see home computers blocked for reasons of convenience, library computers blocked for reasons of politics, and workplace computers blocked for reasons of profit. Even one university temporarily installed blocking software in its computer labs, in aid of a policy "prohibit[ing] the display in public labs of pornographic material unrelated to educational programs."[110] The result may be that large amounts of content may end up off-limits to a substantial fraction of the *adult* population.[111]

There are limits to this—sex sells. Many home Internet users will be loathe to cut themselves off from the full range of available speech. Most online services and Internet access providers, while attempting to make parents feel secure about their children's exposure to sexually explicit material on the Internet, will still host such material for adults who wish to view it.[112] It seems safe to conclude, though, that blocking software will have the practical effect of restricting the access of a substantial number of adults.

This should affect the way we think about filtering software. Any filtering system necessarily incorporates value judgments about the speech being blocked. These value judgments are not so controversial if we think of the typical user of blocking software as a parent restricting his children's access. It is part of a parent's job, after all, to make value judgments regarding his own child's upbringing. The value judgments are much more controversial, though, if we think of the typical "blockee" as an adult using a library computer, or using a corporate computer after hours. If we are concerned about these users' access to speech, then we need to think hard about the way blocking software works, the extent to which it can be accurate, and the extent to which it is likely to exclude the sort of speech that makes the Internet worthwhile.

IX. CONCLUSION

Across the world, governments and industry are turning to filtering software as the answer to the problem of sexually explicit material on the Internet. In the United Kingdom, service providers and police have endorsed a proposal recommending that Internet service providers require users to rate their own Web pages, and that the providers remove Web pages that their creators have "persistently and deliberately misrated."[113] The European Commission has urged the adoption of similar codes of conduct to ensure "systematic self-rating of content" by all European content providers.[114] Some U.S. companies have been leaning the same way: Compuserve has decided to "encourage" its users and other content providers to self-rate using RSACi.[115]

Ratings, though, come at a cost. It seems likely that a substantial number of adults, in the near future, will view the Internet through filters administered by blocking software. Intermediaries—employers, libraries, and others—will gain greater control over the things these adults read and see. Sites may be stripped out of the filtered universe because of deliberate political choices on the part of rating service administrators, and because of inaccuracies inherent in the ratings process. If a rating service is to categorize a large number of sites, it cannot simultaneously achieve consistency and nuance; the techniques it must rely on to achieve consistency make it more difficult to capture nuance and make it less likely that users will find the ratings useful. The necessity of excluding unrated sites may flatten speech on the Net, disproportionately excluding speech that was not created by commercial providers for a mass audience.

This is not to say that ratings are bad. The cost they impose, in return for the comforting feeling that we can avert a threat to our children, is surely much less than that imposed by the Communications Decency Act. Ratings provide an impressive second-best solution. We should not fool ourselves, though, into thinking that they impose no cost at all.

Notes

* I am grateful to Jessica Litman, whose comments greatly improved this article. An earlier version of this article was presented at the 1996 Telecommunications Policy Research Conference; I am indebted to the participants in that conference, in particular Paul Resnick and Rivkah Sass, for their perspectives. This article attempts to take a snapshot of an extraordinarily fast-moving field; it reflects developments through the spring of 1997.

1. 117 S. Ct. 2329 (1997).

2. See Brief of Appellees at PartII.B.2, Reno v. ACLU, 117 S. Ct. 2329 (1997), <http://www.aclu.org/court/renovaclu.html>.

3. The White House Office of the Press Secretary, Statement by the President (June 12, 1996) <http://www.eff.org/pub/Legal/Cases/EFF_ACLU_v_DoJ/960612_clinton_cda_decision.statement>.

4. Peter H. Lewis, Microsoft Backs Ratings System for Internet, N.Y. TIMES, Mar.1, 1996, at D5 (quoting Daniel Weitzner, Deputy Director, Center for Democracy and Technology); see Jerry Berman & Daniel J. Weitzner, Abundance and User Control: Renewing the Democratic Heart of the First Amendment in the Age of Interactive Media, 104 YALE L.J. 1619, 1634–35 (1995).

5. Antipornography activists, by contrast, have been decidedly less enthusiastic. Some express concern that such software leaves "the parent . . . responsible to go out and buy the software, become educated about how to apply it, how to install it, how to use it, and how to then monitor it to make sure your child or his friends have not gotten around it." Pornography on the Internet: Straight Talk from the Family Research Council (radio broadcast transcript) (last modified July 3, 1996) <http://www.townhall.com/townhall/FRC/netst96g1.html> (statement of Colby May, Senior Counsel, American Center for Law and Justice). To say that blocking software obviates the need for government speech restrictions is "saying . . . that we are free to pollute out cultural environment, and parents have to buy the gas masks." Id. (Statement of Kristi Hamrick, moderator).

6. See Paul Resnick & James Miller, PICS: Internet Access Controls Without Censorship, 39 COMMUNICATIONS OF THE ACM 89 (1996). PICS was developed by the World Wide Web Consortium, the body responsible for developing common protocols and reference codes for the evolution of the Web, with the participation of Apple, America Online, AT&T, the Center for Democracy and Technology, Compuserve, DEC, IBM, MCI, the MIT Laboratory for Computer Science, Microsoft, Netscape, Prodigy, the Recreational Software Advisory Council, SafeSurf, SurfWatch, Time Warner Pathfinder, and others.

7. Microsoft calls its World Wide Web browser Internet Explorer; Content Advisor first appeared in Internet Explorer's version 3.0. Content Advisor makes it easiest to use RSACi ratings. RSACi is an Internet ratings system established by the Recreational Software Advisory Council (RSAC), which was created by the Software Publishers Association in 1994 to create a rating system for computer games. RSAC formed a working party in late 1995, including representatives from Time Warner Pathfinder, AT&T, PICS and Microsoft, to develop RSACi. See infra note 13 and accompanying text.

For Content Advisor to use ratings from a PICS-compliant rating service other than RSACi, the user must copy that service's .RAT file into his Windows System folder and then click on "Add A New

Rating service" in the IE Options menu. See SafeSurf News (visited Feb. 7, 1997) <http://www.safesurf.com/nletter/summ96.htm>.

8. Shea v. Reno, 930 F.Supp. 916, 931 (S.D.N.Y. 1996):

    > While it is difficult to ascertain with any certainty how many sexually explicit sites are accessible through the Internet, the president of a manufacturer of software designed to block access to sites containing sexually explicit material testified in the Philadelphia litigation that there are approximately 5,000 to 8,000 such sites, with the higher estimate reflecting the inclusion of multiple pages (each with a unique URL) attached to a single site. The record also suggests that there are at least thirty-seven million unique URLs. Accordingly, even if there were twice as many unique pages on the Internet containing sexually explicit materials as this undisputed testimony suggests, the percentage of Internet addresses providing sexually explicit content would be well less than one tenth of one percent of such addresses.

    Id. (citations omitted).

9. "URL" is an acronym for "Uniform Resource Locator." See Internet Engineering Task Force, Uniform Resource Locators [RFC-1738] (Dec. 1994) <http://ds.internic.net/rfc/rfc1738.txt>.

10. See Shea, 930 F.Supp. at 932.

11. See Resnick & Miller, supra note 6.

12. See id.

13. The heavy hitters behind RSACi have been RSAC, established in 1994 by the Software Publishers Association, and such industry players as Microsoft, AT&T, and Time Warner Pathfinder. See supra note 6. As of April 15, 1996, content providers have been able to rate their own sites using the RSACi system by completing a questionnaire at the RSAC Web site, <http://www.rsac.org> (visited March 27, 1997).

14. SafeSurf describes itself as an "international no-fee parents' organization formed to protect children on the Internet and the rights of parents through technology and education." SafeSurf press release (Apr. 18, 1996) <http://www.safesurf.com/press/press12.htm>. It uses the CyberAngels, an offshoot of Curtis Sliwa's Guardian Angels, to patrol sites whose owners have rated them as suitable for "All Ages," verifying that the sites do not contain adult content. E-mail from Wendy Simpson, President, SafeSurf to Declan McCullagh (Apr. 28, 1996) (on file with author).

15. The categories are: profanity, heterosexual themes, homosexual themes, nudity, violence, intolerance, glorifying drug use, other adult themes, and gambling. See SafeSurf Rating System (visited Feb. 7, 1997) <http://www.safesurf.com/classify/index.html>.

16. See CyberNOT List Criteria (last modified May 9, 1996) <http://www.microsys.com/cyber/cp_list.htm>.

17. See Specs Glossary (visited Feb. 7, 1997) <http://www.newview.com/cust/ss_sg_lv13a_cf_fcs.html>.

18. See CYBERSitter Product Information (visited Feb. 7, 1997) <http://solidoak.com/cysitter.htm>. CYBERSitter characterizes its customers as "strong family-oriented people with traditional family values." The product is sold by Focus on the Family. See Brock N. Meeks & Declan B. McCullagh, Jacking In from the 'Keys to the Kingdom' Port, CYBERWIRE DISPATCH (July 3, 1996) <http://www.eff.org/pub/Publications/Declan McCullagh/cwd.keys.to.the.kingdom.0796.article>.

19. For the most part, Cyber Patrol drops all but the first three characters of the file name in the URL, thus blocking innocuous pages. See Meeks & McCullagh, supra note 18. In some instances, Cyber Patrol blocks at a higher level, so that, for example, it excluded all of Jewish.com because personal ads were not stored in a separate subdirectory. Eric Berlin & Andrew Kantor, Who Will Watch the Watchmen?, INTERNET WORLD (Oct. 1996) <http://www.iw.com/1996/ll/surf.html>.

20. According to an article in the electronic version of Internet World, CYBERSitter blocks all sites hosted by cris.com. A CYBERSitter representative suggests that Internet service providers "are responsible for their content," and that the owners of cris.com are to blame because they "will not monitor their [customers'] sites." Berlin & Kantor, supra note 19. According to another recent report, CYBERSitter now blocks all sites at a variety of Internet service providers including the WELL, the pioneering California electronic community. See K.K. Campbell, Who's Watching the 'Watchers'?, TORONTO STAR, Jan. 30, 1997, at J3. Cyber Patrol blocks all pages hosted by crl.com (including a real estate agency's Web pages). A Cyber Patrol representative says that the company is reviewing its policy of blocking entire domains. Berlin & Kantor, supra note 19.

21. The RSACi and SafeSurf systems allow content providers to label each page individually. At a recent PICS developers' workshop, the prevailing view was that filtering software should expect to find PICS-compliant labels only in the individual documents, not in the directories or elsewhere in the site. See PICS Developers' Workshop Summary (visited Feb. 7, 1997) <http://www.w3.org/pub/WWW/

PICS/picsdev-wkshp1.html>. This makes sense only in the context of software that makes the blocking decision for each page individually.

The more difficult question is whether the problem will persist in connection with third-party rating services. At least one third-party rating service (Specs for Kids) does rate on the document level, and such a service should be more attractive to many users; the question is whether the increased sales will outweigh the added expense of that granularity.

22. The on-line service solved the problem, to its own satisfaction, by advising its customers from that city to pretend they were from "Sconthorpe" instead. See Clive Feather, AOL Censors British Town's Name!, 18 RISKS DIGEST, Issue 7 (Apr. 25, 1996) <http://catless.ncl.ac.uk/Risks/18.07.html#subj3.1>. On string-recognition software, see infra notes 63 and 77 and accompanying text.

23. See Internet Censorship and Blocking Software, WEB4LIB ARCHIVE (visited Mar. 18, 1997) <http://www.lib.berkeley.edu/Web4Lib/archive/9703/0120.html>.

24. See e-mail from Solid Oak Software Technical Support to Bob Stock (Oct. 24, 1996) (on file with author).

25. See Meeks & McCullagh, supra note 18; Cyber Patrol Censors Animal Rights Web Sites (visited Feb. 7, 1997) <http://www.mit.edu/activities/safe/labeling/cp-bans-animal-rights>.

26. Id.

27. Id.

28. Queer Resources Directory (visited Feb. 9, 1997) <http://www.qrd.org>. The Health/AIDS directory at QRD, for example, contains information from the Centers for Disease Control and Prevention, the AIDS Book Review Journal, and AIDS Treatment News. See Meeks & McCullagh, supra note 18.

29. See SurfWatch Censorship Against Lesbigay WWW Pages (visited Feb. 7, 1997) <http://www.utopia. com/mailings/censorship/SurfWatch.Censorship.Against.Lesbigay.WW>; e-mail from Chris Kryzan for wide distribution (June 15, 1995) (on file with author).

30. See Meeks & McCullagh, supra note 18.

31. Id.

32. Id. Indeed, Cyber Patrol apparently blocks all of the alt.support groups (including, for example, alt.support.shyness and alt.support.depression), along with such groups as alt.war.vietnam and alt.fan.frank-zappa. E-mail from Declan McCullagh to the fight-censorship mailing list (Oct. 4, 1996) (on file with author); CyberPatrol: The Truth (visited Feb. 7, 1997) <http://www.canucksoup.net/ CYBERWHY.HTM>.

33. Meeks & McCullagh, supra note 18. Among the other WWW sites blocked by Cyber Patrol is that of the Campaign for Real Ale, a British consumer group dedicated to preserving and promoting traditional pubs and independent breweries. Cyber Patrol lists it as an alcohol & tobacco CyberNOT. Charles Arthur, Real Ale is Too Strong for the American Moralists, INDEPENDENT (London), July 22, 1996, at 11.

34. See e-mail from Ari Herzog to the fight-censorship mailing list, Feb. 27, 1997 (on file with author).

35. Meeks & McCullagh, supra note 18. It also refuses any site whose URL contains "sinnfein" or "fascism." Berlin & Kantor, supra note 19.

36. See The Penal Lexicon: What's New Page (visited Mar. 18, 1997) <http://www.penlex.org.uk/wnarc51. html>.

37. See Campbell, supra note 20; Pamela Mendels, Publishers Say CYBERSitter Filter is Screening Out Their Criticism (Feb. 9, 1997) <http://www.nytimes.com/web/docsroot/library/cyber/week/020997cybersitter. html>.

38. See David Pescovitz, Site-Filtering Controversy Likely to Heat Up, L.A. TIMES, Jan. 6, 1997, at D3.

39. See Censorware Search Engine (visited Mar. 18, 1997) <http://www.pathfinder.com/netly/spoofcentral/ censored>.

40. Jonathan Wallace, An Auschwitz Alphabet (visited Feb. 7, 1997) <http://www.spectacle.org/695/ausch. html>.

41. Jonathan Wallace, Why I Will Not Rate My Site (visited Feb. 7, 1997) <http://www.spectacle.org/cda/ rate.html#report>.

42. Id.

43. Or she could take an approach falling somewhere in between. The polar models I describe in the text, though, provide a useful way of looking at the problem.

44. See Duncan Kennedy, Form and Substance in Private Law Adjudication, 89 HARV. L. REV. 1685, 1685, 1688–89 (1976); Pierre Schlag, Rules and Standards, 33 UCLA L. REV. 379, 379–80 (1985); Kathleen Sullivan, The Supreme Court, 1991 Term—Forward: The Justices of Rules and Standards, 106 HARV. L. REV. 22, 58–59 (1992); JONATHAN WEINBERG, Broadcasting and Speech, 81 CAL. L. REV. 1101, 1167–69 (1993); see also Cass R. Sunstein, Problems with Rules, 83 CAL. L. REV. 953, 956 (1995) (adopting somewhat different terminology, but contrasting "two stylized conceptions of legal judgment":

"clear, abstract rules laid down in advance of actual applications" and "law-making at the point of application through case-by-case decisions, narrowly tailored to the particulars of individual circumstances").

45. See Jim Miller et al., Rating Services and Rating Systems (and their Machine Readable Descriptions) (last modified Oct. 31, 1996) <http://www.w3.org/pub/WWW/PICS/services.html>, at Appendix B. There is a slightly different description of the RSACi categories at Rating the Web <http://www.rsac.org/why.html>.

46. See The Net Labeling Delusion: Protection or Oppression (visited Jan. 14, 1997) <http://www.thehub.com.au/~rene/liberty/label3.html>.

47. See SafeSurf Rating System (visited Feb. 7, 1997) <http://www.safesurf.com/classify/index.html>.

48. See Solid Oak Software, Inc. VCR Rating System (visited Feb. 7, 1997) <http://www.solidoak.com/vcr.htm>.

49. Specs Glossary (visited Feb. 7, 1997) <http://www.newview.com/cust/ss_sg_lvl3a_cf_fcs.html>.

50. It is inevitable that people will disagree as to the consequences of an item of speech being pigeonholed in a particular category—whether, for example, youngsters should be exposed to scenes of murder and mayhem. My point about the examples in the text is that individuals will come to different conclusions regarding which pigeonhole a given item of speech should be deemed to occupy in the first place.

51. Elsewhere in the Specs rating system, one can find definitions that seem standard-like because it is doubtful that they mean what they say. For example, the Specs default settings do not allow persons under eighteen to view Web sites that "[a]ttempt[] to persuade the viewer to join a specific political group." Specs Glossary (visited Feb. 7, 1997) <http://www.newview.com/cust/ss_sg_lvl3a_cf_fcs.html>. If this is not to exclude the Democratic and Republican parties (say), the test must embody some unarticulated assumptions about which political appeals are the pernicious ones—rendering the de facto category standard-like and unconstrained.

52. See sources cited supra note 44.

53. See Kennedy, supra note 44, at 1688–89; Sullivan, supra note 44, at 62–63; Sunstein, supra note 44, at 972–77.

54. See Frederick Schauer, Formalism, 97 YALE L.J. 509, 512 n.8 (1988) [hereinafter Schauer, Formalism]:

> [Consider] the transformation of the "honor codes" at various venerable universities. These codes were phrased in quite general terms at their inception in the 18th and 19th centuries because these schools contained homogenous student bodies who shared a common conception of the type of conduct definitionally incorporated within the word "honor." If a person thought that purchasing a term paper from a professional term paper service was consistent with being honorable, then that person simply did not know what "honor" meant. As values have changed and as student bodies have become less homogenous, however, shared definitions of terms such as "honor" have broken down. Some people now do think that buying a term paper can be honorable, and this breakdown in shared meaning has caused general references to "honor" to be displaced in such codes by more detailed rules. There may now be little shared agreement about what the precept "be honorable" means, but there is considerable agreement about what the rule "do not purchase a term paper" requires.

See also id. at 539–40.

55. Steve G. Steinberg, Seek and Ye Shall Find (Maybe), WIRED, May 1996, at 108, 112 13.

56. Id. at 113; see also Leslie Walker, On the Web, a Catalogue of Complexity, WASH. POST, Nov. 20, 1996, at F17; The Total Librarian, ECONOMIST (visited Feb. 7, 1997) <http://www.economist.com/review/rev9/rv12/review.html>.

57. RSAC Specifics About the Rating Process, Questionnaire, the PICS Standard and Granularity (visited Feb. 7, 1997) <http://www.rsac.org/start.html>.

58. Indeed, for just that reason, First Amendment philosophy largely proscribes standards on the level of operative First Amendment doctrine. Speech-regulatory law, the Supreme Court has explained, must be expressed in hard-edged, nondiscretionary terms so as to minimize the possibility of government arbitrariness or bias. Situationally sensitive judgment by government officials, making speech-regulatory decisions turn on "the exercise of judgment and the formation of an opinion," is forbidden. Forsyth County v. Nationalist Movement, 112 S.Ct. 2395, 2401–02 (1992) (quoting Cantwell v. Connecticut, 310 U.S. 296, 303 (1940)); see Weinberg, supra note 44, at 1169–70; see also Frederick Schauer, The Second-Best First Amendment, 31 WM. & MARY L. REV. 1, 14–17 (1989).

59. See Kennedy, supra note 44, at 1689.

60. Schauer, Formalism, supra note 44, at 510.

61. See id. at 534–37; Sunstein, supra note 44, at 992–93.
62. See Kennedy, supra note 44, at 1689; Sullivan, supra note 44, at 62; Sunstein, supra note 44 at 994; Weinberg, supra note 44, at 1168–69.
63. See Richard A. Knox, Women Go On Line to Decry Ban on 'Breast,' BOSTON GLOBE, Dec. 1, 1995, at A12. This incident was likely the result of string-identification software. String-identification programs are excellent examples of rules-based filtering systems.
64. In fact, RSACi is seriously flawed for reasons having nothing to do with rules and standards. The original RSAC rating system was designed for video games. RSACi carries over the categories and language of the earlier video game rating system even where they are completely inappropriate. Thus, for example, RSACi's definition of "aggressive violence" on a Web page excludes acts of nature "such as flood, earthquake, tornado, hurricane, etc., unless the act is CAUSED by Sentient Beings or Non-sentient Objects in the game or where the game caused the act." See RSACi Ratings Dissected (visited Mar. 18, 1997) <http://www.antipope.demon.co.uk/charlie/nonfiction/rant/rsaci.html>. One consequence of RSAC's approach is that the Internet rating system nowhere acknowledges a distinction between images and text.
65. In the wake of recent political speculation about bomb-making recipes on the Internet, five major rating services agreed to work together to "ensure that parents can block Internet sites containing weapons and bomb making information and recipes." Press Release, SafeSurf Enables Parents to Block Internet Bomb Sites (Aug. 1, 1996) <http://www.safesurf.com/press/press16.htm>.
66. The Specs default settings, for example, would deny to persons under eighteen any "[m]aterial defaming one or more social groups or members of such groups." See Specs Glossary (visited Feb. 9, 1997) <http://www.newview.com/cust/ss_sg_ lvl3a_cf_fcs.html>; Specs: Age Defaults (visited Feb. 9, 1997) <http:// www.newview.com/cust/ss_stsp_lvl2_fcs.html>.
67. Specs classes all nudity as either "in an artistic or educational context," or "with the principal purpose of exciting the viewer." Specs Glossary, supra note 66.
68. See supra text accompanying note 19.
69. To the extent that a user does not agree, the service will block sites he would want admitted, or let through sites he would want shut out, or both.
70. See Using Content Advisor (visited Feb. 9, 1997) <http://microsoft.com/ie/most/howto/ratings.htm>.
71. As a ratings system multiplies parental choice, it becomes more complex and, perhaps, harder to use. As a practical matter, rating system designers will have to balance fine differentiation of the ratings system against ease of use. See J.M. Balkin, Media Filters, the V-Chip, and the Foundations of Broadcast Regulation, 45 DUKE L.J. 1131, 1172 (1996). Cf. Solid Oak Software's Voluntary Web Site Rating System (visited Feb. 9, 1997) <http://www.solidoak.com/vcr.htm> (arguing self-rating system should be "extremely simple," in contrast to "PICS compliant ratings systems where there are several dozen possible ratings").
72. The Federal Communications Commission relies on an emphatically standard-like guide to determine whether speech broadcast on television and radio is "indecent." The resulting uncertainties have subjected the agency to critical attack. See generally JONATHAN WEINBERG, Vagueness and Indecency, 3 VILL. SPORTS & ENT. L.J. 221 (1996). The FCC, though, is a single entity; its choices will display far more consistency than those of millions of disconnected content providers each evaluating their own sites.
73. All of these areas of speech trigger Cyber Patrol blocking (except for "tattooing and body piercing," which constitute a CyberNOT only to the extent they result in "gross depictions"). See Cyber Patrol Cyber NOT List Criteria (visited Feb. 9, 1997) <http://www.microsys.com/cyber/cp_list.htm>. Tattooing and body piercing are specifically blocked by Specs (in a category, called "subjects of maturity," that lumps them in with "illegal drugs, weapon making . . . [and] some diseases." Specs Glossary, supra note 66. Cf. Balkin, supra note 71, at 1166–68 (discussing competing images of "what characteristics count in making programming unsuitable for children").
74. RSAC Rating the Web (visited Feb. 9, 1997) <http://www.rsac.org/why.html>.
75. If unrated sites are either all innocuous or all verboten, we have an exceptional case; blocking software can then treat all according to a single rule.
76. Rating services are only beginning to confront the issue of updating ratings for particular sites as their contents change. RSACi provides one-year expiration dates for its labels. SafeSurf is providing no expiration dates, instead simply enjoining content providers to update their ratings if there is a material change in the content of their speech. See PICS Developers' Workshop Summary, supra note 21.
77. See Douglas Bailey, Couplegate, BOSTON GLOBE, Feb. 22, 1996, at 54. The page displays pictures of Bill and Hillary Clinton and Al and Tipper Gore.

78. The PICS Standard (visited Feb. 7, 1997) <http://www.microsoft.com/intdev/sdk/docs/ratings/ratng002.htm>.

79. See Whit Andrews, Site-Rating System Slow to Catch On, WEB WEEK (July 8, 1996) <http://www.webweek.com/96July8/comm/rating.html> (quoting Compuserve representative Jeff Shafer); Specs FAQs: Quick Quest: General Info (visited Feb. 9, 1997) <http://www.newview.com/cust/ss_qq_lvl3a_reg.html> (recommending users select option of blocking all unrated sites "to ensure a safe Internet environment"); e-mail from Andy Oram, O'Reilly and Associates, to telecomreg mailing list (May 21, 1996) (on file with author).

80. Few Web sites today carry self-rating labels. See Andrews, supra note 80 (only two of the "more than 50" sites listed in the Entertainment Magazine: Sex category at Yahoo! carry self-ratings); see also Hiawatha Bray, Rated P for Preemptive: System to Shield Kids From Adult Web Material Also Seeks to Keep Censors Off Net, BOSTON GLOBE, Jul. 25, 1996, at E4 ("only a tiny percentage" of Web sites have RSACi ratings).

81. See Lewis, supra note 4; RSAC Rating the Web (visited Feb. 9, 1997)< http://www.rsac.org/why.html>. Cf. Balkin, supra note 71, at 1164 (discussing the V-chip).

82. See Andrews, supra note 79. There are two separate problems here. The less important one is the technical issue of affixing a rating to each individual page. As noted supra note 21, the prevailing view at a recent PICS developers' workshop was that filtering software should expect to find PICS-compliant labels in each document; content providers cannot get away with supplying "blanket" ratings at the directory level or higher. On the other hand, it should be easy to develop software that will automatically insert labels into Web pages, so long as all of the pages on a site carry the same rating.

    The more important problem arises when a content provider must audit each page of a large archive to determine what rating that page should receive. Robert Croneberger, director of the Carnegie Library in Pittsburgh, testified at the ACLU v. Reno trial that he would have to hire 180 additional staff in order to search the library's online materials (in particular, its online card catalogue) so as to be able to tag individual, potentially indecent items. Trial Transcript for Mar. 22, 1996 at 101–02, ACLU v. Reno, 929 F.Supp. 824 (E.D. Pa. 1996) (No. 96-963) <http://www.eff.org/pub/Legal/Cases/ EFF_ACLU_v_DoJ/960322_croneberger.testimony>. It would be a huge task for MSNBC, say, to rate its news stories individually for descriptions or pictures of violent behavior—and perhaps for that reason, as of this writing, MSNBC does not provide RSACi ratings. See Declan McCullagh, RSACi-Hacky, NETLY NEWS (Mar. 18, 1997) <http://cgi.pathfinder.com/ALRDzgcACqLjhGnr/netly/1,1039,740,00. html>.

83. See e-mail from Stephen Balkam, RSACi, to Irene Graham (Feb. 14, 1997) (on file with author).

84. See 3 Trial Transcript at 192:3–4, ACLU v. Reno, 929 F.Supp. 984 (E.D. Pa. 1996) (No. 96-963) (testimony of Barry Steinhardt), and Reno v. ACLU, 117 S. Ct. 2329 (1997).

85. 487 U.S. 781 (1988).

86. Id. at 795.

87. Id. at 798, 800. The Court noted that "[p]urely commercial speech is more susceptible to compelled disclosure requirements." Id. at 796 n.9 (citing Zauderer v. Office of Disciplinary Counsel, 471 U.S. 626 (1985)); see also Hurley v. Irish-American Gay, Lesbian and Bisexual Group, 115 S.Ct. 2338, 2347 (1995). A self-rating requirement, though, would affect noncommercial as well as commercial speech. The Justices have noted that a state can compel doctors to make certain disclosures as part of the practice of medicine, see Planned Parenthood v. Casey, 505 U.S. 833, 884 (1992) (opinion of O'Connor, Kennedy, & Souter, JJ.), but that isn't this case either.

88. 115 S.Ct. 1511 (1995).

89. Id. at 1518.

90. Id. at 1519–20.

91. See also Hurley, 115 S.Ct. at 2347–48:

> [O]ne important manifestation of the principle of free speech is that one who chooses to speak may also decide what not to say. . . . [Except in the context of commercial advertising,] this general rule, that the speaker has the right to tailor the speech, applies not only to expressions of value, opinion, or endorsement, but equally to statements of fact the speaker would rather avoid. . . . Nor is the rule's benefit restricted to the press, being enjoyed by business corporations generally and by ordinary people engaged in unsophisticated expression as well as by professional publishers. Its point is simply the point of all speech protection, which is to shield just those choices of content that in someone's eyes are misguided, or even hurtful.

Id. (citations and internal quotation marks omitted).

92. Meese v. Keene, 481 U.S. 465 (1987), is not to the contrary. The Court in that case approved statutory provisions pursuant to which the Justice Department characterized speech distributed by foreign agents as "political propaganda." The disseminator of the speech, however, was not required to characterize it in that manner. The case was about the extent to which the government can pejoratively characterize a person's speech, not about the extent to which government can force a person to characterize her own speech, pejoratively or otherwise.

93. See Hurley, 115 S.Ct. at 2347–48; Pacific Gas & Elec. Co. v. Public Utils. Comm'n, 475 U.S. 1, 15 (1986) (plurality opinion) (holding government may not "require [speakers] to associate with speech with which [they] may disagree," nor force them to "alter their speech to conform with an agenda they do not set"); Wooley v. Maynard, 430 U.S. 705, 714 (1977) (holding government may not compel citizen to "be an instrument for fostering public adherence to an ideological point of view he finds unacceptable"); West Va. State Bd. of Educ. v. Barnette, 319 U.S. 624, 642 (1943) (holding government may not prescribe an orthodoxy and "force citizens to confess [it] by word").

94. Baggett v. Bullitt, 377 U.S. 360, 372 (1964) (quoting Speiser v. Randall, 357 U.S. 513, 526 (1958)).

95. Interstate Circuit, Inc. v. City of Dallas, 390 U.S. 676, 688 (1968); see also Motion Picture Ass'n of Am., Inc. v. Specter, 315 F.Supp. 824 (E.D. Pa. 1970).

96. The Court followed a similar reasoning process in McIntyre. The state in that case supported its ban on anonymous election materials by pointing to its interest in policing fraudulent statements and libel in election campaigns. The Court noted, though, that other provisions of state election law barred the making or dissemination of false statements. The value of the challenged provision was merely incremental. That incremental benefit could not justify the damage the provision did to free speech. McIntyre v. Ohio Elections Comm'n, 115 S.Ct. 1511, 1520–22 (1995).

97. ACLU v. Reno, 929 F.Supp. 824, 883 (E.D. Pa.) (Dalzell, J.), prob. juris. noted, 117 S.Ct. 554 (1996).

98. Id. at 883.

99. Id. at 877.

100. Id. at 881–82 (quoting Leathers v. Medlock, 499 U.S. 439, 448–49 (1991)).

101. This concern is most salient in connection with blocking programs, such as Microsoft's Content Advisor, that block *any* access to restricted sites through the computer on which the program is installed unless the program is disabled. Other programs, including Cyber Patrol, offer a more advanced feature known as "multiple user profiles." Each family member can have his or her own password, and the program can be configured at the start to grant the different password holders different levels of access. These programs make it easy for a parent to access the sites he seeks to exclude his child from. See PICS Developers' Workshop Summary, supra note 21 (noting formation of working group to specify formats for describing PICS user profiles). Parents may be wary of this feature, though, since the exclusion is only as secure as the parent's (frequently used) password.

102. See, e.g., BESS.NET: The Service (visited Feb. 9, 1997) <http://demo.bess.net/about_bess/the_service.html>. SafeSurf is now providing technology—the SafeSurf Internet Filtering Solution—that allows any ISP to offer parents this easy option. See Rose Aguilar, Site Filters Criticized, THE NET (Oct. 18, 1996) <http://www.news.com/News/Item/0,4,4609,00.html>. Even some households without children, if blocking software comes bundled with their Web browser, may choose to enable that software because they believe that otherwise they may be confronted with smut.

103. When a user running blocking software seeks to conduct a search using an Internet search engine such as Alta Vista, the software will transmit the user's filtering rules to the search engine. The search engine will tailor its search so as not to return any sites excluded by the filter. Participants at the recent PICS Developers' Workshop agreed that this was the preferable approach, in part because it would be undesirable for users to get search results like "'here's the first 10 responses, but 9 of them were censored by your browser.'" PICS Developers' Workshop Summary; see also PICS Frequently Asked Questions (visited Feb. 9, 1997) <http://www.w3.org/pub/WWW/PICS>.

104. See, e.g., Gary Chapman, Universal Service Must First Serve Community, L.A. TIMES, June 3, 1996, at D1. See generally ROBERT H. ANDERSON ET AL., UNIVERSAL ACCESS TO E-MAIL: FEASIBILITY AND SOCIETAL IMPLICATIONS (1995) (discussing pros and cons of locating devices for e-mail access in home, at work, in schools, and in libraries, post offices, community centers, and kiosks).

105. See QUESTIONS AND ANSWERS: Access to Electronic Information, Services, and Networks: An Interpretation of the Library Bill of Rights (visited Feb. 9, 1997) <http://ala1.ala.org:70/0/alagophx/alagophxfreedom/electacc.qa>; Access to Electronic Information, Services, and Networks: An Interpretation of the Library Bill of Rights (visited Feb. 9, 1997) <http:// ala1.ala.org:70/0/alagophx/alagophxfreedom/electacc.fin>.

106. See, e.g., Alan Boyle, Resolving the Information Battle (visited Mar. 17, 1997) <http://www.msnbc.

com.news/59459.asp> (explaining that Bakersfield, Cal. public libraries have installed blocking software on all terminals); Pamela Mendels, Censoring Web Sites Poses Dilemma for Librarians (Mar. 9, 1997) <http://nytimes.com/library/cyber/week/030997libraries.html> (Austin Tex. and Connetquot, N.Y.; same); Rebbeca Vesely, Library Blocks Porn, and May Block Rights, WIRED NEWS (visited Jan. 7, 1997) <http:// www.wired.com/news/story/1289.html> (Orange County, Fla.; same). I do not want to overplay this point. Many libraries have decided not to install blocking software. See, e.g., Ramon McLeod & Carolyne Zinko, Online Smut in the Reading Room, S.F. CHRON., Mar. 1, 1997, at A1. Other libraries have installed the software only on terminals intended for use by children. See, e.g., Geeta Anand, Library Ok's Limits on 'Net Access, BOSTON GLOBE, Mar. 22, 1997, at A1. I am grateful to Linda Mielke, President of the Public Library Association and Director of the Carroll County (Maryland) Public Library, Kathleen Reif, Director of the Wicomoco County (Maryland) Free Library, and Naomi Weinberg, President, Board of Trustees, Peninsula Public Library Lawrence, New York for educating me on these issues.

107. Pornography and Gambling are Inappropriate in a Library (visited Feb. 9, 1997) <http://www.librarysafe.com/library.html> (typeface in original). The vendor is the Library Safe Internet System.

    Librarians have shown great courage in their decisions to carry controversial books and artworks. They have repeatedly demonstrated their willingness to carry items of sexually explicit material that they consider valuable. Recent cases litigated by the Freedom to Read Foundation include Lowe v. Kiesling, 882 P.2d 91 (Or. Ct. App. 1994), rev. dismissed, 889 P.2d 916 (Or. 1995), challenging a proposed Oregon ballot measure that, among other things, would have forbidden public libraries from collecting any materials on homosexuality written for children, and Ong v. Salt Lake City Public Library, in which plaintiffs sought to bar a public library from exhibiting art including nudity. See Freedom to Read Foundation Annual Report For 1994–1995, 20 Freedom to Read Foundation News, Nos. 3–4 (1995). (visited Apr. 17, 1997) <http://www.sirs.com/partner/read/v20n3.htm>; Reports to Council, 19 Freedom to Read Foundation News, Nos. 3–4 (1994). (visited Apr. 17, 1997) <http://www.sirs.com/partner/read/v19n2.htm>. By providing an uncensored Internet feed, though, a library makes available material much more difficult to defend in a political context.

108. See Rosilind Retkwa, Corporate Censors, INTERNET WORLD, Sept. 1996, at 60; see also, e.g., Microsystems Announces Immediate Availability of Cyber Patrol Proxy for Microsoft's Proxy Server (July 31, 1996) <http://www.microsys.com/prfiles/proxy796.htm>.

109. Retkwa, supra note 108, at 61.

110. The university was the University of Arkansas at Monticello. See e-mail from Carl Kadie to fight-censorship mailing list (Oct. 22, 1996); e-mail from Tyrone Adams to amend1-L mailing list (Oct. 22, 1996); e-mail from Stephen Smith to Jonathan Weinberg (Oct. 22, 1996) (all on file with author).

111. It is possible that Disney or a similar entity will get a large market share with a kid-centered interface limiting users to a specific list of kid-friendly sites, and that that interface will be so aggressively child-oriented that adults won't use it (and can't be suckered into using it). Even so, employers and similar entities using the Internet will still have an interest in installing a grown-up interface with blocking capabilities and, presumably, the market will respond to that.

112. Consider America Online. AOL markets itself as a family-friendly service. It allows parents to confine their children to a "Kids Only" area, or to disallow their access to chat rooms and Usenet news. AOL monitors the use of forbidden words in various contexts. It censors messages posted in the advertisers' area called "Downtown AOL," removing advertisements that its manager thinks do not have "the look and feel that best fits [AOL]'s environment." At the same time, though, it allows its members to create chat rooms with names like "m needs bj now," "bond and gaged f4f," and "M4Fenema."

113. R3 Safety-Net: Rating Reporting Responsibility For Child Pornography and Illegal Material on the Internet (last modified Sept. 23, 1996) <http://dtiinfo1.dti.gov.uk/safetynet/r3.htm>. Under the initial proposal, users were to rate with RSACi. See id. The proponents apparently have backed away from that position. The proposal also recommends that Internet service providers take steps to support rating and filtering of Usenet newsgroups. For an explanation of the mechanics of the Usenet proposal, see Turnpike Newsgroups (last modified Sept. 24, 1996) <http://www.turnpike.com /ratings>.

114. See Restricting Access to Illegal and Harmful Content on the Internet: Communication to the European Parliament, the Council, the Economic and Social Committee and the Committee of the Regions (Oct. 16, 1996) <http:// www2.echo.lu/legal/en/internet/content/communic.html>. A recent EU working group document recommends research into new, non-RSAC rating systems, so as to "take account of Europe's cultural and linguistic diversity" and "guarantee respect of [users'] convictions." Report of Working Party on Illegal and Harmful Material on the Internet (visited Mar. 7, 1997) <http://www2.echo.lu/legal/en/internet/ientent/wpen.html>. Other countries have adopted more drastic approaches. See, e.g.,

Kathy Chen, China Bars Access To as many as 100 Internet Web Sites, WALL ST. J., Sept. 5, 1996, at B5; James Kynge, Singapore Cracks Down on Internet, FIN. TIMES (London), July 12, 1996, at 6.

115.   See RSAC Press Release, Compuserve to Rate Internet Content by July 1 (May 9, 1996) <http://www.rsac.org/press/960509-1.html>.

PART FOUR

APPENDIX

CANADA

I. **Report to the Canadian Radio-television and Telecommunications Commission (CRTC)**

II. **The Canadian Television Rating System—A Comprehensive Classification System for Violence and Other Program Content**

I. **Report to the Canadian Radio-television and Telecommunications Commission from The Action Group on Violence on Television, April 30, 1997 (Excerpt)**

. . . .

A CLASSIFICATION SYSTEM FOR VIOLENT CONTENT

The Action Group on Violence on Television is a pan-industry organization, formed in February 1993 to co-ordinate broadcast and cable industry strategies and initiatives to deal with the issue of violence on television. In response to CRTC Public Notice 1996-36, the Action Group re-activated and expanded its Classification Committee in April 1996. A co-ordination secretariat was established and a budget struck. Financial support for the project was provided by all sectors of the industry.

. . . .

As protection of children has been the underpinning of how Canada has addressed the issue of violence on television, the first key question for the Committee was to deal with content in children's programming. As the Classification System will function as a component of the industry's *Voluntary Code on Violence in Television Programming,* it was important to build the ratings for children's programming on the foundation of the Children's Section of the CRTC approved Code, where there are strict rules clearly established for the portrayal of violence in children's programming.

While the Commission itself defined children as all youngsters under the age of twelve, the Committee felt that a single children's category would be too broad an age spectrum, and needed to be divided into two levels. Committee members, many of whom are parents themselves, turned to research undertaken by Dr. Wendy Josephson of the University of Manitoba. In her study prepared for the Department of Canadian Heritage, she noted that age eight has been identified as a watershed period for the effects of television violence on children, particularly in terms of being able to distinguish reality from fantasy.

With these two categories in place, establishing the levels of the rating system for non-children's programming emerged over subsequent committee sessions. In the end, the committee agreed that four classification levels could accommodate the range of programming from that designed for a broad general audience, to programming intended for adult audiences.

The guidelines for violence content were built word by word, to provide useful information for parents. The descriptive information was deliberately kept concise, to ensure ease of comprehension and use. The violence guidelines begin with "minimal and infrequent" in the first of these four classifications. The content gradations conclude at the fourth level with "violence intended for adult audiences," the description used in establishing the criteria for violence in programming which must be scheduled no earlier than the 9:00 P.M. "watershed hour," in the industry's voluntary code.

The challenge in building the classification system was substantial. It would have to be capable of dealing with the wide range of programming offered by English-language services through over-the-air local stations, national networks, and cable-delivered specialty services, ranging from children and youth-oriented services such as YTV to services such as Showcase, and Bravo!.

. . . .

THE 1997 FIELD TRIAL

One of the key reasons AGVOT requested an extension from the CRTC was to allow the necessary time for another V-chip trial. Such a test was viewed as critical to assess consumer response to the proposed classification system, and improved V-chip technology.

Trial Logistics

This trial was the fourth test since early 1995 and the first to test an industry-developed classification system. It was far and away the most ambitious in terms of the number of families and programming services that would participate, as well as the complexity of the technical and software specifications.

There were also significant costs involved. Most of the broadcasters, even those who had taken part in earlier V-chip trials had to acquire new field 2-compatible hardware and software. Their programming and operations personnel had to spend numerous hours first learning, then implementing the procedures for reviewing, rating and encoding the hundreds of hours of programming.

Rogers, Shaw and Cogeco volunteered to test the V-chip with their subscribers in Vancouver, Edmonton, Toronto, Ottawa and Trois-Rivières. The Canadian Cable Television Association (CCTA), on behalf of its members, assumed the costs of the five hundred V-chip boxes and financed and managed the trial research. This included retaining the research company to recruit the families and conduct the post-trial research; writing the technical specifications for the standalone V-chip box; overseeing the design, production and delivery of five hundred V-chip boxes; and writing the bilingual User Manual for the trial families.

V-Chip Decoder Description

The decoder developed for this trial was a standalone V-chip box manufactured by

Tri-Vision Electronics Inc. The decoder was implemented with bilingual user menus and supported four single-category classification systems consisting of six different levels. The menu screens were designed in such a way as to promote simplicity of use. For this test, the user menus were permanently programmed into the five hundred V-chip boxes. However, later versions of decoders will be equipped with chips that can be reprogrammed at the factory if software modifications are required in the future.

The V-chip decoder was controlled by a small but effective remote control unit which consisted of 12 buttons: 10 numbers, plus a "VIEW" and a "MENU" key. The decoder interfaced at RF using CH 3 for the input and output of the box. The decoder did not have tuning capability and therefore required a VCR or external converter box to be placed at the input of the V-chip decoder to act as the tuning device. Stereo sound was fully supported and a 4-digit Personal Identification Number (PIN) assured a fair degree of security.

V-Chip Trial 1997

It was originally expected that the trial would commence at the beginning of January, 1997 and continue for sixty days. However, there were delays in manufacturing and shipping the five hundred V-chip boxes (the largest number ever produced), therefore the test did not officially begin until February 7, 1997. In the meantime, families were being recruited for the trial, and boxes were being installed in homes as they became available. Programming services were testing their new equipment, ensuring that the encoder in particular interfaced smoothly with their existing operational configuration—a critical issue since it would be feeding into their programming stream.

The 1997 V-chip trial saw nearly three times as many broadcasters taking part as in the previous trial, nearly a year earlier. A total of twenty-eight programming services participated:

14 conventional stations in five markets
3 national networks
7 specialty services
4 US border stations

Unfortunately, technical restrictions prohibited several programming services which had been key participants in earlier trials from taking part. They currently use the DigiCipher 1 scrambling system which is unable to support field 2 data. This meant that neither YTV nor any pay-TV services were able to physically encode their programs for the trial. Nevertheless they were significant contributors to the Programming and Technical/Software Committees.

Trial Recruitment

Environics Research Group was commissioned to recruit the five hundred families for the trial, as well as conduct a detailed, evaluative telephone interview at its conclusion. In order to recruit participants, telephone calls were made to a random selection of Canadian households including some households that in earlier representative surveys had indicated their families included small children. To qualify, respondents had to be parents or guardians with children aged 3 to 12. They had to agree to have the V-chip installed in their homes for a 3–4 week period, commit to use the system and participate in a subsequent research interview.

It was much more difficult to recruit families for the trial than either AGVOT or Environics had foreseen. In Trois-Rivières alone, almost 5,000 households were contacted before identifying eighty nine who were eligible and who agreed to participate.

A possible explanation for the difficult recruiting process can be found in questions posed as part of a consumer attitude survey undertaken by Strategic Counsel on behalf of the CCTA this spring. Consumers were asked about their concern regarding the level of violence on television. The results were compared to those from similar surveys in 1995 and 1996. While Canadians' concern remains consistent—73% over two years, their interest in technology to block programming has dropped significantly from 66% to 55% over the same period.

Consequently, there were finally only 374 households participating, rather than the recruitment goal of five hundred. Some households dropped out after agreeing to take part in the trial because of incompatible cable/broadcast services in their area (particularly in Edmonton); being unavailable during the installation period; or simply a change of mind.

For their part, the cable companies made sure that their installers were well-briefed in how to hook-up the V-chip box. Each installation took approximately half an hour, and the families were left with a detailed User Manual.

Research from earlier trials had indicated that a detailed yet easy to understand User Manual could be a critical tool in helping to determine the success of a V-chip trial. If participants became frustrated with the unfamiliar technology or needed a clear explanation of the various ratings choices, they needed to be able to access this information; otherwise there was a risk they would drop out of the trial in frustration. Accordingly, the User Manual was first vetted by a non-profit group specializing in simplifying prose and subsequently it was tested on several families in a focus group.

The results were worth this extra effort. According to the post-trial research, most participants had no problem understanding the Canadian Television Rating System. In all five focus groups, the participants reported that the ratings as described in the User Manual were easy to understand and readily programmed.

Once the trial was underway, each family was contacted by their cable company, to make sure that the equipment was working effectively and that there were no problems, again a lesson learned from earlier trials.

Trial Research

The trial ended March 16, 1997. Research began immediately with the Environics Research Group conducting an extensive telephone survey of all trial families, and The Strategic Counsel Inc. conducting focus groups in each of the five trial location cities.

(i) V-Chip Households Survey

More than eight in ten participants (84%) found the V-chip box easy to use. The majority (80%) also found that it worked properly and they did not experience any difficulties with it.

Also, the improvements which were made to the V-chip since the last trial received good reviews including:

- a larger, multi-digit remote control (65% said they wouldn't change anything about it)
- a new on-screen menu (92% found it easy to understand)
- a PIN number for security (89% felt this was an effective way to control access)
- a Temporary Disable feature (75% found it useful)

Almost one half (49%) said they would be very (21%) or somewhat (28%) interested in having the V-chip system in their home on an on-going basis. The standalone box concept however did not test well. Only 11% chose a standalone box like the one they tested. When given various options two-thirds (64%) said they would prefer the V-chip to be built into their television. 18% said they would like the V-chip to be built into an existing TV converter—which is how the V-chip was offered to participants in earlier trials.

(ii) V-Chip Households—Focus Groups

A series of five focus groups was conducted in the V-chip trial centres. Focus group members were randomly selected from lists of V-chip trial participants provided from Environics Research. At least eight individuals participated in each focus group; all participants had at least one child living in the household with the majority having at least two or three children living in the trial household.

It was very clear from these focus groups that the high awareness of the V-chip prior to participation in the trial affected the participants' expectations for the technology and their subsequent disappointment in it. While most spoke highly of the V-chip technology as an important and very useful means of monitoring their children's television viewing, there was a general unwillingness to acquire the technology at the current time. Interestingly, there was a general feeling that changes and improvements to the technology would be made prior to availability within the marketplace—they were unwilling to believe that what they had tested was in its final form.

As with the telephone survey findings, the majority of participants found the technology easy to program and to use on an on-going basis. However, when able to voice specific problems in the environment of a focus group (compared to a more specific telephone questionnaire), some strong views emerged including:

- significant dislike of an additional set-top box
- significant dislike of an additional remote control
- complaints from those who required an additional converter
- significant frustration with problems using their VCRs

After using the V-chip technology for the period of the trial, very few participants reported they would either purchase or rent the box in its current form. While there was widespread praise for the concept of the V-chip most wanted to see changes in the technology prior to serious consideration of acquisition. Trial participants believe that like other technologies, the V-chip will become more sophisticated and the current technology which they tested is only in its initial stage.

TECHNICAL ISSUES

The AGVOT report filed last September with the Commission identified various technical issues which needed to be resolved during the 1997 V-chip trial, in order to guarantee a successful North American roll-out in the future. The issues identified included:

- the requirement of the V-chip box to handle three to four different ratings systems in both official languages;
- the importance of adhering to international standards and placing the V-chip data in line 21 of field 2;
- the need to field test the V-chip technical modifications by way of another V-chip trial;
- the benefits of a standalone box versus retrofitting converters;
- the belief that any system that Canada develops should be compatible, if not interoperable with that of the Electronic Industries' Association (EIA) published standard;
- the problems with the DigiCipher I and Scientific Atlanta scrambling systems' inability to support field 2 data; and,
- the cost and delivery windows of the Extended Data Service (XDS) encoders, equipped to hold Closed Captioning in field 1 and V-chip data in field 2 of the video signal.

1. The requirement of the V-chip box to handle three to four different ratings systems in both official languages

The V-chip box was equipped with enough memory to handle the following four rating systems:

i.   Canadian Television Rating System (as developed by AGVOT)
ii.   Québec Classification System (modified Régie du cinéma)
iii. Pay and Pay-per-view Classification System
iv.   U.S. Parental Guidelines

While it was found that the complexity of implementing more than one system was not a major factor in manufacturing the V-chip box, the costs associated with the additional memory to store the classification systems information in both official languages could be. In the recent V-chip trial, the classification systems tested were based on a single category system consisting of approximately six levels. If multiple systems were to be adopted, the costs associated with having to store all the relevant information for the various systems in two or more languages would lead to significant cost increases.

This issue is magnified when the V-chip gets implemented in television receivers as the television manufacturing industry designs their systems to the tenth of a cent to manage the costs of their products. Because Canada currently requires at least three classification systems to be adopted for its market alone, the U.S. manufacturers may be less than amenable to implementing the Canadian systems, in order to keep manufacturing costs down.

Survey results also indicate a strong interest from participants to adopt a common classification system to reduce potential confusion between systems and simplify the setting of a classification level for each household. This in return would lead to simpler on-screen menus, a lower cost product and an opportunity to take advantage of the V-chip technology being implemented in all television receivers in the future.

2. The importance of adhering to international standards and placing the V-chip data in line 21 of field 2

This last V-chip trial used technology which was compatible with the EIA technical standard which imbeds V-chip information into line 21 of field 2 of the video signal. This was the first time that line 21, field 2 V-chip services were field tested in North America.

One of the main objectives for carrying V-chip information in field 2 of the video signal was to eliminate the interference that the V-chip information was causing with the Closed Captions. The move to field 2 appears to have been successful, as throughout the trial no perceived interference was experienced between the Closed Captioning and the V-chip rating information.

Another benefit to carrying V-chip information in Field 2 is the increased frequency at which the information can be transmitted to the V-chip decoder, thereby potentially cutting in half the blocking or unblocking reaction time of the decoder. On average the V-chip rating signals were transmitted every three seconds.

Even with this improvement, trial participants claimed that the overall reaction time of the V-chip decoder appeared to be slow. Programs would continue to be blocked if one began channel surfing when the channel that was originally being watched was blocked. The same circumstances occurred in reverse when channel surfing through programs which had higher ratings than the program that was originally tuned to. A recommendation to the EIA may be required to increase the priority and frequency of the V-chip rating information to eliminate that problem.

. . . .

BROADCASTER TECHNICAL ISSUES

From the trial, a number of critical concerns emerged for programming services, at both the programming and engineering/operations levels.

(a) Encoding Promos and Movie Trailers

All twenty eight participating programming services indicate encoding promos and movie trailers cannot be done with the current stand-alone software. There are several issues.

(i) As the current software runs strictly to clock time, it cannot react to circumstances where commercials are not scheduled at an exact time. This is standard in news, sports, and other live-event programming, where the commercial insert breaks are often determined in real time, and thus are unable to be programmed into the encoding software. This means there currently is no way to guarantee the correct encoding for movie commercials and promotional spots is transmitted at the exact time these spots are on the air.

(ii) Only one service, with no live programming, made an attempt to encode for trailers and promos. It took a full 8 hours each day to manually load in the day's log, an unrealistic proposition for most programming services running on minimal staff. For those services which only encoded their programs for the trial, it took about half an hour to load in a day's playlist, once the show data base was built.

A realistic assessment of the problem is that encoding of promos and movie commercials is not feasible until the encoding system is dynamically linked into a station's traffic and automation systems. While traffic system manufacturers are beginning to examine how to do this, no real progress will begin until the US ratings system is finalized.

(iii) The other option for this problem is to stripe the trailers and promos with the encoding information as they are transferred to the in-house tape format or to a file server. However this option has considerable manpower and equipment implications for services which may have to equip as many as three production edit suites with the encoder/computer package, at approximately $12,000 a system. Furthermore, not all file servers support field 2 data, which could be problematic.

(iv) Another consideration is the timeliness of the material's availability. Some movie commercials arrive within hours of airtime. The same situation occurs with many promotional spots, which are cut from episodic material fed to stations in the morning for prime time airplay. Dubbing these spots is one thing. Ensuring that the large number of staff who process the material are fully trained to apply the appropriate encoding information is something else.

Both the AGVOT classification and technical committees are adamant that this part of the encoding regime cannot be implemented with any degree of technical and operational reliability, until the software for traffic and automation systems is re-written to accommodate encoding data. That evolution could take up to two years. Only at that time will the encoding process be transparent to a station's operating system, with the rating information loaded in via the commercial log.

(b) Software

Both programmers and engineers have deep reservations about the current software. They indicate it requires extensive modifications to the point that a new start may have to be made.

(i) Considerable re-design of the screen displays used by programmers to load ratings information is required. The software needs to be modified to allow each service to create their own broadcast day, rather than a clock day.

(ii) At the moment there is no simple way to over-ride the system in situations where live event programming runs past the scheduled time. When that occurs, the Master Control operator has no time to re-program the encoding software to reflect the new schedule. Under the existing software/hardware configuration, this live programming could be blocked, as the encoder assigns a rating to the program it believes is running at that time.

The ability to impose an easy and technically fool-proof over-ride mechanism is vital and needs to be developed before widespread introduction of the encoding regime.

(iii) Members of the AGVOT Technical committee described the need for the software to be more "robust." Some programming services reported circumstances during the trial where the software either became hung-up, failed to apply the correct code, or inserted an incorrect code. They would like direct input into any revisions made to the software.

(iv) There is intense concern that there is currently only one software supplier, itself a modest operation. If the software company is incapacitated in any fashion, programming services will be vulnerable. The view was that the industry would be unwise to implement such an important process based upon one supplier.

Questions remain regarding the expense of modifying the software to meet the needs of programming services, and whether these modifications can be completed and tested by September, 1997.

(c) Hardware

Only one brand of encoder really functioned without difficulty during the trial , the EEG-470. A second make was tested, but was found to be unreliable, and unable to handle both encoding and closed captioning requirements within a single unit. EEG appears to be acceptable on matters of delivery and reliability, and more manufacturers will undoubtedly come on stream over time. But at the moment, there is only one encoder supplier, which is again risky for broadcasters.

(d) Compression/Scrambling Technology Problems

A number of programming services are still facing difficulties with older generation technology which is unable to process field two information. For example, CanCom which uses Scientific Atlanta Phase 2 is unable to pass field 2 of Line 21 for City, CHCH,

BCTV and other conventional services. This means these stations would be encoded in their home markets, but not in the markets where they are a distant signal delivery.

CTV/Baton and several Montreal-based services are still working with Scientific Atlanta Phase 2 and 3 equipment, which is unable to transmit field 2 data, where the encoding information is embedded. A number of specialty services such as WTN and YTV are using DigiCipher 1 equipment which is also unable to transmit field two data. It is uncertain whether any of these services can be upgraded in time for September 1997.

. . . .

II. The Canadian Television Rating System—A Comprehensive Classification System for Violence and Other Program Content

The Canadian Television Rating System has been developed in response to parental concerns over violence in television programming. Violence is the most important consideration when a program is assigned a rating. To provide parents with more information about the suitability of a program, non-violent content elements such as language and sexuality/nudity have also been incorporated into the rating system. The levels of the Canadian rating system are as follows:

EXEMPT

(no icon required)

Exempt programming includes: news, sports, documentaries and other information programming; talk shows, music videos, and variety programming.

CHILDREN

Programming intended for children under age 8.

Violence Guidelines
Careful attention is paid to themes which could threaten children's sense of security and well-being. There will be no realistic scenes of violence. Depictions of aggressive behaviour will be infrequent and limited to portrayals that are clearly imaginary, comedic or unrealistic in nature.

Other Content Guidelines
There will be no offensive language, nudity or sexual content.

CHILDREN 8 AND OLDER

Programming generally considered acceptable for children 8 years and over to watch on their own.

Violence Guidelines
Violence will not be portrayed as the preferred, acceptable, or only way to resolve conflict; or encourage children to imitate dangerous acts which they may see on television. Any realistic depictions of violence will be infrequent, discreet, of low intensity and will show the consequences of the acts.

Other Content Guidelines
There will be no profanity, nudity or sexual content.

GENERAL AUDIENCE

Programming considered acceptable for all age groups. While not designed specifically for children, it is understood younger viewers may be part of the audience.

Violence Guidelines
Will contain very little violence, either physical or verbal or emotional. Will be sensitive to themes which could frighten a younger child, will not depict realistic scenes of violence which minimize or gloss over the effects of violent acts.

Other Content Guidelines
There may be some inoffensive slang, no profanity and no nudity.

PARENTAL GUIDANCE

Programming intended for a general audience but which may not be suitable for younger children (under the age of 8). Parents may consider some content inappropriate for unsupervised viewing by children aged 8–13.

Violence Guidelines
Depictions of conflict and/or aggression will be limited and moderate; may include physical, fantasy, or supernatural violence.

Other Content Guidelines
May contain infrequent mild profanity, or mildly suggestive language. Could also contain brief scenes of nudity.

VIEWERS 14 AND OVER

Programming contains themes or content which may not be suitable for viewers under the age of 14. Parents are strongly cautioned to exercise discretion in permitting viewing by pre-teens and early teens.

Violence Guidelines
May contain intense scenes of violence. Could deal with mature themes and societal issues in a realistic fashion.

Other Content Guidelines
May contain scenes of nudity and/or sexual activity. There could be frequent use of profanity.

ADULTS

Programming intended for adults 18 and older. It may contain elements of violence, language, and sexual content which could make it unsuitable for viewers under 18.

Violence Guidelines
May contain violence integral to the development of the plot, character or theme, intended for adult audiences.

Other Content Guidelines
May contain graphic language and explicit portrayals of nudity and/or sex.

THE UNITED STATES

I. Public Law 104-104, Telecommunications Act of 1996 (Excerpt)

§ 551. PARENTAL CHOICE IN TELEVISION PROGRAMMING.
(a) Findings.—The Congress makes the following findings:
(1) Television influences children's perception of the values and behavior that are common and acceptable in society.
(2) Television station operators, cable television system operators, and video programmers should follow practices in connection with video programming that take into consideration that television broadcast and cable programming has established a uniquely pervasive presence in the lives of American children.
(3) The average American child is exposed to 25 hours of television each week and some children are exposed to as much as 11 hours of television a day.
(4) Studies have shown that children exposed to violent video programming at a young age have a higher tendency for violent and aggressive behavior later in life than children not so exposed, and that children exposed to violent video programming are prone to assume that acts of violence are acceptable behavior.
(5) Children in the United States are, on average, exposed to an estimated 8,000 murders and 100,000 acts of violence on television by the time the child completes elementary school.
(6) Studies indicate that children are affected by the pervasiveness and casual treatment of sexual material on television, eroding the ability of parents to develop responsible attitudes and behavior in their children.
(7) Parents express grave concern over violent and sexual video programming and

strongly support technology that would give them greater control to block video programming in the home that they consider harmful to their children.

(8) There is a compelling governmental interest in empowering parents to limit the negative influences of video programming that is harmful to children.

(9) Providing parents with timely information about the nature of upcoming video programming and with the technological tools that allow them easily to block violent, sexual, or other programming that they believe harmful to their children is a nonintrusive and narrowly tailored means of achieving that compelling governmental interest.

(b) Establishment of Television Rating Code.—
  (1) Amendment.—§ 303 (47 U.S.C. 303) is amended by adding at the end the following:
  "(w) Prescribe—
  "(1) on the basis of recommendations from an advisory committee established by the Commission in accordance with § 551(b)(2) of the Telecommunications Act of 1996, guidelines and recommended procedures for the identification and rating of video programming that contains sexual, violent, or other indecent material about which parents should be informed before it is displayed to children, provided that nothing in this paragraph shall be construed to authorize any rating of video programming on the basis of its political or religious content; and
  "(2) with respect to any video programming that has been rated, and in consultation with the television industry, rules requiring distributors of such video programming to transmit such rating to permit parents to block the display of video programming that they have determined is inappropriate for their children.".
  (2) Advisory committee requirements.—In establishing an advisory committee for purposes of the amendment made by paragraph (1) of this subsection, the Commission shall—
  (A) ensure that such committee is composed of parents, television broadcasters, television programming producers, cable operators, appropriate public interest groups, and other interested individuals from the private sector and is fairly balanced in terms of political affiliation, the points of view represented, and the functions to be performed by the committee;
  (B) provide to the committee such staff and resources as may be necessary to permit it to perform its functions efficiently and promptly; and
  (C) require the committee to submit a final report of its recommendations within one year after the date of the appointment of the initial members.

(c) Requirement for Manufacture of Televisions That Block Programs.—§ 303 (47 U.S.C. 303), as amended by subsection (a), is further amended by adding at the end the following:
  "(x) Require, in the case of an apparatus designed to receive television signals that are shipped in interstate commerce or manufactured in the United States and

that have a picture screen 13 inches or greater in size (measured diagonally), that such apparatus be equipped with a feature designed to enable viewers to block display of all programs with a common rating, except as otherwise permitted by regulations pursuant to § 330(c)(4).".

(d) Shipping of Televisions That Block Programs.—
  (1) Regulations.—§ 330 (47 U.SC. 330) is amended—
    (A) by redesignating subsection (c) as subsection (d); and
    (B) by adding after subsection (b) the following new subsection (c):
  "(c)(1) Except as provided in paragraph (2), no person shall ship in interstate commerce or manufacture in the United States any apparatus described in § 303(x) of this Act except in accordance with rules prescribed by the Commission pursuant to the authority granted by that section.
  "(2) This subsection shall not apply to carriers transporting apparatus referred to in paragraph (1) without trading in it.
  "(3) The rules prescribed by the Commission under this subsection shall provide for the oversight by the Commission of the adoption of standards by industry for blocking technology. Such rules shall require that all such apparatus be able to receive the rating signals which have been transmitted by way of line 21 of the vertical blanking interval and which conform to the signal and blocking specifications established by industry under the supervision of the Commission.
  "(4) As new video technology is developed, the Commission shall take such action as the commission determines appropriate to ensure that blocking service continues to be available to consumers. If the Commission determines that an alternative blocking technology exists that—
    "(A) enables parents to block programming based on identifying programs without ratings,
    "(B) is available to consumers at a cost which is comparable to the cost of technology that allows parents to block programming based on common ratings, and
    "(C) will allow parents to block a broad range of programs on a multichannel system as effectively and as easily as technology that allows parents to block programming based on common ratings, the Commission shall amend the rules prescribed pursuant to § 303(x) to require that the apparatus described in such section be equipped with either the blocking technology described in such section or the alternative blocking technology described in this paragraph.".
  (2) Conforming amendment.—§ 330(d), as redesignated by subsection (d)(1)(A), is amended by striking "§§ 303(s), and 303(u)" and inserting in lieu thereof "and §§ 303(s), 303(u), and 303(x)".

(e) Applicability and Effective Dates.—
  (1) Applicability of rating provision.—The amendment made by subsection (b) of this section shall take effect 1 year after the date of enactment of this Act, but

only if the Commission determines, in consultation with appropriate public interest groups and interested individuals from the private sector, that distributors of video programming have not, by such date—
(A) established voluntary rules for rating video programming that contains sexual, violent, or other indecent material about which parents should be informed before it is displayed to children, and such rules are acceptable to the Commission; and
(B) agreed voluntarily to broadcast signals that contain ratings of such programming.
(2) Effective date of manufacturing provision.—In prescribing regulations to implement the amendment made by subsection (c), the Federal Communications Commission shall, after consultation with the television manufacturing industry, specify the effective date for the applicability of the requirement to the apparatus covered by such amendment, which date shall not be less than two years after the date of enactment of this Act.

§ 552. TECHNOLOGY FUND.
It is the policy of the United States to encourage broadcast television, cable, satellite, syndication, other video programming distributors, and relevant related industries (in consultation with appropriate public interest groups and interested individuals from the private sector) to—
(1) establish a technology fund to encourage television and electronics equipment manufacturers to facilitate the development of technology which would empower parents to block programming they deem inappropriate for their children and to encourage the availability thereof to low income parents;
(2) report to the viewing public on the status of the development of affordable, easy to use blocking technology; and
(3) establish and promote effective procedures, standards, systems, advisories, or other mechanisms for ensuring that users have easy and complete access to the information necessary to effectively utilize blocking technology and to encourage the availability thereof to low income parents.
. . .

§ 503. OBSCENE PROGRAMMING ON CABLE TELEVISION.
Section 639 (47 U.S.C. 559) is amended by striking "not more than $10,000" and inserting "under title 18, United States Code,".

§ 504. SCRAMBLING OF CABLE CHANNELS FOR NONSUBSCRIBERS.
Part IV of title VI (47 U.S.C. 551 et seq.) is amended by adding at the end the following:

"§ 640. SCRAMBLING OF CABLE CHANNELS FOR NONSUBSCRIBERS.
"(a) Subscriber Request.—Upon request by a cable service subscriber, a cable operator shall, without charge, fully scramble or otherwise fully block the audio and

video programming of each channel carrying such programming so that one not
a subscriber does not receive it.
"(b) Definition.—As used in this section, the term 'scramble' means to rearrange
the content of the signal of the programming so that the programming cannot
be viewed or heard in an understandable manner.".

§ 505.SCRAMBLING OF SEXUALLY EXPLICIT ADULT VIDEO SERVICE
PROGRAMMING.
(a) Requirement.—Part IV of title VI (47 U.S.C. 551 et seq.), as amended by this
Act, is further amended by adding at the end the following:

"§ 641. SCRAMBLING OF SEXUALLY EXPLICIT ADULT VIDEO SERVICE
PROGRAMMING.
"(a) Requirement.—In providing sexually explicit adult programming or other
programming that is indecent on any channel of its service primarily dedicated
to sexually-oriented programming, a multichannel video programming distributor shall fully scramble or otherwise fully block the video and audio portion
of such channel so that one not a subscriber to such channel or programming
does not receive it.
"(b) Implementation.—Until a multichannel video programming distributor
complies with the requirement set forth in subsection (a), the distributor shall
limit the access of children to the programming referred to in that subsection by
not providing such programming during the hours of the day (as determined by
the Commission) when a significant number of children are likely to view it.
"(c) Definitions.—As used in this section, the term 'scramble' means to rearrange
the content of the signal of the programming so that the programming cannot
be viewed or heard in an understandable manner.".
. . . .

II.   A Statement by All Segments of the Television Industry

The National Broadcast Networks (including PBS), National Cable Television
Association, National Association of Broadcasters, Motion Picture Association of
America, Association of Local Television Stations, and other participants
February 29, 1996

During the past two months all segments of our industry have discussed a plan to give
more information about TV programs to the parents of America. We have reached the
following conclusions:

1. The television industry, broadcasters, cable and the production community have
unanimously agreed to voluntarily rate TV programs, to encode them to activate an electronic device which in turn responds to parental choice, and to infuse all we do with

integrity and purpose. All elements of the TV industry will rise to this challenge, ready to participate in a national voluntary enterprise which we believe will be useful and valuable to the parents of America.

2. We are going to provide parents with more information about TV programs, similar to parental information provided by the MPAA movie ratings for the past 27 years, which have won consistently high approval from parents. We do this so that parents can more effectively monitor the TV viewing of their young children. All programs will be self-rated consistent with the overall rating guidelines, with ratings applied by the distributor of the programs.

3. We will construct an industry ratings review process, composed of various segments of our industry which will, from time to time, examine the ratings of specific programs and comment as to the appropriateness of the ratings.

4. To carry forward this huge voluntary effort, an Implementation Group under the leadership of Jack Valenti, whose membership will be drawn from all parts of our industry, will begin work immediately to draw up the design and the procedures of this new rating project, which explores unmapped terrain. There is a massive amount of detail to be worked out. We intend to do both technical and audience research, refining and revising our plans that when implementation takes place it is grounded in reality. We hope to have this new rating system in place no later than January, 1997.

5. Our objective is clear and firm. This enterprise is totally voluntary. There will be no government involvement of any kind. Within each of us is a unity of belief that government censorship, in whatever form, no matter how benign in its public declarations, is fundamentally in conflict with more than 200 years of our national heritage of freedom of speech, and collides directly with the Constitutional protection of the First Amendment.

III. TV Parental Guidelines—First Proposed System

January 17, 1997

Mr. William F. Caton
Secretary
Federal Communications Commission
1919 M Street, N.W.
Washington, D.C. 20554

Dear Mr. Caton:

By this letter, we are submitting to the Commission the system of parental guidelines that has been adopted and is being implemented by television broadcasters and networks, cable networks and systems, and television program producers. In the Telecommunications Act, Congress called upon the video programming industry to establish a voluntary system to provide parents with information concerning "programming that contains sexual, violent, or other indecent material about which parents should be informed" that is shown on television.

Last February 29, all segments of the video programming industry pledged to create television program guidelines. That pledge has now been met. The system of voluntary parental guidelines that we are submitting today without question achieves Congress' objectives.

THE TV PARENTAL GUIDELINES

The TV Parental Guidelines will provide parents with ratings of programs based on age and content. Under the Guidelines, television programming will fall into one of six categories. The categories are age-based, with the decision as to which category a program falls into determined by specified content. Two of the categories are for programming designed solely for children. The categories and the descriptions of the categories they signify are:

These categories are for programs designed for children—

All Children. *This program is designed to be appropriate for all children.* Whether animated or live-action, the themes and elements in this program are specifically designed for a very young audience, including children from ages 2–6. This program is not expected to frighten younger children.

Directed to Older Children. *This program is designed for children age 7 and above.* It may be more appropriate for children who have acquired the developmental skills needed to distinguish between make-believe and reality. Themes and elements in this program may include mild physical or comedic violence, or may frighten children under the age of 7. Therefore, parents may wish to consider the suitability of this program for their very young children.

These categories are for programs designed for the entire audience—

General Audience. *Most parents would find this program suitable for all ages.* Although this rating does not signify a program designed specifically for children, most parents may let younger children watch this program unattended. It contains little or no violence, no strong language and little or no sexual dialogue or situations.

Parental Guidance Suggested. *This program may contain some material that some parents would find unsuitable for younger children.* Many parents may want to watch it with their younger children. The theme itself may call for parental guidance. The program may contain infrequent coarse language, limited violence, some suggestive sexual dialogue and situations.

 Parents Strongly Cautioned. *This program may contain some material that many parents would find unsuitable for children under 14 years of age.* Parents are strongly urged to exercise greater care in monitoring this program and are cautioned against letting children under the age of 14 watch unattended. This program may contain sophisticated themes, sexual content, strong language and more intense violence.

 Mature Audience Only. *This program is specially designed to be viewed by adults and therefore may be unsuitable for children under 17.* This program may contain mature themes, profane language, graphic violence and explicit sexual content.

The TV Parental Guidelines using these six categories are designed to give parents a simple, easy-to-use system for deciding which programs are appropriate for children to watch. The Guidelines—which provide parents with information concerning the level and kinds of content in a program that Congress believed would be useful to them—will be widely available to parents. A copy of a brochure explaining the system is attached; it is being made available to parents across the Nation. Further, we expect that newspapers and other program listings, including *TV Guide* and cable's Prevue Channel, will carry full explanations of the six categories, including the types of program content that each category of programming may contain. We have also established a home page on the World Wide Web where parents can obtain information about the Guidelines, as well as telephone numbers in English and Spanish that parents can call to obtain a copy of the Guidelines.[1] Cable networks and television stations will also air public service announcements explaining the TV Parental Guidelines and how parents can use them.

The TV Parental Guidelines will permit parents quickly to decide which categories of programming they wish their children to watch unsupervised, and they can also use the Guidelines to help them decide which programs they should watch with their children. Further, the TV Parental Guidelines will be readily usable with the "V-chip" to give parents another tool to help control their children's television viewing.

Guidelines will be assigned to programs in most cases by broadcast and cable networks and producers. This was the process Congress contemplated in the Telecommunications Act[2], and it is the only feasible way in which the 2,000 hours of television programming distributed every day could be rated. The final say in assigning program guidelines rests with local television stations who will have the right to substitute the rating they deem most suitable for their particular audience for a rating chosen by a program's producer. Each program in a series will be separately rated, so that parents will have notice if a particular episode of a program has content about which they may be concerned.

In addition, we are establishing an Oversight Monitoring Board to ensure that the

Guidelines are applied accurately and consistently to television programming. The Oversight Monitoring Board will have 19 members, six each from the broadcast television industry, the cable industry, and the program production community, in addition to a chairman. This follows the precedent established by the Appeals Board for movie ratings whose members also come from within the industry. The first chairman of the Board will be Jack Valenti, who also chaired the inter-industry committee that established the Guidelines.

The Oversight Monitoring Board will provide information to producers and other program distributors concerning the Guidelines, as well as address complaints and requests from the public about the Guidelines and their implementation. The Oversight Monitoring Board will regularly hear the views of parents through an ongoing effort that will explore attitudes about the TV Parental Guidelines and the way in which they are being applied to programming. The Board will also regularly conduct focus groups and commission quantitative studies to determine whether the Guidelines are in fact providing useful information to parents, and will consider any needed changes to them.

The Guidelines will be applied to all television programming except for news and sports. Unedited movies that are typically shown on premium cable channels will carry their original MPAA ratings. Movies that were produced before the creation of the movie ratings system in 1968 and movies that are edited for television will carry the TV Parental Guidelines. The guideline icon will be displayed for 15 seconds at the beginning of each program in the upper left-hand corner of the screen.[3] It will be displayed again at the beginning of the second hour of longer programs.

All of the national broadcast television networks have agreed to apply the Guidelines to their programming, and much of network programming is already carrying a guideline. Virtually every national cable network has also agreed to rate its programs, and many have already begun to do so. We have provided information about the TV Parental Guidelines to syndicators and we are urging them to rate their own programs. Most of the major producers of syndicated programming will either apply a guideline to their programs themselves, or provide ratings information to stations and other distributors of their programs. Within a short period, therefore, most of the television programming available on broadcast television and cable will carry the Guidelines.

Cable networks and television stations will supply ratings information to newspapers and publishers of printed and electronic program guides. We have asked that they include the appropriate icon or another appropriate printed indication of a program's category in their program listings.

We have also agreed to encode the guideline for each program on line 21 of the Vertical Blanking Interval once the Commission establishes a technical standard. This will enable the "V-chip" and permit parents to use the TV Parental Guidelines to control children's television viewing when parents are not in the home.

The Statutory Framework

Section 551 of the Telecommunications Act of 1996, P. L. 104-104, requires the Commission to prescribe, after consultation with an advisory committee, "guidelines and recommended procedures for the identification and rating of video programming that contains sexual, violent, or other indecent material about which parents should be informed before it is displayed to children." Section 551(e)(1) provides that this requirement shall take effect one year after enactment,

> *only* if the Commission determines, in consultation with appropriate public interest groups and interested individuals from the private sector, that distributors of video programming have not, by such date—
> (A) established voluntary rules for rating video programming that contains sexual, violent, or other indecent material about which parents should be informed before it is displayed to children, and such rules are acceptable to the Commission; and
> (B) agreed voluntarily to broadcast signals that contain ratings of such programming. (Emphasis added)

By its plain terms, the Act does not require the Commission to act at a particular time on guidelines adopted by the industry; it is to appoint an advisory committee and proceed to adopt its own recommended guidelines only if it concludes that, as of one year after enactment, the television industry has not established "acceptable" guidelines. The Conference Report on the Act makes this clear:

> Under subsection (e)(1), the effective date for subsection (b) (regarding the appointment of an advisory committee to recommend a rating system and the rules for transmitting a rating) is no less than one year after the date of enactment. The actual effective date has also been made contingent on a determination by the Commission that distributors of video programming have not, by such date, established a voluntary system for rating video programming and such programming is acceptable to the Commission and have also agreed to include ratings in the transmission of signals to television sets for blocking.

H. REP. NO. 458, 104th Cong., 2d Sess. 196 (1996). The conferees also stated that any guidelines adopted by the Commission would only be "intended to provide industry with a carefully considered and practical system for rating programs if the industry does not develop such a system itself." *Id.* at 195.

The language and structure of the Telecommunications Act and the Conference Report demonstrate, therefore, that Congress hoped that the television industry would voluntarily establish a ratings system and that, if it did, the Commission would not be required to adopt any recommended procedures for rating programs. The debates on the Act confirm that Congress intended the Commission to act only if the industry failed to do so. Congressman Markey, who sponsored the House version of the "V-chip" language (the version that was largely adopted in the conference bill)[4], explained that "[t]his is a voluntary system that is submitted. If the networks do not come up with one on their own, a voluntary rating system that is recommended." 141 CONG. REC. H8487 (daily ed. Aug.

4, 1995). In the debate on the conference bill, Congressman Markey reiterated this understanding: "It will be several years before television sets include the V-chip. First, the industry must develop a ratings system." 142 CONG. REC. H1171 (daily ed. Feb. 1, 1996). The same point was made in the Senate debate on the conference bill: "[I]f the television broadcasters, [and] cable operators have not taken the opportunity to voluntarily develop a rating system to guide parents, the Federal Communications Commission would be authorized to establish an advisory committee to develop recommendations and guidelines for the identification and rating of television programming." *Id.* at S702 (daily ed. Feb. 1, 1996)(Statement of Senator Burns).

Thus, if the television industry develops a voluntary system of guidelines, as it has, Congress did not expect the Commission to develop its own ratings system; the Commission is to act only if the industry fails to. To be sure, the Act authorizes the Commission to appoint the advisory committee if the industry-developed system is not "acceptable." But that proviso does not alter Congress' express understanding that it was principally looking for guidelines adopted by the industry. Nor does it permit the Commission to substitute its own judgment of what might be the "best" system for the industry's choice.

The structure of the Act itself so indicates. If the industry failed to adopt a system, the Commission would be required to appoint a broad-based advisory committee including representatives of "appropriate public interest groups, and other interested individuals from the private sector." No such requirement was imposed upon the industry in its development of guidelines, which shows that Congress did not intend the two processes to be interchangeable.[5]

Further, Congress' use of the word "acceptable" also confirms that it did not intend for the Commission to demand that an industry-developed system of guidelines conform to the Commission's own or anyone else's vision of an ideal program. Given the absence of a specific definition of the term in the Act or its legislative history, the Commission should be guided by its general meaning.[6] *Webster's Third International* defines "acceptable" as a thing that is "capable or worthy of being accepted;" as something that is "satisfactory: conforming to or equal to approved standards;" and as "barely satisfactory or adequate." Thus, if the industry-developed system is designed to accomplish Congress' stated goals, then it must be deemed "acceptable" by the Commission.

The relevant standard that Congress established for guidelines is a system for "rating video programming that contains sexual, violent, or other indecent material about which parents should be informed before it is displayed to children." Telecommunications Act § 551(e)(1)(A). The TV Parental Guidelines the industry has adopted more than meet that test. They identify programs and place them into categories based on specified levels of sexual content, violence, and strong or profane language. Parents who wish to monitor or restrict their children's watching will be informed about the levels of sexual and violent materials and strong language that will be found in non-news or sports television programs. This information will be available to them in program listings, on-screen during each program, and—when the Commission adopts a technical standard—in the Vertical Blanking Interval of television signals (and in a suitable fashion in digital television signals). Further, through the Oversight Monitoring Board, the industry has established a means to address any concerns that develop about the operation of the Guidelines, their usefulness to parents, and complaints about the application of the Guidelines to particular programs.

The TV Parental Guidelines indeed are precisely the kind of system contemplated by the proponents of the "V-chip" provisions of the Telecommunications Act. Congressman Goodlatte told the House that the legislation would:

> empower the parents of this country to do what every one of them does with their children today when they ask if they can go to a movie theater, give them a limited number of choices to help them make decisions that they cannot be in that movie theater when their child asks them to go with another friend to see a movie: G, PG, PG-13, R, and C-17, X, and not rated. The V-chip will give them a similar opportunity to do something with television that they cannot possibly do just by reading the newspaper ads.

141 CONG. REC. H8488 (daily ed. Aug. 14, 1995). Congressman Burton, one of the sponsors of the "V-chip" amendment, stated, "we need a system where a parent can block out a whole category of violence and sexually explicit programs if they want to." *Id.* at H8487. Thus, even if Congress had no precise understanding of the system of guidelines that might be adopted, it clearly preferred to leave development of a system to the industry, and the debate in Congress shows that it would be comfortable with guidelines similar to those that have been in place for movies for 28 years which place programs into categories that parents could readily understand and use. Indeed, if Congress had believed that an MPAA-like age-based ratings system would not achieve its goals, it easily could have said so. Clearly, however, it did not.

The TV Parental Guidelines in fact are based on the MPAA ratings with which parents are familiar and which enjoy broad public support.[7] The rating assigned to individual programs will reflect levels of the precise content that Congress identified as the ones about which parents would be concerned. They provide parents with a useable number of options so that their wishes concerning their children's viewing can be readily implemented. As the descriptions of each category are widely distributed, and as parents see the ratings assigned to different programs, they will become familiar with the Guidelines and will recognize the content of programs in the different categories.

The TV Parental Guidelines, therefore, will achieve Congress' objective of informing parents about television programming. This is the test the Commission must use to determine acceptability, not whether a different system might also achieve Congress' goals, or perhaps serve purposes beyond those Congress identified. If the Guidelines adopted by the industry conform to Congress' expectations — as they clearly do—then the Commission must conclude that they are "acceptable."

As Congress indicated in the Act, we anticipate that the Commission will seek public comment on the TV Parental Guidelines. We look forward to participating in that process.

Please direct any questions concerning this matter to Jill Luckett at NCTA, Jack Goodman at NAB, and Cynthia Merrifield at MPAA.

Respectfully submitted,

Jack Valenti, President and CEO Motion Picture Association of America
Decker Anstrom, President and CEO National Cable Television Association
Eddie Fritts, President and CEO National Association of Broadcasters

Attachments
cc: Chairman and Commissioners
 Meredith J. Jones
 Roy J. Stewart
 Christopher J. Wright

Notes

1. The Web site can be accessed at http://www.tvguidelines.org.
2. *See* 141 CONG. REC. H8486 (daily ed. Aug. 4, 1995)(Statement of Congressman Markey)("All of the ratings will be done voluntarily by the broadcasters."); *id.* at H8495 (Statement of Congressman Moran)("What we do is ask the broadcast industry to rate their own programs.").
3. The icons will occupy 40 scan lines on the television screen. This is twice the size that the Commission determined to be adequate for sponsor identifications on political advertising. *See* 47 C.F.R. § 73.1212(a)(2)(ii); *Codification of the Commission's Political Programming Policies*, 7 FCC Rcd. 1616 (1992). Notably, the Telecommunications Act does not require distributors of video programming to display ratings on-screen, and the legislative history also includes no suggestion that stations would do so. Broadcasters and cable networks nonetheless decided to carry the on-screen icon to ensure that parents would have access to this information before the "v-chip" in [*sic*] available in television sets. By so agreeing, the industry is thus exceeding Congress' expectations.
4. H. REP. No. 458, 104th Cong., 2d Sess. 195 (1996)("The conference agreement adopts the House provisions with modifications.").
5. Nonetheless, the Implementing Group devoted thousand of hours to designing the system, meeting with educators, children's advocacy groups, medical and psychological experts and groups, as well as producers and distributors of television programming, in order to design a system that would at the same time be easy to use and understand and provide the most useful information to parents. A list of these groups is attached. Thus, in developing the Guidelines, the industry went far beyond the process that Congress anticipated.
6. *Perrin v. United States*, 444 U.S. 37, 42 (1979)("A fundamental canon of construction is that, unless otherwise defined, words will be interpreted as taking their ordinary, contemporary, common meaning."). While the Commission's Rules use the term "acceptable" in a variety of contexts, none of them appear to relate to the question before the Commission here. *See, e.g.,* 47 C.F.R. § 1.4000(a)(2)(iii)(preempting local regulation that precludes reception of an "acceptable" quality signal); 47 C.F.R. § 5.207 (applicants for a pioneer's preference may submit an "acceptable" showing of technical feasibility); 47 C.F.R. § 15.117(c)(Note)(discussing "acceptable" television tuning mechanisms); 47 C.F.R. § 68.318(b)(1)(establishing minimum "acceptable" standards for certain terminal equipment); 47 C.F.R. § 73.702(g)(Note)(although FCC prefers field strengths equal to or greater than IFRB standards, lesser field strengths will be "acceptable"); 47 C.F.R. § 73.3522(a)(6)(applicant whose application is not "acceptable" for filing granted opportunity to correct deficiencies). Further, there is no evidence that Congress knew about or considered any of these uses of the word "acceptable" when it drafted the Telecommunications Act.
7. Surveys of parents show that roughly 80 percent believe that the MPAA movie ratings system is useful or very useful as "a guide for deciding what movies children should see." Opinion Research Corporation (Sept. 1996).

IV. PUBLIC NOTICE FCC 97-34

Report No. CS 97-6
February 7, 1997

COMMISSION SEEKS COMMENT ON INDUSTRY
PROPOSAL FOR RATING VIDEO PROGRAMMING

(CS Docket No. 97-55)

1. In the Telecommunications Act of 1996 ("the 1996 Act"),[1] Congress determined that parents should be provided "with timely information about the nature of upcoming video programming and with the technological tools that allow them easily to block violent, sexual, or other programming that they believe harmful to their children."[2] Congress also provided that, in the first instance, distributors of video programming should be given the opportunity to develop a voluntary system to provide such information to parents.[3]

2. On January 17, 1997, the National Association of Broadcasters ("NAB"), the National Cable Television Association ("NCTA") and the Motion Picture Association of America ("MPAA") submitted a joint proposal to the Commission describing a voluntary ratings system for video programming (the "industry proposal"). Under the industry proposal, television programming would fall into one of six categories (the "industry guidelines").[4] For programs designed solely for children, the general industry guidelines are: TV-Y (All Children—*This program is designed to be appropriate for all children*), and TV-Y7 (Directed to Older Children—*This program is designed for children age 7 and above*). For programs designed for the entire audience, the general industry guidelines are: TV-G (General Audience—*Most parents would find this program suitable for all ages*), TV-PG (Parental Guidance Suggested—*This program may contain some material that some parents would find unsuitable for younger children*), TV-14 (Parents Strongly Cautioned—*This program may contain some material that many parents would find unsuitable for children under 14 years of age*), and TV-M (Mature Audience Only—*This program is specially designed to be viewed by adults and therefore may be unsuitable for children under 17*).[5]

3. According to the industry proposal, the industry guidelines typically would be assigned to television programs by broadcast and cable networks and producers.[6] However, local television stations would retain the right to substitute the guideline they deem most suitable for their particular audience.[7] The industry proposal also notes the establishment of an industry Oversight Monitoring Board "to ensure that the Guidelines are applied accurately and consistently to television programming."[8] Under the industry proposal, most of the television programming available on broadcast and cable will soon carry the industry guidelines.[9] The industry proposal states that a guideline icon will be displayed for 15 seconds at the beginning of each program and again at the beginning of the second hour of longer programs.[10] In addition, the proposal states that the guideline for each program will be encoded on line 21 of the Vertical Blanking Interval once the

Commission establishes a technical standard, which will enable the "V-chip" and permit parents to use the guidelines to control their children's television viewing.[11]

4. The above is only a general description of certain aspects of the industry proposal. For a more detailed description, interested parties are directed to review a complete copy of the industry proposal. The industry proposal is attached to this Public Notice as an Appendix. Copies may also be obtained from the Commission's Public Reference Room, Room 239, 1919 M Street, N.W., Washington, D.C., or from the Commission's Internet site (http://www.fcc.gov/vchip),[12] or by calling ITS, the Commission's transcription service, at (202) 857-3800.

5. Under Section 551(e) of the 1996 Act, the Commission must now determine, in consultation with appropriate public interest groups and interested individuals from the private sector, whether: (1) video programming distributors have established, within one year of the 1996 Act's enactment,[13] voluntary rules for rating video programming that contains sexual, violent or other indecent material about which parents should be informed before it is displayed to children; (2) such voluntary rules are acceptable to the Commission; and (3) video programming distributors have agreed voluntarily to broadcast signals that contain ratings of such programming. If the Commission determines that the industry proposal fails to satisfy these criteria, the Commission must establish: (1) on the basis of recommendations from an advisory committee, guidelines and recommended procedures for the identification and rating of video programming that contains violent, sexual or other indecent material about which parents should be informed before it is displayed to children; and (2) in consultation with the television industry, rules requiring the distributors of video programming that has been rated to transmit such rating to permit parents to block the display of video programming that they have determined is inappropriate for their children.[14]

6. Interested parties are invited to provide comment on whether the industry proposal meets the standards set forth in Section 551(e) of the 1996 Act. In particular, we seek comment on whether the industry proposal is "acceptable."[15] Parties should specifically identify the factors they believe that the Commission should consider in making this determination. We also seek comment on whether the industry proposal satisfies Congress' concerns.[16]

. . . .

Notes

1.   Pub. L. 104-104, 110 Stat. 56 (February 8, 1996).
2.   1996 Act, § 551(a)(9).
3.   *Id.*, § 551(c).
4.   Industry Proposal at 1–2.
5.   *Id.*
6.   *Id.* at 3. The industry proposal states that the guidelines will be applied to all television programming except for news and sports. Each program in a series will be separately rated. Unedited movies that are typically shown on premium cable channels will carry their original MPAA ratings. Movies that were produced before the creation of the movie ratings system in 1968 and movies that are edited for television will carry the industry guidelines. *Id.* at 3–4.
7.   *Id.* at 3.
8.   *Id.*

9.   *Id.* at 4. The industry proposal states that all of the national broadcast television networks and virtually every national cable network have agreed to rate their programming, and that many of them are already doing so. In addition, the industry proposal states that most of the producers of syndicated programming will either apply a guideline to their programs themselves, or provide ratings information to stations and other distributors of their programs. *Id.*

10.   *Id.* at 4. The industry proposal also states that cable networks and television stations will supply ratings information to newspapers and publishers of printed and electronic program guides, and that they have asked that the appropriate icon or other appropriate indication of a program's category be included in the program listings. *Id.*

11.   *Id.* at 4–5.

12.   For technical reasons, a brochure that was attached to the industry proposal, entitled "TV Parental Guidelines," cannot be posted on the Commission's Internet site. This brochure can be obtained through the Commission's public reference room or through ITS.

13.   As indicated above, the 1996 Act was signed into law on February 8, 1996.

14.   1996 Act, § 551(b)(1), codified at Section 303(w) of the Communications Act of 1934 ("the Communications Act"), as amended, 47 U.S.C. § 303(w). The 1996 Act also mandated the inclusion in most new television signal receivers of the so-called "V-chip" technology, which will be capable of reading electronic program ratings and blocking the display of video programming with a common rating. 1996 Act, § 551(c), codified at Section 303(x) of the Communications Act, 47 U.S.C. § 303(x); 1996 Act, § 551(d), codified at Section 330(c) of the Communications Act, 47 U.S.C. § 330(c); and 1996 Act, § 551(e). The Commission will initiate a separate proceeding shortly addressing the issues relating to the "V-chip."

15.   1996 Act, § 551(e)(1)(A).

16.   *Id.*, § 551(a).

V.   Joint Statement of Motion Picture of Association of America, National Association of Broadcasters, National Cable Television

July 10, 1997

WASHINGTON, D.C.—The television industry has concluded a long negotiation with public advocacy groups and has come to closure on revisions to the TV PARENTAL GUIDELINES.

The following content information, where appropriate, will be added to all non-exempt programming to supplement the existing Guidelines: in the TV-Y7 category—FV for fantasy violence; in the TV-PG, TV-14 and TV-MA categories—V for violence, S for sexual situations, L for language, and D for dialogue.

Leaders in Congress have said no legislation regarding television ratings, content and program scheduling should be enacted for several years, so that parents will have time to understand and deal with V-chips in television sets, a mechanism which gives them the ability to block out programs they may find inappropriate for young children. Additionally, advocacy group leaders have said this process should proceed unimpeded by pending or new legislation that would undermine the intent of our joint agreement or disrupt the harmony and good faith of the process just concluded.

We are grateful to Vice President Gore, to Chairman John McCain, to Chairman Tom Bliley, Chairman Billy Tauzin, Congressman Ed Markey, among others, who were helpful throughout this process. We also wish to thank the parents of Peoria, Illinois who, in a May town hall meeting, shared with us their thoughts on the subject of television ratings.

As the industry declared on February 29, 1996, in announcing its plans to design parental guidelines for television, we repeat now: Parents will be the arbiters of these new TV PARENTAL GUIDELINES, which will be implemented no later than October 1, 1997. Obviously, until there is a sufficient number of television sets equipped with V-chips in American homes, no evaluation can be properly conducted.

VI. TV Parental Guidelines—Revised Proposal*

September 10, 1997

Mr. William F. Caton
Secretary
Federal Communications Commission
1919 M Street, N.W.
Washington, D.C. 20554

Re: CS Docket No. 97-55

Dear Mr. Caton:

We are formally notifying the Commission by this letter of certain elements we are adding to the system of parental guidelines that the television industry submitted on January 17, 1997. The additions we describe below are supported by television broadcasters, cable systems and networks, and television production companies. We are also pleased that the revised guidelines are supported by leading family and child advocacy groups. These supplements to the existing system of guidelines will be implemented, apart from provisions dealing specifically with the "V-chip," by October 1 of this year.

We are attaching a description of the amended system and statements of the television industry and family and child advocacy groups concerning the revised voluntary TV Parental Guidelines, as well as the agreement between the television industry and the advocacy community concerning additions to the Guidelines.[1]

We are changing some of the descriptors associated with the six age-based categories of television programming and, in certain categories, adding symbols describing the type of material that is included in a particular program. The program categories we will use after October 1 are:

The following categories apply to programs designed solely for children:

TV-Y All Children *This program is designed to be appropriate for all children.* Whether animated or live-action, the themes and elements in this program are specifically designed for a very young audience, including children from ages 2–6. This program is not expected to frighten younger children.

TV-Y7 Directed to Older Children *This program is designed for children age 7 and* *above.* It may be more appropriate for children who have acquired the developmental skills needed to distinguish between make-believe and reality. Themes and elements in this program may include mild fantasy violence or comedic violence, or may frighten children under the age of 7. Therefore, parents may wish to consider the suitability of this program for their very young children. Note: For those programs where fantasy violence may be more intense or more combative than other programs in this category, such programs will be designated **TV-Y7-FV**.

The following categories apply to programs designed for the entire audience:

TV-G General Audience *Most parents would find this program suitable for all ages.* Although this rating does not signify a program designed specifically for children, most parents may let younger children watch this program unattended. It contains little or no violence, no strong language and little or no sexual dialogue or situations.

TV-PG Parental Guidance Suggested *This program contains material that parents may find unsuitable for younger children.* Many parents may want to watch it with their younger children. The theme itself may call for parental guidance and/or the program contains one or more of the following: moderate violence (V), some sexual situations (S), infrequent coarse language (L), or some suggestive dialogue (D).

TV-14 Parents Strongly Cautioned *This program contains some material that many parents would find unsuitable for children under 14 years of age.* Parents are strongly urged to exercise greater care in monitoring this program and are cautioned against letting children under the age of 14 watch unattended. This program contains one or more of the following: intense violence (V), intense sexual situations (S), strong coarse language (L), or intensely suggestive dialogue (D).

TV-MA Mature Audience Only *This program is specifically designed to be viewed by adults and therefore may be unsuitable for children under 17.* This program contains one or more of the following: graphic violence (V), explicit sexual activity (S), or crude indecent language (L).

These refinements maintain the broad six-category structure of the system of ratings we previously submitted to the Commission and add symbols indicating the particular content of each program, as appropriate. Together, the category and program-specific content indicators will provide parents with information that will help them make informed decisions about what their children should watch on television.

The icons and associated content symbols will appear for 15 seconds at the beginning of all rated programming, and the size of the icons will be increased from those shown presently.

In addition, five representatives of the advocacy community will be added to the monitoring board which we have established to ensure that the Guidelines are applied accurately and consistently to television programming. This will provide input from representatives of parents and family and child advocacy groups about the way in which the Guidelines operate in practice.

Consistent with the operation of the TV Parental Guidelines since January, cable networks and television stations will supply ratings information to newspapers and publishers of printed and electronic program guides so that the ratings can be included in program guides. Also unchanged is the right of local television stations to substitute the rating they deem appropriate for their audience for ratings assigned by producers and distributors. The TV Parental Guidelines will continue to apply to all television programming except for news and sports and unedited MPAA-rated movies that are shown on premium cable channels. The latter will continue to carry their original MPAA ratings and the additional advisories currently used by several premium services.

Section 551(e)(1) of the Telecommunications Act of 1996, Pub. L. No. 104-104, requires the Commission to determine if "distributors of video programming have . . . established voluntary rules for rating video programming that contains sexual, violent, or other indecent material about which parents should be informed," and that the industry-adopted ratings system is "acceptable." As we pointed out in submitting the TV Parental Guidelines on January 17 and in comments submitted on May 8, 1997,[2] the ratings system we adopted achieved Congress' goals of providing information that would give parents an effective tool to control their children's television viewing, a tool whose effectiveness would become even greater when the "V-chip" becomes available.

By adding information to the Guidelines, parents will have additional information to help them decide which television programs their children will watch. Parents who wish to prevent their children from seeing a whole category of programs oriented in theme or content to older viewers will be able to do so; parents who instead are interested in controlling their children's access to particular types of content will also be provided with the information they need. Each network or television station also will continue to have the right to provide additional advisories to parents when they believe their audience will benefit from particular information about a specific program.

When coupled with the "V-chip," the TV Parental Guidelines will allow parents flexible options to ensure that their children see only the programs that they deem suitable for them. The content symbols added to the ratings categories meet many of the concerns expressed in comments to the Commission,[3] and the addition of representatives of advocacy groups to the Oversight Monitoring Board address the concerns of others that decisions about ratings should reflect input from outside the television industry.[4]

The TV Parental Guidelines are voluntary and broadly supported by the television industry which has pledged to begin transmitting ratings information on line 21 of the Vertical Blanking Interval (VBI) within six months. While the Telecommunications Act contemplated that a ratings system would be incorporated into the "V-chip," Congress specifically eschewed any requirement that distributors of programming be required to use that system. The Commission is only authorized to require transmission of blocking codes "with respect to video programming that has been rated." 47 U.S.C. § 303(w)(2). The Conference Report emphasized that "the conferees do not intend that the Commission require the adoption of the recommended rating system *nor that any particular program be rated.*" H. REP. NO. 458, 104th Cong., 2d Sess. 195 (1996)(emphasis added).

Program producers and distributors were thus explicitly left by Congress with the discretion to determine whether they will rate their own programming, subject only to the requirement that they cannot strip ratings information from the VBI. Congress undoubtedly adopted this approach to avoid the obvious constitutional questions that would arise if programmers were required to display government-approved messages about program content. Thus, whether certain program producers or distributors decide that they will not rate programs at all (as some did after the TV Parental Guidelines were adopted last December), or others do not utilize the additional content symbols, has no impact on the decision as to whether the ratings system adopted by the industry is "acceptable" under Section 551(e)(1).

In order to bring the full benefits of the TV Parental Guidelines to the American people, we urge the Commission promptly to conclude that this system is acceptable and to adopt the technical standards needed for its incorporation into television receivers.

Please direct any questions concerning this matter to Jill Luckett at NCTA, Jack Goodman at NAB, and Cynthia Merrifield at MPAA.

Respectfully submitted,

Jack Valenti, President and CEO Motion Picture Association of America
Decker Anstrom, President and CEO National Cable Television Association
Eddie Fritts, President and CEO National Association of Broadcasters

Attachments
cc: Chairman and Commissioners
       Meredith J. Jones
       Roy J. Stewart
       Christopher J. Wright

Agreement on Modifications to the TV Parental Guidelines

July 10, 1997

1.   Content Information: The following content information, where appropriate, will be added to all non-exempt programming to supplement the existing TV Parental Guidelines: in the TV-Y7 category—FV for fantasy violence; in the TV-PG, TV-14 and TV-MA categories—V for violence, S for sexual situations, L for language, and D for dialogue.

2.   Descriptions of the Guidelines: Modifications will be made to the category descriptions as specified in Attachment 1.

3.   Monitoring Board: Five non-industry members, drawn from the advocacy community and selected by the Chairman, will be appointed to the Monitoring Board as full voting members. Recommendations for appointment to the Board will be offered by advocacy groups and Monitoring Board members.

4.   V-chip: The industry and advocacy groups will recommend to the FCC that the MPAA movie rating system and the universal television rating system be the only systems mandated for inclusion on the V-chip.

5. **Icons:** Larger icons will appear on-screen for 15 seconds at the beginning of all rated programming and through use of a display button thereafter.

6. **Assurances:** Attachment 2 reflects the agreement reached between the industry and advocacy groups on treatment of the relevant proceedings at the FCC and pending and future legislation.

7. **Research and Evaluation:** Independent, scientific research and evaluation will be undertaken once the V-chip has been in the marketplace.

8. **Effective Date:** Networks will begin to rate programming using the new universal television rating system by October 1, 1997. The industry agrees to encode and transmit the rating information in Line 21 of the vertical blanking interval within 180 days of the date of this agreement.

Attachment #1

The following categories apply to programs designed solely for children:

TV-Y **All Children.** *This program is designed to be appropriate for all children.* Whether animated or live-action, the themes and elements in this program are specifically designed for a very young audience, including children from ages 2–6. This program is not expected to frighten younger children.

TV-Y7 **Directed to Older Children.** *This program is designed for children age 7 and above.* It may be more appropriate for children who have acquired the developmental skills needed to distinguish between make-believe and reality. Themes and elements in this program may include mild fantasy violence or comedic violence, or may frighten children under the age of 7. Therefore, parents may wish to consider the suitability of this program for their very young children. Note: For those programs where fantasy violence may be more intense or more combative than other programs in this category, such programs will be designated **TV-Y7-FV**.

The following categories apply to programs designed for the entire audience:

TV-G **General Audience.** *Most parents would find this program suitable for all ages.* Although this rating does not signify a program designed specifically for children, most parents may let younger children watch this program unattended. It contains little or no violence, no strong language and little or no sexual dialogue or situations.

TV-PG **Parental Guidance Suggested.** *This program contains material that parents may find unsuitable for younger children.* Many parents may want to watch it with their younger children. The theme itself may call for parental guidance and/or the program contains one or more of the following: moderate violence (V), some sexual situations (S), infrequent coarse language (L), or some suggestive dialogue (D).

TV-14 **Parents Strongly Cautioned.** *This program contains some material that many parents would find unsuitable for children under 14 years of age.* Parents are strongly urged to exercise greater care in monitor ing this program and are cautioned against letting children under the age of 14 watch unattended. This program contains one or more of the following: intense violence (V), intense sexual situations (S), strong coarse language (L), or intensely suggestive dialogue (D).

TV-MA   **Mature Audience Only.** *This program is specifically designed to be viewed by adults and therefore may be unsuitable for children under 17.* This program contains one or more of the following: graphic violence (V), explicit sexual activity (S), or crude indecent language (L).

Attachment # 2

The attached modifications of the TV Parental Guideline System have been developed collaboratively by members of the industry and the advocacy community. We find this combined age and content based system to be acceptable and believe that it should be designated as the mandated system on the V-chip and used to rate all television programming, except for news and sports, which are exempt, and unedited movies with an MPAA rating aired on premium cable channels. We urge the FCC to so rule as expeditiously as possible.

We further believe that the system deserves a fair chance to work in the marketplace to allow parents an opportunity to understand and use the system. Accordingly, the undersigned organizations will work to: educate the public and parents about the V-chip and the TV Parental Guideline System; encourage publishers of TV periodicals, newspapers and journals to include the ratings with their program listings; and evaluate the system. Therefore, we urge governmental leaders to allow this process to proceed unimpeded by pending or new legislation that would undermine the intent of this agreement or disrupt the harmony and good faith of this process.

Motion Picture Association of America
National Association of Broadcasters
National Cable Television Association
Center for Media Education
Children Now
National Education Association

American Medical Association
American Academy of Pediatrics
American Psychological Association
Children's Defense Fund
National Association of Elementary
School Principals
National PTA

Notes

*   The industry proposal was found acceptable by the FCC on March 12, 1998 [Editor's note].
1.   We are also providing a copy of this submission and the attachments on diskette to the Cable Services Bureau.
2.   Joint Reply Comments of the National Association of Broadcasters, The National Cable Television Association, and The Motion Picture Association of America, CS Dkt. No. 97-55 (May 8, 1997).
3.   *See, e.g.,* Comments of the Center for Media Education, CS Dkt. No. 97-55 (April 8, 1977); Comments of the National Association for Family and Community Education, CS Dkt. No. 97-55 (Aprii 8, 1977).
4.   *See, e.g.,* Comments of Morality in Media, CS Dkt. No. 97-55 (April 8, 1977).

VII. TV Parental Guidelines—Examples of On-Screen Icons

VIII.   The UCLA Television Violence Report 1996*

The UCLA Center for Communication Policy

. . . .

B.   Historical Background

Concerns about media violence have been with us since long before the advent of television. Throughout the nineteenth century, moralists and critics warned that newspapers were the cause of juvenile crime. There was concern that the great flow of stories about crime and vice would lead people to imitate the vividly described immoral behavior. In the 1920s many were alarmed at what they saw as rampant sex, violence and general lawlessness on the movie screen. During that era the motion picture industry was not protected by the First Amendment. This protection did not come until the Supreme Court's *Miracle* decision in the 1950s. To forestall governmental regulation the film industry created its own production standards under the supervision of the Motion Picture Producers and Distributors of America (MPPDA). The man the MPPDA chose to supervise the film industry, Harding Administration Postmaster General Will H. Hays, became so powerful that the organization became known as the Hays Office.

The Hays Office Codes, which discuss sexuality as well as violence, established the following standards regarding criminal violence:

1.   Murder
     (a) The technique of murder must be presented in a way that will not inspire imitation.
     (b) Brutal killings are not to be presented in detail.
     (c) Revenge in modern times shall not be justified.

2.   Methods of crimes should not be explicitly presented.
     (a) Theft, robbery, safe-cracking and dynamiting of trains, mines, buildings, etc. should not be detailed in method.
     (b) Arson must be subject to the same safeguards.
     (c) The use of firearms should be restricted to essentials.

The codes list brutality, gruesomeness and cruelty to children or animals as repellent subjects. In justifying some of the codes, the Hays Office reasoned that crimes should not:

1.   Teach methods of crime.
2.   Inspire potential criminals with a desire for imitation.
3.   Make criminals seem heroic and justified.

The concerns embodied in the Hays Codes regarding the effects of film images, particularly on the young, led to the landmark Payne Fund studies (1933–1935). These studies concluded that movies contradicted social norms in regard to crime (and sex) and that motion pictures directly influenced youngsters to become juvenile delinquents and criminals. When the production codes finally disappeared in the 1960s, they were replaced by the voluntary rating of motion pictures by the Classification and Ratings Administration (CARA) administered by the Motion Picture Association of America (MPAA). Originally created in 1968 as G, M, R and X, these ratings still exist today, with some changes, as G, PG, PG-13, R and NC-17.

After World War II, there was concern about violence and gruesomeness in comic books such as *Tales from the Crypt, Haunt of Fear* and *Vault of Horror*. The comic book industry was attacked for contributing to juvenile delinquency. This led to the establishment in 1947 of the Association of Comic Magazine Publishers, which drafted a code in the 1950s banning, among other things, torture, sadism and detailed descriptions of criminal acts. A seal of approval then was printed on the cover of acceptable comics.

Significant penetration of television into American households began after World War II. By 1960, 150 million Americans lived in homes with television. Homes with children were more than twice as likely to have a television as those without children. By 1960, children were spending more time with television than they were with radio, comic books, babysitters or even playmates. As television became a staple of the American home, concern grew over what effect the medium might have on children. Would it stimulate or stunt intellectual development and creativity? Would it make kids passive or aggressive, friendly or empathic? Would it corrupt children by prematurely introducing them to an adult world of sex, smoking, liquor and violence? Or would it make them better able to cope with the real world around them?

Congressional interest in television violence began in 1954 with the creation of a Senate Subcommittee to Investigate Juvenile Delinquency, chaired by Senator Robert Hendrickson. Estes Kefauver took over the chairmanship a year later and extended the inquiry. In 1961 and 1962 Connecticut's Thomas Dodd, with support from President John F. Kennedy and Attorney General Robert F. Kennedy, followed up with intensive hearings leading the three networks to consider a joint effort to reduce television violence. Attorney General Kennedy even promised to protect such an effort against an antitrust challenge but the President was assassinated and the Attorney General resigned before any action could be taken.

The concerns in the 1950s and early 1960s about the violence in television series focused on television programs such as *The Rifleman* and *The Untouchables*. In 1961 the results of the first major investigation of the effects of television on children in North America were published. *Television in the Lives of Our Children* (Wilbur Schramm, Jack Lyle and Edwin Parker) presented the findings and conclusions from 11 studies conducted in ten American and Canadian communities between 1958 and 1960. This investigation covered a wide variety of topics and research areas, including the physical, emotional, cognitive and behavioral effects of television on children. The study addressed the most common concern about television: that it contributed to delinquent and violent behavior. The researchers found the content of television to be "extremely violent." Fighting, shooting and murder were common, as were themes of crime. Violence constituted an important part of programs in more than half of the hours monitored.

The researchers argued that television could contribute to violent and delinquent behavior in some cases. This might result, for example, in the case of a child who confuses the rules of the fantasy world, as seen on television, with the rules of reality, or an already aggressive child whose aggression is increased by identifying with a successful "bad" character on television. But the researchers cautioned that television was, at most, a contributing factor in causing violent and delinquent behaviors, or any behaviors for that matter. For example, they noted, "Delinquency is a complex behavior growing usually out of a number of roots, the chief one usually being some great lack in the child's life—often a broken home or a feeling of rejection by parents or peer groups. Television is, at best, a contributing cause."

Schramm and his associates summed up their conclusions in regard to the possible behavioral effects of television as follows: "For *some* children, under *some* conditions, *some* television is harmful. For *other* children, under the same conditions, or for the same children under *other* conditions, it may be beneficial. For *most* children, under *most* conditions, *most* television is probably neither harmful nor particularly beneficial." They also stressed that parents had little to fear from television if they provided their children with a warm, loving, interesting, secure family environment.

The 1960s was a tumultuous decade in the United States. Violent street demonstrations related to civil rights, inner-city turmoil, student activism and antiwar protests shook the country. The rate of violent crime soared. Major political assassinations occurred. Americans saw brutal images of the world on their television sets, including the Vietnam War (called "The Living Room War" by Michael Arlen), the suppression of antiwar demonstrators at the Democratic National Convention in Chicago in 1968 and the assassinations of President John F. Kennedy, Martin Luther King, Jr. and Robert F. Kennedy. In June 1968, President Lyndon B. Johnson, in response to concerns about societal violence and the recent assassinations, convened the National Commission on the Causes and Prevention of Violence. While looking at all sources of societal violence, the commission devoted much attention to the mass media, particularly television. This effort produced the massive *Violence and the Media* (1969), edited by Sandra Ball (now Ball-Rokeach) and Robert Baker. The third part of this three-part work focused on entertainment television and the issue of violence. It included summaries of past research assembled by experts in the field and new research prepared specifically for the report.

The media task force was concerned not only with the quantity of violence on entertainment television, but also with its quality. In other words, how was the violence portrayed? Who killed whom? Which weapons were used? Where did the violence take place? Was the violence justified? Were the aggressors rewarded or punished? Were the consequences of the violence fully shown? To conduct a content analysis of entertainment programs on television, the task force chose Professor George Gerbner of the Annenberg School for Communication at the University of Pennsylvania, a leading expert in the study of media violence. Gerbner defined violence as "the overt expression of force intended to hurt or kill."

It is important to reiterate that Gerbner and his staff analyzed both the extent of violence on television and the qualitative context of the violence. They not only quantified what portion of crime, comedy and cartoon shows contained violence, they also qualitatively examined the context in which the violence occurred. They noted, for example, that most violence was portrayed as serious rather than funny, and that most occurred between strangers at close range and involved weapons. They found that the consequences of television violence were unrealistic since little pain or gore was visible. They distinguished the violence of good guys from that of bad guys (good guys were as violent, but did not suffer negative consequences). Among their other qualitative findings were the following: police officers were nearly as violent as criminals; criminals usually received punishment from their enemies or the police rather than from the judicial system; most violence was committed by young or middle-aged unmarried males; nonwhites and foreigners also committed more than their share of violence (and were usually villains); and violence was rarely punished. Historical setting was another important contextual factor analyzed. While nearly three-quarters of programs set in contemporary times contained violence, almost all programs set in the past and the future contained violence.

From Gerbner's content analysis, the media task force reported what it saw as the basic messages or norms in regard to violence portrayed on broadcast television. Overall, the task force concluded that violence was shown as a useful means of resolving problems and achieving goals. Viewers learned from television that conflicts are best resolved through the use of violence. There was a notable absence of alternative means of conflict resolution, such as debate, cooperation and compromise.

From a comprehensive review of the effects-related research, the task force concluded that television's portrayal of violence was "one major contributory factor which must be considered in attempts to explain the many forms of violent behavior that mark American society today."

The media task force report was criticized for making assertions that were not well grounded in the data. There were many suppositions and conjectures in their conclusions about the effects of violence on viewers. Nevertheless, the work was considered important and stimulated further research.

Many felt that, although the report of the President's Commission on the Causes and Prevention of Violence pointed to a link between media violence and violence in the real world, a more detailed examination of the issue was desirable. In the political arena, Senator John Pastore (D-R.I.) argued that a "public health risk" might be at stake. If television was responsible for making the children of America more aggressive, he asserted, then government might have to pressure the industry to clean up its act. Even if the First Amendment prohibited government censorship, scientific evidence showing a link between television violence and real world violence might be used to convince the industry to restrain itself. With this in mind, Congress appropriated $1 million to fund research studies focusing on television violence and its effect on children and adolescents.

The result was a massive, six-volume Report of the Surgeon General of the United States, which included extensive reviews of existing literature and specially commissioned research. The project was managed by the Surgeon General and coordinated and administered by the National Institute of Mental Health (NIMH). An advisory committee composed of distinguished scholars was created to draw up the Report's conclusions.

The content analysis in the Surgeon General's Report was again provided by George Gerbner. He compared programming in 1969 with the results of the analyses he had completed for 1967 and 1968. Again, he applied both a quantitative and qualitative analysis. One important conclusion of his work was the lack of reality in television violence. The people, relationships, settings, places and times of television violence, he argued, all differed dramatically from those in real life.

Muriel Cantor ("The Role of the Producer in Choosing Children's Television Content") and Thomas Baldwin and Colby Lewis ("Violence in Television: The Industry Looks at Itself") reported on interviews with television professionals to provide insight into how television content was created. The professionals tended to see violence as synonymous with "action," which they argued was the best tool to keep the interest and attention of viewers, young and old. They claimed that they limited violence to those places where it was contextually appropriate, for example, where it was essential to plot or character development. They insisted that violence was portrayed as immoral unless it was used for self-defense or by law enforcement officials. Heroes only resorted to violence when absolutely necessary and, even then, always obeyed the law. Generally discounting criticism of television violence, they argued that television violence accurately reflected the real world and cited influences other than television as responsible for the real violence in society. They also criticized parents for blaming television while ignoring their own responsibilities.

In a major effects-related study, Robert Liebert and Robert Baron ("Short-Term Effects of Televised Aggression on Children's Aggressive Behavior") found that viewing a violent act on television increased the willingness of children to be aggressors in a laboratory situation. Liebert, summarizing the research from his own and other studies within the Surgeon General's Report, as well as 54 earlier experimental studies, concluded that children who see violence rewarded in the mass media subsequently act more violently themselves.

Monroe Lefkowitz and his associates ("Television Violence and Child Aggression: A Follow-up Study") conducted a ten-year longitudinal study that found the television habits established by an eight-year-old boy would influence his aggressive behavior throughout his childhood and into his adolescent years. The more violence an eight-year-old boy watched, the more aggressive his behavior would be at age eight and at age 18. The link between his television viewing at eight and his aggressive behavior at 18 was even stronger than the link between his television watching at eight and his aggressive behavior at 8. Carefully controlling for other variables, Lefkowitz and his associates concluded that regular viewing of media violence seemed to lead to aggressive behavior.

This is but a brief taste of the many different studies that constituted the Surgeon General's Report. Surveying the whole report, the advisory committee concluded, "Thus the two sets of findings (laboratory and survey) converge in three respects: a preliminary and tentative indication of a causal relation between viewing violence on television and aggressive behavior; an indication that any such causal operation operates only on some children (who are predisposed to be aggressive); and an indication that it operates only in some environmental contexts. Such tentative and limited conclusions are not very satisfying [yet] they represent substantially more knowledge than we had two years ago."

Each of the individual studies can be criticized, especially for methodological flaws. For example, one can question whether findings from a laboratory experiment can be applied to the "real world." In some instances, the sample sizes studied were quite small.

In many instances, a host of additional variables might account for the correlations found. Moving beyond individual studies, the report can be faulted for its general focus on short-term and direct effects. For example, some critics have argued the most profound influences of television are long-term and indirect. Nevertheless, overall, the accumulation of evidence supported the hypothesis that viewing of violence on television may increase the likelihood of aggressive behavior.

There was some criticism that the conclusions of the advisory committee were overly tentative and cautious. In the 1972 Senate hearings on the committee's conclusions, the Surgeon General himself, Jessie Steinfeld, expressed this view:

> While the Committee report is carefully phrased and qualified in language acceptable to social scientists, it is clear to me that the causal relation between televised violence and antisocial behavior is sufficient to warrant appropriate and immediate remedial action. The data on social phenomena such as television and social violence will never be clear enough for all social scientists to agree on the formulation of a succinct statement of causality. But there comes a time when the data are sufficient to justify action. That time has come.

During the 1970s there were a number of widely publicized crimes attributed to imitation of televised violence. In 1977 Ronnie Zamora, a 15-year-old Florida youth, was charged with the murder of his neighbor, an 80-year-old woman. His attorney, Ellis Rubin, used "television intoxication" as Zamora's defense, arguing that a steady diet of violent television caused him to act as he did. Believing that television could not be held accountable for the crime, the jury was not persuaded and Zamora was convicted of first-degree murder. About the same time, in Boston a young woman was beaten to death and burned in a vacant lot by a group of youths. When arrested for her murder, the youths claimed they had gotten the idea for the crime from television the night before. Fearful of the potential effect of television, interested groups began protesting against television violence. The American Medical Association argued that it was a threat to the social health of the country. The National PTA sponsored forums on its effects. The National Citizens' Committee for Broadcasting publicly identified advertisers that sponsored programming with violent content.

In the summary of the Surgeon General's Report of 1971, the advisory committee called for investigation into previously unexplored areas of television's influence, such as its influence on prosocial behaviors, and the study of its effects in the home environment rather than in the laboratory. The scientific community responded to this call with a huge outpouring of research. So much information was produced (over 3,000 titles), that Surgeon General Julius Richard suggested that a synthesis and evaluation of the literature be conducted by the NIMH. This project began in 1979 and was coordinated by David Pearl of NIMH. The resulting report consisted only of reviews of the existing literature and its focus was much broader than that of the 1971 Surgeon General's Report. The two-volume report, *Television and Behavior: Ten Years of Scientific Progress and Implications for the Eighties*, was edited by Pearl, along with Lorraine Bouthilet and Joyce Lazar, also of NIMH.

In the 1970s there was more of an emphasis on field studies, in part because many researchers believed that links between violent programming and aggressive behavior had already been well established in the laboratory. Two field investigations conducted by J.L. Singer and D.G. Singer related children's viewing habits at home with their behavior during free-play periods at day-care centers (*Television Imagination and Aggression: A Study of Preschoolers' Play*, 1980). Those children who watched a lot of violent television at home tended to exhibit much more unwarranted aggression in free play. A field study by E.D. McCarthy and his associates showed that watching television violence is related to fights with peers, conflict with parents and delinquency ("Violence and Behavior Disorders," *Journal of Communication*, 1975). L.D. Eron and L.R. Huesmann found a significant positive relationship between viewing television violence and aggressive behavior in both boys and girls in the United States, Finland and Poland ("Adolescent Aggression and Television," *Annals of the New York Academy of Sciences*, 1980). This study was especially significant because in earlier research the relationship had only been found for boys.

Not all of the research reviewed supported the causal relationship between television violence and aggressive behavior. One significant study that did not was conducted by J. Ronald Milavsky and his associates (Milavsky, Ronald Kessler, Horst Stipp and William S. Rubens, "Television and Aggression: Results of a Panel Study," 1982). While they did not disagree that viewing television violence was associated with short-term aggressive behavior, their findings concluded that no long-term, cumulative relationship existed.

Some still doubted that the existence of a link between viewing violence and aggressive behavior could be shown. Nevertheless, many scientists argued that researchers should move beyond the accumulation of further evidence establishing a link and instead shift the focus to the processes that are responsible for this relationship. Therefore, researchers were urged to develop theories that explain why and how that relationship exists.

Observational learning theory, which deals with the imitation of an observed model, was tested in field studies and expanded, and was linked to other factors, such as age. Some researchers attempted to link observational learning with how the brain learns and stores information (cognitive-processing psychology). They showed how certain aggressive behaviors may be learned and stored in the brain for future reference. For example, a young viewer watches a violent television episode. Later in life, when a situation arises similar to the one seen on television, the young viewer may retrieve and perform the violent act once viewed. Included in one study is an analysis of cases in which youths apparently imitated criminal acts they had viewed on television (C.W. Turner and M.R. Fern, "Effects of White Noise and Memory Cues on Verbal Aggression," presented at meetings of the International Society for Research on Aggression, 1978). In each case, specific visual cues that were present in the television portrayal were also present in the environment in which the criminal act was imitated.

Attitude change theory also received attention. Some of the research suggests that the more violent television a child watches, the more that child tends to have favorable attitudes toward aggressive behavior. This seems to occur largely because viewers of much televised violence come to see violent behavior as normal. Some scientists contended that television violence leads to aggressive behavior by overstimulating children. In this regard, some research suggested that aggression can be stimulated by large amounts of action programming, even without a high level of violent content. However, others claimed that children are anesthetized or desensitized by the same overloading process. One study showed that boys who watch a lot of violent television programming tend to exhibit less physiological arousal when shown new violent programs than do boys who regularly watch less violent fare (V.B. Cline, R.G. Croft, S. Courrier, "Desensitization of Children to Television Violence," *Journal of Personality and Social Psychology*, 1973).

There was some discussion of the catharsis theory which argues that viewing violent behavior serves to "release steam" and dissipate the need or desire to be aggressive. This theory predicts that watching violence on television will reduce aggressiveness. Some have argued that this explains the low levels of social violence in Japan, a country with a high level of media violence. But the Japanese case might be better explained by cultural variables. While one cannot dismiss the Japanese example, most American studies point to an increase in aggressive behavior from viewing violence on television, and thus the available American data tend to contradict catharsis theory.

This is not an exhaustive review of the theories that explain the relationship between aggressive behavior and television violence. But these theories do indicate that researchers moved beyond trying to establish that a positive relationship exists to the matter of explaining why that relationship exists.

It was also significant that the NIMH report moved beyond the violence issue to deal with many other effects of television. Prosocial behavior was one area that received considerable attention. The report concluded that television portrayals of prosocial behavior, such as friendliness, cooperation, delay of gratification and generosity, can lead to similar behaviors in viewers. Both laboratory and field studies tended to confirm that observational learning applies to good behaviors on television as well as bad, suggesting television's power as an overall socializing force. An example of this prosocial modeling behavior, which was looked at by other studies beyond the NIMH report, was the television industry's emphasis on showing people fastening their seat belts before driving. Evidence suggests this may have had an important effect on encouraging viewers to buckle up. The television industry has made similar strides in deglamorizing the use of cigarettes and alcohol.

Not only did the NIMH report expand the focus beyond the violence issue, it also shifted from examining short-term direct effects to long-term indirect effects. Television was presented as an educator, albeit an informal one, that helps construct the social reality in which we live. The following statement from the summary captures the report's overall conclusion:

> Almost all evidence testifies to television's role as a formidable educator whose effects are both pervasive and cumulative. Television can no longer be considered as a casual part of daily life, as an electronic toy. Research findings have long since destroyed the illusion that television is merely innocuous entertainment. While the learning it provides is mainly incidental, rather than direct and formal, it is a significant part of the total acculturation process.

Despite the healthy redirection of energy, the popular media uniformly focused on the single conclusion that children who watch violence on television might be influenced to behave aggressively. (For a more thorough review of the television-effects literature, see Shearon Lowery and Melvin DeFleur's *Milestones in Mass Communication Research*, 1995, upon which much of the above discussion is based.)

Although research has continued over the past decade, the overall conclusions have changed little. While skeptics remain, most social scientists find the evidence from so many studies compelling. Taken together, the many different studies point to a statistically significant connection between watching violence on television and behaving aggressively. In 1992 the American Psychological Association issued a report entitled "Big World, Small Screen: The Role of Television in American Society." The report concluded, "The accumulated research clearly demonstrates a correlation between viewing violence and aggressive behavior. Children and adults who watch a large number of aggressive programs also tend to hold attitudes and values that favor the use of violence."

Some researchers have gone so far as to assign a numerical value to the connection between violence on television and violence in the real world. Leonard Eron has stated that 10% of societal violence is attributable to exposure to violent television images.

The accumulated scientific evidence is compelling, but the complex relationship between violence on television and violence in the real world must not be oversimplified. Many of the nuances, qualifications and complexities of the research have, out of necessity, been omitted from the foregoing discussion. Scientific evidence strongly suggests that there is a link between violence on television and that in the real world. The degree and nature of that link is not so clear. More of the possible effects are known than the probable effects. It is known that television does not have simple, direct stimulus-response effects on its audiences. It is further known that the way television affects people is influenced by many other factors, including: habits, interests, attitudes and prior knowledge; how individuals and our institutions use television; and the socio-cultural environment in which the communication occurs. Television does not have uniform effects. As television has a different impact on different types of cultures, the same television program has different effects on different people. When the impact of television is discussed or when television is blamed for having caused something to happen, it should never be suggested that television alone is a sufficient cause. Anything as complex as human behavior is not shaped by a single factor. Each behavior is caused by a large set of factors. In different individuals, the same behavior might well be caused by different factors. Given these difficulties, the precise influences of television are very hard to determine.

There are some who think it is a mistake to focus on whether media violence directly causes social violence. These critics argue that long-term indirect effects are of more importance. They believe that the accumulated perceptions and attitudes acquired from watching violent television content over the long term are of greater significance. For example, George Gerbner contends that the wrong question is being asked. "The contribution of television to the committing of violence is relatively minor, maybe 5%. Whereas the contribution of television to the perception of violence is much higher. People are almost paralyzed by fear" (*The New York Times*, December 14, 1994). Gerbner argues that frequent television viewers tend to suffer from the "mean world syndrome." They are more likely to overestimate the amount of violence that is actually in the world than those who watch less television. They are more likely to believe the crime rate is rising, whether it actually is or not. They are also more likely to believe that their neighborhood is unsafe and that they might encounter violence there. With these fears, they are more likely to take self-protective measures, such as purchasing and carrying a gun.

Though our study seeks to address the problem of television violence, it also acknowledges the very real danger of making television into a scapegoat for violence in America. A focus on television violence must not divert attention from deadlier and more significant causes: inadequate parenting, drugs, underclass rage, unemployment and availability of weaponry. Compared to problems of this magnitude, television is a tempting target simply because it is so easy to attack. Television's role in contributing to violence in America must be kept in perspective. It will take much more than sanitizing the television schedule to begin to deal with the problem of violence in America.

Although we have been reviewing the scientific literature on the effects of television violence, this report is not an effects study. The public is concerned about media effects and it is important to know what science says about these matters. The effects research serves as important background information for our study. We acknowledge that television violence is a potential danger. If it were not, we would never have been asked to conduct this study. But our effort is a content analysis of television, with a focus on programming which may raise concerns with regard to violence. We make no attempt to draw inferences about the behavior of audience members based on the content of the programs.

The scientific evidence, although valuable, gives the public little guidance in regards to specific television programs. Our contextual analysis attempts to fill that void. To a significant extent, our contextual examination builds on the qualitative analyses conducted by Gerbner and his associates beginning in the late 1960s. Specifically, we expanded upon the idea of delineating the qualitative world of television violence using a detailed contextual analysis of every scene of violence in a program. Every scene is subjected to a whole panoply of contextual criteria as will be described. Ours is the most thorough application of a qualitative contextual analysis of violence on broadcast television to date.

For over a century, the issue of violence in the media has been a prominent area of concern for government officials, academics and the general public. Research has been conducted and conferences convened, but the issue remains as contentious as ever.

PART II. THE STUDY

. . . .

D.   Methodology

1. Rationale and Definitions of Violence. The rationale and methodology of this monitoring project are based on the belief that not all violence is created equal. While parents, critics and others complain about the problem of violence on television, it is not the mere presence of violence that is the problem. If violence alone was the problem and V-chips or other methods did away with violent scenes or programs, viewers might never see a historical drama like *Roots* or such outstanding theatrical films as *Beauty and the Beast, The Lion King, Forrest Gump* and *Schindler's List.* In many instances, the use of violence may be critical to a story that actually sends an anti-violence message. Some important stories, such as Shakespeare's *Hamlet,* a history of World War II or a biography of Abraham Lincoln, would be impossible to convey accurately without including portrayals of violence.

For centuries, violence has been an important element of storytelling, and violent themes have been found in the Bible, *The Iliad* and *The Odyssey*, fairy tales, theater, literature, film and, of course, television. Descriptions of violence in the Bible have been important for teaching lessons and establishing a moral code. Lessons of the evils of jealousy and revenge are learned from the story of Cain and Abel. Early fairy tales were filled with violence and gruesomeness designed to frighten children into behaving and to teach them right from wrong. It was only when fairy tales were portrayed on the big screen by Walt Disney and others that the violence contained in the stories was substantially sanitized.

The issue is not the mere presence of violence but the nature of the violence and the context in which it occurs. Context is key to the determination of whether or not the violence is appropriate. If parents could preview all television, film and literature for their children, we do not believe they would remove all violence regardless of its nature or surrounding context. Parents know that violence can be instructive in teaching their children important lessons about life. What parents would do if they could preview all content for their children is remove or modify the inappropriate or improper uses of violence. Examples of these are applications of violence which glorify the act or teach that violence is always the way to resolve conflict. Our discussions with parents indicate that they know violence is a part of storytelling, but that there are appropriate and inappropriate ways of depicting violence. For example, the consequences of violence should be shown and those persons using violence inappropriately should be punished. We would also note that when violence is used realistically, it is more desirable to accurately portray the consequences than to sanitize the violence in a manner designed to make it acceptable.

Over the years, scientific research has focused both on the quality and quantity of violence on television. For example, the most important and prominent scholar to investigate this issue, George Gerbner, whose work stretches back into the 1960s, conducted extensive quantitative and qualitative analyses of violence on television. Most attention, however, was focused on the quantitative aspect of the content analyses of Gerbner, including his mechanism to determine whether the amount of violence was increasing or decreasing.

Some of the early quantitative research that counted acts was limited in its ability to examine the context of television violence. The same is true of the numerical counts often favored by public interest groups. (Numerical counts generate big headlines but we believe they do not fully address the issue of television violence.) That work required elaborate and exact definitions of violence to determine whether the act was counted or not. It was necessary to decide if verbal violence should be counted or whether comedic violence such as cartoons (what Gerbner calls "happy violence") would be registered. A precise definition determined whether the particular act would be counted. Everything had to be neatly included or excluded so that the conclusions with regard to the amount of violence would be consistent with the definition of violence.

No matter how well the definitions were drawn, there would be those who felt that some important aspect of the problem should or should not have been included. Almost everyone has his or her own definition of violence. People have often attempted to validate or invalidate quantitative research based on how much the scholar's definition resembles their own. Children's animation is a good example of this phenomenon. Consider a cartoon in which a character is hit over the head with a two-by-four, a funny sound effect is heard, the character shakes his head and merrily continues on his way. Some people consider this the worst type of violence because it is unrealistic, there are no consequences and it might encourage children to imitate it precisely because it shows no consequences. Others feel they watched these cartoons growing up and did not imitate them because they knew these cartoons obviously were not "real." Scholars have had to decide whether to count this type of violence and usually have included it. Anyone who feels this inclusion is silly would reject the entire definition and might ignore the conclusions of the research. The same is true with slapstick humor. Sports programming provides yet another example. Many feel that violent sports such as football or hockey make violence an acceptable or even desirable part of American life. Whether to count unrealistic cartoon violence, slapstick humor or sports within a definition of violence is a difficult decision.

Looking at violence within a contextual framework makes these definitional distinctions less critical. There is less need for a narrow definition because the focus is not on inclusion or exclusion in a count. We avoid the problems associated with narrow definitions by defining violence broadly. We put our focus not on establishing a correct, narrow definition of violence, but rather on distinguishing between violence that raises issues of concern and that which does not. Our broad definition includes sports violence, cartoon violence, slapstick violence—anything that involves or immediately threatens physical harm of any sort, intentional or unintentional, self-inflicted or inflicted by someone or something else. More precisely, violence is the act of, attempt at, physical threat of or the consequences of physical force. We also occasionally considered verbal threats of physical violence, although these were of secondary importance. Verbal phrases such as a teenager exclaiming, "If I don't get home by midnight, my dad'll kill me," would only raise issues if the teenager's father was a homicidal maniac.

Our broad definition might yield high numbers of scenes of violence on a given show. However, unlike previous studies, this is not our primary focus which is instead on whether the violence raises concerns within the context of the show. It is possible that a situation comedy such as *Home Improvement* or *3rd Rock from the Sun* might yield several scenes of "violence." But the nature of the violence and the context in which it occurs might lead us to conclude that none of these scenes raised concerns.

In sum, all violence, in our view, is not created equal. The focus of the project is not on counting the number of acts of violence but on the contextual analysis of each of these acts. We examine acts of violence and the context in which they occur to distinguish between uses of violence which raise concern and those acts which, because of their nature and the context in which they occur, do not raise such concerns.

. . . .

4.   *Criteria.* Essential to a strong, contextual analysis was the establishment of a set of criteria that could be applied to every scene we monitored and clearly understood by readers of this report. From these criteria we could derive a comprehensive understanding of the context of that scene. The goal of these criteria was to make ultimate distinctions between programs which:

- contain no violence
- raise no concerns because of the appropriateness of the violence in the context of the story
- raise concerns because of the inappropriateness of the violence in the context of the story

The analyses from the scene sheets coupled with the viewing and discussions from the weekly meetings allowed us to make these distinctions, which underlie the conclusions found in parts III and IV of this report.

As previously indicated, our definition of violence is so all-inclusive that any program deemed to contain no violence is so free of problematic violent content that it would be acceptable to almost anyone. The real burden of our work is to look at those programs that do contain violence and determine whether the violence raises concerns within the context of the story.

The ultimate decision as to whether the program raises concerns regarding its use of violence is contingent upon whether it is deemed contextually appropriate. This determination is based on the application of the following criteria:

a. What time is it shown? Children are less able to comprehend context than adults. The earlier the show is aired, the more likely it is for violence to raise concerns. Conversely, the later the show is aired, the less likely it is for the violence to raise concerns. Shows aired at a later time, appealing more to adults, deserve more latitude to use violence to tell the story. Nevertheless, only in a few instances can time slot alone become a decisive factor.

b. Is an advisory used? If a program contains scenes of violence, an advisory is considered an important warning, especially for parents and their children. An advisory alone does not excuse all that follows, but it does provide important information for viewers. While an advisory by itself seldom alleviates concerns, the lack of an advisory in some instances can raise concerns.

c. Is the violence integral to the story? Violence historically has been important in the telling of some stories. If violent scenes are included, they should be used to move the story or in some way add to viewers' understanding of the characters or the plot. Violent scenes should not be included only to attract viewers. Some programs use only one scene of violence but repeat it as many as 11 times. If the same violent scene is shown repeatedly, it must continue to be contextually relevant. Whether the violence was integral is the measure of gratuitousness. A frequent test of gratuitousness was whether the integrity of the story would be compromised without the violence. A character's motivation for using violence and the overall justification of that violence are also important aspects to consider when examining the relevance of the violence to the story. Violence, for example, used by the hero or protagonist tends to be justified. Research suggests that such violence may be more likely to produce acceptance, if not aggressive behavior, in the viewer. This violence is more prone to be imitated and lessens social inhibitions against aggression. On the other hand, unjustified violence is more likely to make viewers more fearful.

d. Are alternatives to violence considered? Is violence a knee-jerk reaction or do the characters consider alternatives to violence? The use of violence as a well-considered action after other alternatives have been exhausted raises fewer concerns than merely reflexively resorting to violence.

e. Is the violence unprovoked or reactive? Do the lead characters resort to violence freely or only when provoked? A character resorting to violence only when provoked raises fewer concerns than a character who instigates the violence or deliberately seeks a confrontation. Self-defense is also considered here.

f. How many scenes of violence are included and what percentage of the show did they comprise? This is the closest our research gets to counting. Normally, a judgment is made about a violent act or acts within the context of an individual scene. The number of scenes becomes a concern only when there are so many acts of violence that the context of the show is little else but violence. There is no magic number for how many violent scenes are appropriate. "Tonnage" can be a problem when there are so many scenes of violence that they serve as the thread holding the story together. This is seen in some action theatrical films such as the Rambo films and a few television series. Too much violence may desensitize the viewer and/or promote the "mean world syndrome."

g. How long are the scenes of violence? The scenes should be as long as they need to be to tell the story. There is no standard for appropriate length. If the scene containing violence seems unnecessarily elongated simply to fill out the time allotted, it may raise concerns. Some series routinely end with scenes of violence as long as five minutes, while some theatricals have violent finales as long as 15 minutes. If the scene continues to add to the story, it is less likely to raise concerns. A related concern is the repetition of the same scene throughout the program. Last season, one program, *Hard Copy*, repeated the same scene of violence 11 times.

h. How graphic is the violence? Graphicness in and of itself is not a problem. In *Psycho* it is necessary to see Norman Bates' decomposed dead mother to understand the full depths of his mental illness. In that scene, the graphicness adds something important to the story. If scenes are graphic just to illustrate gore or demonstrate some cinematic special effect, that graphicness may raise concerns. We endorse the networks' 1992 statement which said that graphic violence should not be used to shock or stimulate the viewer. It must have a contextual purpose to not raise concerns. A few of the scenes monitored this season, showing throats being slowly slit or people impaled on spikes, added nothing important to the story. Graphicness for the sake of graphicness was a frequent problem. Repeated graphic portrayals may desensitize the viewer and/or promote the "mean world syndrome."

i. Is the violence glorified? Does the story serve to make the violence exciting? Music, sound effects and other techniques can frequently enhance or mitigate the sense of excitement. Are the other characters shown supporting the use of violence? Is the decision to use violence ratified and supported or do the other characters disapprove? What does the viewer learn about the acceptability of violence? Glamorized violence can be seen in the James Bond films, particularly when the acts are accompanied by exciting theme music.

j. Who commits the act of violence? Is it a hero or an appealing character with whom the audience identifies or is it an unsympathetic villain who commits the violence? Audiences naturally identify with the hero. If the hero easily uses violence or does not carefully consider his/her actions, violence may be affirmed as a desirable tactic. Conversely, a sympathetic character's reluctance to use violence, or decision to use it only as a last resort and with some measure of restraint, sends an important message to viewers and raises fewer concerns. A hero committing acts of violence, particularly without examining alternatives, such as Dirty Harry or Billy Jack, does raise concerns. In addition, if a character is like the viewer in terms of sex, age, race, etc., the viewer may be more likely to imitate that character. These same considerations also apply to the victim of the violence.

k. How realistic is the act of violence? Few viewers expect animation to be very realistic. Shows that contain a "realistic" sense, however, are under an obligation to portray acts of violence close to how they would occur in real life. Most police shows, reality shows and anything that purports to show life "the way it is" are examined for the realistic nature of violence. A show resembling "real life" in all other ways would also be expected to be realistic with regard to violence. *Grand Canyon,* Lawrence Kasdan's story about life in Los Angeles in the 1990s, would be held to a standard of realism in its use of violence and it does portray the shooting of Steve Martin in the leg very realistically. The same would be true of some war films such as *Braveheart,* but not many contemporary action films. Anything that makes realistic violence seem less serious than it really is may raise some concerns.

l. What are the consequences of the violence? Similar in some ways to the above concept of realism is the concept of consequences of violence. Those shows that portray real life (most urban police shows, for example) should also demonstrate the realistic consequences of violence. Few would expect to see excessive bleeding in a cartoon or situation comedy, but would, in some instances, in a police drama. Psychological or emotional consequences can be as significant as physical consequences in dealing with scenes of violence. Studies show that the portrayal of consequences, i.e., pain and suffering, elicits sympathy, inhibits the learning of violent behavior, and decreases the likelihood that the violence will be imitated. An important question regarding the consequences of the violence is whether the violent act is rewarded or punished. Acts of violence that are rewarded are more likely to be imitated and encourage aggressive behaviors.

m. Is the violence used as a hook to attract viewers? Is it the promise of violence coming from a promo or theatrical advertisement that is attracting the viewer? Some programming uses violence as the salable quality of the show. This is true of many martial arts films. In some instances, there is a commercial break just before or in the middle of a scene of violence. Is the violent scene used as a vehicle to ensure the viewer continues watching?

n. What kinds of weapons are used? Do characters respond with much more force than is necessary? Do they use unusually brutal weapons designed to inflict the maximum amount of pain and damage? Is the use of excessive weaponry endorsed or glorified? The police in urban dramas such as *NYPD Blue* use realistic weaponry, while the Dirty Harry films are filled with enormous guns capable of overwhelming fire power. Also of greater concern because of possible imitation is the use of ordinary, readily available household implements such as scissors or kitchen knives as weapons.

All of these factors are weighed together. No one factor determines whether a program does or does not raise concerns. For example, the simple use of an advisory does not excuse all that follows. If it did, then the networks could use advisories and air anything under the protection of that advisory. Similarly, a programmer cannot air gratuitous violence at 10:00 p.m. without raising concerns simply because the show aired in a later time slot. All criteria are considered and related to the specifics of the show and, as a consequence, each program is treated uniquely. For example, there are some similarities between *Beavis and Butt-Head* and *The Simpsons* (they are both animated and contain subversive humor) and, therefore, it might be tempting to evaluate them similarly. However, the programs are quite different in the level of satire they use. Moreover, *Beavis and Butt-Head* uses an advisory and runs late in the evening while *The Simpsons* runs at 8:00 p.m. without one. Thus they warrant separate and different treatment. Another consideration is the presence of graphic violence which by itself does not necessarily mean that a show raises concerns. That decision is based on why the program contains graphic violence and how it is integrated into the story. As mentioned earlier, *Schindler's List* does contain graphic violence but because of its historical importance and necessity to the plot, the violence does not raise concerns.

All of the above factors are part of a formula that leads to the decision of whether a show raises concerns. We recognize this is not as clean or simple as counting acts of violence. At times when we were buried in scene sheets or mired in endless discussions applying the above criteria, we longed for the ease of counting. Even though our method necessitated long, difficult applications of standards, we feel it ultimately produced the kind of results people needed in order to assess the problem of media violence. We are particularly sensitive to the concerns of parents. Unfortunately, parents in America in the 1990s do not have the time or opportunity to preview all programming for their children. This report aims to provide illumination for parents on the issue of televised violence. In fact, our methods are quite similar to those of a parent previewing television programming for his or her child.

From a practical point of view, there are four types of programs containing violence:

1. Shows that raise concerns and almost everyone agrees they raise concerns. These are shows such as slasher movies. An extreme example is the film *Faces of Death* (even though it has only been available on home video), which is a collection of real people being killed on camera.
2. Shows that contain scenes of violence but almost no one would feel they raise concerns. This would include shows like *Home Improvement,* which contains workshop "accidents" within a wholesome family comedy.

These two categories are easy to deal with. They produce near unanimous agreement. Harder to achieve consensus on are:

3.   Shows that do not have high levels of violence or in which the violence is not graphic, glamorized or gratuitous, but, because of context, the violence does raise concern. These are shows such as *America's Funniest Home Videos* or theatrical films such as *Home Alone,* which are elaborated upon later in the report. These are the shows that are likely to produce the "Oh, come on" response from some.

4.   Shows that contain high levels of violence or very graphic violence, but in which the violence is appropriate to the story and therefore does not raise concerns. This is where *Schindler's List* or the television series *M*A*S*II* fits in. The violence is absolutely necessary to tell the story.

Television violence is a complex issue and everyone approaches it differently. Trying to deal with an equally difficult subject, pornography, Supreme Court Justice Potter Stewart threw up his hands in frustration and declared, "I know it when I see it." Although we sympathize with his dilemma, it is not enough that we know problematic violence when we see it. Our goal is to explain this problem in a way that has meaning for everyone concerned about the issue. Therefore, as readers examine our results section, they will be able to look over our shoulder and evaluate how our decisions were made. Most other research on this issue was written for either the academic community or special interest groups and then interpreted for the public, usually by the media. It is our strong desire that this study—its purpose, methodology and results—be directly accessible and understandable to anyone interested enough to read this report.

E.   Operating Premises and Stipulations

There are some fundamental premises emerging from the aforementioned criteria that must be understood before one can examine whether an act of violence within the context of a story raises concerns. Awareness of these basic premises should help the reader to understand the monitoring process and the ultimate decisions that have been made. Our operating premises have been as follows:

1. There is no such thing as an accident in fictional programming. In the course of the monitoring, questions frequently arose about accidental violence. Examples of this include a tree falling on someone during a hurricane and someone losing his or her footing and falling down the stairs. Clearly this violence is unintentional and unprovoked. Nevertheless, in the world of fictional programming everything is created by a screen-writer (with input by, and perhaps at the instigation of, the network, producer or director). There are no real "accidents" in these cases. A screenwriter has to decide that there will be a hurricane and that a tree will fall on the character in a particular way. Then the screen-writer has to decide on the extent of the resulting injuries. In fiction, a screenwriter has a whole range of choices, and the decision to have something violent happen is only one of a variety of options. The director also has a variety of options with which to depict the "accident." Camera angles, musical score and level of graphicness are all within his control. Nevertheless, the motivation of the character is important. In our contextual analysis, accidentally running into a wall is less serious than a character consciously and intentionally hitting someone else.

The obvious exception is non-fiction programming, in which the screenwriter is following a set of facts established by what really happened. Although decisions are still made about how to interpret the actual event and how much dramatic license to take, there does not exist the wide variety of choices available in creating fictional programming. In fiction, all violence is the result of writers' and producers' decisions that violence should occur.

2. Violence is important in character and plot development to establish the bad guy as the bad guy. Establishing the villain as a key character in many stories is important. Even stories that virtually no one would find objectionable feature a villain. Disney's *Beauty and the Beast* needs to establish why Belle could not possibly be interested in Gaston, the handsome muscle man who is determined to make her his wife. Viewers know that Belle is interested in ideas and books and not just an attractive partner. We learn Gaston's villainous nature when, to the tune of the song bearing his name, he punches innocent townspeople in a bar and acts like an all-around brute. These scenes are necessary to establish what kind of person he is and why Belle will turn her attentions later to the far less attractive but more caring and sensitive Beast. Likewise, in *Schindler's List,* the commandant of the camp is shown exploding in rage and shooting prisoners without purpose or warning. We also see him shoot random human targets with his rifle from his balcony. All of this is necessary to demonstrate his character and the evil and vicious nature of the Nazis.

We may respect creators' needs to demonstrate why and how certain characters are bad or evil but this, of course, has its limits. In *Beauty and the Beast,* a family entertainment, establishing Gaston's brutishness allows him to engage in violence but does not include entitling him to break townspeople's necks or sever their heads. On the other hand, at least two theatrical films this season contained graphic throat slashings or decapitations, clearly exceeding the demands of character development.

3. Audiences like to see the bad guy "get it good." After watching a series for an hour, a film for two hours or a mini-series for as long as five hours, there is a natural tendency for the audience to want to see the conflict resolved and the villain punished or killed—getting what he or she deserves. The worse the villain, the more the audience wants some kind of vengeance, justice or final resolution. Sometimes viewers even want to see the bad guy die a gruesome, brutal death. Everyone has been to a movie theater and witnessed the audience cheer as the bad guy is shot, knifed or impaled. This desire to see the villain suffer and pay for his evil deeds is exemplified by the conclusions of the following theatrical films that aired on broadcast television: *The Last of the Mohicans, In the Line of Fire* and *Cliffhanger.* While each of these films contained an intense climactic scene where the score is settled with the bad guy, those scenes were generally well edited by the broadcast networks. ABC's cut of *The Last of the Mohicans* was a model of how to limit excessive violence without affecting the integrity of the story or the film maker's vision. There is a need for the viewer to see the evil villain punished, but there are limits as to how this should be depicted on television.

    4. Time slot does make a difference. The earlier a program is shown, the more likely children are to be a significant part of the audience. For the networks, prime time television consists of the three hours from 8:00 to 11:00 P.M. On Sunday, network prime time begins at 7:00 P.M. On Fox, prime time ends at 10:00 P.M. Until this season the FCC maintained a prime time access rule allowing the broadcast networks to program no more than 22 hours of prime time a week. Now that this rule has been eliminated, there may be more hours of network programming in the future. A network can demonstrate its responsibility by scheduling more violent programs later in the evening. Such responsibility has been exhibited when prime time has been extended to 11:30 P.M. in order to accommodate a theatrical film with violent themes. (Television movies are produced to run with commercials in a two-hour block. Theatrical films, however, are made for the movie theater with no such constraints and, when commercials are added, they may end up at odd lengths for the purposes of television.) Extending prime time usually incurs the wrath of affiliates which have turned their 11:00 P.M. hour into a lucrative franchise with advertising revenues that are not shared with the networks. If prime time were not extended, films with violent themes would have to start at 8:00 or 8:30 P.M. This has been a particular problem for Fox Broadcasting since it does not have a 10:00 P.M. block of prime time and therefore must start its theatricals and television movies at 8:00 P.M.

    Time slot is an important consideration on Saturday morning children's programming as well. Networks schedule the tamest programming at 7:00–8:30 A.M. when the youngest children dominate the audience. When their older brothers and sisters start watching at 9:00 or 10:00 A.M., they see more action and violence. Viewers would not expect to see the most intense programming in the earliest hours and, in most cases, they do not.

    In 1975, FCC Chairman Richard Wiley and the broadcast networks tried to establish the earliest hour of prime time as a "Family Viewing Hour." While many in the nation applauded this goal, it had the effect of censoring situation comedies like *All in the Family* and *M*A*S*H.* The creative community filed suit, charging that the rule violated the First Amendment. After the courts struck down the hour, the networks announced a voluntary effort to be sensitive to family viewing concerns during the earliest hours in prime time. The 8:00 P.M. period was seen as a time when families could sit down together and watch programming free of most violence and sexuality. But the voluntary effort never really worked. Fox runs *Melrose Place* and *Beverly Hills 90210* at 8:00. Audiences responded favorably to these shows at 8:00 and NBC responded by scheduling its popular adult situation comedy *Mad About You* at 8:00. The following season NBC did the same with *Friends.* CBS ran *Due South* and ABC switched *Roseanne* to 8:00. Most of these shows raised issues involving matters of sexuality which are beyond the scope of this report. In terms of violence, we think that the networks should be sensitive to the fact that there are a large number of children in the 8:00 P.M. audience. There are other time slots, especially 10:00 P.M. (except at Fox), that can be used for more adult programs. Typically programs with violent themes are appropriately scheduled in the 10:00 P.M. time period. Many of these programs are of high quality and reached new levels of popularity in the 1995–96 television season.

5. *Consequences or punishment must occur within the specific episode for context to have an impact.* In some shows, the consequences or punishment might not come until several or many episodes later. But the nature of television does not ensure that the viewer who watched a violent act will definitely be watching to see it punished or resolved several episodes or months later. The consequences or punishment must occur within a particular episode of the program or movie. While there is no guarantee that the viewer who watched a violent act will be there 15 minutes later when it is resolved, without this assumption there would be no way to allow for normal plot and character development. The only exception to this is the mini-series in which there is a reasonable expectation that the person who watches the beginning installment will also watch the final episode.

There has been some discussion over the past year whether some viewers, particularly children, need to see the consequences immediately following an act of violence. Not all children may be able to fully discern consequences if they occur later in the program. However, to compel a program to show consequences immediately after a scene of violence is to interfere with the processes of creativity, character development and the unfolding of the story. Under such a narrowly defined stricture, Sherlock Holmes would be required to immediately identify the perpetrator of a violent crime and see him punished within moments of the crime.

6. *Advisories do what they are intended to do.* There are issues regarding the way advisories are used and whether they are used at all. We would like to see advisories used more often than they are, especially in the case of made-for-television movies. Many critics, perhaps with a tinge of cynicism, argue that advisories promising scenes of sex and/or violence actually do the opposite of what is intended: they encourage people who might not otherwise watch to do so. In fact, a recent study by Joanne Cantor of the University of Wisconsin suggests that for boys, particularly those aged 10–14, parental discretion advisories and PG-13 and R ratings make movies and programs more attractive. Advisories are designed to provide warnings to concerned viewers, especially parents. But even if they do encourage some such viewing, we accept them as primarily providing beneficial warnings to prospective viewers. Advisories might be more effective if they were made more available ahead of time in printed materials describing upcoming programming, such as *TV Guide*. (It should be noted that there is some reluctance to use advisories because of advertiser concern about what might be perceived as problematic or controversial content.)

7. *Music is a very important part of context.* Music adds texture to the story and often, in regard to violence, a cue to warn or reassure the viewer. Sound tracks can exaggerate, intensify or glorify the violence on screen. Scary movies are not nearly as frightening without the music, and some viewers turn off the sound during some scenes to lessen their fright. On the other hand, music can trivialize the seriousness of violence or make it seem acceptable.

It is impossible to separate the violent shower scene in *Psycho* from Bernard Herrmann's musical score that accompanies it. The music sends a message about the evil and appalling nature of the crime. Similarly, the James Bond theme frequently accompanies shootings, chases and other scenes of violence and tends to glamorize or glorify the acts on screen.

Television music is equally important in telling the viewer about what he or she is watching. Light or funny music implies that what the viewer is seeing is not so serious or profound. The same scene of a shooting or stabbing can leave vastly different impressions depending upon the background music. In our monitoring meetings, there were frequent discussions about music. We often scrutinized the music to discern the producer's intent or goals. Music helps viewers understand the context of a scene or program.

Some shows use music as an important, if not essential, part of the show. *New York Undercover* uses hip hop, rap and R&B music to establish an urban grittiness. *The Mighty Morphin' Power Rangers* uses fast, upbeat music to energize the scenes of combat and involve the audience, while *America's Most Wanted* uses music to create a sense of foreboding or impending danger. The music on *Murder, She Wrote* serves to downplay the violence of the crime so viewers will instead focus on the mystery. Sometimes the music in *Due South* serves to emphasize and underscore the violence.

8. Cinematic techniques can also affect the context of violence. Many cinematic techniques are used in an attempt to lessen the impact of the violence or to make it seem more artistic. On *Melrose Place* and other dramas, slow motion is used to emphasize or draw attention to an act of violence. Police dramas like *Homicide* use a stroboscopic effect to break up the horror of a murder scene. The strobe simulates a police photographer rapidly snapping pictures to create a record of the scene. Sound effects also are used in a variety of shows, especially comedies, in an attempt to mitigate the severity and impact of "funny" violence. Such sound effects are a staple of *America's Funniest Home Videos* where they are used to accompany people getting hit in the head or crashing into objects. *Walker, Texas Ranger* also uses sound effects to add emphasis to punches during fist fights. *New York Undercover* frequently uses music and lyrics (as in a music video) as virtually the only sounds accompanying an act of violence. Sometimes the lyrics are relevant to what is on screen and other times they are not. The only sound viewers hear other than the music is that of the violence, usually a gun shot. While some may feel that the music frames the act of violence and gives it a sense of realistic grittiness, repeated monitoring found that it minimized a serious act and created a surreal sense of distance from the act and its horrific impact.

We found that the use of sound and music in *America's Funniest Home Videos*, *New York Undercover* and *Walker, Texas Ranger* tends to aggravate the violence and increase concerns, while the use of the flash technique in *Homicide* tends to lessen concerns about the violence in the scene. Therefore, it is not possible to draw hard and fast rules about whether the use of these different cinematic techniques tends to raise or to reduce concerns. Their use is examined on an individual basis. In many cases the music and sound effects constitute a crucial contextual factor heavily influencing our overall judgment of the violence in the scene.

9. "Pseudo" guns are only slightly better than real guns, if at all. In some television movies and science fiction series, such as *Space: Above and Beyond* and *SeaQuest,* characters shoot futuristic ray guns. Some networks and producers argue that using these kinds of guns is an improvement over regular guns with bullets and that the futuristic context further fictionalizes the gunplay; in either event, making it less realistic and, therefore, less likely to be imitated. This raises an interesting issue since a child cannot grab his or her parents' ray gun, but he or she may grab their real gun. Moreover, the scene still involves a gun and shooting and, therefore, we treat these kinds of weapons in the same way we treat real guns. At most, in our judgment the use of non-realistic weapons represents only a slight improvement and, in most cases, not even that.

10. "Real" reality is given more latitude than re-creations. After reaching a high point in popularity several seasons ago, the reality genre on television seems to be diminishing in appeal. Next season promises to see even fewer reality shows. Within the reality genre, there are shows, such as *Cops* and *America's Funniest Home Videos,* that use actual footage of a crime or some other incident, and there are shows that re-create situations, such as *Rescue 911, America's Most Wanted, Unsolved Mysteries* or *Real Stories of the Highway Patrol.* Shows using real footage need responsible editing and cannot use the fact that "it really happened" to justify showing anything on television. Nevertheless, we did hold shows using re-creations or re-enactments to a higher standard in determining whether their use of violence raised concerns for the following reasons.

In many instances, real film footage comes from actual events in which there is no pre-planned intent to use the tape on television. There is a compelling human interest in seeing the real tape of the real situation with real people. Programs such as *Cops* provide a more genuine view of what police are like and how they handle the pressures of the job than what is seen on shows with actors as police. Since *Cops* is real and uses actual film, we gave it more latitude to make its case. Still, producers must exercise care in their editing.

Re-creations, however, have all the choices in the world. Unlike "real" tape shows, they hire actors to portray characters. This allows them to influence how viewers process the scene. Producers can choose between sympathetic actors who will elicit support and unattractive "thugs" who incur anger. Producers of re-enactments can decide how close the camera will get during a crime and whether there should be a gallon of blood or a thimble-full. Producers of "real" tape shows cannot make these decisions; they are limited by what is on the tape. Re-enactment shows have a wide range of options and alternatives not available to the other shows and, therefore, we hold them more accountable for what ends up on the television screen.

. . . .

*   This report has been excerpted for republication in this book. For a copy of the report in its entirety, readers are directed to contact the UCLA Center for Communication Policy at Box 951586, Los Angeles, CA 90095-1586. The editor expresses his deepest thanks to Dr. Jeffrey Cole, Director of the Center, for his permission to include the study in this book.

EUROPE

I. European Union, Television Without Frontiers Directive II
II. European Union, Green Paper on the Protection of Minors and Human Dignity in Audiovisual and Information Services
III. French Audiovisual Council, Violence on Television: Steps in the Cooperation between the French Audiovisual Council (CSA) and Broadcasters
IV. French Audiovisual Council, The Protection of Minors, Excerpts from the TF1 and M6 Licences

---

I. European Union, Television Without Frontiers Directive II (Excerpt)

Directive 97/36/EC of the European Parliament and of the Council of 30 June 1997 amending Council Directive 89/552/EEC on the coordination of certain provisions laid down by law, regulation or administrative action in Member States concerning the pursuit of television broadcasting activities

Official journal NO. L 202 , 30/07/1997 P. 0060 - 0071

. . . .

27. Article 22 shall be replaced by the following:
    "Article 22
    1. Member States shall take appropriate measures to ensure that television broadcasts by broadcasters under their jurisdiction do not include any programmes which might seriously impair the physical, mental or moral development of minors, in particular programmes that involve pornography or gratuitous violence.
    2. The measures provided for in paragraph 1 shall also extend to other programmes which are likely to impair the physical, mental or moral development of minors, except where it is ensured, by selecting the time of the broadcast or by any technical measure, that minors in the area of transmission will not normally hear or see such broadcasts.
    3. Furthermore, when such programmes are broadcast in unencoded form

Member States shall ensure that they are preceded by an acoustic warning or are identified by the presence of a visual symbol throughout their duration.";

28. the following Article shall be inserted:
    "Article 22a
    Member States shall ensure that broadcasts do not contain any incitement to hatred on grounds of race, sex, religion or nationality.";

29. the following Article shall be inserted:
    "Article 22b
    1. The Commission shall attach particular importance to application of this Chapter in the report provided for in Article 26.
    2. The Commission shall within one year from the date of publication of this Directive, in liaison with the competent Member State authorities, carry out an investigation of the possible advantages and drawbacks of further measures with a view to facilitating the control exercised by parents or guardians over the programmes that minors may watch. This study shall consider, inter alia, the desirability of:
        *   the requirement for new television sets to be equipped with a technical device enabling parents or guardians to filter out certain programmes;
        *   the setting up of appropriate rating systems,
        *   encouraging family viewing policies and other educational and awareness measures,
        *   taking into account experience gained in this field in Europe and elsewhere as well as the views of interested parties such as broadcasters, producers, educationalists, media specialists and relevant associations."

    . . . .

II. European Union, Green Paper on the Protection of Minors and Human Dignity in Audiovisual and Information Services, COM (96) 483, November 1996 (Excerpt)

. . . .

CHAPTER II
RULES AND ENFORCEMENT MEASURES APPLICABLE TO PROTECTION OF MINORS AND HUMAN DIGNITY

2.2 The protection of minors

In some Member States, the general principle of the protection of minors takes the form of ***provisions of criminal law banning the supply to minors of material that may be harmful to their development*** but which is lawfully available to adults. These provisions are of general application: they apply regardless of the manner in which the material in question is supplied to the minor. In Member States which do not have general rules of this type, the same sort of protection is afforded by *rules applying specifically to the individual media.*

Any system for protecting minors needs a reasonable way of ensuring that minors do not normally have access to material which could damage their physical or mental development, while at the same time allowing adults access to such material.

2.2.1   Controlling access by minors to questionable material

Rules governing access by minors to certain types of material depend very much on the type of service. Despite certain similarities between the world of broadcasting and that of on-line services, we shall study these two areas separately to simplify the layout (see Annex IV).

a)   Broadcast services

With conventional television, the *time of transmission of programmes* can be scheduled in such a way as to protect minors: potentially harmful programmes may be transmitted only late in the evening, when children are presumed not to be watching. Technically, this "watershed" system can be applied to any television service, but it will not always necessarily correspond to the logic of tomorrow's television. Some private and public broadcasters have also developed, usually on a voluntary basis, a *system of symbols* to inform viewers of the nature of the programmes broadcast. Various logos are used to classify programmes potentially harmful to minors.

The new broadcasting services offer new solutions for the protection of minors. *The conditional access inherent in all pay-as-you-view services offers a wide range of possibilities for controlling access by minors:*

- firstly, subscription is in itself a means for parents to check that the service they choose does not contain material liable to upset their children;
- secondly, the privileged relationship between the subscriber and the pay-per-view service has often led the services involved to develop a consumer information policy on the programmes offered which includes advice for parents;
- finally, a variety of technical features are sometimes offered to facilitate parental control: this could be a simple locking system allowing parents to prevent access to programmes, for example in their absence, or a system for giving access to programmes (which are normally scrambled) only by means of a personal identification number (PIN), special card or credit card. In the case of adult services, this type of system would enable parents to ensure that they alone have access to programmes.

The emergence of *technical methods of parental control* has led to an extensive debate, particularly on whether or not they should be used for non-encoded television. Based on the Canadian example and the interest that it generated in the United States, the possibility of linking a systematic classification of content to a parental control mechanism attracted special interest in the European Parliament and the Council in the course of the review of the Television Without Frontiers Directive.[1] The question was also debated in several Member States. The various debates on this system have quickly highlighted not only the problems of the implementation of the system (notably as regards classification of material) but also a more fundamental problem that has not yet been settled.

The industries concerned have also recognized the importance of the protection of minors and are developing practical solutions. Electronic guides for navigating through the wide range of television programmes will soon be available on the market and will offer various possibilities in terms of parental control. Originally designed to assist and automate the programming of video recorders in a multi-channel environment, these electronic guides will be able to decipher a wide range of information about programmes, including whether they contain material that could pose a problem for minors.

In the field of *digital television*, the use of a decoder and the need for electronic guides to cope with the large number of programmes available provide two opportunities for developing devices for providing the viewer with information and controlling content. In the initial stages, pressure on the price of digital decoders has not so far made it possible to incorporate this dimension. As the market develops, however, and if it seems to meet the consumers' needs, this type of function could be introduced at a reasonable cost.

b)   On-line services

Unlike broadcast services, on-line services do not lend themselves to a segregation of material based on the time of broadcast. All available material can be consulted at any time. Moreover, material is accessed on an individual basis (choice of a specific item) at a time selected by the user. Access to sensitive material will therefore rarely be accidental. In this specific context, the question of the protection of minors takes the following form: how can adults be offered a maximum freedom of expression while ensuring that minors are not exposed to material which is likely to harm their physical, mental or moral development. Possible ways of protecting minors will vary according to the degree of openness of the networks.

*   Closed networks

Video-on-demand systems, at their current stage of development, have a number of features which can be used to protect minors.

Operators are clearly identifiable and relatively few in number. When they do not offer material themselves they have contractual links with information providers. This structure makes it possible to install a *transparent system of responsibility for the material shown*. While it is clearly out of all proportion to ban all material which could be harmful to minors from such services, it is perfectly reasonable, in cooperation with the operators concerned, to work out ways of protecting minors effectively:

- *identification or classification of controversial material* by means of electronic programme guides (for example, identification of a space reserved for adult entertainment);
- *proof of age* on payment for or on access to the programme (using a bank card or a personal identification number);
- possibility of *opting out* of certain categories of programmes at the user's request (the user would then only have access to part of the material available);
- *parental control devices* preventing access to certain categories of programme.

Similarly, in *proprietary on-line services*, the *editorial content* (material provided by the service itself or provided on the basis of a contract between the service and the information providers) is similar in some ways and therefore offers similar solutions. The size of the network plays an important role here, however: it could be difficult, on a worldwide network, to find solutions which would be acceptable in all the countries covered by the service.

*   **Open networks**

The protection of minors becomes more difficult on open networks where every user is a potential information provider. On the *proprietary networks or on the Internet*, thousands of items are created, consulted and exchanged via facilities permitting varying degrees of interactivity between users which require the intervention of various intermediaries between the information provider and the users accessing it.

Given the threat of joint liability, notably criminal liability, for distribution of material harmful to minors, the industry has spontaneously developed a series of mechanisms for the protection of minors. These mechanisms can be broken down according to the level at which they operate: the level of information providers, access providers or the user.

Only systems developed by the user offer a truly comprehensive solution enabling parents to enjoy full access to Internet (or a proprietary on-line service) while controlling or restricting access by minors. They are all based on software the security of which depends substantially on the level of sophistication of the product.

In addition to the prior identification of users, which is common to all systems, various other functionalities are proposed:

- *restrictions on computer use* enable parents to limit access by children to times when they are present;
- *memory storage of navigation on the networks* (sites accessed, messages exchanged, etc.) enables parents to monitor the use their children actually make of services;
- *systematic filtering of material* allows controversial material to be intercepted automatically. The first generation of systems of this type operates mainly on the basis of key words and the identification of certain types of material (images). This limits the effectiveness of the protection (a few key words may

not be sufficient to determine the scope of material which could shock minors) while imposing considerable limits on access to harmless material;
* *blocking sites on a selective basis* on the basis of a labelling system allowing material to be filtered by suitable software.

All services may be adapted to incorporate control devices, notably parental control. However, such systems are not yet available on all services under development and existing systems are not as secure as they might be. Exploration of the potential in this field offered by all digital services should be a priority. In view of the potentially transnational nature of all of these services, the European Union is concerned by all aspects of such developments.

4   Should the approach taken in the area of parental control devices be based on legislation or on self-regulation (possibly supervised)? What rules should be introduced, particularly at Union level?

5   In what cases (types of service or other criteria) should parental control devices be incorporated in a service automatically? Should this be compulsory? If so, what form should it take and which operators would be affected? In these different cases, what are the essential functions which the device should perform?

2.2.2   Labelling of material

At first glance, the identification of material which could be harmful to minors presents a basic problem: firstly, a consensus does not necessarily exist, even in medical circles, as to what is likely to affect the moral or physical development of minors; secondly, the term "minors" does not cover a uniform group and it is doubtful whether children of four have the same problems as adolescents of 15.

These two problems lead in practice to a *wide variety of national classifications* introduced for certain media (especially films) which are *often incompatible*. In the services context, this diversity has repercussions for the circulation of the material concerned.

To combine the use of the new means of controlling content with the free movement of services assumes a *trend away from centralized classification systems towards decentralized labelling systems which take better account of differences in attitudes*. The urgency of this development varies according to the nature of the services.

a)   Broadcasting services

In the absence of parental control facilities, broadcasters have to base their scheduling on a centralized classification operated by the broadcaster in accordance with more or less detailed rules and recommendations.

In the context of the development of electronic programme guides and navigation systems, ways can be found that will respect national sensitivities in transnational services:

- information on the programmes offered can be differentiated according to the country served (for a given service available in countries A and B, different classifications might be used, e.g. A in country A and B in country B, for the same programme);
- the classification and labelling of programmes might be decentralized (the service sets up a classification and labelling structures in each country served).

b)   On-line services

Video-on-demand and proprietary on-line services can also classify the material they offer themselves (or via contracts with other information providers). While it is not yet systematic on the proprietary services, user information on the potentially harmful nature of certain material for minors is becoming more common.

The open structure of the Internet, on the other hand, as well as the user-friendly and highly interactive applications of the proprietary services, raise the question of the classification of material in radically different terms. The variety of ways of publishing material and the fact that each user is a potential publisher makes it necessary to filter the material that is available. Three different types of filter have been developed.

- **Black list** filtering aims to block access to sites identified as problematic in view of the material they distribute (nudity, violence, sex, etc.); black lists are difficult to update.
- **White list** filtering authorizes access only to pre-determined sites; access to material is heavily limited.
- Filtering based on **neutral labelling** gives users access to information on material loaded by suppliers or third parties on the basis of their own selection criteria.

A combination of these various forms of classification enables the user to make up an operating environment that is generally safe as regards Internet access by minors. But only the generalized introduction of the neutral labelling filtering system would make it possible to regulate the question comprehensively.

As can be seen from the Communication on Illegal and harmful Content on the Internet, PICS (Platform for Internet Content Selection) offers an open global standard to make this neutral labelling possible. **For European Union purposes, PICS has the decisive advantage that it offers a very flexible framework for classifying and indexing material and enables the same material to be classified under different labels supplied by different third parties and containing different types of information, so that it can have regard to differing national, regional and local sensitivities.** A large number of filtering systems already incorporate the PICS system (PICS compatible) but the real challenge is still to reach a critical mass of sites and labelled content.

For all services operating according to the individual consumer demand principle, encouraging material suppliers and third parties to label the material

they make available is a priority for the harmonious development of control of material in general and parental control in particular.

6   How can the labelling of material be decentralized in the case of transnational services so as to reflects the diversity of national, local and personal sensitivities?

7   What standardization efforts are needed to ensure the coherent development of material labelling at European level, particularly for digital services (standardization of the types of information supplied, coding and decoding of this or other information)?

ANNEX IV
TECHNICAL AND OTHER NON-REGULATORY
PROTECTION MEASURES

1.   Parental control devices applied to television broadcasting

Canada has been a pioneer in this field: in the 1990s the Conseil de la Radiodiffusion et des Télécommunications (CRTC) launched a strategy to curb violence on television. From the outset this strategy has been shaped by five guiding principles:

- collaboration based on the principle that violence on television is a cause of psychological problems among children;
- protection of children and not censorship of adults;
- concentration on gratuitous or idealized violence without involving eroticism or other moral considerations;
- involvement of all those concerned: broadcasters, advertisers, producers, parents, teachers and specialists in mental health;
- adoption of a dual perspective, one short-term and one long-term.

In more practical terms, the strategy is based on a raft of complementary measures:

- codes of conduct worked out with the industry;
- classification of programmes;
- anti-violence or "V" chip;[2]
- information campaign to increase public awareness, and media education programme.

In terms of the relative importance of these different measures in the overall strategy, the Canadian authorities believe that the first three account for a mere 20% of the answer (with the V-chip accounting for 10%), the main thing being to change attitudes in the long term through information, awareness-raising and education (80%).

The United States, which has been involved with this Canadian initiative from a very early stage, has up to a point adopted the same approach: the Telecommunication Act was amended to require TV manufacturers to incorporate the anti-violence chip into their products. Since then, the industries involved have been working on the introduction of a programme classification and encoding system which should be operational by January 1997. The Children's Programming Act also requires broadcasters to make an effort to broadcast children's programmes.

In Europe, as in the USA, the debate at once centred on whether a parental control system should be imposed, whether at national or Community level, before the objectives of a system of this type have been clearly established.

On the general philosophy of the system, the main arguments propounded in Europe can be summarized as follows:

- *Supporters* of the system point out that it does away with programme censorship *a priori* and offers every parent the opportunity to control their children's access to television according to their own set of values, even in their absence; this type of system would therefore allow broadcasters greater freedom of expression while respecting the individual values and child-rearing philosophy of parents. What is more, no-one has pointed out the advantages of such a system for cross-border services if it could be used to replace sometimes incompatible regulations.

- *Opponents* of the system point out the dangers of a complete transfer of broadcasters' responsibilities to the parents: firstly, the system could be used to justify slippages in broadcasters' schedules; secondly, not all parents are willing or able to exercise the responsibility that this system would place on them. As this is a system designed for use with non-encoded services, many minors could thus be exposed to programmes harmful to their development.

This basic controversy shows how relatively little attention has been paid in Europe to the Canadian experience, since the CRTC defined and limited its strategy precisely to avoid this clash of principles. In Canada, the anti-violence chip was considered neither as an end in itself nor as a universal panacea capable of resolving all problems single-handed. The two most important elements of the Canadian approach are still the identification of a specific objective and the definition of a long-term strategy. Even the CRTC views the anti-violence chip as no more than a gizmo which would be useless if the awareness-raising campaign failed to bear fruit within a time span of ten years or so.

In addition to the debate on the philosophy of parental control, various practical difficulties have been highlighted.

- The adoption of a common system by several broadcasters implies a common and systematic classification of all programmes broadcast. The introduction of a common system raises the question of responsibility for classification, supervision and possible penalties (a central authority or self-regulation by the operators). This question grows in complexity as the number of broadcasters concerned increases, and culminates in the question of cross-border operation.
- The quantity and diversity of programmes to be classified raises a great many questions on how to evaluate the impact of certain material according to

context (e.g. violent images shown on the news) or whether it is actually possible to classify certain programmes (a live debate can lead to unexpected remarks or behaviour).

- Making a parental control device compulsory for television sets would require a lengthy transitional period depending on the rate of renewal of existing sets. Moreover, old sets often end their life in children's rooms. The choice of a specific device would concentrate technological innovation in this particular field, depriving consumers of solutions which might have been better suited to their needs.

- Finally, the introduction of this type of system would create relative economic uncertainty, since audience ratings, on which the economy of broadcasting financed by advertising is largely based, would be undermined to some extent by the difficulty of analysing the use parents would actually make of the device.

These various problems are not unsurmountable, since Canada and the United States have decided to tackle them, but it must be said that, in the Member States which have discussed this matter, the compulsory introduction of parental control devices has been rejected in favour of other types of action.[3] The debate in Europe, launched by the European Parliament, is still going on.

Consumer electronics manufacturers are particularly concerned by the development of parental control devices. The EACEM[4] in particular has adopted very clear positions on this matter. It recognizes the advantages of developing systems to provide parents with better ways of controlling what children watch and consequently supports any initiative on the classification of material, including compulsory measures. On the other hand, it points out that the imposition of one particular technical device would be counter-productive, notably because a single specific technology cannot be the best option for every system for processing and labelling material now or in the future, and because a large number of formulas are possible depending on the way in which parents wish to use the information offered by the classification of material.

2.   Parental control devices applied to on-line services

While the proprietary on-line services and some information providers have always been conscious of the need to protect minors from certain types of material, the threat followed by the enactment of special legislation in the United States has turned the whole question upside down.

The Telecommunication Act, signed by President Clinton on 8 February 1996, introduced a number of rules on material circulating on electronic networks.[5] In substance, these rules made it illegal knowingly to provide indecent or manifestly shocking material to minors via electronic computer networks.

The industry reacted in two ways:

- first, a coalition of publishers, material providers, access providers and civil liberties associations, attacked the legislation, claiming it violated the First

Amendment (freedom of expression), and having the Act invalidated by the Philadelphia Federal Court of Appeals;
- then it stepped up its efforts to find an alternative solution to legislation as soon as the Bill appeared.

The basis for the invalidation of the Act was primarily the fact that, as there was no reasonable way in which information suppliers could ensure that no minor would have access to it, the Act would require them to censor all indecent material despite the fact that adults had a constitutional right to access it.[6]

Control mechanisms have been developed at different levels.

The mechanisms used *at the level of information providers* are as follows:

- insertion of a warning page alerting the user to the potentially controversial nature of the site or the material he wishes to access; this is intended more as information than protection, the risk being that it will be more of an incentive than a deterrent, particularly for minors;
- pre-access age check: the information provider states the conditions for access to the material in a cover page. Many of the commercial sites require a variety of guarantees in the form of written requests for access (by e-mail or post) or payment by credit card. Some companies are also trying to centralize this process, particularly so that non-commercial sites can benefit: on payment of a modest sum by credit card, the user receives a personal identification code giving him access to all the affiliated sites;
- putting the material offered on special servers (cache-based systems): in this case an operator creates a closed network giving access only to certain material selected from all the information available on the Internet. This approved material can be classified and differential access given on the basis of personal identification codes. Although the choice of material is limited to what has been approved, this type of system provides a high level of security. It is particularly used for providing cable and school access to the Internet.

It is not the place of *access providers*, who seldom if ever provide material themselves, to introduce systematic controls on information. They may, however, be required to help control illegal material by blocking pre-identified sites (black lists). Apart from the problems created by the difficulty of constantly updating these lists and the risk of withholding access to legitimate material, it is clear that this type of measure would not solve the specific problem of protecting minors (it would require the systematic blocking of material which adults must be able to access).

On the other hand, some access providers can offer restricted access (for minors, for example) by using various filters, blocks or preselection of sites. This is an additional service which requires special investment and must be distinguished from the straightforward provision of access.

. . . .

3.   Media education

Most of the different aspects of media education are relevant to the protection of minors and human dignity in the new services.

Schools still need to provide more encouragement for the acquisition of skills in the use of new tools, especially involving computers. The most appropriate method of media education is still the hands-on approach. However, parental enlightenment is also crucially important. What is the point of a parental control device if the parents have to ask their children to instal or programme it? Education in the visual image would serve to develop a critical attitude in adolescents and a new type of demand as regards the quality and diversity of audiovisual content. Furthermore, this type of education would produce long-term effects enabling future generations of parents to perform their child-rearing responsibilities more effectively. Measures to improve parental awareness and information as to the various types of harm to which their children may be exposed are an inevitable corollary to their increasing level of responsibility.

There is recurring debate on these issues in educational circles in all the Member States, and experiments and research are being run on a sporadic basis, notably at local levels. Efforts to increase adult awareness and involvement in media education are much less developed, there are a number of measures which offer themselves as possible examples:

- In the Netherlands, the Kinderkast, a non-governmental organization, has the task of increasing awareness of various aspects of the child/television relationship. This organization performs a variety of activities: production of newsletters, teaching materials for children, parents and educators, research into children's viewing habits, monitoring of television programme schedules, etc;
- In Spain, the Ministry for Social Affairs has published an awareness booklet on the place and use of television and the new services in the home;[7]
- In the United Kingdom, the National Council for Educational Technology devises measures to help teachers and pupils to take advantage of the new technologies. It has published various papers on the new communications networks, most notably a schools booklet on the problems of pornography on the Internet suggesting various initiatives which schools could take in this area;
- In the United States, the National Center for Missing and Exploited Children and the Interactive Services Association have published a joint booklet entitled "Child Safety on the Information Superhighway", intended to help parents to understand the nature of on-line services, the Internet and BBS.

Apart from the organization of a few European-scale meetings on these various facets of media education, the exchange of information and good practice and the establishment of networks on the European or world scale are still in their infancy.

4.   Promotion of high-quality material intended for minors

In some Member States, analysis of the relationship between the media and minors has resulted in the improvement of the programme supply for minors being deemed a priority. In view of the difficulties specific to the production and distribution of such programmes (How should programmes be adapted to different age groups? How are programmes intended for a segment of the population which has not yet the status of solvent consumers to be funded? How are outlets to be found for these niche programmes?), the public authorities and/or the operators themselves have devised policies for the promotion of high-quality programmes.

These policies mainly concern cinema and television. In the field of on-line services and the Internet, everything still remains to be done to promote the development of high-quality sites for minors. The classification and labelling of contents adapted to minors (particularly in the form of white lists) is a first step in this direction. Other forms of encouragement on the lines of those introduced for other media could also be appropriate.

*   Promoting parental control systems and the labelling of material

The development of filtering systems based on labelled material meets in full the preconditions for genuine responsibility on the part of parents and teachers: it provides as much information as possible on the material available so that access can be selected automatically using control devices, on the basis of the family's own criteria (children's age, sensitivity and educational choices). These tools, which are vital in a decentralized services environment, could also prove a useful adjunct to other systems in centralized services.

This type of system can be applied in practice only by following certain steps:

- information must be supplied on the material in question (classification/labelling);
- this information is enclosed as a message with the material (coding);
- the message is transmitted as a substitute for access to the material (transmission);
- the message is read by an control device (decoding);
- control devices are supplied to users.

Classification/labelling of material, irrespective of the media or networks transmitting it, is clearly a priority: without it there is no point in developing solutions for the other stages in the process. To ensure perfect compatibility of the various sources of labelling, it would be useful to define common categories (nudity, sexuality, violence, bad language, etc.) based on a set of age-groups.

The next three stages (encoding, transmission and decoding) are neutral. However, they do raise the question of the compatibility of labels from different sources and the proliferation of control devices (hardware or software) designed to use them. It is important here to secure the greatest possible degree of compatibility on the basis of non-proprietary open standards.

The provision of control devices raises two separate issues: the first concerns their development and production by industry and the second their marketing and supply to users.

The spontaneous development of a wide variety of parental control systems for the Internet and other services shows that industry can very quickly come up with systems which take into account users' needs and the general environment of available services. Measures to promote standardization and the labelling of material as outlined above can only reinforce this tendency and bring product prices down. However, any attempt to define or prescribe a specific system would run the risk of placing an artificial barrier on promising developments.

The marketing and supply of parental control devices to users raises more complex questions. In services where parental control devices are the only effective means of protecting minors, they should automatically be supplied—or offered—to users. However, these automatic supply arrangements must not interfere with competition between different types of device, which is an inherent guarantee of progress in the systems offered.

Notes

1. Directive 89/552.
2. The anti-violence chip is a technical device developed by Professor Tim Collins at Simon Fraser University, Vancouver. This microchip, incorporated in a television set, a cable selector or a decoder, reads the classification code of each programme. The viewer can programme this chip to block the signal of programmes with a classification which exceeds the level considered acceptable for that family. Thus, if the viewer selects the violence level V3, programmes coded V4 and V5 will not appear on the screen. Programme classification codes could be applied to aspects other than violence as required (nudity, sex, bad language, etc.).
   It should be noted that the expressions "anti-violence chip" or "V-chip" relate directly to this Canadian proprietary system. We therefore prefer, in relating to a broader concept, to refer to parental control systems or devices.
3. In France, the CSA asked non-encrypted broadcasters (private and public) to develop common classifications and identifiers for programmes which could be harmful to minors and a code of conduct for television news programmes.
4. European Association of Consumer Electronics Manufacturers.
5. Attached to the provisions on the V-chip, these rules are now known as the Communications Decency Act (CDA).
6. "A wealth of persuasive evidence ... proved that it is either technologically impossible or economically prohibitive for many of the plaintiffs to comply with the CDA without seriously impeding their posting of on-line material which adults have a constitutional right to access."
7. "¿Qué Miras?, ¿Qué Haces?—La familia, las niñas y los niños ante la televisión y las nuevas pantallas."

III. French Audiovisual Council, Violence on Television: Steps in the Cooperation between the French Audiovisual Council (CSA) and Broadcasters

October 1995: The French Audiovisual Council publishes a quantitave first of-its-kind study of which shows the importance of violence in works of fiction broadcast by French stations.

November 8, 1995:As a follow-up on the study, the Council meets with all broadcasters and asks them to make an engagement to limit the amount of violent programming in order to help protect the young viewing public.

The French Audiovisual Council makes clear to all broadcasters that it wishes to forge a code of good conduct applicable to all networks no later than summer of 1996, in time for the signature of new licencing agreements for TF1 and M6. The code will then be included in all agreements for licencing of private networks and in programming requirements for public networks.

January–June 1996: Broadcasters make propositions which are then examined by the CSA, and which are molded to form a single plan applicable to all networks, public and private.

At the same time the Council requests that networks broadcast at 8:30 P.M. only exceptionally films which are forbidden to children under 12. From January to June, only six films in this category are programmed at 8:30 P.M. on the entirety of the networks (out of total of 250 films broadcast at that hour).

July 2, 1996 : The CSA asks networks to subscribe to a definitive version of the code for the protection of minors applicable to all networks and which includes:

- the creation of a viewing commission at each network.
- the classification, by this commission, of programs into five categories.
- the adoption of on-screen symbols.
- the designation of certain hours for each class of programs.

July 31, 1996: The signature of licencing agreements for TF1 and M6.1 These licences include articles specifically aimed at the protection of minors.

August 1996: The CSA asks the government to include the articles protecting minors of the TF1 and M6 licences in the programming requirements for public networks. Prime Minister Juppe' responds affirmatively to this request.

Networks are asked to formulate a range of on-screen symbols visible during and before programs which will be operational by January 1, 1997.

September 1996: The debate surrounding the effect of violence on TV is heightened by the violent deaths of two highschool students. The CSA and national networks decide to unite in the application, by mid-November, of measures to protect minors, notably in the use of on-screen symbols.

October 1996: France 2, France 3, TF1 and M6 finalize the on-screen symbols plan which will be used from November 18. They create their viewing commissions and begin program classification.

October 23, 1996: Presentation of standard on-screen symbols to the press.

November 18, 1996: The on-screen symbols program takes effect.

IV. French Audiovisual Council, The Protection of Minors, Excerpts from the TF1 and M6 Licences

Article 11

The broadcasters family programming should be aired between 6:00 A.M. and 10:00 P.M., hours when young people are most likely to be in front of the television. In this time slot and particularly in the period dedicated to children's programs, violence, even psychological violence, should not be perceptible as continuous, omnipresent or as the sole solution to conflicts.

The broadcaster shall classify films and audiovisual creations[1] into five categories of acceptability in order to promote the protection of minors.

- *Category I* General public
- *Category II*: Programs containing scenes likely to shock a young public.
- *Category III*: Films forbidden to children under 12, as well as broadcasts likely to disturb a young public, notably when their scenario uses repeated scenes of physical or psychological violence.
- *Category IV*: Films forbidden to children under 16, as well as pornographic and extremely violent works, likely to endanger the physical, mental and moral development of minors of 16 years of age.
- *Category V*: Works of a pornographic or extremely violent nature likely to endanger the physical, psychological and moral development of minors.

The classification given films at the time of their release in theaters may be used as a classification method for television. It is, however, the duty of the broadcaster to verify it this classification is suitable for application to television audiences.

Each station will create a viewing commission which will make recommendations concerning program classification. A list of members of this commission should be made known to the French Audiovisual Council.

Article 12

Each company will apply an on-screen symbol to programs it has classified in adherence with Article 11 of the present agreement with the CSA. This on-screen symbol, with the exception of Category I, should be brought to the attention of the public at the time of programming, in advance advertising and in published TV schedules. This rating system does not exonerate the broadcaster from respecting decree No 90-74 of January 23, 1990 concerning a public warnings previous to programs forbidden to minors and the advance advertising concerning them.

Article 13

Broadcasters must respect the following conditions for programming, for each of the categories laid out in Article 11.

- *Category II*: Programming time is left at the discretion of the network insofar as they are not aired during children's programs.

    The broadcaster must take particular care as concerns advance advertising for programs in this category during or in proximity to children's programs.
- *Category III*: Programming should not take place before 10:00 P.M. Such programming may, exceptionally, be made on condition that it is accompanied by a permanent on -screen symbol, but never before 10:00 P.M. on Tuesdays, Fridays, Saturdays or the eve of holidays.

    Advance advertising for these program should not contain scenes likely to shock a young public. They may not be aired in proximity to children's programs.
- *Category IV*: Adults only, to be programmed only after 10:30 P.M.

    Advance advertising for these programs should not contain scenes likely to shock a young public. They may not be aired before 8:30 P.M.
- *Category V*: Broadcast is strictly forbidden.

Article 14

It is left to the discretion of broadcasters to take precautions when particularly shocking scenes or testimony are evoked in news coverage. The public should, in such cases, be notified in advance.

Notes

1.   Mainly TV fiction and also cartoon and documentary.

Bibliography

Marlene Gebauer and Barry Sherman

BOOKS

Barendt, E. M. (1995). *Broadcasting law: A comparative study.* Oxford University Press: New York.

Bellamy, R. V. Jr., and Walker J. R. (1996). *Television and the remote control: Grazing on a vast wasteland.* The Guilford Press: New York.

Brown, A. (1986). *Commercial media in Australia: Economics, ownership, technology and regulation.* University of Queensland Press: New York.

Cowan, G. (1979). *See no evil: The backstage battle over sex and violence in television.* Simon and Schuster: New York.

Federman, J. (1990). *Media ratings: design, use and consequences.* Mediascope: Studio City, California.

Klinger, R. (1996). *The new information industry: Regulatory challenges and the First Amendment.* Brookings Institution Press: Washington, D.C.

Krasnow, E. G., Longley, L. D., and Terry, H. A. (1982). *The politics of broadcast regulation* (3rd ed.). St. Martin's Press: New York.

Krattenmaker, T. G., and Powe, L. A. Jr. (1994). *Regulating broadcast programming.* MIT Press: Cambridge, MA, and AEI Press: Washington, D.C.

Kreech, K. (1996). *Electronic media law and regulation* (2nd ed.). Focal Press: Boston.

Lipschultz, J. H. (1997). *Broadcast indecency: F.C.C. regulation and the First Amendment.* Focal Press: Boston.

Noam, E. M. (ed.). (1985). *Video media competition: Regulation, economics and technology.* Columbia Press: New York.

Pally, M. (1994). *Sex and sensibility: Reflections on forbidden mirrors and the will to censor.* The Ecco Press: Hopewell, NJ.

Paraschos, E. E., and Paraschos, M. (1997). *Media law and regulation in the European Union: National, transnational and U.S. perspectives.* Iowa State University Press: Ames, Iowa.

Roth, H. F. (1996). *Cable TV: Regulation or competition?* Brookings Institution: Washington, D.C.

JOURNAL ARTICLES

Albert, J. A. (1978). Constitutional regulation of televised violence. *Virginia Law Review* 64, 1299.

Association of American Law Schools, Section on mass communications law (Summer, 1997). 1997 annual conference panel: Sex, violence, children & the media: Legal, historical and empirical perspectives. *Catholic University of America Commlaw Conspectus* 5, 341.

Balkin, J. M. (April, 1996). Media filters, the V-chip, and the foundations of broadcast regulation. *Duke Law Journal* 45, 1131.

Corn-Revere, R. (Summer, 1994). New technology and the First Amendment: Breaking the cycle of repression. *Hastings Communication and Entertainment Law Journal* 17, 247.

Corn-Revere, R. (Winter, 1995). Television violence and the limits of voluntarism. *Yale Journal on Regulation* 12, 187.

Corn-Revere, R. (Summer, 1997). Symposium, Rationales and rationalizations: Chapter 1: Red Lion and the culture of regulation. *Catholic University of America Commlaw Conspectus* 5, 173

Dean, B. M. (Spring, 1997). The age-based ratings system: An unfortunate response to the V-chip legislation. *Virginia Journal of Social Policy and the Law* 4, 743.

Deutsch, B. P. (Fall, 1994). Note: Wile E. Coyote, Acme Explosives and the First Amendment: The unconstitutionality of regulating violence on broadcast television. *Brooklyn Law Review* 60, 1101.

Feldman, S. D. (Winter, 1996). The V-chip: Protecting children from violence or doing violence to the Constitution. *Howard Law Journal* 39, 587.

Hamilton, M. A. (1996) Regulating the Internet: Should pornography get a free ride on the information superhighway? A panel discussion. *Cardozo Arts & Entertainment Law Journal* 14, 343.

Hamilton, M. A. (1997). Reconceptualizing ratings: From censorship to marketplace. *Cardozo Arts & Entertainment Law Journal* 15, 403.

Hazlett, T. W. (Fall, 1996). Explaining the Telecommunications Act of 1996: Comment of Thomas G. Krattenmaker. *Connecticut Law Review* 29, 217.

Kelly, C. M. (Summer, 1997). Note, The specter of a 'wired' nation: Denver Area Educational Telecommunications Consortium v. FCC and First Amendment analysis in cyberspace. *Harvard Journal of Law and Technology* 10, 559.

Kim, S. J. (April, 1994). Comment: 'Viewer discretion is advised': A structural approach to the issue of television violence. *University of Pennsylvania Law Review* 142, 1383.

Krattenmaker, T. G., and Powe, L. A. Jr. (December, 1978). Televised violence: First Amendment principles and social science theory. *Virginia Law Review* 64(8), 1123.

Krattenmaker, T. G. (November, 1996). The Telecommunications Act of 1996. *Federal Communications Law Journal* 49, 1.

Lessig, L. (Summer, 1997). Symposium, The state of the First Amendment at the approach of the millennium. The Constitution of code: Limitations on choice-based critiques of cyberspace regulation. *Catholic University of America Commlaw Conspectus* 5, 181.

Lipschultz, J. H. (April, 1993). Article Digest, Conceptual problems of broadcast indecency, 14 Comm. & Law 3. *Federal Communications Law Journal* 45, 339.

MacCarthy, M. M. (1995). Broadcast self-regulation: The NAB codes, family viewing hour, and television violence. *Cardozo Arts and Entertainment Law Journal* 3, 667.

Popham, J. J. (Summer, 1997). Passion, politics and the public interest: The perilous path to a quantitative standard in the regulation of children's television programming. *Catholic University of America Commlaw Conspectus* 5, 1.

Price, M. E., and Duffy, J. F. (May, 1997). Symposium, Technological change and doctrinal persistence: Telecommunications reform in Congress and the Court. *Columbia Law Review* 97, 905.

Saunders, K. W. (Summer, 1994). Media violence and the obscenity exception to the First Amendment. *William and Mary Bill of Rights Journal* 3, 107.

Saunders, K. W. (Fall, 1994). Media self-regulation of depictions of violence: A last opportunity. *Oklahoma Law Review* 47, 445.

Schneider, L. B. (Winter, 1994). Warning: Television violence may be harmful to children, but the First Amendment may foil congressional attempts to legislate against it. *University of Miami Law Review* 49, 477.

Scott, D. V. (1996). The V-chip debate: Blocking television sex, violence and the First Amendment. *Loyola of Los Angeles Entertainment Law Journal* 16, 741.

Smolla, R. A. (Summer, 1997). Symposium, The state of the First Amendment at the approach of the millennium: The culture of regulation. *Catholic University of America Commlaw Conspectus* 5, 193.

Spitzer, M. (Fall, 1996). Dean Krattenmaker's road not taken: The political economy of broadcasting in the Telecommunications Act of 1996. *Connecticut Law Review* 29, 353.

Spitzer, M. L. (1997). An introduction to the law and economics of the V-chip. *Cardozo Arts & Entertainment Law Journal* 15, 429.

Wolfson, N. (Fall, 1994). Eroticism, obscenity, pornography and free speech. *Brooklyn Law Review* 60, 1037.

Windhausen, J. (Summer, 1994). Symposium, Television and violence: Congressional interest in the problem of television and violence. *Hofstra Law Review* 22, 783.

Wise, E. (1996). Symposium, Safe harbors and stern warnings. FCC regulation of indecent broadcasting: A historical perspective on the protection of children from broadcast indecency. *Villanova Sports & Entertainment Law Journal* 3, 15.

FCC RECORD AND REPORTS

In the Matter of Implementation of Section 551 of the Telecommunications Act of 1996; Video Programming Ratings. FCC 98-35. (March 12, 1998). [1998 FCC LEXIS 1241].

In the Matter of Technical Requirements to Enable Blocking of Video Programming Based on Program Ratings; Implementation of Sections 551(c), (d), and (e) of the Telecommunications Act of 1996. FCC 98-36. (March 12, 1998). [1998 FCC LEXIS 1246].

Commission seeks Comment on Industry Proposal for Rating Video Programming, FCC 75-202, FCC Record 3260. (February 7, 1997). [1997 FCC LEXIS 688].

Commissioner Chong Calls for "First Amendment Friendly Framework" for Regulating Media Content. (September 25, 1996). [1996 FCC LEXIS 5339].

Commissioner Chong Challenges Radio Broadcasters to Fight for First Amendment Freedom. (September 19, 1997). [1997 FCC LEXIS 5138].

In the Matter of Policies and Rules Concerning Children's Television Programming Revision of Programming Policies for Television Broadcasting Stations. FCC 96-335, 11 FCC Record 10660. (August 8, 1996). [1996 FCC LEXIS 4304].

In the Matter of Technical Requirements to Implementation of Sections 551(c), (d) and (e) of the Telecommunications Act of 1996. FCC 97-340. (September 26, 1997). [1997 FCC LEXIS 5331].

Remarks by Commissioner James H. Quello before the National Religious Broadcasters Association, Washington D.C. (February 1, 1994). [11994 FCC LEXIS 462].

Remarks of Commissioner Rachel B. Chong to the American Advertising Federation National Government Affairs Conference, Washington, D.C. (March 13, 1997). [1997 FCC LEXIS 1301].

Remarks of Reed E. Hunt, Chairman of the Federal Communications Commission: The Hard Road Ahead: An Agenda for the FCC in 1997. (December 26, 1996). [1996 FCC LEXIS 7111].

Report of the Broadcast of Violent, Indecent and Obscene Material, FCC 75-202, 51 FCC 2d 418. (February 19, 1975). [1975 FCC Lexis 2228].

CONGRESSIONAL RECORD

E124 Television Violence, Proceedings and Debates of the 104th Congress, Second Session, Wednesday, January 31, 1996. [142 Cong. Rec. E124-03].

E240 TV Ratings, 105th Congress, First Session, Wednesday, February 12, 1997. [143 Cong. Rec. E240-18].

E365 The Introduction of the Children's Protection from Violent Programming, 105th Congress, First Session, Tuesday, March 4, 1997. [143 Cong. Rec. E365-26].

E378 Introduction of the Markey-Burton Bill To Encourage Content-Based TV Ratings, 105th Congress, First Session, Thursday, March 6, 1997. [143 Cong. Rec. E378-03] [1997 WL 93061 (Cong. Rec.)].

E800-03 Extension of Remarks, The Telecommunications Revolution, 104th Congress, Second Session, Tuesday, May 14, 1996. [142 Cong. Rec. E800-03] [1996 WL 252200].

E957 The Loss of the Family Hour, Extensions, 104th Congress, First Session, Monday, May 19, 1997. [143 Cong. Rec. E957-66].

E1436 Introducing the Parental Choice in Television Act of 1995, Proceedings and Debates of the 104th Congress, First Session, Thursday, July 13, 1995. [141 Cong. Rec. E1436-03].

E1565 Introducing the Markey-Moran-Burton-Spratt Amendment on Parental Blocking of TV Shows that Harm Children, Proceedings and Debates of the 104th Congress, First Session, Monday, July 31, 1995. [141 Cong. Rec.E1565-04].

E1909-02 Extensions of Remarks; How Bureaucrats Rewrite Laws, 104th Congress, Second Session, Thursday, October 3, 1996. [142 Cong. Rec. E1909-02] [1996 WL 562356 (Cong. Rec.)].

E2011 Television Violence Reduction Through Parental Empowerment Act of 1993, Proceedings and Debates of the 103rd Congress, First Session, Thursday, August 5, 1993. [1139 Cong. Rec. E2011-01].

E5780 Changing the Diet that Is Poisoning the Minds of Our Children, Proceedings and Debates of the 104th Congress, First Session, Tuesday, June 13, 1995. [141 Cong. Rec. H5780-01].

H650 New Television Program Rating System Not Providing Enough Information for Parents To Make Choices for Their Children's TV Viewing, 105th Congress, First Session, Wednesday, February 26, 1997. [143 Cong. Rec. H650-02].

H3208 The Children's Television Act Rulemaking, 104th Congress, First Session, Friday, March 29, 1996. [142 Cong. Rec. H3208-09] [1996 WL 288310 (Cong. Rec.)].

H8541 Television Decoder Circuitry Act of 1990, Proceedings and Debates of the 101st Congress, Second Session, Tuesday, October 1, 1990. [136 Cong. Rec. H8541].

H6745 The V-Chip, Proceedings and Debates of the 104th Congress, First Session, Tuesday, July 11, 1995. [141 Cong. Rec. H6745-02].

*S309 Report of the State of the Union Address—Message from the President—*Proceedings and Debates of the 104th Congress, Second Session, Tuesday, January 23, 1996. [142 Cong. Rec. S309-02].

S540 Empowering Parents and the Public: The Key to a Solution for Television Violence, Proceedings and Debates of the 103rd Congress, Second Session, Tuesday, February 1, 1994. [140 Cong. Rec. S540-02] [1994 WL 26636 (Cong. Rec.)].

S1467 Agreement to Create TV Rating System, Proceedings and Debates of the 104th Congress, Second Session, Thursday, February 29, 1996. [142 Cong. Rec. S1467-01].

S1631 Joint Standards on Violence, Proceedings and Debates of the 104th Congress, Second Session, Thursday, March 7, 1996. [142 Cong. Rec. S1631-02] [1996 WL 99496 (Cong. Rec.)].

S1659 Statements on Introduced Bills and Joint Resolutions, 105th Congress, First Session, Wednesday, February 26, 1997. [143 Cong. Rec. S1659-22].

S2021 TV Rating System Legislation, 105th Congress, First Session, Thursday, March 6, 1997. [143 Cong. Rec. S2021-28].

S5653 Radio and Television News Directors' Foundation Annual Banquet and Celebration of the First Amendment, Proceedings and Debates of the 104th Congress, Second Session, Friday, May 24, 1996. [142 Cong. Rec. S5653-01] [1996 WL 277287 (Cong. Rec.)].

S10438 The Media, Censorship, and Parental Empowerment, Proceedings and Debates of the 104th Congress, First Session, Thursday, July 20, 1995. [141 Cong. Rec. 10438-01] [1995 WL 428813 (Cong. Rec.)].

S10661 The V-Chip, Proceedings and Debates of the 104th Congress, First Session, Tuesday, July 25, 1995. [141 Cong. Rec. S10661-03].

S10208 A Call To Tone Down the Violence, 104th Congress, Second Session, Tuesday, September 10, 1996. [142 Cong. Rec. S10208-01] [1996 WL 511135 (Cong. Rec.)].

S11470 Television Violence, Proceedings and Debates of the 103rd Congress, First Session, Friday, September 10, 1993. [139 Cong. Rec. S11470-01] [1993 WL 344847 (Cong. Rec.)].

S12208 The Mysterious V-Chip, Proceedings and Debates of the 104th Congress, First Session, Thursday, August 10, 1995. [141 Cong. Rec. S12208-03].

S12333 FCC's Implementation of the Telecommunications Act of 1996, 104th Congress, Second Session, Thursday, October 3, 1996. [142 Cong. Rec. S12333-02][1996 WL 562266 (Cong. Rec.)].

S15153 Children's Television, Proceedings and Debates of the 104th Congress, First Session, Friday, October 13, 1995. [141 Cong. Rec. S15153-01].

Markey, Rep. Edward, *How the V-Chip Came to Pass: A Paradoxical History. Ironically, the Story Begins in 1990 with a Bill that Had Nothing at All To Do with Television Violence,* Roll Call March 11, 1996.

CONGRESSIONAL TESTIMONY

Baumann, H. L., *Testimony of Henry L. Baumann before the House of Representatives Committee of Commerce,* S652, Telecommunications Act of 1996. (May 19, 1997). [1997 WL 454428 (F.D.C.H.)].

Britt, D. V. B. *Testimony of David V. B. Britt before the House of Representatives Subcommittee of Telecommunications, Trade and Consumer Protection,* S652, Telecommunications Act of 1996. (February 29, 1996). [1996 WL 103647 (F.D.C.H.)].

Markey, E. J. *Testimony of Edward J. Markey before the House of Representatives Subcommittee of Telecommunications and Finance.* (June 30, 1997). [1997 WL 313437 (F.D.C.H.)].

Markey, E. J. *Testimony of Edward J. Markey before the Senate Committee of Commerce,* S652, Telecommunications Act of 1996. (February 27, 1997). [1997 WL 90701 (F.D.C.H.)].

Markey, E. J. *Testimony of Edward J. Markey before the Senate Committee of Commerce,* S652, Telecommunications Act of 1996. (July 12, 1995). [1995 WL 431092 (F.D.C.H.)].

Valenti, J., Fritts, E. and Anstrom D., *Testimony of J. Valenti, E. Fritts and D. Anstrom before the House of Representatives Subcommittee of Telecommunications, Trade and Consumer Protection,* S652, Telecommunication Act of 1996. (May 19, 1997). [1997 WL 309259 (F.D.C.H.)].

Valenti, J. *Testimony of Jack Valenti before the Senate Committee of Commerce,* S652, Telecommunications Act of 1996. (February 27, 1997). [1997 WL 85030 (F.D.C.H.)].

CONGRESSIONAL REPORTS AND PUBLIC LAW

Children's Protection from Violent Programming Act of 1995, 104th Congress, 1st Session, Senate Report 104-171, November 9, 1995. [104 S. Rpt. 171].

Public Law 104-104 Sec. 551. Parental Choice in Television Programming, February 8, 1996.

MAGAZINE, WIRE SERVICES, PRESS RELEASES AND NEWSLETTERS

Anti-violence TV efforts by independents OK's. (1994, January 31). *FTC Watch.*

Attention business/news editors: Canwest Global applauds efforts of CRTC on violence hearing decision. (1996, March 14). *Canada NewsWire.*

Attention business/news editors: CRTC sets deadline for a V-chip based television classification system. (1996, March 14). *Canada NewsWire.*

Attention entertainment editors: Action group tackles program classification and improved V-chip. (1996, April 4). *Canada News Wire.*

Aversa, J. (1997, August 2). 'V,' 'S,' 'L,' and 'D' could show up in TV ratings: Television industry submits revamped plan to government, *Peoria Journal Star.* [1997 WL 7671395].

Bainbridge, J. (1996, April 4). Ads are at risk when the V-chips are down, *ASAP,* 6.

Beatty cautions broadcasters after receiving 1.2 million signatures protesting TV violence. (1992, November 18). *Canada Newswire.*

Boliek, B. (1994, January 26). Details of TV violence plan may come today, *The Hollywood Reporter.*

Broadcasters endorse petition against gratuitous violence on TV. (1992, November 18). *Canada Newswire.*

Came, B. (1992, December 7). A child's crusade: More than a million Canadians back a young Quebecer who abhors TV violence, *Maclean's,* 46.

Canada's V-chip test, polls find criticism of TV. (July 1996). *Newsletter on Intellectual Freedom* XLV (4) 115.

Canadian company to make first V-chip product. (1996, May 15). *Reuters Financial Service.*

Canwest Global applauds efforts of CRTC on violence: Hearing decision. (1996, March 14). *Canada Newswire.*

Chidley, J. (1996, June 17). The V-chip made in Canada stirs controversy, *Maclean's,* 42.

Chisolm, P. (1993, January 4). The fear index, *Maclean's,* 24.

Chisolm, P. (1996, March 25). Disarming the tube, *Maclean's,* 56.

Clark, K. R. (1988, December 20). Television censorship isn't what it used to be, *The Record,* E10.

Clayton, M. (1993, December 20). Canadian broadcasters set violence standards for TV, *The Christian Science Monitor,* 15.

Coe, S. (1993, July 19). Salhany supports violence-warning plan; Fox CEO Lucie Salhany, *Broadcasting & Cable,* 24.

Cohen, S. (1996, March 25). V-chip impact on industry weighed: Industry trend or event?, *Electronic News,* 1.

Conrad, K. (1996, May 21). Canada following similar paths in fight against TV violence, *Congressional Press Releases.*

Corry, J. (1995, August). Dole and the depraved, *The American Spectator,* 50.

CRTC salutes Virginia Larivière and outlines its actions against TV violence. (1992, November 18). *Canada Newswire.*

CRTC: Respecting children: A Canadian approach to helping families deal with television violence. (1996, March 22). *Presswire.*

Dahir, M. S. (1995, July). Sticker shock; sound recording labels, *Reason,* 60.

Dickson, G. (1996, February 12). How's it work? The V-chip is based on closed-captioning technology, *Broadcasting and Cable,* 24.

European Parental TV sex & violence chip plans 02/28/96. (1996, February 28). *Newsbyte News Network.*

Excerpt of the hearing of the Senate Judiciary Committee, Constitution Subcommittee Paul Simon, subject: Violence on television. (1993, May 21). *Federal News Service Washington Package.*

Fitzgerald, N. (1997, August 11). Moral prescriptions: Congress adds sex, language and violence to the TV ratings system, *Adweek.* [1997 WL 9317282]

Flint, J. and Stern, C. (1996, September 30). V-chip falls where it may, *Variety,* 57

Frank, B. (1996, May 15). The great content debate; television censorship; V-chip, *Inside Media,* 38.

Foster, C. (1994, February 22). Australia creates new system to classify explicit video games, *The Christian Science Monitor* 6, 262.

Gray, T. E. (1996, April 15). V-chip, the Betamax of the 90's, *Broadcasting & Cable,* 30.

Halonen, D. (1989, March 20). Senator renews push to limit TV violence, *Electronic Media,* 8.

Halonen, D. (1996, March 18). Canada pushes U.S. on TV ratings code, *Electronic Media,* 3.

Halonen, D. (1997, September 8). NAB readies for First Amendment battle, *Electronic Media.* [1997 WL 8290169].

Healey, J. (1995, July 8). Proposed electronic 'V-chip' complicates the view, *CQ,* 1994.

Hernandez, D. G. (1995, August 26). Controlling cyberporn: Numerous First Amendment questions arise as the government attempts to regulate content of online information services, *Editor and Publisher Magazine*, 14.

Henry, W. A. III. (1995, July 6). Another kind of ratings war; the campaign to take the sex out of television, *Time*, 17.

Kelly, B. (1996, June 17). Arts funding, V-chip hot buttons at Banff, *Variety*, 30.

Kelly, B. (1996 June 11). Victory for the V-chip: Canadians love device, loathe ratings plan, *Daily Variety*, 34.

Kerr, G. (1988, July 8). A Q & A with Tipper Gore, *Gannet News Service*.

Kornhauser, A. (1988, April 18). Brothers bet on lobbying venture, *Legal Times*, 1.

Krumlitsch, K. and Grower, A. (1993 November 1). Public enemy no. 17: Most adults are offended by television sex and violence, *Mediaweek*, 18.

Life after the Telecom Act. (1996, April 15). *Broadcasting & Cable*, 20.

Mahoney, W. (1988, September 19). ABC makes staff cuts in its standard division, *Electronic Media*, 3.

Martin, E. (1991, August 7). News shows, old controversies: From the makers of "Soap" and "The Golden Girls" comes two shows that could spark concern: "Nurses," "Good and Evil," *Inside Media*, 15.

McConnell, C. (1997, May 12). Two countries, one rating system: Canadian TV group comes up with system similar to one in US, *Broadcasting & Cable*, 19.

McDonald, M. (1997, May 5). A V-chip tug-of-war, *Maclean's*, 60.

Parents make the best TV guides: Cable TV industry. (1995, September 6). *Canada Newswire*.

Powell, B. (1988, November 14). Whatever happened to the 'content police'?, *Newsday*, A41.

Radomski, J. K. (1994, January 4). Broadside on TV violence: Voluntary Canadian code already having far-reaching consequences, *The Hollywood Reporter*.

Sanger, E. (1995, June 9). Balancing act for record execs: Review set for album lyric labels, *Newsday*, A41.

Schneider, M. (1996, March 11). Two US stations give Canada's V-chip rating test high marks, *Electronic Media*.

Scott, V. (1985, May 23). TV censorship eases, *UPI*.

Shaw announces Rogers, CF Cable and Ontario & Quebec broadcasters and pay television networks to join "V" chip testing. (1995, August 10). *Business Wire*.

Spring, G. (1997, August 18). Kids don't rate: Syndicators won't label cartoon violence, *Electronic Media*. [1997 WL 8290071].

Stern, C. (1995, July 17). Clinton puts V-chip on fast track, *Broadcasting & Cable*, 6.

Stern, C. (1996, February 12). Clinton: V-chip is not enough, *Broadcasting & Cable*, 4.

Stern, C. (1996, February 12). The V-chip: First Amendment infringement v. empowerment tool, *Broadcasting & Cable*, 20.

The ratings conundrum. (1996, September 30). *Electronic Media*, 10.

TV violence ratings system mandated. (1996, March 21). *Facts on File World News Digest*, 28.

Wagner, D. (1986, May 23). The new right and the new pluralism, *National Review*, 28.

Waters, H. F. (1978, February 20). Sex and TV. *Newsweek,* 54.

West, D. and Stern, C. (1996, March 18). Jack of all trades: The man in the middle on the V-chip. Motion Picture Association of America President Jack Valenti, *Broadcasting & Cable,* 26.

Whalen, J. (1995 October 18). Myers seeking panel to rate TV violence, *Advertising Age.*

Why the Markey chip won't hurt you; Edward Markey; interview. (1995, August 14). *Broadcasting and Cable,* 10.

Wulf, S., Fedarko, K., Fowlner, D., Chandrani, G. and Savaiano, J. (1997, September 8). TV or not TV: Faced with the new fall offerings for kids and an already dizzying array of channels, parents must ponder whether to turn it on and tune into it or—dare we say it?—turn it off, *Time.* [1997 WL 13375756].

Zogglin, R. (1996, February 19). Chips ahoy: As new study warns that violence saturates the airwaves, a technical quick fix promises to help, but will the V-chip really protect our children?, *Time,* 58.

Zoglin, R. (1988, December 12). Where are the censors? A titillating fall raises questions about new standards, *Time,* 95.

NEWSPAPER ARTICLES

Allan, M. D. (1996, September 11). Record labels, retailers stick to their stickers, *The Indianapolis Star,* p. C1.

Andrews, K. A. (1996, June 26). Australia: Pain and shame of a violent culture, *Australian Financial Review.*

AOL's case pushes interactive industry role in public service. (1997, October 8). *Communications Daily.*

Armstrong, D. (1996, March 10). V-chip more than a concept in Canada: North of the border, technology to block TV programming may be in place by fall, *The San Francisco Examiner,* p. D1.

Backers say TV ratings provide 'precisely' what Congress intended. (1997, October 8). *Communications Daily.*

Bash, A. (1996, March 14). A test case for TV ratings Canadian V-chip experiment has lessons for US networks, *USA Today,* p. 3D.

Bash, A. (1996, October 2). V-chip system to get creative input, *USA Today,* p. 3D.

Blummer, R. E. (1997, August 31). Ratings could chill cyberspace. *St. Petersburg Times.* [1997 WL 6216309].

Bowers, M. (1995, November 7). Parenting: Warning about explicit lyrics often ignored, *The Virginian-Pilot* (Norfolk), p. E1.

Boyer, P. J. (1988, August 29). The media business. Television of profanity and profits: A network's new focus, *The New York Times,* p. D6.

Bradner, S. (1997, July 14). Reflections on Independence Day, *Network World,* p. 36.

Braxton, G. (1996, October 4). Confusion, anger mark discussion about V-chip, *Los Angeles Times,* p. F1.

Cerone, D. H. (1995, September 1). Let buyers beware: Ratings formulas may be complex television. Last year, the video game industry was under congressional pressure to devise a ratings system, but after disagreeing on how to classify content, it ended up with not one, but two, *Los Angeles Times,* p. F1.

Clinton announces plan for kid-friendly Internet despite court ruling. (1997, July 21). *Communications Daily.*

Cole, G. (1996, April 22). What's in it? Read the label. George Cole on a new rating system for the World Wide Web, *The Independent,* p. 17.

Comm. Daily Notebook. (1997, September 19). *Communications Daily.*

Congressional panel to conduct second hearing on TV violence. (1993, June 23). *Chicago Sun-Times.*

CRTC sets September as V-chip deadline. (April 1996). *Television Business International,* p. 22.

CRTC to conduct public hearings on the issue of violence in television programming. (1995, April 12). *Presswire.*

Cuthbert, W. (1993, February 20). Canada: Ottowa to fight TV violence: Cooperative effort, *Financial Post.*

Dickinson, B. (1996, June 26). Duke meeting to brainstorm solutions to violent television. V-chip inventor sees creation as important for parental control, *The Herald Sun,* p. C1.

Dorsey, T. (1996, April 15). Devising TV-show rating code a big order: Multiple labels, program volume complicate task, *The Courier-Journal,* p. C5.

Farber, S. (1987, April 4). TV deals with sex more candidly, *The New York Times,* Sec. 2 p. 50.

Farhi, P. (1994, December 24). A waiting game for ratings game: When it comes to video play, few products carry promised content warnings, *The Washington Post,* p. D1.

Federman, J. (1996, December 9). Let's pave a high road for TV ratings system. *Los Angeles Times.* [1996 WL 12764004].

Fotheringham, A. (1996, April 2). V-chip is not one of Spicer's better ideas, *The Toronto Sun,* p. 12.

Garner, M. R. (1997, September 5). Perspective on the First Amendment. Democrats' 'value agenda' imperils quality TV: Producers think their programming is protected with 'friendly' Democrats Clinton and Gore in charge, *Los Angeles Times.* [1997 WL 13976980].

Gay, V. (1996, February 15). Taking control of your TV: The chip that blocks television sex and violence has become law. Now the real battle begins, *Newsday,* p. B4.

Goldman, K. (1988, August 17). Change in TV 'standards': CBS, NBC phasing out offices of program review, *Newsday* (Nassau and Suffolk Edition), Part II, p. 15.

Grattan, M. An Australian minister backs TV block on violence, *The Age.*

Griest, S. (1995, August 28). Mortal Kombat's bloodless coup: Kids say hit martial-arts film lacks video game's gory details, *The Washington Post,* p. D1.

Harrington, R. (1995, April 26). A harder spin: Debate on stricter label laws, penalties heat up again, *The Washington Post,* p. C7.

Hohler, B. (1993, January 29). Finding a turnoff for TV: Parents use technology to limit children's screen time, *The Boston Globe,* p. 1.

Jost, K. (1997, September 9). Will a new ratings system and new shows bring about improved TV for children?, *Portland Oregonian.* [1997 WL 13118629].

Kaplan, K. (1995, September 13). Clueless about song lyrics? Translations are now available, *Los Angeles Times,* p. F1.

Kolbert E. (1993, May 23). What's a network censor to do?, *The New York Times,* Sec. 2, p. 1.

Kolbert, E. (1994, January 11). Canadians curbing TV violence, *The New York Times,* p. C15.

Mass Media. (1997, July 23). *Communications Daily.*

Mass Media. (1997, August 8). *Communications Daily.*

Mass Media. (1997, September 29). *Communications Daily.*

Mass Media. (1997, October 1). *Communications Daily.*

Microsystems takes the lead in creating the industry's first PICS based on its CyberNot ratings system: Microsoft to offer developers FREE PICS client test program. (1996, January 25). *Business Wire.*

Murphy, K. (1996, July 10). Australia govt. backs V-chip to censor violence, *Australian Financial Review.*

Nagler, E. (1987, August 30). Company meets concern on MTV, *The New York Times,* Sec. 2, p. 10.

Overset: Television and radio. (1997, October 1). *Media Daily.*

Poulter, S. (1996, March 19). Why I will be viewing the V-chip by Virginia, *Daily Mail,* p. 15.

Recreational software advisory: Council gives Microsoft Internet Explorer 3.0 top rating: Launch of Microsoft browser solution advances industry acceptance of prominent Internet content labeling system. (1996, August 13). *Business Wire.*

Riley, S. (1996, March 15). V-chip to regulate Canadian television viewing. *Southam Newspapers.*

Robbins, L. (1995, June 23). Discordant reaction: Parental advisory explicit lyrics, *St. Petersburg Times,* p. 1D.

Rodgers, E. (1996, February 12). Ratings games. *The Idaho Statesman,* p. 1D.

Rohn, L. (1996, January 2). X-files, V-chips and off switches, *The Indianapolis News,* p. A4.

Saunders, K.W. (1996, August 6). Defining what's 'obscene' and what's on television, *The Washington Times.* [1996 WL 2962044].

Shaw Comms <SCLA.AL> Announcement. (1996, March 14). *Reuters Financial Service.*

Shaw welcomes CRTC endorsement of V-chip. (1996, March 14). *Business Wire.*

Sinclair, D. (1994, November 25). Ratings are name of the game for this season, *Chicago Tribune,* p. 81.

Stern, C. (1996, October 4). H'wood, D.C. spar in V-chip teleconference, *Daily Variety,* p. 5.

Swisher, K. (1995, December 13). The games people rate: Software industry awaits review of video, computer game labeling, *The Washington Post,* p. F1.

Traherne, D. (1996, March 24). Digital future means a high price for V-chip censorship, *The Observer,* p. 18.

TV set makers say V-chip for new TV ratings system is no problem. (1997, July 21). *Communications Daily.*

Turner, C. (1995, September 3). V-chip to censor TVs get weak reception by Canadian tuned in during screenings, *The Commercial Appeal* (Memphis), p. 2C.

Turner, C. (1995, September 4). No victory for V-chips in Canada: Nonviolent-TV experiment draws tepid reactions, *Los Angeles Times,* p. F15.

Turner, C. (1996, March 31). Canada's V-chip test pairs broadcasters, gut instincts: TV using technology to block adult content is proving easier than many in the US industry had warned, *Los Angeles Times,* p. A1.

Viewpoint: Weigh in on TV ratings: Smart old dog. (1997, July 21). *Advertising Age,* p. 13.

Walker, D. (1997, August 29). Declining viewership. Losses to cable. A confused ratings system. As the fall season approaches, TV executives must be wondering what's a network to do?, *The Arizona Republic.* [1997 WL 8389474].

Woellert, L. (1996, February 2). Ratings system lags 'V-chip' technology, *The Washington Times,* p. A2.

Woellert, L. (1996, March 23). Canada wants to chip in with TV ratings system, *The Washington Times,* p. A1.

TELEVISION TRANSCRIPTS

Insider says Clinton on right track despite concerns. (1993, June 4). Atlanta Georgia, CNN News, Transcript #419-4.

Crossfire. (1995, June 9). Atlanta Georgia: CNN News Transcript #609.

Russert, T. (producer). (1997, August 2). *Interview, Senator John McCain, Republican, Arizona, discusses the agreement on the budget and taxes, the fund-raising issue and television ratings.* Washington, DC: CNBC, Inc.

Contributors

JACK M. BALKIN is Lafayette S. Foster Professor and Director of the Information Society Project at Yale Law School. He teaches courses in constitutional law (with a special emphasis on the First Amendment), torts, jurisprudence, telecommunications and cyberspace law, multiculturalism, social theory, and the theory of ideology. He has written over forty articles on various aspects of constitutional law, civil liberties, jurisprudence, and legal theory, and is the author of *Cultural Software: A Theory of Ideology* (Yale University Press 1988).

JOEL FEDERMAN is Director of the Center for Communication and Social Policy at the University of California, Santa Barbara. Among other projects, the Center coordinates the National Television Violence Study, a three-year research effort involving the Universities of California, Texas, North Carolina and Wisconsin. He is the author of *Media Ratings: Design, Use and Consequences* (Mediascope, 1996).

MARLENE C. GEBAUER received her J.D. from Case Western Reserve University School of Law. She is currently an M.L.S. student at Rutgers, the State University of New Jersey's School of Communications and Library and Information Science. Ms. Gebauer practiced law for several years, specializing in health care and hospitalization litigation. She is presently a Library Research Assistant at both the Benjamin N. Cardozo School of Law and Rutgers University School of Law.

JAMES T. HAMILTON is Director of the Duke Program on Violence and the Media and

Assistant Professor of public policy, economics, and political science at Duke University. He is the author of *Channeling Violence: The Economic Market for Violent Television Programming* (Princeton University Press, 1998). He received his Ph.D. in economics from Harvard University in 1991.

ANDREA MILLWOOD HARGRAVE is Research Director of the British Broadcasting Standards Commission. The Commission's role is to produce codes of practice, consider audience complaints and to conduct research and monitoring on standards and fairness in broadcasting.

MARJORIE HEINS is the former director and staff counsel to the American Civil Liberties Union Arts Censorship Project; and is the author of *Sex, Sin and Blasphemy: A Guide to America's Censorship Wars* (New Press 1993), and "Indecency: The Ongoing American Debate Over Sex, Children, Free Speech, and Dirty Words" (Andy Warhol Foundation for the Visual Arts, Paper Series on the Arts, Culture, and Society 1997).

AL MACKAY is a broadcast and communications consultant based in Ottawa, Canada. As an executive in private broadcasting, he was heavily involved in developing industry codes dealing with the portrayal of violence on television and the establishment of the Canadian Broadcast Standards Council. He was retained by the Action Group on Violence on Television to co-chair the industry committee which developed and tested the Canadian classification system.

CARLEEN MAITLAND is a doctoral candidate in the Department of Telecommunication at Michigan State University. She has research interests in electronic commerce, new technologies, and international communication.

C. DIANNE MARTIN is an Associate Professor in the Department of Electrical Engineering and Computer Science at George Washington University. She received a B.A. in economics and mathematics education from Western Maryland College, an M.S. in computer science from the University of Maryland, and an Ed.D. in teacher education from the George Washington University. She is Chair of the ACM Special Interest Group on Computers and Society (SIGCAS), served as a member of the Task Force to revise the ACM Code of Professional Ethics, and is President of the Recreational Software Advisory Council (RSAC) Board of Directors.

STEPHEN D. MCDOWELL teaches in the Department of Communication at Florida State University. His research interests include political economy of communication, and new technologies. He has examined communications policies in Canada, India, and the United States.

RICHARD M. MOSK is Chairman of the Motion Picture Association of America Classification and Rating Administration. He is a California attorney, specializing in litigation and international arbitration. He has served as a member of the staff of the Warren Commission, a deputy federal public defender, a judge on the Iran-U.S. claims Tribunal, and a member of the Christopher Commission. He received an A.B. from Stanford University and J.D. from Harvard University

MONROE E. PRICE is a Markle Fellow and Danciger Professor of Law at the Benjamin N. Cardozo School of Law, Yeshiva University, New York and founder and co-director of the Oxford Programme in Comparative Media Law and Policy, Wolfson College, Oxford University. During completion of this book he was a Fellow at the Media Studies Center of the Freedom Forum. He is also Director of Cardozo's Howard M. Squadron Program in Law, Media and Society. His book, *Television, National Identity and the Public Sphere*, was published by Oxford University Press.

DONALD F. ROBERTS is the Thomas More Storke Professor in the Department of Communication at Stanford University. His research and teaching focus on issues related to children and media, a topic on which he has published extensively. He was part of the team that developed the RSAC (Recreational Software Advisory Council) content labeling system currently used to advise parents about computer games and Internet content.

BARRY SHERMAN is Lambdin Kay Professor and Director of the George Foster Peabody Awards program in the Department of Telecommunications at the Grady College of Journalism and Mass Communication, University of Georgia. He is the author of *Telecommunications Management: Broadcasting/Cable and the New Technologies* (McGraw-Hill, 1996) and *Broadcasting/Cable and Beyond: An Introduction to Modern Electronic Media* (McGraw-Hill, 1995). In 1995, he was named Frank Stanton Fellow by the International Radio & Television Society, and, in 1996, he was a Fellow at the Freedom Forum Media Studies Center in New York.

JONATHAN WEINBERG is an Associate Professor at Wayne State University Law School. He has been a law clerk for Justice Thurgood Marshall and then-Judge Ruth Bader Ginsburg, a legal-scholar-in-residence at the Federal Communications Commission, a professor-in-residence at the Department of Justice, and a visiting scholar at the University of Tokyo. He writes about the Internet, First Amendment law and communications regulation.

DANIEL J. WEITZNER is Deputy Director of the Center for Democracy and Technology. His chief areas of responsibility include advocacy and research on the policies related to the Internet and other interactive communications networks. His publications on communications policy have appeared in a number of magazines and journals. He is editor of *Electronic Democracy,* by Graeme Browning, and a commentator for NPR's Marketplace Radio.

AUTHOR INDEX

SUBJECT INDEX

A

AC (Adult Content), cable rating (US), 121, 146
"Acceptable," (FCC requirements for television ratings), 33, 39, 73, 139
   advocacy group disagreement with, 134–135
   unclear definition of, 133–134, 148–149, 269
Access providers, *see* Internet Service Providers
Accused, The, 54
ACLU, *see* American Civil Liberties Union
Action Group on Violence on Television
      (AGVOT) (Canada), 5, 21, 27, 36
   development of rating system, 9–13
   field trial of V-chip, 6, 10, 13, 248–252
   industry relationships, 40
   interest groups relationships, 41
   public opinion surveys, 13–16, 21, 30, 250–252
   rating violent content only, 12, 16, 29
   use of on-screen icons, 17–18, 19, 20
   V-chip report, 16–19, 29–30, 247–256
Adolescents
   attracted to restricted ratings, 119, 128, 140, 167–168, 301
   effect of media violence on, 283–291
   ignoring classification systems, 97
   perspective on advertising, 92
   strategies to attract, 136, 296
Adult Assistance May Be Needed, software packaging label (US), 124
Adult Content (AC), cable rating (US), 121, 146
Adult Language (AL), cable rating (US), 121, 145
Adult themes, amount allowed in rated films (Australia), 101–103
Adults Only (AO), software rating (US), 123
Adults rating (Canada), 258
Advertisements
   adolescents' perspective on, 92
   filtering, xiv
   movie
      rating of, (UK), 113–114
      rating of (US), 117–118, 198
   software
      rating of (US), 124, 125
   television

      rating of (Canada), 15, 16
      and technical issues with V-chip, 253–254
Advertisers
   effect of ratings on, 55, 80, 82, 96, 135, 141–143, 149
   and prescreening of shows, 144
   and unrated programming, 77
Advertising Administration (film) (US), 198
Advisories, *see also* Age-based ratings;
      Content-based ratings; Labeling
cable (US), 37–38, 146
music (US), 122
programmer reaction to, 141–142
software (US), 182
television
      Australia, 111–112
      Canada, 20
      in UCLA study, 294, 301
      viewer reaction to, 139–140
Advocacy groups, *see* Public interest groups
Age, and television time slots, *see* Channeling
Age-based ratings
   boomerang effect of, 119, 128, 140, 167–168, 301
   combined with labels (US), 37, 146, 149
   computer games
      Australia, 105
      Germany, 112–113
      United Kingdom, 114–115
      United States, 123
   content-based preferred over, xvii, 134–135, 138–139, 169, 170, 192
   effect on advertisers, 149
   as evaluative, *see* Evaluative ratings
   film
      Australia, 100–104
      Germany, 112–113
      Sweden, 115–116
      United Kingdom, 113–114
      United States, 116–118
   Internet, 225
   as judgmental, *see* Judgmental ratings
   Motion Picture Association of America (MPAA), xvii
   printed material, Australia, 106–107